The Contemporary
MOSQUE

The Contemporary
MOSQUE

Architects, Clients and Designs since the 1950s

Renata Holod and Hasan-Uddin Khan
With the assistance of Kimberly Mims

RIZZOLI NEW YORK

To my mother, Maria Prokopowych Holod, model and inspiration and to the memory of my late father, Roman Holod.

Renata Holod

To my parents, Bilquis Jehan and Naser-Ud-Deen Khan, who have always actively encouraged me to explore new paths.

Hasan-Uddin Khan

First published in the United States of America in 1997 by
Rizzoli International Publications, Inc.
300 Park Avenue South, New York, NY 10010

First published in Great Britain in 1997 by
Thames and Hudson Ltd, London, under the title *The Mosque and the Modern World: Architects, Patrons and Designs since the 1950s*

© 1997 Thames and Hudson Ltd, London

ISBN 0-8478-2043-2
LC 97-68124

Book design by Adam Hay, London

Printed and bound in Singapore

Page 1. *Bismillah* in the entrance hall of the London Ismaili Centre (see p. 43).

Frontispiece (p. 2). The King Faisal Masjid, Islamabad: detail of roof showing symbolic crescent moon finial (see p. 76).

Contents

Preface

The last four decades of the twentieth century have seen a radical transformation of the built environment, especially within many regions of the Islamic world. Cities have exploded in terms of population and extent. Central business districts have been transformed through the introduction of high-rise buildings. Myriad new neighbourhoods have come into being, whether as government-sponsored housing developments, commercial undertakings or unplanned squatter settlements. New roads, bridges and highways have changed every city dweller's perception of the urban environment. The massive influx of people from rural areas into the old city centres has transformed their character irrevocably. Conversely, rural settlements are assuming an urban character. Large-scale migrations and emigrations have caused previously geographically cohesive Muslim communities to become widely scattered throughout the world. Throughout, the divergence of these restless and burgeoning populations is countered by a corresponding centripetal tendency either to seek to create new, or to recreate old, communities and enclaves. Such attempts to re-establish order and cohesion are as continuous as uncontrolled growth itself. A sure indicator of their success has been the construction of thousands of new mosques which now form part of the streetscape, even if they do not amount to landmarks on the horizon.

Many different aspects of the explosion of metropolises can be examined, and many approaches can be taken in attempting to acquire a measure of understanding of these important changes. We have focused on the mosque as a building type because, in our view, the treatment of its formal as well as functional characteristics serves as a barometer of taste, of identity and of symbolic values. In this initial study of the recent history of a traditional building type, we present a variety of examples built since the 1950s; we hope that the issues raised by this presentation can be further explored by future students of contemporary Muslim societies and their architecture.

This book, with its wide geographical coverage, has been almost a decade in the making, partly because of our wish to visit as many mosques as we could, and partly because at the outset we were living on different continents and had heavy commitments elsewhere. We probably would not have embarked on the venture at all had we not become closely engaged with the issues stemming from the physical transformation of the contemporary Islamic world through our association with His Highness the Aga Khan and the Aga Khan Award for Architecture. This privileged vantage point afforded us the opportunity to view hundreds of buildings, to learn from our colleagues, and to meet architects and clients alike. Renata Holod was the first Convenor of the Aga Khan Award for Architecture (1977–80), and in the 1990s became a member of its Master Jury and of the Steering Committee. Hasan-Uddin Khan worked for His Highness the Aga Khan for seventeen years (1977–94) in various capacities, as Convenor of the Award and as a member of its Steering Committee, as head of Architecture at his Secretariat, as a director at the Aga Khan Trust for Culture, and as Editor-in-Chief of the journal *Mimar: Architecture in Development*. Many of our observations are based on personal experiences in this milieu.

Having visited almost all the mosques covered in this book, we have found that although they are products of very different material conditions in various regions of the world, they share an expressive intent which has been shaped by similar external and internal forces. The simultaneous realities of the existence of global and local cultures are ever present: these multiple actualities are now merely aspects of the same web in which all of us find ourselves entangled and with which we must all deal in various ways. In the late twentieth century, multi-national economies, multi-cultural societies and concomitant global communications have also brought with them expressions of a common denominator in mosque design – a cross-cultural architectural idiom understood by individuals, communities and nation-states alike, wherever Muslims constitute a significant presence.

The resulting buildings are representations of Muslim communities in transition and raise wider issues about cultural heterogeneity and assimilation, and about hybrid forms and meanings. The architecture of the mosque provides a window on the nature of indigenous Islamic states, and on the dreams of the increasing numbers of recent Muslim migrants living in societies with more diverse backgrounds. If public buildings and spaces are to reflect these realities, the many fragmented boundaries and enclaves created by this diversity of populations need to find a place and a voice. Long-held notions of 'otherness' must now be gradually replaced by more pluralistic, inclusive formulations of new societies and a new world order for the twenty-first century. The ways in which Muslims view and represent themselves within such contexts will be a key indicator of the progress of this new understanding and development. It is our hope that this initial examination of contemporary mosque architecture in all its aspects, the first of its kind, will be a useful tool to this end.

Acknowledgments

Our association with the Aga Khan Award for Architecture provided the impetus for embarking on the preparation of this book. Over a period of several years we, as travellers through ever more rapidly changing landscapes and cityscapes, remarked again and again upon the insistent appearance of a key landmark feature, the mosque. It appeared in many guises, simple or elaborate, marking a corner or a coastline, serene or overwhelming, modern or traditional, or both. To record this phenomenon took the energy, the time and the goodwill of numerous individuals and organizations. We can only hope that we have faithfully recorded all those who helped. To all our sincere thanks; our apologies for any inadvertent omissions.

Unique opportunities were afforded us for travel, for making contact with architects and clients, and for close examination of the buildings themselves through our association with the Aga Khan Award for Architecture and associated organizations and publications, including the journal *Mimar: Architecture in Development*. To the founder of these organizations, His Highness the Aga Khan, our heartfelt thanks for his challenge to see and to understand and for his inspiration to persevere with the task.

Special thanks are due to the architects of the mosques featured in this book and to the clients who commissioned them. They provided us with often unpublished briefs and drawings, and through conversations with them, as well as exchanges of correspondence, it became possible for us to enter into the world of the formation of an architectural expression. Without these contributions, the book would have had little immediacy of experience or liveliness of detail.

A significant amount of the archival information comes from the archives of the Aga Khan Award for Architecture in Geneva. The staff of the Award, Said Zulficar, Suha Özkan, Jack Kennedy, Farroukh Derrakhshani and William O'Reilly were always ready to help in discussing individual projects as well as with the provision of access to materials. Their openness, generosity and engagement were unwavering. Their sympathetic criticism and continuous support have sustained us as authors through the years and have been very much appreciated.

It has been a pleasure and a constant challenge to be associated with a number of scholars and architects whose opinions and criticism have helped to shape our thinking about the contemporary architectural expression in the Islamic world. Oleg Grabar was ever willing to exchange views and provide information; we thank him for his careful critique of our drafts. Our conversations with Mohammed Arkoun alerted us to the complex nature of modernization and contemporary Islam. Serge Santelli, Brian Brace Taylor and Said Mouline have provided assistance in identifying new projects, as well as information about individual building processes. The work of Osamah El-Gohary, Sibel Bozdoğan and Mohammad Al-Asad supported our initial interpretation of some key examples. Soedermadji Damais and Rifat Chadirji elucidated important details about the interrelationship between architecture and patronage in practice.

Preliminary aspects of this study of the contemporary mosque were presented before several audiences, among them a College Art Association Session in 1989, the Aga Khan Award Seminar in Indonesia in 1990, the South Asia Seminar of 1990 and the Colloquium of the History of Art Department of 1991 (both of them held at the University of Pennsylvania), the 1992 Lansdowne Lecture at the School of Fine Arts, University of Victoria, the Royal Institute of British Architects in 1993 and the conference on the Contemporary Mosque in North America at the Massachusetts Institute of Technology in 1995. Many helpful and perceptive questions and comments of the audiences resulted in corrections, clarifications and new interpretations.

Photographs and drawings are a crucial part of any study of this nature. Our special thanks to all the photographers whose work is reproduced; individual names are listed in the Sources of Illustrations on p. 286. In addition, Richard and Kelly Gutman of Slide Factor generously provided us with key rare images. We also wish to thank Merrill Smith, Omar Khalidi and Ahmet Annabal of the Rotch Library at the Massachusetts Institute of Technology and Jeffrey Spurr at the Fine Arts Library, Harvard University, for assistance in locating visual material. Drawings provided by the architects were supplemented by those prepared by Amin Ahmad, Rajive Choudhry, Shakeel Hossain, Minakski Mani, Ivaylo Vassilev, Wang Qinhua and Bijay Ramachandran.

For help in research tasks large and small we acknowledge the help of Quaney Porter, Antonia Bryson, Pascal Dufieux, David Roxburgh, James Hargrove, Michelle Rein and Kena Frank. Miloš Jovik provided assistance with translation from Serbo-Croat. Nasser Rabbat was generous with his time in locating Qur'anic quotations and in providing other source references. To Kimberly Mims, assistant *extraordinaire*, we give a special mention on the title page. Her attention to detail kept us alerted to discrepancies and mistakes, while her cheerful enthusiasm made the most tedious of tasks a joy to perform.

The realization of the final manuscript was made possible thanks to the superb editorial and technical skills of Karen Longeteig. To her we express our sincere gratitude. Without her patience, forbearance and support, and without the support of Oleh Tretiak, who also gave technical advice, we would never have been able to bring this venture to a successful conclusion. Lastly, we thank the publishers and their staff for their support and patience in seeing the project to fruition. We credit and thanks all the individuals mentioned for their invaluable contributions to the book and, as is customary, take any faults upon ourselves.

Renata Holod, Philadelphia, PA
Hasan-Uddin Khan, Cambridge, MA   January 1996

Authors' note

Spellings of proper names and place names

In the case of transliterated words or names which may be found in slightly varying forms in English usage, we have opted to use, for example, 'Qur'an' in preference to 'Koran', Muslim rather than Moslem, and '*sura*' and '*madrasa*' rather than '*surah*' and '*madrasah*'; a few exceptional localized usages, e.g. in Indonesia and Pakistan, are explained in context, while terms in more general use are defined in the Glossary (p. 285). In references to the Prophet Muhammad this spelling has been employed throughout, while in the case of individuals named after the Prophet the variant spellings follow the form preferred by those concerned, e.g. Mohamed Makiya or Mohammad Al-Asad. Apart from a few place names better known in familiar forms in English usage, e.g. Mecca rather than Makkah, the spellings adopted are as listed in the *Times Atlas*, whether transliterated (e.g. from Arabic or Persian) or normally written in the Roman alphabet (including Turkish).

Dates

For the sake of convenience the dates cited in this book are generally in accordance with the Gregorian calendar. Exceptionally, in the case of dates having special symbolic significance in the Muslim calendar – a lunar system, the commencement of which coincides with the Prophet Muhammad's departure on his journey (*hijra*) from Mecca to Medina (16 July, AD 622) – the appropriate details are specified in context.

Dimensions and statistics

The sizes and areas of individual buildings etc. are expressed in the text in accordance with the system of measurement originally employed by the architect(s). Thus, in the majority of cases the measurements are provided first in metric units followed in parentheses by the equivalent in feet; conversely, original measurements expressed in feet are followed by metric equivalents. In both situations the conversion may not be exact and will often represent a close approximation reflecting a slight rounding up or down for convenience.

In references to costs, the term 'billion' signifies 'thousand million', following the standard American practice.

Plans and elevations of mosques

In addition to the conventional north point, the direction of Mecca (*qibla*), which governs the orientation of each building in accordance with Islamic tradition, is indicated by an arrow in site plans and floor plans.

The scale is shown in all cases in both metres and feet (see note above).

The mosque in Muslim society: past, present and future

Friday prayers at the Darul Aman Mosque (1986), Singapore.

This volume presents a survey of a selection of mosques built worldwide between the 1950s and the 1990s. Islam is the fastest growing major religion, and recently built mosques are to be found not only in the various countries of the Islamic world, but also in regions where significant Muslim communities have been established in recent decades. Thus, some were part of the building programmes of new states, some a direct reflection of the wealth derived from oil revenues of the 1970s, some part of the massive urbanization within the Islamic world, and still others are manifestations of a Muslim diaspora. We have chosen as representative examples over seventy completed buildings, as well as a number of unbuilt but significant projects, and have examined over a hundred more.

Most of the hundreds of recent new mosques are products of the collaboration between clients and architects (though a few were raised through the efforts and skills of local communities and builders). The design of most individual buildings is based on a specifically articulated brief and design statement, the specific language and terms of which are often as important and as revealing as the resulting buildings themselves. Therefore, our analysis, though architectural in the main, does include an important social component reflecting the intentions and the opinions of client and architect as recorded in these texts. Only secondarily does a larger and more nuanced historical picture begin to emerge.

As a type, the mosque is ubiquitous, and at once old and very new. It is a culture-bound place of worship, representing local and regional architectural traditions, and a trans- or supra-regional expression of a contemporaneity which has acquired a pan-Islamic, worldwide character. This quintessential Muslim symbol provides a way of viewing the mechanisms of representation of state and authority within the nations of the Islamic world, and of Muslim community and self-identity within it as well as outside it. Examples of mosques in this book have been selected because they are significant architecturally or because they demonstrate particular social concerns or technical issues. We have chosen to present these recent buildings according to the

The Salman Mosque (1959–72) in Bandung, Indonesia, designed by Achmad Noe'man, is an example of a building the International Style used to express modern Islam.

type of client who commissioned them and the design response by the architect in each case, and then in a chronological and/or formal sequence. The primacy of the role of the clients reflects the process by which such buildings are commissioned. Also, this manner of grouping reveals patterns of taste on the part of the clients, responses to them on the part of the architects and builders, as well as the symbolic value placed on the style and programme of the mosques themselves.

The period under consideration naturally begins with the first burst of building activity of the post-colonial era. Many new Muslim independent nation-states created out of former colonial territories in the late 1940s and the 1950s felt challenged by their new status and by the external world to represent themselves as 'modern' through their new buildings, particularly mosques.

In the Islamic world, modernity as image and programme had already been embraced in the 1920s and 1930s by republican, statist Turkey.[1] After World War II, Syria, Iraq, Egypt and later Algeria declared themselves socialist republics.[2] They opted for buildings in the prevailing International Style. As had happened in Turkey, the state played the major role in the reshaping of the built environment, but the mosque played no real part in this modernist presentation at the time.[3] Contemporaneously, in Pakistan – the new state specially created for Muslims following the partition of India – the central government was also a prime mover in the new building programmes. Here, however, mosques were included, particularly in the plans for its new capital, Islamabad.[4] Likewise, the state acted as prime client in newly independent Indonesia and Malaysia. Although consisting of heterogeneous populations, these countries nevertheless opted to utilize the building of state mosques in particular as an element in establishing their new identity. In the ensuing decade, several polyvalent trends, at times contradictory, shaped the building of mosques. The strictures of modernism and the International Style, already challenged by the late 1960s, were being further displaced by the development of a cultural and architectural regionalism.[5]

The vast new building programmes of the oil-rich states, such as Kuwait, Saudi Arabia (and to an extent Iran),[6] called for mosques of every scale and in various locations ranging from recreational areas to those attached to airports and universities.[7] Previously avowed secularist or socialist regimes, e.g. those in Iraq, Algeria or Yugoslavia, saw the construction of mosques as an extension of social control and political manipulation. Clients were continuing to demand buildings that were 'modern' but which would somehow be associated with their own region or recognizable as their own. The brief for each of these mosques specified a design with so-called historic or Islamic, as well as modern, features.

Individuals emerge as important clients because of their political, religious or social status, which gives them the 'right' to build, very much in the fashion of the historical élite. Alternatively, individual patronage appears because the centralized state authority can no longer control and fund all major building activity. In the same way, a local community may initiate its own mosque outside the embrace of state authority. By the early 1990s, groups vying for power have moved to utilize the mosque as a symbolic marker in the context of the expanding metropolis, and, in many cases, as an ideological space for the propagation of traditionalist and Islamist thinking.

Finally, throughout the period under review, but more so in the last two decades, numerous mosques outside the boundaries of the traditionally defined Islamic world were built as a result of large-scale migration, emigration and settlement. The development of a Muslim diaspora has meant that the mosque has become a repository of identity and authenticity for those who have found themselves distanced from their home countries. In such cases Muslims from a variety of regions with disparate cultural roots have created in their new mosques a locus of a new identity, and, through them also a connection with their new physical surroundings; that identity has come to be increasingly represented in hybridized, 'creolized' forms in today's post-modern climate.[8] The newly developed 'global mosque' allows for little movement away from the use of the formulaic dome and minaret.[9] Such a formula is in keeping with the clients' consistent desire to preserve remembered places and practices even as, due to their current circumstances, they become ever more distanced from them, and despite the fact that the pace of changes in the home countries may be rapid. These formulas in turn rebound throughout the world, and eventually back to the home regions as well.[10]

The mosques featured in this book are divided into six categories. The first chapter deals with projects initiated and in most cases funded and controlled by an individual patron. The second discusses the nation-state as client and the role that the representatives of the state played in shaping the programme and style of 'state mosques'. The third considers the role of local government agencies, and the fourth covers mosques built in Muslim countries for specialized educational, social, commercial and other institutions constituted as semi-autonomous bodies. The fifth looks at mosques created by Muslim communities and groups (such as students) as independent entities, whether found in traditional settings, in newly urbanized areas of old cities or in newly acquired spaces in non-Muslim countries. The final chapter takes up the particular case of major mosques and Islamic Centres built as symbolic representations of the Islamic presence in Western countries such as the United Kingdom, the USA, Italy and Switzerland, often in the context of international organizations with permanent Muslim delegates or diplomatic representation. In developing these categories we were conscious of the fact that at times some overlapping of boundaries occurs and that the categories cannot be viewed as entirely separate. However, there was a need to differentiate between the scale of the mosques and their intended users, to focus on the desire of the client and the requirements of the users, all the while recognizing the defining role of the architect in each case. We have thus adopted one possible approach to the phenomenon of the mosque – in fact, to a building type which takes many forms but has a single purpose.

There is no single narrative in this book; rather, a series of case studies of individual buildings which yield the outlines of a still fragmentary picture of the history of contemporary mosque architecture. Access to rich, if uneven, documentation has enabled us to expand the narrative into a consideration of corollary issues, such as the special circumstances of the commissioning of certain projects or the training or design philosophy of a particular architect. The participation in this venture of architects ranging from internationally known practitioners to respected regional masters to local

In Visoko, Bosnia, the minaret of Sherefuddin's White Mosque (1970–80) by Zlatko Ugljen projected an uncompromisingly modern image for the town's Muslim community.

Al-Qiblatain Mosque (1989), Medina, is one of a number of mosques in Saudi Arabia designed by the Egyptian architect, Abdel Wahed El-Wakil, in which easily recognizable traditional elements such as minarets, dome, and a prominent entrance portal are employed.

Close links between traditional local craft skills and the architecture of the mosque still continue in modern contexts, as seen in tile work executed for the Bhong Mosque in Pakistan.

The modernist minaret in the Islamic Centre for Technical and Vocational Training and Research (1986) near Dhaka, Bangladesh, not only indicates the presence of a mosque in this educational institution but also serves as an architectural orientation device.

The simplest expression of a mosque as a place of prayer is an open-air enclosure oriented towards Mecca. Here, laid out on the grounds of a hotel in Saidu Sharif, Pakistan, each space is marked in marble and a stone marker serves as a *mihrab* indicating the direction of prayer.

beginners, all linked through education and publications (and sometimes through professional collaboration in practice), introduces mosque-building into the global culture of architects. Fuller development of the narrative must be left to future researchers interested in recording and analyzing the complete story of building in the late twentieth century.

For our part, we have set out to present individual descriptions, documentation and opinions of relatively unknown but significant buildings, clients and architects. We wish to bear witness to the myriad examples of the will to build, with all its psychological implications, on the part of individuals, groups, organizations and states which have yet to enter the mainstream of architectural or critical consciousness.

Several issues concerning the design and structure of contemporary mosques have appeared with consistency. The first is centred on the type of image chosen for a building. The second focuses on new mosque building as the locus of, and opportunity for, the practice of other arts and crafts. Another deals with the challenges of architectural scale and of harmonizing it with the visual and acoustical unity within the mosque space. Competitions, juries and committees have provided a stimulus in the development of contemporary mosque design, as do, of course, individual designers in their efforts to meet the need of the client and user.

The obligatory requirements are few, but must be met in every mosque design: the orienting *mihrab* in the *qibla* wall and a place for prayer alongside it; a *minbar* for the *khutba* (oration) at Friday prayers; and facilities for ritual ablutions. Other elements – even the ever present dome and minaret – are optional. The mosques presented here feature a multiplicity of styles that range from vernacular and vernacularist, modern and modernist, to the historicist and post-modern. Throughout, even when the client has stipulated a 'modern' design, this has been accompanied by a clearly expressed desire to offer an 'Islamic' image. This image is primarily characterized by a vaulted covering in the form of a dome and a distinguishing tower (minaret), and it may also include other ornamental components. Thus, those architects who would normally have worked in a totally contemporary idiom have usually had to turn to historic models for inspiration or, as importantly, for validation of their own designs on the basis of precedents.

This 'Islamic' image has been generated in the imagination of the client and of the architect partly through travel, as will be seen in, for instance, the case of the architect of the Masjid Negara of Malaysia (see Chapter 2). Significantly though, the main crucible for the creation of the image for the mosque was the series of classic nineteenth- and early twentieth-century publications on the great monuments of the Islamic world, such as those by Prisse d'Avennes, Goury and Jones, Creswell, Pope and others, and increasingly by the publications which have appeared since the 1970s.[11] These published works have been the mediators and led the way back to a far-removed past of architectural thinking and building traditions, from which the contemporary viewer has become cut off by the passage of time and by the transition from a pre-industrial to an industrialized society.[12] Based on this historical model, there are several versions of the new 'Islamic' image which have been created and disseminated worldwide: the Andalusian/Maghrebi version, the Ottoman and Mamluk version, and the Indo-Persian version. The link with the past is not a real one, but a wilfully manufactured myth which

Contemporary mosques feature many contrasting styles, as seen for instance in the modernist concrete shell of the Defence Officers' Housing Society Mosque in Karachi (top), a village mosque near Jakarta with pitched roof in the local vernacular style (middle), and a seaside mosque in Freetown, Sierra Leone, which is a hybrid building embellished with a dome as a sign of its function and identity.

Prefabricated 'instant domes' in the Indian Mughal style offered for sale at a roadside stand in Indonesia.

has allowed for the realization of the new expression – an expression which has been named pan-Islamic, or even post-Islamic, architecture.[13] This expression draws indiscriminately on a variety of sources, often abstracting the original meanings from particular units and elements of decoration and form, and sometimes assigning newly coined explanations and histories, e.g. the Rome Islamic Centre Mosque (Chapter 6) or the al-Ghadir Mosque (Chapter 5). Ultimately, the term 'Islamic' has gained a new meaning when applied to contemporary visual manifestations: it is an amalgam of a variety of sources and elements refashioned for current use – a pan-Islamic design vocabulary. This kind of all-embracing designation is widely utilized by clients, architects and users alike.[14]

The insistence on the part of many clients on the inclusion of a dome has forced architects to undertake the design of a form which no longer lies at the centre of design achievement in architecture, either formally or technically. The results have been mixed. The architect has often been challenged to find appropriate proportions and profile, and to produce a harmonious solution on the required scale. Yet, so beloved is the dome as a feature that there are more new mosques with such a covering than there are of any other type. The ubiquitous images of Ottoman, Mamluk, Safavid or Mughal monuments now familiar from the popular media, the postcard, the travel poster and the printed page have played a crucial, though as yet unstudied, role in the anchoring the idea of the dome in the popular nostalgia for the 'authentic'.

In Turkey, for instance, where the modernist image has been thoroughly developed in architecture, innovation in mosque forms has had a mixed history; there have been a variety of reasons for this, not the least the establishment of a secular state in the 1920s. Nevertheless, designs for some small mosques and, more importantly, for the Parliament Mosque in Ankara (Chapter 2) have eschewed many of the formal conventions in the choice of roof cover, inclusion of a *mihrab* niche and a tower. Populist taste, however, has challenged architects again and again, and has even exerted political pressure to conform. (The most notorious example of the success of such pressure was the termination of construction of the modernist shell of the Kocatepe Mosque by Dalokay: see Chapter 2.) The great majority of new mosques can be designated 'Ottomanesque' – as if one were seeing a sixteenth-century Ottoman mosque by Sinan in a distorting mirror. Such buildings are typical of the urban sprawl of Ankara and Istanbul, having been crudely constructed in concrete by contractors without the participation of the architectural profession.

Populist taste has had a clear impact on the profile of the mosque in Indonesia and Malaysia. Expressed through the use of small metal prefabricated domed coverings or finials, which are fast becoming a standard feature of new mosques, this taste could be understood as expressing a desire to belong to a non-regional, pan-Islamic world.[15] (Such prefabricated domes, be they in metal or fibreglass, can also be ordered in many other countries, including the USA.) This ubiquitous image of the domed mosque may be viewed as the triumph of petty bourgeois taste.[16]

The building boom in mosques generated extensive opportunities for their decoration involving traditional Muslim arts and crafts. The design of the *mihrab* and the *minbar* and the development of epigraphy for these two key elements as well as for entrances

Al-Harithy Mosque (1986), Jeddah, Saudi Arabia. An example of traditional *muqarnas* decoration executed in modern materials: decoration below the gallery of one of the Ottoman-style minarets.

Architect's drawing of the Great Mosque (1976–84), Kuwait City, by Mohamed Makiya. One of the many major mosques on a grand scale in the post-colonial era, it combines the symbolic representation of national independence and religion.

and ceilings have presented a challenge to artists and craftsmen. Indeed, major examples of calligraphic inscriptions, woodworking, sculpting and tile working have been executed (see for example, the King Faisal Masjid in Islamabad discussed in Chapter 2). We have been careful to note the work of individual artists, particularly if their contribution added significantly to the expressive qualities of a building. In this context, the lack of skilled building and decorating craftsmen, brought on by the ruptures in building technologies mentioned previously, was sorely felt. Thus, much reinvention has been necessary to achieve the effect desired by the artist, architect and client in the fields of monumental calligraphy, of geometric ornament and of *muqarnas* construction.[17] In fact, the client's desire to embellish the mosque was often so strong, and the vision of how such completion to the building should appear, that at times the intentions of the architect were overwhelmed, as for example in the Kuwait Great Mosque (Chapter 2) or in the King Khaled International Airport Mosque in Riyadh (Chapter 4). Such embellishment has been understood to be the very hallmark of authenticity, regardless of the fact that any number of artists and craftsmen from all parts of the world were called upon to participate in the programme of ornamentation. In this context, the work of the remaining reservoir of Moroccan crafts, plaster workers, tile cutters and wood carvers, whose traditional skills appear to go back unbroken to a pre-industrial age, have, in the clients' eyes, been assigned a value beyond that of the building itself.

The demand for building on a grand scale, at times exceeding that of any previously existing mosque, has meant that acoustic and visual communication had to be recalibrated. Acoustical needs have been provided for through the use of modern loudspeakers and amplification technology. The traditional focus of the *mihrab* as the orienting element of any mosque tends to get lost in a covered space as large as, for instance, the Great Mosque of Kuwait, the Hassan II Mosque in Casablanca, or in designs for the projected State Mosque of Iraq. Likewise, the vastness of the space (and, at the same time, the demands for security) have often worked to separate rather than unite the congregation. In such cases, the huge size dominates all other considerations.

Competitions, whether open or limited, for the design of mosque buildings and complexes have had a key effect in raising interest among architects in the problems of contemporary mosque design. Juries with members drawn from the national and international ranks of the profession and the publication of competition results have helped focus attention on the myriad problems of, and the few successful solutions achieved in designing a mosque for present-day use.[18] Competitions also engaged individual clients in developing a language for the building that would convey to architects specific details of size and use and, as importantly, the hoped for effect on the eventual user. The fact that the client is more often a committee than an individual has expanded the participation in these decisions for some (but, as we shall see later, not all) influential sectors of society. Participants in these processes have formed an interconnected network of opinion-makers, and could also be considered part of the trend of the development of the pan-Islamic contemporary mosque.

In cases other than competitions, the architect is expected to develop the detailed programme from a general brief or instruction given by the client. If the architect is a

Madrid Competition 1980

Architectural competitions attracting entries from all over the world are an important means by which major mosques are commissioned. In February 1980, the prize-winning design for the Islamic Cultural Centre of Madrid was submitted by Jan Czarny, Jolanta Singer-Zemla and Marek Zemla of Czechoslovakia. The winners' design is illustrated below in their proposal for the north-south section of the complex and the overall site plan.

Second prize went to the team of Biernacky-Poray, Tadeusz, Prazdej, Jastrzebska and Janczewski of Poland. Their treatment of the north-south section and plan of the Islamic Centre is shown below.

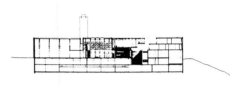

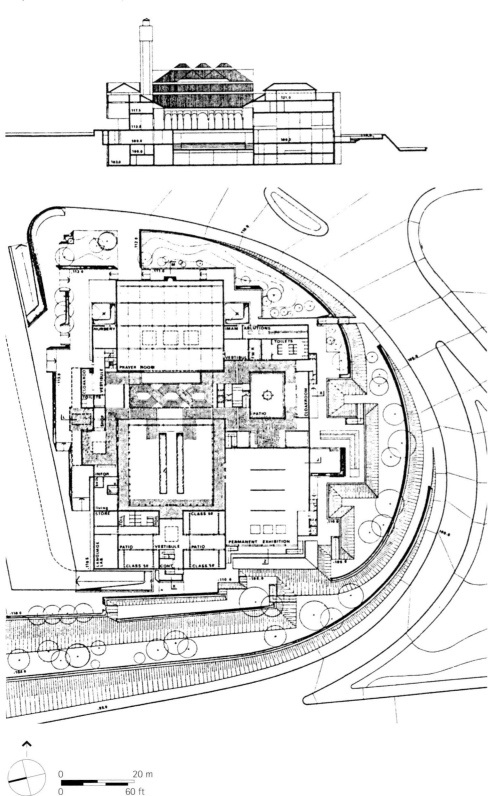

Muslim, an additional onus is placed on him, in that he will be expected to volunteer professional services 'for Islam' or at least to work for a reduced fee. In the design development phase the plan is likely to be changed radically by the client and the architect, sometimes as the construction proceeds. Often, even in competition settings, such changes are made to the winning design after it has been announced. The collective nature of the funding effort, whether within a country or through internationally orchestrated fundraising, tends to prolong the construction periods of many mosques and further dissipate the initial design vision.[19]

An area which deserves a complete study of its own, and to which we have paid some attention only in passing, is the current usage of the mosques featured in this book. One aspect is the significance of the individual designation of each mosque. Connected to this, but extending well beyond it, is the nature and role of the users of the mosque space. To begin with, the mosques discussed are designated by their official names in the form in which these names initially appeared and in their local usage: the name of every mosque is reproduced exactly as it has been used. Thus, terms such as *jami*, *masjid, masjid-i jami, juma masjid,* Friday Mosque, Great Mosque, community mosque and congregational mosque occur throughout the book, and have been employed interchangeably in their contexts (for definitions of terms see the Glossary, p. 286): a large mosque might be designated a *jami*, even though it has no official connection with political authority, and a state mosque a *masjid,* despite the fact that it purports to be emblematic of state authority. These terms have only an indirect connection with the usage for *masjid* and *masjid-i jami* as generally defined by Islamic jurisprudence in pre-modern periods.

There is clear precedent for designating types of mosques recorded in history and differentiated through Islamic jurisprudence.[20] Specifically, the differentiation is made between *jami* (a congregational mosque) and *masjid* (a prayer hall). Such a differentiation was a very early one in Islamic history and had to do with the direct connection of the congregational mosque with political authority, where the official sermon or oration (the *khutba*) was proclaimed and where oaths of loyalty were sworn. Over time, the distinction between the two types has lost its significance progressively, and currently it has been largely eroded by scale and usage, as well as by the new formulations of political authority.

The development of the Muslim nation-state, a modern phenomenon, has had an impact on the nature and typology of mosques. Kemal Atatürk's declaration of a secular state in Turkey in 1923 had led to the separation of political authority and the mosque. The regime of the Pahlavi dynasty in Iran partially followed the example of Atatürk by challenging the authority and the wealth of the religious establishment, but never went as far as declaring the establishment of a secular state. Where newly independent states turned avowedly socialist, e.g. Algeria, Egypt, Syria and Iraq, no early attempts were made to equate nationhood with the symbolic display of a state mosque. Yet, in these cases, as well as in the earlier case of Turkey, the idea of state control over many aspects of everyday life was promulgated. The centralization of decision-making has also been a feature of the new nations further to the east, such as Pakistan, Malaysia and Indonesia. The creation of a state mosque and the programme of mosque building generated by central government via its local branches represented, in effect, an attempt to control the *jami*, leaving *masjid* projects to more localized initiatives.

In our discussion of individual cases, we have made only passing references to aspects of ownership of the individual mosque, the administration of its activities and maintenance arrangements.[21] The full detailing of these aspects was not possible and does not fall within the scope of this volume. Nevertheless, some general comments may already be appropriate at this juncture. The question of the ownership and control of the space of the mosque, if not of the precise designation of the space, has not disappeared. If anything, it has become even more acute. Access to the mosque, the appointment of its personnel, especially the *imam*, and, in parallel, the control of the content of the *khutba* have been matters of keen interest to state authorities; they are considered as important as, if not more important than, the founding and funding of mosques in the name of the state (see Chapter 3).

Certainly, the mosque as public space can have high potential for anti-state activities. Even those governments which had previously manipulated Islamist movements became increasingly aware of the fact that the political dimension of the mosque's teaching role and of mosque associations might jeopardize governmental authority. When such potential is realized, as has been demonstrated by the Iranian Revolution of 1979 and in Algeria in the 1990s, the mosque can function as a rallying ground for those wishing to challenge the state and overthrow the existing regime. The findings of a preliminary study show that in practice the governments of many other Muslim countries have been alert to the dangers inherent in this phenomenon. Thus, for example, Morocco, Algeria, Tunisia, Egypt and Oman have passed laws intended to control all aspects of mosque life.[22]

In the case of Morocco, a 1984 decree (*dahir*) prescribed that authorization to build a mosque is granted by the governor of a province or town who acts only after having sought the advice of both the Ministry of Pious Foundations (*habous*) and Islamic Affairs and the Ministry of Habitation and National Territorial Planning. In addition, the founder of a new mosque is obliged to buy or build real estate and to transform that property into a pious foundation, thus providing a rental income by which the mosque and the its personnel will be sustained. The mosque personnel will then be appointed by the Ministry of Pious Affairs acting in conjunction with the governor and the regional council of religious scholars. Private initiative is restricted to the application for authorization to build the mosque and to providing the money for its construction and for the foundation that will sustain the mosque and the personnel. (In the Moroccan case, even the style is determined; see Chapters 1 and 3.) The appointment of the personnel and the administration of the mosque and its day-to-day functioning are vested in the authorities. After prayer hours, the mosque is kept shut.[23]

In Algeria, the intention was clearly the same when the decree relating to mosques was published in 1988.[24] The state control of religious institutions is central to these decrees.[25] In the Tunisian law drafted at the same time, but not promulgated, the degree of control over every mosque community would have been even more extensive.[26] Room was left for private initiative (and pious intention) only in the funding and founding of a mosque, but once completed the building would become public property.

Authors' note

Spellings of proper names and place names

In the case of transliterated words or names which may be found in slightly varying forms in English usage, we have opted to use, for example, 'Qur'an' in preference to 'Koran', Muslim rather than Moslem, and '*sura*' and '*madrasa*' rather than '*surah*' and '*madrasah*'; a few exceptional localized usages, e.g. in Indonesia and Pakistan, are explained in context, while terms in more general use are defined in the Glossary (p. 285). In references to the Prophet Muhammad this spelling has been employed throughout, while in the case of individuals named after the Prophet the variant spellings follow the form preferred by those concerned, e.g. Mohamed Makiya or Mohammad Al-Asad. Apart from a few place names better known in familiar forms in English usage, e.g. Mecca rather than Makkah, the spellings adopted are as listed in the *Times Atlas*, whether transliterated (e.g. from Arabic or Persian) or normally written in the Roman alphabet (including Turkish).

Dates

For the sake of convenience the dates cited in this book are generally in accordance with the Gregorian calendar. Exceptionally, in the case of dates having special symbolic significance in the Muslim calendar – a lunar system, the commencement of which coincides with the Prophet Muhammad's departure on his journey (*hijra*) from Mecca to Medina (16 July, AD 622) – the appropriate details are specified in context.

Dimensions and statistics

The sizes and areas of individual buildings etc. are expressed in the text in accordance with the system of measurement originally employed by the architect(s). Thus, in the majority of cases the measurements are provided first in metric units followed in parentheses by the equivalent in feet; conversely, original measurements expressed in feet are followed by metric equivalents. In both situations the conversion may not be exact and will often represent a close approximation reflecting a slight rounding up or down for convenience.

In references to costs, the term 'billion' signifies 'thousand million', following the standard American practice.

Plans and elevations of mosques

In addition to the conventional north point, the direction of Mecca (*qibla*), which governs the orientation of each building in accordance with Islamic tradition, is indicated by an arrow in site plans and floor plans.

The scale is shown in all cases in both metres and feet (see note above).

Introduction

The mosque in Muslim society: past, present and future

Friday prayers at the Darul Aman Mosque (1986), Singapore.

This volume presents a survey of a selection of mosques built worldwide between the 1950s and the 1990s. Islam is the fastest growing major religion, and recently built mosques are to be found not only in the various countries of the Islamic world, but also in regions where significant Muslim communities have been established in recent decades. Thus, some were part of the building programmes of new states, some a direct reflection of the wealth derived from oil revenues of the 1970s, some part of the massive urbanization within the Islamic world, and still others are manifestations of a Muslim diaspora. We have chosen as representative examples over seventy completed buildings, as well as a number of unbuilt but significant projects, and have examined over a hundred more.

Most of the hundreds of recent new mosques are products of the collaboration between clients and architects (though a few were raised through the efforts and skills of local communities and builders). The design of most individual buildings is based on a specifically articulated brief and design statement, the specific language and terms of which are often as important and as revealing as the resulting buildings themselves. Therefore, our analysis, though architectural in the main, does include an important social component reflecting the intentions and the opinions of client and architect as recorded in these texts. Only secondarily does a larger and more nuanced historical picture begin to emerge.

As a type, the mosque is ubiquitous, and at once old and very new. It is a culture-bound place of worship, representing local and regional architectural traditions, and a trans- or supra-regional expression of a contemporaneity which has acquired a pan-Islamic, worldwide character. This quintessential Muslim symbol provides a way of viewing the mechanisms of representation of state and authority within the nations of the Islamic world, and of Muslim community and self-identity within it as well as outside it. Examples of mosques in this book have been selected because they are significant architecturally or because they demonstrate particular social concerns or technical issues. We have chosen to present these recent buildings according to the

Members of a North American Muslim community gather for religious classes in the Dar al-Islam Mosque (1981), Abiquiu, New Mexico.

The Jamatkhana and Centre (1985) in Burnaby, British Columbia, built for the Ismaili Community of Canada, is a contemporary building with only a distant echo of historic architectural references.

When compared to traditional Islamic law, legislation concerning the mosque, such as the decrees promulgated or drafted by Maghrebi states, underlines the role of the state as the controller, if not the provider (client) of mosques (see Chapter 3). The aim of such recent legislation is certain to exert control even over small mosques and over the communities served by them. (The form of these laws, coincidentally, follows some of the strictures controlling places of worship found in French law.) Historically, however, the small community has been a feature of mosque usage and is recognized as such in Islamic legal tradition. Such a community was seen as an autonomous group which met regularly for worship and whose members were known to each other. Jurists defined the people of the quarter (*ahl al-mahal*) as an autonomous mosque community. The observance of Friday prayers was understood as the hallmark of civilized society, and separate from state authority.[27]

The community mosque, rather than the state mosque, serves as the model for mosques resulting from the Muslim diaspora. The small mosque, funded primarily by a community and wholly maintained by it is, at once, economically feasible and reproducible. It can be a shop-front rented space, a converted synagogue or church or a purpose-built mosque, depending on available resources. Whatever their physical form, such mosques fulfil a key religious and social integrative function. It is through the mosque that each diaspora community (migrant, emigrant or settled) connects to the larger non-Muslim society and is represented through its very form and location. More than new community mosques in Muslim countries, these buildings, in addition to being places for prayer, often take the form of a complex intended to serve all the socio-religious needs of the community – family functions, education, activities for women, provision of a library, and even food preparation.

In countries where other immigrant groups of whatever religious persuasion have their own places of worship, as for instance in Canada or the United States, the mosque functions in the same way as any other religious/cultic building. There is no relationship to the state as such, except to establish the client community according to local laws, and to obtain building permits and planning approval from the relevant authority. These are sometimes easily obtained, but in certain situations formal applications may be considered politically or culturally sensitive.[28] The question of control over the content of sermons and mosque personnel, and control of property and maintenance of the complex simply does not arise. Similarly, the distinction between a *masjid* and a *jami* does not reflect any engagement with, connection with or control by political authority. Paradoxically, then, the mosque community has greater freedom to develop in the diaspora, away from controls imposed by Muslim governments in their own lands.

In many programmes, the size of the mosque is specified in terms of the number of worshippers, who are understood to be male, praying together shoulder to shoulder, disposed in rows facing the *mihrab*. Women are relegated to other smaller spaces within the mosque, such as a gallery, a mezzanine level or a separate side hall. In the case of larger mosques and state mosques, the programmes foresaw the participation of women worshippers by specifying these spaces – see for example the specifications for the State Mosque in Baghdad (Chapter 2), or the Zagreb Mosque (Chapter 3). The ratios of the space allocated to women and men respectively in these mosques range from 1:4 to

In the prayer hall of a recent mosque (1986) in Pahang State, Malaysia, by CSL Associates a simple curtain is used to segregate women worshippers during prayers.

1:20. In smaller mosques, women are provided with either a small gallery or barriers such as curtains or screens, as for example in the Said Naum Mosque in Jakarta (Chapter 5) or the Jondishapur University Mosque (Chapter 4). Sometimes, however, they are allocated no space at all. Rarely has there been any expectation that there would be parity in the amount of space assigned to men and women. Faced with these programmatic demands, many architects have had to contend with the problem of developing a mezzanine or gallery, as well as separate entrances and ablutions facilities. The solutions have been successful in varying degrees. The fact that such galleries, though quite infrequent in earlier buildings, have appeared in new mosques throughout the world has had a paradoxical impact on the place of women in the mosque. Insistence on a clearly defined physical separation for them, unlike the more flexible arrangements adopted in the past, has in practice limited the actual and potential use of the space by women. On the other hand, by making the provision of some space for them nearly obligatory in a new mosque, the programming has ensured the inclusion of facilities for women in instances where they had previously been denied access.

The contemporary building boom has taken account of the changing circumstances of women in Muslim societies by recognizing that they do have a place in (some) mosques.[29] Yet neither their greater participation in economic life as income earners nor their participation in the life of community and state as professionals, activists or political leaders are adequately reflected in the space allocated to them in mosques. The construction of new (civil) societies through mosque communities still posits only a minimal presence there. Nor are women noticeable as patrons of this type of building: in fact, they are largely unrepresented on committees, whether appointed by the state or as members of communities, acting as the new clients or as architects of these buildings. Concurrently, the historic role of élite women as important individual patrons of mosques has been curtailed. The disappearance of the ruling dynasties within which such activity was a right or privilege for women may be one of the reasons for this.[30] Another may be that élite women are no longer content to be represented by a building to which they themselves will never have equality of access. In states where the composition of ruling circles is based not on family ties but on membership of military, political or religious associations, women do not seem to have developed parallel élite groups which would provide them with a base for action as clients. Nor have local mosque communities been open to their participation.

The inclusion of women in the activities of the mosque has not yet been the subject of a detailed historical study, either separately or as part of a more general study of women's socio-religious life.[31] In the early Islamic world their religious space was in the home and, as importantly, in shrines. The interior space of the shrine has never been subject to the same strict separation of the sexes and is in many ways not bounded by the strictures of society. Hence equal access to them was accorded to men and women.[32] There exist, however, considerable regional and chronological variations. In some regions, women never participated in mosque activity, specifically in congregational prayer or attending sermons held there at other times, while in others they seem to have been present at one or both.[33] Pre-modern legal opinion on the subject is considerable and varied: some jurists supported the participation of women in mosque activities, others were solidly against it. The range of legal opinion is based largely on the school of the particular jurist and his own reflection on local custom.[34] The heterogeneity of these opinions has led in turn to the choice of one or another of them to justify the individual inclinations of current client committees.[35]

The practice of segregation of the sexes in places of worship has very old roots in the Mediterranean area and the ancient Near East, and in Jewish, Eastern Christian and Islamic settings.[36] This gendering of space has been a persistent, primary feature of mosques. The idea of segregated prayer goes back to the conception that members of the opposite sexes must be separated so as not to distract each other, or more specifically that the presence of women must not distract men. In the case of men, prayer – and particularly Friday prayer – is not valid if polluted by touch and sometimes even by the sight of a woman, according to some opinions. Women's participation in prayer was condoned as long as they were not visible to the male members of the congregation.[37] Whether in monumental buildings or in smaller settings, women were separated by curtains or screens, and in some cases they used special galleries.[38]

For the purposes of this book, it is sufficient to note that the contemporary massive building campaigns have not, on the whole, yielded any programmatic changes for the location of women's spaces in mosques. These must come from different impulses, from changes in the role of women in a traditionally male-dominated society, from their aspirations and the level of their participation in mosque life.[39] Modern design programmes have served only to locate and specify their place in subordinate locations within the mosque space.

Finally, how do these contemporary buildings, these manifestations of present-day culture, shed light on the characteristics of Islamic societies? The fact that the mosques are powerful emblematic buildings has been recognized by Muslims and by non-Muslims alike. They accommodate collective acts of prayer and are public affirmations of being and of being seen to be Muslim. Their existence can provide emotional support in old neighbourhoods, as well as in new settlements and new communities. As a result of their very visible presence, they can also become magnets for strife, whether sectarian or political.[40] They are spaces serving social and political as well as religious purposes, and the uses to which they are put fluctuate constantly.

Mosques express a collective identity, and glimpses of that identity can be discerned in the client's words of intent, the shapes of design, the pragmatism of realization, in the theatre of their inauguration, and in the realities of the everyday use of these special buildings. Through them, the process of the creation of state identities can be charted. Through them, the dynamics of regional politics can be discerned. In them, finally, the growth of a trans-regional worldwide Islamic community and its culture can be mapped. Reflected in terms of their numbers alone is the emergence of a global Muslim community – the *umma* – aided by the missionary activities of a variety of separate organizations. However, the variegated appearance of contemporary mosques – historicist, vernacularist or modernist – with no single type of expression predominating, provides evidence of the growing numbers of this community, adapting itself to and being transformed by the world in which it lives.

Bait ul-Mukkarram (1959–86), Dhaka, Bangladesh, provides a complex to serve religious, social and cultural needs in the city's main business district; the form of the mosque is a cube inspired by the Ka'ba in Mecca (see p. 204).

Chapter 1

Personal patronage

In the past mosques have been financed and built by
wealthy individual patrons and given by them to their own
communities and, in some cases, to communities other than
their own, as manifestations of their piety and social status.
Such patrons were generally members of a ruling or social
élite, such as a monarch, a prince or princess, a sheikh or a
religious leader, a landowner or merchant. The building of a
mosque was considered to be a charitable act on the part of
the patron, and was generally accompanied by the provision
of an endowment in perpetuity through the creation of
a *waqf* or pious foundation. It was widely believed that
charitable acts constitute one of the three enduring legacies
of a Muslim's life.[1] Yet, at the same time, many patrons were
surely motivated to build mosques as symbols of political or
dynastic power, or of the presence of the ruling power in a
land conquered by the forces of Islam. In the pre-modern
periods such acts could also be categorized as acts of the
state if the patron was a ruler and if no real distinction
between private and state acts could be made. In today's
world, individual patronage, though far outnumbered by
other forms, continues to be overwhelmingly by men, and
is only rarely also an act of state.[2]

Featured in this chapter are mosques that were initiated
and financed by individuals who did not normally have
recourse to extensive governmental or community funding
and retained control over design decisions. Such personal
control does not necessarily yield more daring departures
from type or produce innovations of mosque design, for the
taste of the individual patron is usually limited by that of
the group or the society. In practice, individual patrons have
often sought the services of architects already known for
specific types of design, leaving little room for the architect
to press for a design which departed in any major way from
the easily recognizable and understood features of the
mosque. Only in rare instances does the patron set the
overall stylistic and architectural agenda, as can be seen in
the case of King Hassan II of Morocco or of the Aga Khan.

Because the examples discussed have been drawn from a
large but not comprehensive sample, it may be too early to
make a definitive characterization. An impression emerges,

(Above) A view into the main dome of the
Al-Harithy Mosque (1986), Jeddah (see p. 39),
one of the series of mosques designed by Abdel
Wahed El-Wakil, showing the intricate brick
construction of the pendentives and the
geometric pattern of the chandelier.

(Opposite) The upper part of the minaret of
the Mosque of Hassan II in Casablanca, the
tallest structure associated with a religious
building anywhere in the world (see p. 54). It
houses a computer centre from which technical
services throughout the mosque complex are
controlled; on important occasions a powerful
laser beam can be projected from the summit.

however, that, unlike other instances of patronage in architectural history which have been documented elsewhere, the individual, non-corporate nature of the client has not necessarily yielded the most radical departure from the popular and populist architectural language associated with the mosque. Nonetheless, individual visions for contemporary mosque architecture do leave room for some novel departures, mainly in their desire to rely completely on the use of modern and readily available building materials. Through them a design vocabulary which draws upon modernism and the contemporary city as a source of inspiration has made its appearance since the mid-1970s.

Shafiq Amash Mosque, Beirut, Lebanon

This building, completed in 1984, addresses modernist formal and contextual issues in contemporary urban mosque architecture. In the early 1980s, Beirut – the Mediterranean metropolis of the Levant coast – was scarred by bombings and explosions; on the other hand, it was simultaneously notable for the continuous commercial development of concrete-box apartment buildings and for the division of the city into sectors based on the religious affiliations of the population. Nevertheless, efforts to reconstruct and reorganize continued. It was against this background of conflict and tension that the Shafiq Amash Mosque was conceived to replace an existing community mosque located at the heart of the city and run by the Mohammad Al-Amine Islamic Association. Since it had become too dangerous to use the existing mosque for

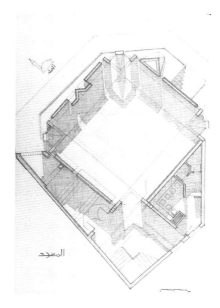
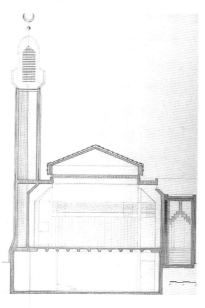

The Shafiq Amash Mosque (1984), Beirut, by Nabbil Tabbara.

(Above) Axonometric view; the main area of the mosque is inserted into a restricted site, with ancillary facilities below ground level.

(Above right) Section of the mosque showing the gateway and the minaret placed outside the main mass of the prayer hall.

(Below) Interior of the prayer hall, showing the *qibla* wall separated from the structural elements of the mosque by rows of windows; the corners are articulated as glazed niches permitting views into the street.

prayers, the Association decided to move to a new location. A couple whose identity remains obscure generously donated land for this purpose in the safer Ras-Beirut district. Saeb Salaam, the former Prime Minister of Lebanon and president of the Mohammad Al-Amine Islamic Association, was a prime mover in the project, and Rabih Amache, Chairman of Ramco Construction Company, offered to finance the construction of the mosque in memory of his late father.[3] Though technically this mosque was funded by a number of people, clearly the major voice in the design decision was that of the person of greatest renown and authority, who can be considered as the primary patron, if not the patron of record.

Saeb Salaam commissioned Nabbil Tabbara, a Lebanese architect, to prepare the drawings for a new mosque with a small community centre. Before starting the design, the architect conducted a thorough survey of existing mosques in the city in an attempt to discover and identify the particular characteristics of mosque design in Beirut. These characteristics, he determined, were basically defined by the building materials most commonly used in the city, such as local sandstone and terracotta tiles. In order to reflect this visual aspect in his design conceived in a modern idiom, he used travertine slab walls to suggest sandstone, while keeping traditional roof tiles.

The design and technology employed in the case of this mosque are based on variations of square and cube. The site was very restricted, with an area of only 200 sq. m (2,150 sq. ft) and was bordered on two sides by busy streets. The

Exterior views showing the *qibla* wall (above) and a detail of the *mihrab* (left); carefully crafted in local sandstone, elements of the *muqarnas* and the portal are given a monumental expression. The siting of the minaret (far left) at one corner ensures that both it and the mosque as a whole are prominently visible despite the presence of nearby high-rise buildings.

25

architect used almost the entire ground-floor space for the building's outer envelope and had to locate the ancillary facilities, such as the community centre, underground. The prayer hall is square in plan and is covered by a truncated pyramidal structure supported by pairs of columns at each corner which are referred to by the architect as 'inverse pendentives'. In this way, the walls of the prayer hall are left free and are separated from the structural elements by glass partitions running both horizontally and vertically. The windows extend to full height at each corner of the mosque, allowing the street activity and passers-by to be seen from within.

The openness of the prayer hall in relation to the street is a daring departure from traditional mosque design, in which the prayer hall is treated as the most protected space. This innovation is rendered all the more astonishing in the context of the busy urban site.[4] Indeed, the users of the mosque have in subsequent years blocked the vista out to the street immediately around the *mihrab* so as to eliminate the distractions created by passing traffic.

While proximity to and, particularly, visual contact with the outside world may not be conducive to spiritual reflection, Tabbara's solution creates an aesthetic of natural light in the interior. The criss-crossed patterns created by sunlight filtering through the windows into the prayer hall produce a stunning effect. The constrained character of the site as well as the chosen modernist aesthetic forced the architect and patrons away from the easy consideration of the dome as a symbolic feature. Likewise, the concept of the minaret is transformed through the use of a simple shaft topped by stainless steel arches which join at the crown. What remain as easily recognizable signs identifying the building as a mosque are specifically the stone inlay work and *muqarnas* on the *mihrab* and at the entrance.

Bin Madiya Mosque, Dubai, UAE

This is another example of a modern mosque donated for public use by a private patron. Majid Al Futtaim, one of Dubai's leading businessmen, commissioned the design in 1982 from the firm A.N. Tombazis & Associates, based in Athens. The prominent Greek architect Alexandros Tombazis,

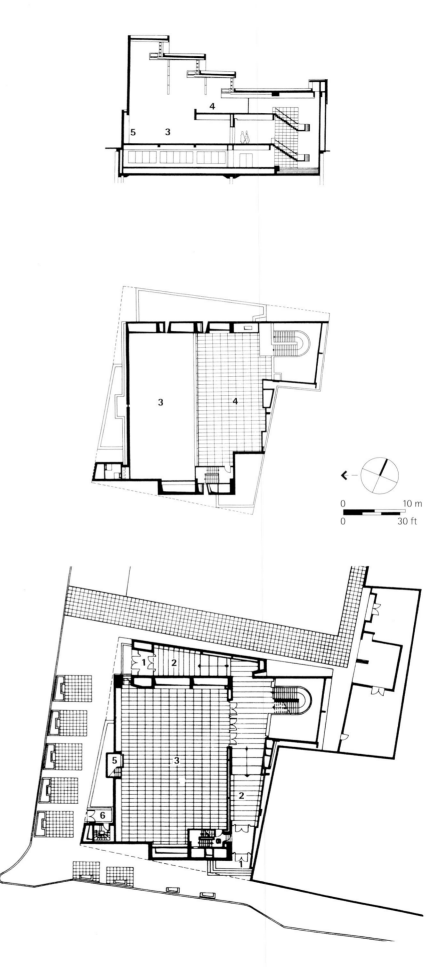

The Bin Madiya Mosque (1987–90), Dubai, by A.N. Tombazis Associates.

(Right) Section and mezzanine and ground-floor plans. The use of a stepped roof and clerestory windows admits natural light, successfully avoiding the problem of providing a domed covering.

1 Entrances
2 Shoe-racks
3 Prayer hall
4 Women's mezzanine
5 *Mihrab*
6 Minaret

(Right) The striking *mihrab* niche, with shimmering blue and beige decoration incorporating Qur'anic quotations in glass mosaic.

(Below) The brick-clad exterior of the mosque contrasts with the square minaret with its white balcony and oblique edge.

trained in Athens, had worked on a wide range of building designs, but this was his first mosque project. The design was finished in 1987 and, with the construction completed, the building was handed over to the client in 1990.[5]

The mosque is situated near Al Nasser Square in the centre of the town of Dubai, surrounded by busy streets and tall buildings. (It replaced a poorly built mosque of the 1970s.) It can accommodate 500 men in the main prayer hall on a raised ground floor, 230 women in the mezzanine balcony and a further 360 worshippers in the basement. The outer walls, clad in sand-coloured hand-made brick, have few openings; the interiors are finished in marble panelling and smooth white-painted plaster. The most interesting aspects of the building are its section featuring a stepped roof and clerestory windows to admit natural light and the *mihrab* wall, above which a vertical slit also lets in light. The wall itself, with mosaic-patterns in blue and beige glass, shimmers in this light, which illuminates quotations from the Qur'an, selected by the local *ulema* and given to the interior designers to develop. The building is fully air-conditioned and the artificial lighting follows the pattern of the natural light sources. The total building area is 2,100 sq. m (22,600 sq. ft) and the minaret rises to a height of 45 m (148 ft). The total project cost (excluding land) was equivalent to US$2 million.

The strength and simplicity of the Bin Madiya Mosque are comparable to those of the Shafiq Amash Mosque in its form and its successful way in which the structure has been oriented while retaining a clear relationship to the street. This example deals with the manipulation of natural light,

27

but achieves a better volumetric expression. Both mosques make a significant contribution as solutions to the problems presented by difficult urban sites.

Bhong Mosque, near Rahimyar Khan, Pakistan

The rural setting, as much as the taste of the patron, was the determining factor of the shape and appearance of the mosque complex at Bhong. The construction of a mosque in this village, near Rahimyar Khan in the Punjab Province of Pakistan, was under the total control of the landowner, Rais Ghazi Muhammad. This project, comprising a variety of buildings in addition to the mosque and initiated in 1932 by his father, was for the most part shaped, financed and directed by Rais. His plan was to develop an infrastructure and services to include roads, a market, electricity and running water, irrigation and public transport for the 5,000 inhabitants of the village. The project also generated local employment, as well as providing training for over 1,000 workers and craftsmen over its duration. Most of the work and the mosque were substantially completed by 1983.

The site lies within the family compound and comprises, in addition to the mosque, residences for Rais and his family, a library, a *madrasa* and student housing, geometrically laid-out gardens with fountains, and a guest house adjacent to a market on the through road. The new mosque was the second one to be built on the site; the earlier smaller building is now used as the women's prayer hall. The new mosque compound is entered from the road by passing through a monumental portal and the four-part garden, then up a main staircase to reach the gate leading to a raised platform, beneath which is located an ablutions pool. The platform, 3 m (10 ft) above ground level, serves to protect the mosque and the library against flooding during the rainy season and allows these two structures to dominate the rest of the compound and the village.[6]

Approached from the side through the gateway, the mosque and library form a pendant pair of buildings typical of Mughal architecture: the mosque with its three domes and verandah is the traditional statement or question (*sual*); the response (*jawab*) on the opposite side of the courtyard is the library with a single dome. Each corner is marked by a *chhatri* (umbrella) and *jaroka* (finial), common elements in Indian architecture. The marble-clad verandah precedes the red-brick prayer hall, which measures 18 x 8 m (60 x 26 ft). The hemispherical *mihrab* niche is emphasized externally by a semi-dome. The minaret, completed only to its first two stages, is situated to the southwest of the mosque and is connected to it by a bridge.

Having accepted the norms of the Mughal architectural language chosen by Rais, his craftsmen worked on the embellishment and enlargement of the ornamentation.

(Opposite) The triple-domed Bhong Mosque (1983), featuring elaborate ornament. The verandah (below) leading to the prayer hall is covered with carved marble and mother-of-pearl inlay.

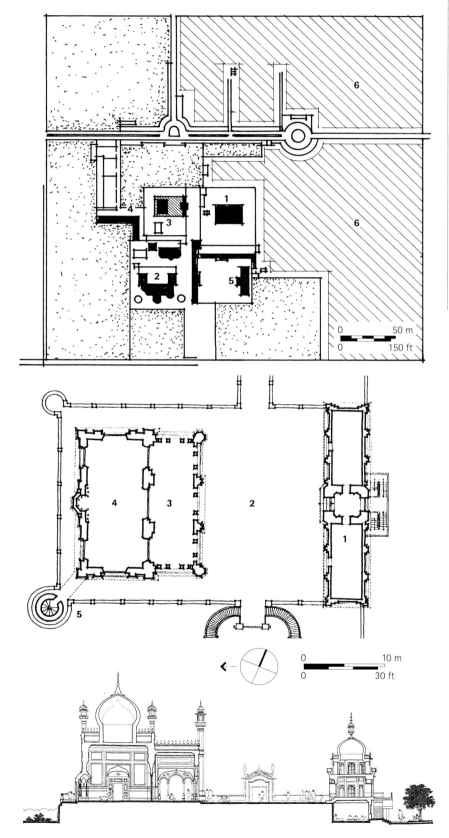

(Below) Site plan of the mosque complex showing its relationship to the village.

1 Palace
2 Main house
3 Mosque and library
4 *Madrasa*
5 New house
6 Village

(Bottom) Plan and section of the mosque and library, showing the raised platform.

1 Entrance and library
2 Courtyard
3 Verandah
4 Prayer hall
5 Minaret

0   50 m
0   150 ft

0   10 m
0   30 ft

(Opposite) Decorative Multani tile work on the dome of the library pavilion; the three domes of the mosque are similarly finished.

(Top) General view of the complex; the overdetermined ornamentation reflects the prevailing contemporary popular taste of the area and of Pakistan in general.

(Above) An example of the geometric patterns derived from the Multani tile-working tradition that were used extensively in the embellishment of the Bhong Mosque.

(Right) The *mihrab* niche; lavish ornament covers every surface in the prayer hall. The inclusion of ornate clocks follows a common trend in mosque interiors.

The styles of ornament are eclectic, incorporating motifs and materials derived from Mughal, Multani and even Victorian colonial traditions.[7] The verandah is embellished with carved marble tracery and with mother-of-pearl inlay, while blue Multani tile work decorates the three concrete domes, the *mihrab* semi-dome and the top of every wall. Ornament – painted, gilded, tiled and mirrored – covers every surface of the interior of the mosque hall, but especially the tripartite *mihrab*. Its three golden canopies echo the three domes. The *qibla* wall is further enriched with clocks and pictures of the Ka'ba, both of which were nineteenth-century additions to many important buildings in the region. Throughout the complex, traditional materials – teak, ivory, coloured glass, onyx, gilded tracery and calligraphy, glazed tiles, mirrors and mother-of-pearl inlay – are juxtaposed with more modern materials such as marbleized patterned industrial tiles, artificial stone facing, terrazzo and wrought iron. However, Rais reserved the best, costliest, and most skilful and traditional hand-crafted ornamentation for the mosque.

The Bhong Mosque and its complex represent a reprise of an architectural language with which Rais had familiarized himself by visiting major Mughal sites in India as well as Pakistan. Replicating the massing and layout, without resorting to the services of an architect, he applied his energies and the skills of his craftsmen to the realization of his personal vision of a newly embellished whole. The over-determined ornamentation programme which resulted is defined by this desire, and is located solidly within the prevailing contemporary popular visual culture of the area and of Pakistan in general, as evident in advertising, films, wedding decorations, illustrated books and popular prints.[8]

One of the hundreds of mosques built in Libya, Egypt and Syria in a neo-Mamluk style in the second half of the twentieth century, the El-Sayyida Safiyya Mosque (1980), designed by Mohammed Abdallah Eissa, was built for the use of a local community in Cairo.

(Below) Ground-floor plan and entrance façade.

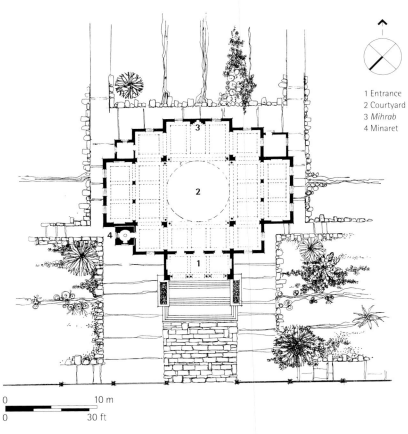

1 Entrance
2 Courtyard
3 *Mihrab*
4 Minaret

0   10 m
0   30 ft

A similar taste for the bold juxtaposition of colours and materials can also be noted in other contexts in the region, for example in the decoration of trucks and rickshaws.[9] The power of popular taste and a purposeful reimagination of past architecture are the hallmarks of this complex.

El-Sayyida Safiyya Mosque, Cairo, Egypt

The urge to reconnect with monumental architecture of the past is also a well-documented motivation associated with the many mosques of Egypt, Libya and Syria for which the central model has been Mamluk architecture of the thirteenth to fifteenth centuries.[10] Among hundreds of these imitations, which include the Othman Mosque in Damascus (1961–74),[11] the El-Sayyida Safiyya Mosque, completed in 1980, is also the result of individual patronage. It was conceived by Mohamed El Sharkawy to provide a place of worship for the community of Nasr City in Cairo which was also badly in need of a social centre. The mosque itself was financed entirely by him, while the land was provided free of charge by the government. The project, proposed in 1977, was to embrace facilities for prayer, a community centre and a social services office for the elderly. In this instance, the patron, El Sharkawy, sought an architect to help him realize his wish: a mosque that would be immediately recognizable by every inhabitant of the city through the use of familiar architectural features. El Sharkawy and his architect, Mohammed Abdallah Eissa, based in Cairo, determined that the design for the mosque should stay within the narrow limits of the idioms of Mamluk architecture of Cairo itself. However, unlike the first Mamluk revival, undertaken largely by the Fahmy Brothers, Herz Bey and others at the turn of the twentieth century, this revivalism can be characterized, in the main, by a simple repetition of stylistic features, such as the dome, the minaret and certain decorative practices, but with no attempt at a contemporary re-evaluation of these models and no deep understanding of their historical generative aesthetics.[12]

Mosque and Cultural Centre, Marbella, Spain

The creation of a building in a style that is at once familiar and connected to the architecture of the past was also the intention of the patron of the mosque in Marbella, on the southern coast of Spain. In the late 1970s, many Arab families, particularly from the Persian Gulf area, began to spend the summer months in Spain, while more and more Algerians and Moroccans started working in the coastal area. Since then, the popular holiday resort of Marbella has enjoyed major Arab investment and boasts a highly influential Muslim community. The Mosque and Cultural Centre, sometimes called the Mosque of the King, was designed in 1979 by the Spanish architect Juan Mora Urbano, who was chosen because of his knowledge of Andalusian architecture. The client of record, Aradico Invest Trading, a private organization that financed the entire project as well as donating the land, wanted a building that would fit into its surroundings and yet be immediately recognizable as a mosque.[13] Work on the mosque was completed in June 1981.

The mosque is entered from the courtyard. It has a rectangular hypostyle-type hall with, over the *mihrab*, a large clerestoried dome supported by columns. A separate entrance for the *imam* is located in the *qibla* wall, providing direct access to the *imam's* office situated behind the *mihrab*. The main entrance leads to a vestibule from which

(Below) Sometimes called the Mosque of the King, the mosque at the Spanish resort of Marbella (1981), designed by Juan Mora Urbano, was intended to recall traditional features of the architecture of Andalusia, but insistence on the inclusion of an ill-proportioned dome has partly vitiated this stylistic expression, as shown in the southeast elevation drawing.

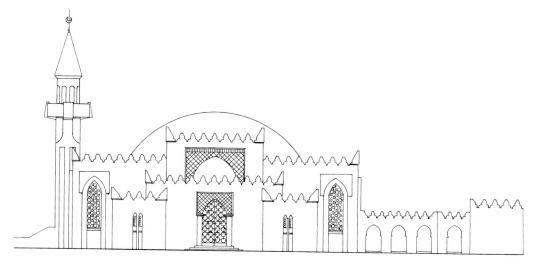

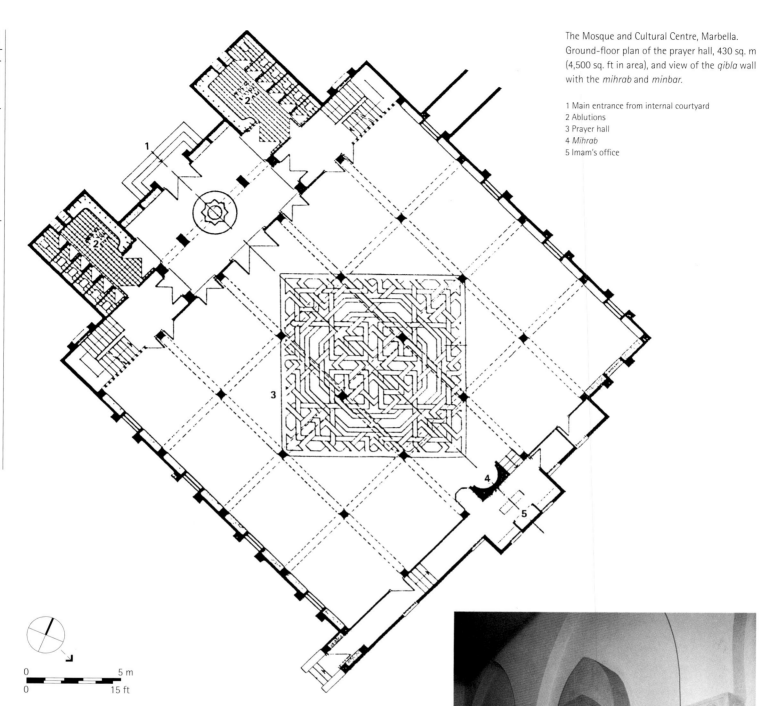

The Mosque and Cultural Centre, Marbella. Ground-floor plan of the prayer hall, 430 sq. m (4,500 sq. ft in area), and view of the *qibla* wall with the *mihrab* and *minbar*.

1 Main entrance from internal courtyard
2 Ablutions
3 Prayer hall
4 *Mihrab*
5 Imam's office

0   5 m
0   15 ft

worshippers gain access to the prayer hall. The vestibule is flanked by the ablutions rooms for men and women respectively to the right and left. Separate entrances to the prayer hall (for men) and to the gallery (for women) are provided by way of two small side halls.

The prayer hall can accommodate 600 worshippers – a capacity ample to meet the requirements of the Muslim community of Marbella; it is recognizable to the casual passer-by and to Muslims alike from the use of elements most clearly associated with Andalusian architecture: the decorated portal featuring crenellations and tile work. Such a clear symbol is not enough, however, to compensate for the ill-proportioned dome behind it. Taken together, these elements form a rather dissonant whole, falling far short of the desired Alhambra-like ambience.

Al-Ibrahim Jami, Caracas, Venezuela

Continuing the tradition of building mosques in countries other than one's own, the mosque of Sheikh Ibrahim bin Abdulaziz al-Ibrahim in Caracas,[14] completed early in 1993, is similar in nature to the preceding Cairo and Marbella examples in that it features clearly the historic elements of dome, minaret and portal in order to express its presence in its urban surroundings. The client of record is the Al-Ibrahim Foundation in Riyadh, but two individuals in particular promoted and controlled the project – Sheikh Abdulaziz al-Ibrahim and the Saudi Ambassador to Venezuela, Sheikh Bakar Khomais.[15]

A leading Venezuelan architect, Oscar Bracho, was selected to develop the design and to co-ordinate the work.[16] He saw this commission as a unique opportunity to produce 'an emblematic cultural sign . . . conceived with the intention of integrating the mosque's strict functionalism to the city's dynamics.'[17] The building was completed some three years after being commissioned, and it is intended that a *madrasa* will be added later.

The mosque is usually referred to as the Caracas Great Mosque; it was inserted into the urban context of a rapidly changing area, and complements a series of religious, cultural and museum buildings along the Santa Rosa Boulevard. The tall concrete and brick minaret is the pivot of

Al-Ibrahim Jami (1993), Caracas, by Oscar Bracho.

(Above) Standing on the Santa Rosa Boulevard, the building holds its own in competing for attention with a series of major religious, cultural and museum buildings along this street.

(Below) The exterior of the *qibla* wall. The upper part of the crystalline *mihrab* incorporates stained glass.

the building, which is located at the junction of an avenue and the boulevard, and acts as a landmark. The visual impact of the building is partially due to its distinctive architectural style, which provides the transition from exuberant urban surroundings to its self-contained peaceful interior.

The mosque stands on a large platform which supports the main elements of the building. The entrance is marked by a series of freestanding portals (with the main one facing the street) leading to the main prayer hall or to the ablutions areas from the raised plaza. As the visitor enters the building, mirrors covering the base of the minaret produce constantly changing reflections of the exterior and of movement through the plaza which also serves as a visual barrier to the busy streets beyond. At the lower level are the ablutions areas and a car park. Separate stairways lead from the men's and women's ablutions chambers to their respective prayer areas.

The prayer hall volume rises from the square base as an octagon and finally makes a transition to the hemispherical dome which serves to define the space both internally and externally. The men's prayer space is on the main level and the women's area on the upper mezzanine level, visually separated by a screen (*mashrabiya*). The interior ornamentation, defined by a horizontal band of calligraphy in bronze, becomes progressively more elaborate towards the *qibla* wall, stopping at the protruding crystalline *mihrab*. The stained-glass *mihrab* is flanked by two other glazed openings through which natural light floods into the prayer hall, illuminating the *qibla* wall area. On either side of the *qibla* wall are deep elevated niches, recalling *muqarnas*, which also admit light. Light also enters the prayer hall from around the perimeter of the dome, so illuminating the method of suspension employed in the structure. In this a metal structural skeleton supports the dome and the ceiling is suspended from a stepped steel girder; as the ceiling in the prayer hall ascends, it is gradually transformed into a series of rings. Stucco work extends partially over the walls and ceilings, and wooden screens with geometric motifs create an inner homogeneous border. The steel-and-concrete structure is faced on the exterior with marble, as are the columns.

'The balance – established by both Western and Islamic architectural systems – turns out to be something without reference or context. Here, it is not a question of pure historicism, nor of selecting from various architectural elements, it is a question of defining this particular balance.'[18] The manner in which the major features that characterize the mosque and the balance of these elements are considerations which are addressed in the majority of contemporary mosque designs.

Turning to the Islamic architectures of the past does not have to be a hollow copying process or an ill-considered pastiche. It can involve a creative dialogue between the designer and the visual languages of the past. Abdel Wahed

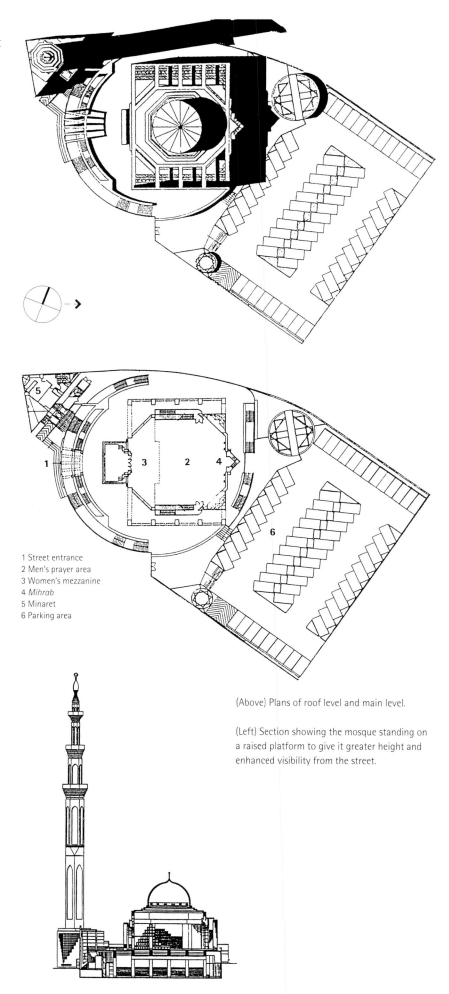

1 Street entrance
2 Men's prayer area
3 Women's mezzanine
4 *Mihrab*
5 Minaret
6 Parking area

(Above) Plans of roof level and main level.

(Left) Section showing the mosque standing on a raised platform to give it greater height and enhanced visibility from the street.

El-Wakil pursued just such a dialogue intensively and extensively in the 1970s and 1980s. Born in 1943 in Cairo, he studied architecture in the faculty of engineering at Ain Shams University. He is a former student and disciple of the Egyptian architect Hassan Fathy. In 1971, he went into professional practice, establishing offices in Cairo and soon afterwards in England (in London and Ashford, Kent).[19] He is noted for an approach to architectural design which stresses continuity within, or the revisiting of tradition as the architect's guiding principle. His work combines traditional vocabularies, historical models and building traditions often from very different sources from within the Arab and Mediterranean regions. He has designed a number of mosques in Saudi Arabia, some for local authorities, like the Corniche and Island mosques (see Chapter 3), some for the Ministry of Hajj and Awqaf, and several others for private patrons.[20] So continuous and consistent has been El-Wakil's series of some eleven mosque projects in terms of their development of a unified visual and constructional language that he has himself called them a 'programme of mosques' rather than individual buildings funded by separate patrons.[21] In actuality, his mosques in Jeddah form only a proportion of the new mosques constructed the 1970s and 1980s by a variety of individual patrons and sited at locations decided in the context of the Master Plan for Jeddah. Other architects, too, were commissioned to build mosques, though few seem to have succeeded in obtaining several commissions, which they could then call a building programme.[21] The choice of El-Wakil as architect by individual as well as by corporate patrons was guided, it seems, by several factors. First was the conservative nature of the clients; second, their acceptance of the discipline of this 'programme'; and, third, the persuasiveness of the architect concerning his intention to recreate the visual impression created by, and also the craftsmanship of, earlier monumental building traditions. The powerful backing of the Mayor of Jeddah, Mohammad Said Al-Farsi, and of Sheikh Husam Khashoggi, the Deputy Minister of Awqaf, seems to have helped to persuade these private patrons to go along with his design and constructional proposals.

Sulaiman Mosque, Jeddah, Saudi Arabia

The earliest of El-Wakil's mosques is the Sulaiman Mosque of 1980, commissioned by Sheikh Abdel Aziz al-Sulaiman and his brothers, for whom the architect had designed a palace.[22] As the first of what would become a series, this mosque was dependent on the faith of the client in the architect's intentions: to design a building which not only looked like the traditional Mamluk/Rasulid mosque, but also to generate these forms using historic materials (brick and stone in contrasting colours) and to employ traditional means of construction, such as the creation of vaults without scaffolding. The mosque is located close to the Jeddah Corniche in the Hamra district; it stands near the Sulaiman Palace, on a site 10,000 sq. m (107,500 sq. ft)

(Below) The Sulaiman Mosque (1980) in Jeddah was the earliest of Abdel Wahed El-Wakil's mosques to be built using traditional materials and construction methods such as the building of vaults without the aid of scaffolding; axonometric projection and the south façade showing the separate entrance used by women.

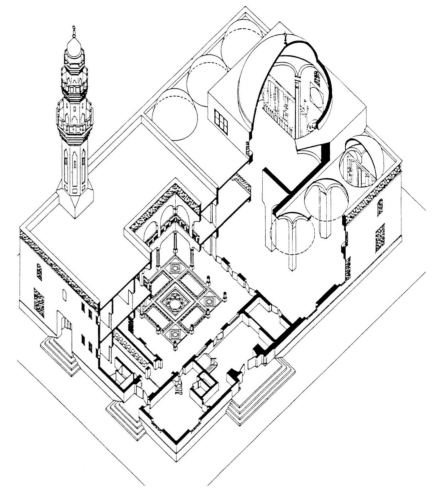

in area. The total area of the mosque itself, which can accommodate about 1,000 worshippers, is approximately 1,500 sq. m (16,100 sq. ft). A raised platform of consolidated earth was used instead of piles to construct the foundation. The layout is based on an Ottoman-style model with two main entrances that lead into an enclosed courtyard, from which the main prayer hall is reached. The entrance on the south side is reserved for women; a staircase on the left leads to a gallery which surrounds the courtyard and which gives access to the women's prayer mezzanine. The prayer hall is surmounted by a large central dome that is supported by six piers and has a span of 12 m (39 ft), flanked by six smaller domes arranged in groups of three, each 6 m (19 ft 6 in.) in diameter.[23] The domes were built without the aid of scaffolding by means of corbelling and other bricklaying techniques rediscovered in Upper Egypt and previously used by El-Wakil's mentor, Hassan Fathy. In this case, the span is larger than any achieved by Fathy, and must be considered a technical feat. According to the architect, it was only the contractors' lack of previous experience in this method of construction which obliged him to agree to the minimal introduction of reinforced concrete into columns and tie beams as a safety measure.

The success of the first of El-Wakil's large mosque projects lent credibility to the design vision and the constructional discipline of the architect. An additional dividend was the development of the skills necessary to

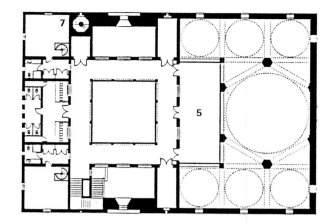

1 Entrances
2 Women's entrance
3 Internal courtyard
4 Men's prayer area
5 Women's gallery
6 *Mihrab*
7 Minaret

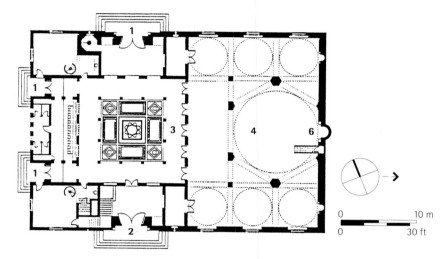

0   10 m
0   30 ft

(Top right) Plans at the mezzanine and ground-floor levels. The layout is based on an Ottoman model, with a courtyard preceding the prayer hall. Flanked by two rows of three smaller domes, the main dome supported on six piers has a span of 12 m (39 ft).

(Above) View into the main dome.

(Right) The interior with the chandelier beneath the dome and an oblique view of the women's gallery.

produce the variety of ornamentation employed in the mosque, such as *muqarnas* and marble paving. The marble floors display rich and varied geometric patterns which harmonize with the scale and the hierarchy of spaces of the building as a whole, while the *muqarnas* have been faithfully reintroduced to areas such as the minaret balconies, the entrance portals and the *mihrab*.

Al-Harithy Mosque, Jeddah, Saudi Arabia

The Al-Harithy Mosque, completed in 1986, was funded by Muwaffak Al-Harithy and built by his own construction company. It has roughly the same floor area as the Sulaiman Mosque and a similar layout, apart from the relative proportions of open and covered areas. The courtyard is situated at the centre with a fountain and some planting; not only is it smaller than the courtyard in the Sulaiman Mosque, but it is also shaded by a retractable canopy tent, so that effectively the entire area of the building becomes usable as prayer space, even at the hottest time of day. In this instance the women's gallery is approached from the rear (west) façade by means of staircases adjacent to the two minarets. The dome over the prayer hall sits on pendentives and was left bare in order to show off the intricate brickwork. The two Ottoman-style minarets at the northwest and southwest corners rise from the body of the building, in contrast to the earlier mosque in which a single minaret is located on the north side of the building.

Al-Harithy Mosque (1986), Jeddah, by Abdel Wahed El-Wakil.

(Above right) View along the *qibla* wall with the carved wooden *minbar*. El-Wakil's mosques all contributed to the revival of traditional crafts; the chandeliers as well as the tile work were carefully planned to complement the overall interior design.

(Right) A view into the small courtyard, which can be adapted to an interior space protected from the sun by closing the retractable cover.

Just as the dome represents the fruits of a re-learned and reintroduced construction technique, so too the elements of ornament – be they the marble paving, the tile work from Kütahya, the hanging metal chandeliers, or the carefully proportioned *muqarnas* – constitute a purposeful revival of specific craft traditions from various centres around the Mediterranean. The ceramic tiles and carved marble finishes of the *mihrab* were made in Turkey. The interior spaces of the Al-Harithy Mosque are more successful and more developed than those of the Sulaiman Mosque, and because of its orientation to the street and its framing pair of minarets, the later building also makes a stronger visual statement in its urban context.

In both mosques, as in all El-Wakil's work, the guiding principle has been the reintegration and reconciliation of traditional design and materials with a contemporary architectural expression. Modernist architects' rejection of ornament for its own sake is countered by El-Wakil, who sees decorative elements as a natural and divinely inspired element in architectural design: '. . . ornament and pattern in building do enlighten architectural space and should be an integral function of form. . . . In fact patterns are the crystallization of beauty. If we see nature as beautiful it is in a sense because we are seeing it as a pattern. Even the mighty creation of the planets, when seen as a pattern, becomes an ornament to the observer expanding his heart through divine beauty.'[24]

The use of direct quotation in his buildings can usually be traced to works of Islamic architecture, particularly in Egypt and Syria, dating from the fourteenth–sixteenth centuries. The architect's adherence to traditional historical forms has been criticized. For example, Mohammad Al-Asad has pointed out: 'Any assessment of architectural historicism should take into consideration the primary role of revivals in the development of western architecture. . . . Renaissance, Baroque and Neo-classical architecture are all historicist in nature and the dependence on past prototypes has not diminished the value of works by Michelangelo, Bernini or

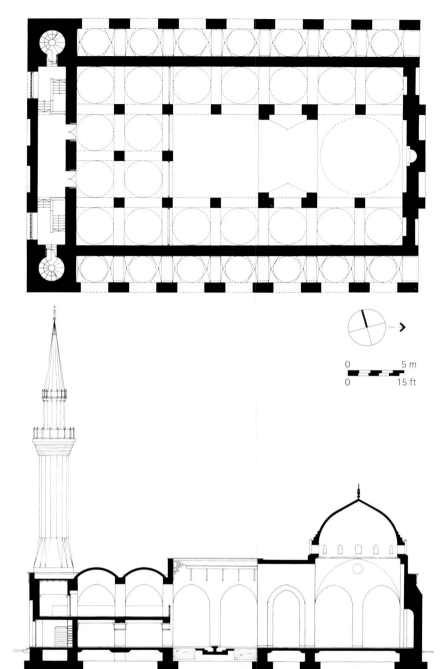

(Above) Plan and section showing the much diminished courtyard space.

(Left) A view of the exterior showing the *qibla* wall and flanking porches which connect the building to the street.

Soane.'[25] El-Wakil's use of past models stems, however, from his dissatisfaction with the rootlessness of modernism. His method encompasses different approaches and produces an eclectic result which, because of his skill as a designer, counts amongst the most interesting architecture of the contemporary Islamic world.

Jumma Masjid, Johannesburg, South Africa

The style of architectural expression developed by El-Wakil began as a regional model, but has subsequently come to be regarded widely throughout the world as an 'authentic' Islamic expression. The articulation and displacement of this model occurs in the design by Muhammad Mayet, advised by El-Wakil, for the Jumma Masjid in Johannesburg, due to be completed in 1997.[26]

The first Muslim community became established in Johannesburg in the late nineteenth century, soon after the town came into existence as the direct result of the discovery of gold deposits there in 1886. During the apartheid era the community, mainly of Indian origin, had been exiled to the peripheral township of Lenasia, but after the abolition of apartheid members of the community returned to re-establish their presence in the city centre and to build a new congregational mosque. The project was financed and commissioned by a single wealthy Indian family and was controlled by three of its members. The architect Muhammad Mayet, whose work was known to the family and who is a member of the local community, was selected for the task. He in turn involved El-Wakil, for whom he had once worked. Construction work on the mosque commenced in 1992.

Within Johannesburg's formal nineteenth-century grid layout the new mosque on Kerk Street in the heart of the Central Business District replaces an inadequate and structurally unsound building of the 1920s on a site with an area of 740 sq. m (7,950 sq. ft). According to the architects, the mosque ' . . . has drawn deeply and reflectively on the traditional disciplines of Islamic sacred art and architecture to produce a building that embodies spiritual constancy and social focus.'[27] This statement, emphasizing the 'sacred' in terms of El-Wakil's own theories of design, makes no reference to local building styles or to Indian architectural traditions, nor does it attempt to introduce a contemporary architectural language. In this respect the transplantation of architecture is similar to the alien use of the Mughal-style dome in Southeast Asia – a form of cultural domination. However, as a building the new mosque provides a striking physical presence in its urban context.

The external walls of the Masjid follow the line of the existing street grid, but internally the prayer hall, which dominates the structure, is rotated to conform with the required orientation towards Mecca. The directional axis is emphasized by the presence of a large dome raised on a drum, allowing natural light to filter onto the *mihrab* located on the north façade. The prayer hall, with its massive structure of loadbearing brick walls and piers,

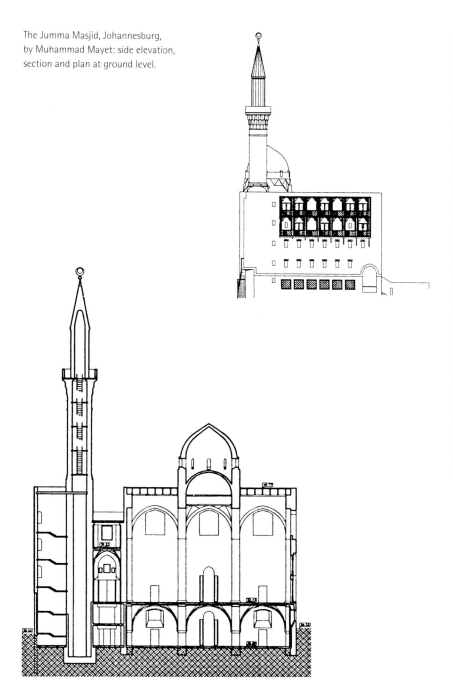

The Jumma Masjid, Johannesburg, by Muhammad Mayet: side elevation, section and plan at ground level.

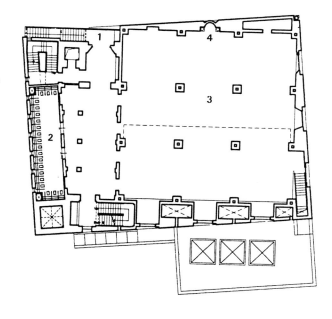

1 Entrance
2 Ablutions
3 Prayer hall
4 *Mihrab*

41

rises from basement level to support arches and vaults that run perpendicular to the *qibla* wall. The building can be entered at street level via an arched opening leading to a hallway from which staircases provide access to the prayer hall and ablutions facilities situated on the upper level; they can also be reached by a dramatic open flight of stairs directly from the street. The architects brought masons (who had worked with El-Wakil on his mosque projects in Saudi Arabia) from Egypt in order to supervise the elegant masonry corbelling. Unfortunately, the nature of the structure is concealed, having been plastered over and painted white. The disproportionately tall minaret, built to compete with the surrounding high-rise buildings, acts as a marker in the cityscape; Mamluk influence is evident in its *muqarnas* balcony. The interiors of the building feature plaster-worked screened openings and the use of the *muqarnas* in the *mihrab* and dome. The design and ornamentation are similar to those used by El-Wakil in the Al-Harithy Mosque (see above) and elsewhere.

Despite the mosque's alien appearance in the urban context of Johannesburg, it is a powerful design statement that is well detailed and built. Instead of choosing an image that could communicate the roots of the local community and its longstanding presence in South Africa, the clients preferred to represent themselves in an overtly Islamic form articulated by the architect. The strength of El-Wakil's architectural vision has been a major factor in shaping the clients' vision of new mosques both in Saudi Arabia and in Johannesburg. Elsewhere, however, there are clients with coherent and articulate vision and ideas who play an active role in shaping project design.

Perhaps the most important patron of new architecture for Muslim societies in recent decades has been His Highness Prince Karim Aga Khan, whose architectural award, educational programmes and commissioned buildings have most consistently explored a contemporary expression of architecture. As the 49th hereditary *Imam* of the Shiite Ismaili Muslim sect, whose members are now scattered throughout the world, the Aga Khan exerts considerable influence on the expression of their major buildings. These are to be found in many regions of the world, from Canada to Bangladesh, and in many other places where Ismaili communities have been established in recent history. The Aga Khan regards architecture as a manifestation of culture and a tool to express both modernity and unity for his diverse followers. Ismaili centres and *jamatkhanas* (places of gathering for the community) now exist all over the world, and under his patronage a common idiom appears to be emerging. These new centres are programmatically comparable to many others that have been completed since the 1960s, in that they are conceived as multi-functional projects containing not only the prayer hall, but meeting areas, educational facilities and libraries, recreational and social spaces, and other facilities such as living quarters for

(Below) The Ismaili Centre (1985) in London, designed by Neville Conder of the Casson Conder Partnership, emulates the scale of the surrounding buildings, such as the Victoria and Albert Museum (seen in the background), while simultaneously reflecting the mood of Islamic architectural tradition.

(Opposite) The generous octagonal entrance hall with its central fountain creates an effect reminiscent of a courtyard and at the same time echoes the transitional spaces typical of Iranian architecture. On entering, the visitor is reminded of the nature of the building by the presence of the prominently displayed *bismillah*; the calligraphy is by Karl Schlamminger (see p. 1).

the staff. The Ismaili community worldwide has already built a number of such centres in the Indian subcontinent, East Africa, the United Kingdom, the United States and Canada, and schemes exist for others elsewhere in Europe and parts of the Arab world not previously inhabited by its members. Although each local Ismaili Council establishes a legal entity that is usually the client of record in these projects, the Aga Khan himself has been the decision-maker and as such can be considered an individual patron whose concerns and tastes dictate the design. By comparing two of these centres, common characteristics and the approach of their patron can be discerned.

Ismaili Centre, London, UK

The first major Ismaili Centre to be built in the West was in central London. In order to meet the growing need for a new centre, a site had been identified in 1971, but this was abandoned later in favour of the present one in South Kensington. The architects, the Casson Conder Partnership (with Neville Conder as the partner-in-charge, working with his associate Kenneth Price), were asked to design a building compatible with its central London setting, to meet the programmatic requirements of the Ismaili community and to reflect the mood of Islamic architectural tradition. (The

The quiet contemplative environment of the
prayer hall is enhanced by modulated light and
a harmonized programme of ornamentation
that is at once rich and disciplined.

(Below) Detail of decorative panels in the prayer hall.

(Right) The architects exploited the irregular shape of the site which provided opportunities for developing special corner articulations, while at the same time responding skilfully to the overall requirements of a complex design programme.

(Bottom) The upper floor of the Ismaili Centre includes the library and meeting rooms, which are disposed around an exquisite small courtyard roof garden providing a restful haven amidst busy urban surroundings.

choice of the word 'mood' in the brief was important, for it signalled that the building was not to be a mere pastiche of past architectural styles but should capture what might be perceived as the spirit of Islam.) Besides the main prayer facilities, space was required for religious education, senior citizens' and youth activities, as well as meeting, seminar and reception rooms. In addition, the design was to include a substantial public exhibition gallery.

The island site occupying some 1,730 sq. m (18,600 sq. ft) bordered by the very busy Cromwell Road presented a problem not only of layout but of circulation in having to deal with the entrance and egress of large numbers of people. Moreover, the site is surrounded by buildings in a variety of styles (neo-Venetian Gothic, neo-Baroque and Edwardian terraced houses). Typical materials and colours used in nearby buildings are brick, stone, terracotta and white stucco. The architectural task was a substantial one, given the restricted nature of the site and the scale and complexity of the requirements. The foundation stone was laid in September 1979, and construction started a year later. The building was completed in 1984 and inaugurated in April 1985.[28]

Almost all of the site area is occupied, with four floors above ground and two basement levels. The interior spaces and the roof garden have been designed for specific community use, as well as for public functions. At ground-floor level there is a generous octagonal entrance hall with a central fountain creating an effect reminiscent of a courtyard, as well as a large reception hall and circulation space that minimizes the impact of crowds outside the building during periods of peak use. This level also houses some offices, a cloakroom, washrooms, and a large kitchen accessible from a small service yard at the rear. On the first floor there is a large hall for events which also serves as a gathering place for worshippers before and after prayers. The main focus of the plan is the wide prayer hall which occupies much of the second floor. It is reached via generous foyers and staircases and provides a quiet and contemplative environment. In relation to its area the richly tiled and carpeted hall has a low ceiling which emphasizes the sense of intimacy, horizontality and equality that is so often absent in major spaces intended for prayer due to the soaring verticality of the interior. The top level contains a small library with meeting rooms around a small but beautiful courtyard garden designed by the American Don Olson of Sasaki Associates of Watertown, Massachusetts. The art gallery (later transformed into meeting rooms), which has a separate entrance, was located mainly in the lower basement with storage and service spaces. There is no provision for parking on the site.

The exterior of the building is clad in vertically corrugated granite and is modulated with alcoves and protrusions that have teak window frames and doors. In planning the interior design the architects were assisted by several specialists.[29] The architectural vocabulary of the interior harmonizes with the exterior and the great care that was devoted to detailing

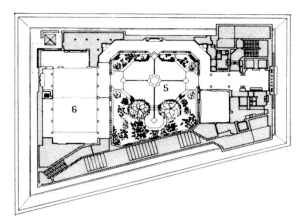

Third floor

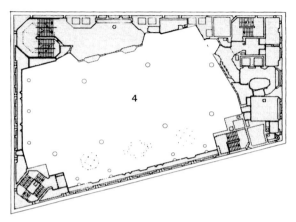

Second floor

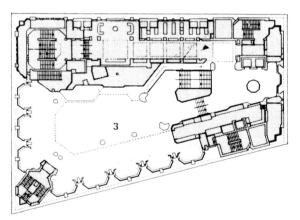

First floor

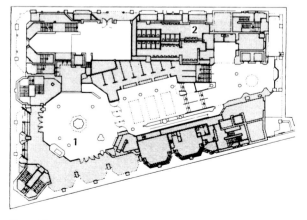

Ground floor

Floor plans of the Ismaili Centre, showing the prayer hall and roof garden at second and third levels respectively.

1 Entrance hall
2 Toilets/ablutions
3 Social hall
4 Prayer hall
5 Roof garden
6 Council chamber/ conference room

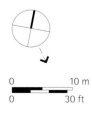

| 0 | 10 m |
| 0 | 30 ft |

is apparent throughout. Materials such as marble, wood, bevelled glass and stainless steel and brass are all employed in a modern style. The carpets, tile work, fountains, intricate moulded plaster ceilings, cast-iron grills, screens and other elements are abstractions of well-known traditional designs. Calligraphy is also used in several carefully selected places. Although the building seems over-designed and detailed in some respects, it is nonetheless a showcase for arts and crafts associated with Muslim cultures.

Ismaili Jamatkhana and Centre, Burnaby, British Columbia, Canada

Similar to the London Ismaili Centre in terms of its scope and programme, this building is located in a suburb of Vancouver, where the first Ismaili congregation in Canada was established. The Centre caters to Ismailis who began arriving in the mid-1960s and then in greater numbers in the 1970s, largely due to political upheavals in East and Central Africa.

The Burnaby site is very different from the London one: it is a flat suburban lot with an area of just under 15,000 sq. m (161,500 sq. ft), more than eight times that of the London site. It was acquired in 1979 and a prominent local architect, Bruno Freschi (who was also the chief architect for Expo '86 held in Vancouver), was commissioned to prepare designs. Construction began in 1982 and was finished in October 1984. The building was officially opened in August 1985. The site offered the architect far greater freedom of design than did the London one, and the result is comparable in quality, although it is simpler and the detailing less intricate. The building has an area of 3,870 sq. m (41,600 sq. ft) and is arranged on two floors plus a basement level. On-site parking facilities are limited to space for a maximum of 134 cars, and it was found necessary to supplement this by leasing land across the street. The architect explained his

The Ismaili Jamatkhana and Centre (1985) in Burnaby, B.C., by Bruno Freschi.

(Left) The complex is preceded by an elegantly landscaped forecourt; the sandstone façade features a massive central portal and is further articulated by complex lateral fenestration.

(Opposite) A view of the citadel-like exterior, and the interior of the double-height prayer hall showing the *qibla* wall decorated with panels of coral and marble. The sculptural ceiling features a series of shallow Ottomanesque octagonal domes.

(Right) Detail of one of the three-dimensional window openings seen from within. The striking glass construction resulted from systematic exploration of the traditional *muqarnas* and dialogue between architect and patron.

(Below) Ground-level plan of the Ismaili Jamatkhana and Centre.

1 Landscaped forecourt
2 Entrance loggia
3 Ablutions/shoe-racks
4 Prayer hall

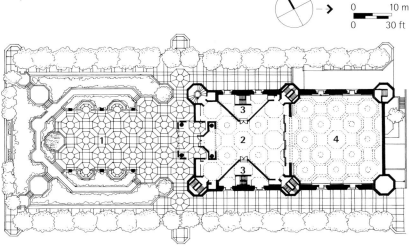

design thus: 'A pursuit of geometry, enclosure, symmetry, mass and layering of symbolic decorations have generated the architectural concept . . . these architectural principles and use of materials have structured and characterized the building.'[30]

Unlike London, the main approach is by car. The building lies along an axis perpendicular to the street, preceded by an elegantly landscaped forecourt,[31] but the access roadway skirts this to reach the open parking area, while pedestrian entrance to the court is from the side, detracting from the initial visual impact of the approach. The building is clad in warm beige sandstone, its citadel-like exterior being punctuated by a soaring portal entrance and unusual three-dimensional window niches featuring glazed geometric patterns. The prayer hall, situated off the entrance loggia, is an impressive carpeted double-height space, whose architectonic elements are carefully balanced to produce a quiet and warm environment. The *qibla* wall is articulated in rectangular sand-blasted white coral and rose-coloured marble panels, combined with Italian Marmorina tiles from Carrara; the decorative panels incorporate the names Allah, Muhammad and Ali inlaid in brass. The natural lighting, which enters from the windows and the thirteen octagonal domes with skylights above, fills the interior with a subdued golden glow. Although the prayer hall is more successful than its London counterpart, the multi-purpose social hall on the upper floor is not as flexible in terms of use, for here visitors have to pass through the entrance loggia to reach it, so mingling with those who have come to pray. The lower basement level, which also benefits from natural light, contains administrative offices and classrooms.

On the occasion of the Burnaby foundation ceremony in July 1982, the Aga Khan's speech was directly relevant to all major Ismaili Centres in the West. In it he said: 'It will be a place of congregation, of order, of peace, of prayer, of hope, of humility and brotherhood . . . It is my hope that it will become a symbol of a growing understanding in the West of a very deep and real meaning of Islam.'[32] Architecturally, the London and Burnaby buildings share a similar language: both are modern, inward-looking, reveal careful attention paid to detail and landscaping, and are of a high quality. In them one can observe a systematic exploration of reinterpreted Islamic themes and motifs that result from an intensive dialogue between patron and architect.

The Aga Khan's personal patronage has given rise to the construction of a number of modern buildings in which overt historicist references have been avoided. By contrast, the architectural patronage of King Hassan II of Morocco can be designated a building programme with a specific cultural, and stylistic bias and aim – namely, to ensure the continuity of Moroccan craft traditions in building and ornamentation. Thus, the numerous buildings which have been started as a result of his initiative and funding almost invariably reflect a very specific visual idiom associated with Moroccan (Andalusian/Maghrebi) traditional architecture. So strong has been this insistence on using the same idiom in mosque building in Morocco that there are very few examples that do not conform with this style. This idiom has also been promulgated as the official style of architecture for all new mosques in Morocco, and has also been exported,

The square minaret of the Great Mosque, Dakar (left), a building dating from the 1970s; closely modelled on the historic ninth-century Qarawiyyin Mosque in Fez (the courtyard of which is seen below), the new mosque was a gift from the people of Morocco to the republic of Senegal.

and easy to use, it belongs inevitably to the past. However, this modern use of an Andalusian/Maghrebi style in Morocco has become the norm; it is a style which every major architectural gesture, both governmental and institutional, seeks to emulate. Indeed, it is now commonly referred to locally as the 'Hassanian style'.

Lalla Soukaina Mosque, Rabat, Morocco

Among the numerous recent religious buildings, a notable example is the Lalla Soukaina Mosque in Rabat. Built in honour of King Hassan's first granddaughter and named after her, it was completed in 1988. Its architects, Youssef Mouline, Mohammed Said and Moustafa Zeghart of Rabat were provided with a considerable budget for innovative roof design and a luxurious programme of ornament. The site has an area of 1 hectare (2¹/₂ acres) and the built area occupies 5,400 sq. m (58,100 sq. ft). With its single square minaret, it dominates the approach to Rabat on the road from Casablanca. The city of Rabat has expanded in this direction and further growth is anticipated. The mosque can accommodate 1,000 worshippers in its prayer hall and another 1,500 in overflow space, including the side gardens

as in the case of the Great Mosque of Dakar, Senegal. Built in the mid-1970s as a gift from the king and country of Morocco to the newly independent republic of Senegal and gradually taking on the role of a State Mosque, it was closely modelled on the Qarawiyyin Mosque in Fez.

The question of architectural language is very important to King Hassan II. An advocate of 'authentic Moroccan architecture', the king had let it be known at a colloquium on construction in December 1979 that the historical precedents of Almohad building style and craftsmanship were the correct ones. In an affirmation of traditional architectural values, expressed in unequivocal moral terms, he said: '... aesthetic aspects must be in harmony with our cities, our past, and the requirements of modern times. ... In preserving the originality of our architecture we can protect family cohesion and the children, the adults and the elderly, from that moral and intellectual pollution of which we spoke already.'[33] In this process King Hassan has championed the continuation and revival of indigenous handicrafts and building craftsmanship, and initiated the publication of an authoritative two-volume study by André Paccard.[34] Traditional Moroccan architecture has typically featured rectangular structures involving the use of beige-coloured stone, green-tiled roofs, intricately carved plaster work and stucco, *zellij* mosaic work, the characteristic blue, green and white wall- and floor-tiles with geometric patterns, the beautiful brightly painted wooden ceilings and beams, and epigraphy in various styles. Interiors are adorned with rich coverings, fabrics and carpets derived from both tribal and local urban cultures. Although Andalusian architecture includes some of the world's greatest buildings, and its formal language is exceptional

(Above) Aerial view and courtyard of the Lalla Soukaina Mosque (1988), Rabat, by Mouline, Said and Zeghait. Here, standard traditional features employed in the decoration of Moroccan mosques – tile mosaic, carved plaster, wooden ceiling and square minaret – veil major changes in layout and the roof design, in which retractable covers are used.

and the side and front esplanades. While the visual programme of the mosque, its tile mosaics, carved plaster, complex wooden ceiling, multi-lobed arches and green tiled roofs represent clear aspects of the familiar, they also serve to mask or make palatable to the client and to the user the real innovations of the building's design and construction. First, the layout of the plan has been significantly altered. The ubiquitous courtyard (*sahn*) has been reduced to no more than a small landscaped area with fountain and flanking porticoed gardens which can only by regarded as a remembrance of the traditional functional courtyard. Second, the roofs, seemingly traditional in appearance, are in fact great sliding covers over a trellis, operated by a complex computerized hydraulic system. (This feature was later taken to its monumental conclusion in the Hassan II Mosque in Casablanca, discussed below.) Thus, the large interior spaces can be lit by either direct or diffused light.

King Abdul Aziz Mosque and Foundation, Casablanca, Morocco

Similar to the previous examples in intent and style is the King Abdul Aziz Mosque and Foundation in Casablanca, completed five years earlier. A gift from Prince Abdullah Ibn Abdul Aziz al-Saud of Saudi Arabia to the Kingdom of Morocco, the semi-autonomous Foundation in Casablanca was set up as a *waqf*, with headquarters in Riyadh.[35] The Mosque and Foundation were designed by Rashid Sabunji, and the contract was awarded to the French firm Coteba International, which undertook the construction on land owned by King Abdul Aziz adjacent to the Corniche. The project was completed in June 1983, within the strict time limit of ten months imposed by the client and within the budget of 27.6 million *dirham* (US$3.7 million). It comprises a mosque with accommodation for 2,200 worshippers using separate men's and women's prayer halls, as well as reading rooms and a library with a capacity for 200,000 books, two *hammams*, residences and a bakery.

While its massing may be fortress-like and its layout different, lacking the great gardens and the use of sliding roofs, this mosque is nevertheless dressed in the acceptable garb of tile mosaic (*zellij*) and carved plaster interiors. The presence of the mosque is signalled by a tall and slender minaret, square in plan, that resembles older traditional Moroccan minarets such as that of the Maulay Idris Zawiya in Fez. The roof is covered typically in green tiles. A covered rectangular courtyard is overlooked by the library housed on the upper storey. The prayer hall, also rectangular in plan, measures approximately 40 x 60 m (130 x 195 ft), with a ceiling 6.50 m (21 ft) in height and a dome rising to 16 m (52 ft). The interior is lit by 90 copper chandeliers.

In order to comply with the time demand, the contractors used many prefabricated elements – such as beams and arches – and the main structure is in reinforced concrete. The extensive decorative programme was executed by a large workforce. Up to 800 specialized craftsmen were employed to carry out the intricate carved stucco work on

(Above) The street façade of the King Abdul Aziz Mosque and Foundation, Casablanca, by Coteba International. Completed in 1983 and dressed in acceptable ornamental garb, the mosque was built and decorated in the space of ten months using many prefabricated elements.

(Below) View of the interior, the decoration of which was executed by a workforce of 800 craftsmen, carvers, tile cutters and painters.

the arches and capitals in the prayer hall and on the façade. Also notable are the extensive tile work and the decorative woodwork in cedar used for doors and screens, while the ceilings were executed in painted wood (*zouaq*). Although the building is rich in ornamentation, the result does, however, betray a lack of careful detailing and finishing.

Mosque of Hassan II, Casablanca, Morocco

In the past, individual patron rulers would make gestures on behalf of the state – a situation that has become rare in the contemporary world. One such gesture is exemplified in the largest new mosque in the world, the Mosque of Hassan II in Casablanca, completed in 1993. It is worth recalling the historical and social context within which the work has been realized. For the first five hundred years of Islam, the fact of descent from the Prophet had not been an aspect of monarchical rule in Morocco. However, since the sixteenth century, soon after the founding of the Sa'di dynasty, Moroccan rulers came to consolidate their power both as rulers and as guardians of Islam on the basis of their descent from the Prophet Muhammad. The Alawid dynasty came to the forefront in 1666 and still exists today in the person of King Hassan II, who came to the throne in 1961. As a patron of the arts, the king seems always to have been conscious of the power of building to impart a sense of dynasty and stability, having inherited a state rich in historic buildings, including palaces, *madrasas* and mosques, such as those in Fez and Marrakech. It is hardly surprising that the monarch

The Great Mosque of Hassan II (1986–93), Casablanca, by Michel Pinseau. The imposing substructure, and the lower elements of the complex, such as the semicircular education centre, help to modulate the massive scale of prayer hall and the minaret.

(Opposite) General view from the southeast.

(Opposite below) Detail of the arcades and decorative panels in the forecourt (see also p. 60). The pattern of intersecting lobes recalls the relief decoration on the upper part of the minaret of the twelfth-century Mosque of Hassan in Rabat, the capital of Morocco.

(Below) Site plan and aerial view of the entire complex. The relationship of the site to the sea and the city is clearly shown.

1 Entrance forecourt
2 Minaret
3 Prayer hall
4 *Madrasa*/education centre

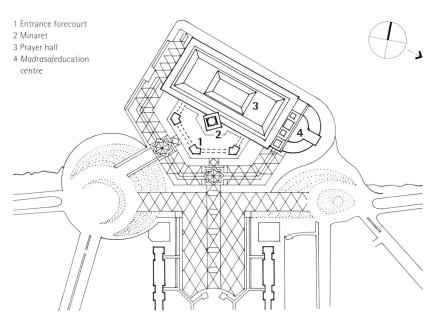

should regard the continuation of building traditions linked to a continuing ruling dynasty as part of his own social responsibility. In 1962, he commissioned a mausoleum for his father, the late King Mohammed V, to be built in Rabat opposite the historic twelfth-century Mosque of Hassan, which also served as one of the models for the minaret of the Hassan II Mosque (the other being the minaret of the twelfth-century Almohad mosque, the Kutubiyya, in Marrakech). The king's desire to build a mosque by the sea came about in the context of plans for the mausoleum project, which he at first wanted to be in Casablanca, but later decided to build in the capital. However, Casablanca lacked a focal point or major monument, even though it was the country's leading economic centre, and in 1986 the king announced his decision to build the mosque there.

It is said, as has often been quoted, that the siting of the mosque was inspired by the Qur'anic verse describing the Creation of the World: '... and His throne was over the waters' (Sura XI:7). Casablanca's location at the western end of the Arab-Islamic world and close to the West was also seen as a vantage point from which to signal the presence of Islam in the form of a major monument. Thus, it is no accident that the idea of building a massive minaret serving both as a landmark and as a beacon is an important one – one that achieves architectural monumentality on an unprecedented scale in the Mosque of Hassan II. The issue of scale, of representation of the importance of the kingdom and its ruler, became translated into the dictum whereby greatness is conveyed by size. In terms of area, the mosque was to be second only to the holy mosque in Mecca (to exceed which might have been seen as an unacceptable act of self-aggrandisement). The Casablanca mosque is the largest contemporary building of its kind and it is therefore not surprising that it is often referred to as the Great Mosque of Hassan II.[36]

Another issue that comes to mind is by its very nature more subtle and psychological. The architectural language that existed in the buildings of past centuries is seen as being 'permanent and legitimate', and the link with the distant past, unsullied by a more recent colonial presence, could only lend weight to the permanence of the faith and its spiritual leader amid the uncertainty of modern political circumstances. As Mohammed Arkoun, a prominent historian of Islamic thought, has written: '... in Muslim societies today there exists a crisis of meaning because the long-established roots of religious authority have been replaced by a pluralistic outlook based on post-modern ideas which no longer recognize the concept of a single reality ... In traditional Muslim societies governmental authority was formerly rendered legitimate only by having a religious basis. In modern times, however, the role of places of worship as dynamic sources of spiritual energy and creativity has declined ... '.[37]

This idea is an important one today because the basis of authority needs to be conveyed to the population at large as legitimate, and the architectural language of legitimacy is that of the past. Hence, the contemporary monarch instructs the architect to follow historical precedent clearly and unambiguously. Given this formidable task, Michel Pinseau, the French architect of the Hassan II Mosque, had limited scope for interpretation and innovation, but was given the opportunity to use and express his planning and technical skills.[38]

The mosque combines provision for the act of worship with facilities for learning and social interaction. In this respect it has much in common with the many recent Islamic Centres built all over the world as multi-functional spaces. The Hassan II Mosque consists of five principal elements: the mosque itself incorporates a prayer hall which can accommodate 25,000 worshippers, areas for ablutions, thermal baths, meeting and VIP rooms, in addition to other ancillary spaces and the tall minaret. The *madrasa* covers some 4,200 sq. m (45,200 sq. ft) as a semicircular protrusion containing a Qur'anic school, a library specializing in Islamic

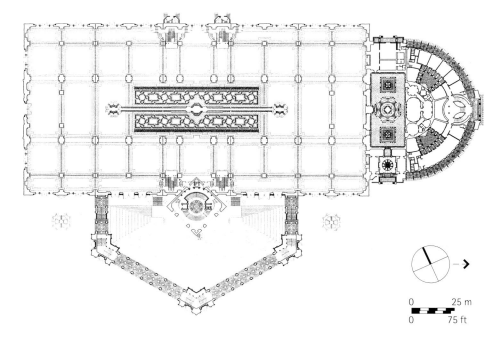

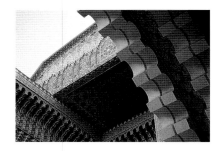

(Left) Plan of the Great Mosque complex, with forecourt, arcade and minaret, large rectangular prayer hall and semicircular *madrasa*/education centre.

(Opposite) The highly ornamented roof which, when opened (see detail above), creates an internal courtyard in the prayer hall.

(Overleaf) A view of the prayer hall looking towards the *mihrab*.

0   25 m
0   75 ft

Sciences and other conference and audio-visual spaces. The third element is the Public Library and Museum which constitute two symmetrically arranged separate buildings along the main access plaza. Another major element is the esplanade itself, a huge open space covering some 30,000 sq. m (323,000 sq. ft) and surrounded by columns; this outdoor area can be used as an extension of the prayer hall to accommodate over 80,000 people. The fifth element is that of transport facilities, with an underground road and the provision of parking space for up to 1,100 vehicles, including 40 coaches.

The work was undoubtedly a major architectural and constructional undertaking. It was overseen by one of the world's major engineering, project management and construction companies, the French Bouygues group, which has worked in Morocco over many years. The technical problems associated with the seaside location and with land reclamation were only a starting point. The deep foundations extending down through the water, provision for anti-swell and anti-seismic stabilizing structures, and protection of the site and the building itself required the use of 300,000 m³ of concrete and 40,000 tonnes of steel. The mining, cutting and layering of marble sufficient to cover an area of 220,000 sq. m (approx. 2.4 million sq. ft), and the chiseling and carving of 30,000 sq. m (323,000 sq. ft) of plaster work, and the painting and carving of wood covering some 40,000 sq. m (430,500 sq. ft) were major logistical tasks in themselves. Over 30,000 technicians, masons, craftsmen and workmen were employed to spend 50 million man-hours over the construction period of nearly seven years.[39] The very scale of the programme – a grand vision and a truly *grand projet* – is staggering. The work was financed mainly through the subscriptions of about 13 million people amounting to over 3 billion *dirham* (approximately US$400 million). Taxes and other cash contributions from individuals, corporations and the royal treasury made up the rest of the funds, but the real cost of the project remains unclear, though the figure most often quoted in the press at the time of its opening was US$700 million.[40] In 1995, another appeal was made, this time for funds to maintain the complex.[41]

There are a few aspects of the design that are worth stressing. Pinseau was working on a scale well beyond that of any of the structures that served as his points of reference. The human being seems lost within the vast new structure, which stands aloof and richly decorated as an object of wonder rather than a welcoming building within which the act of prayer can be made in simple comfort.

The minaret takes the form of a square tower with lantern topped by a finial made of copper, rising to a height of 200 m (650 ft) from a base measuring 25 x 25 m (56 x 56 ft); it is literally a lighthouse, from which a laser beam with a 30 km (20 mile) range is projected from the summit in the direction of Mecca. Owing to the weight of this tower, the structure supporting it had to be reinforced greatly; it is reported to have four times the strength of the tunnel under

Details taken from the mosque's extensive ornamental programme. The walls, ceiling and structural supports feature decorative finishes in tile mosaic (*zellij*), carved plaster and painted woodwork, all executed with craftsmanship of the highest order.

the English Channel. The relationship of the height and size of the minaret to the mass of the building does not represent a proportionate increase following traditional practice, and as a result the tower appears out of scale.

The rectangular prayer hall (200 x 100 m/650 ft x 325 ft) is oriented with the short side adjacent to the *qibla* wall – an unconventional layout given that it is customary for the rows of worshippers facing Mecca to be as wide as possible rather than extend further back – but this only becomes a consideration when the mosque is full. The retractable roof (3,400 sq. m/36,500 sq. ft) in area over the central part of the prayer hall can be opened to form an internal courtyard when weather conditions permit. This roof construction is a technological feat in itself, requiring roof tiles identical in appearance to the clay tiles in the Qarawiyyin Mosque in Fez but cast in aluminium in order to achieve a substantial reduction in weight. The effect of the roof being opened is dramatic, in that the natural top-lighting changes one's perception of the interior space. The effect of combining granite and marble for the floor covering is reminiscent of the design of Moroccan floor rugs. The walls, featuring *zellij* ceramic tile mosaic and intricate plaster work, and the painted ceilings are all decorative works of the highest level of craftsmanship. Two mezzanine floors along each side of the hall serve as the women's prayer galleries with their own direct access from the ablutions facilities. The stepped ceilings are at 65 m (210 ft) above the floor at the highest level, 38 m (125 ft) for the intermediate section, and 27 m (90 ft) for the lateral parts. The crystal chandeliers made in Venice have diameters ranging from 3 m to 6 m (10 to 20 ft).

The ablutions chambers below the prayer hall present a labyrinthine forest of columns, with lotus-blossom basins[42] and fountains placed within spaces covered in tile work. They are the most elaborate facilities of their kind anywhere in the world. In addition, there are *hammams* (the Moroccan or Turkish thermal baths) and a heated swimming pool that, in the Western mind, may well conjure up images like those in Orientalist paintings by Ingres or Gérôme. In this area the architecture enters the realm of fantasy and transforms the interior into an underground house of wonder.

Viewed from the outside, the complex is broken down in scale by the juxtaposition of lower elements and roofs that to some extent disguise the bulk of the prayer hall. From the esplanade on the south side the hall is also bisected by the minaret which is turned to form a 45° angle with it. External courts, arcades and changes in level also help to offset the massiveness of the structure. These devices are successful to some extent and the façades are modulated further by their decorative treatment. The entrance porch and the long sides of the building are covered with carved and polished marble. The three doors on the west façade shine dramatically when reflecting the setting sun. The esplanade acts as a giant plaza, and is also used by the populace as a promenade area during the evenings and weekends. Architecturally, it provides an open space around the mosque to set the building off against the sea.

The sumptuousness of the interiors contrasts with the subdued elegance of the exterior finish. The natural beige Moroccan marble, the green tile work, the copper and brass doors and the traditional green roofs work well over the exterior and help unify the complex. Surprisingly enough, even though the monumental nature of the structure raises certain questions associated with scale, modesty and sense of place, the building situated on the very edge of the city is not overwhelming in its urban context. It is, however, overwhelming when one is close to it. The grandiose aspect of the building, with its rich materials and decoration, attracts hundreds of visitors from within the country and tourists from without, and as a result organized tours have become an important feature of the life of this complex.

After years in the making and with alleged cost overruns, the building was finally inaugurated in August 1993 on the eleventh day of the month of Rabi' al-Awwal (the eve of the anniversary of the Prophet Muhammad's birth) in the year 1414 of the Muslim calendar, four hundred years after al-Mansur inaugurated his Baadi Palace in Marrakech on the same anniversary occasion and in the same way, as has been pointed out by the anthropologist Elaine Combs-Schilling. She notes that 'The significance of such a gesture is not accidental. The ceremony itself, almost identical in content and form to the one centuries earlier, reaffirms nationhood and the King's secular and religious roles. The prayer hall is full to capacity; the King and his cortege enter watched by his subjects, and presidents and diplomats from around the world, and some one thousand media people. The candle-lit procession, the prayers led by the King, and the incantation of poems of praise to the Prophet by the three winners of a poetry competition culminate in a new symbolic event. The King asks the female winner of the fourth award to read her own poem – probably unprecedented in a mosque – and the ceremony closes with this reading.'[43]

The values that the monarch stands for and his role as both the Guardian of the Faith and the father of his people are played out to the nation at large, and to the nations represented at the inaugural ceremony, either in their presence or through the mass media. In the twentieth century the national reaffirmation is extended into the international arena.

In the Mosque of Hassan II the architect, spurred on by the client, has produced an enigmatic and undoubtedly major architectural statement – the building is at once brutal and poetic and one cannot but be moved to react to it. The architectural concerns of place, scale, quality, materials and craftsmanship, as well as the technical feats embodied in the work, are strongly influenced by cultural, social and symbolic meanings and rituals. The creation of this complex has raised some difficult questions about representation, expression of authority and legitimacy of the state. The building presents in microcosm much larger issues concerning the nature and role of nations today, and of architecture as symbol – in this instance, blurring the line between individual and state patronage.

Chapter 2

The State as client

The processes which engendered the concept of the state mosque are intimately tied to those of shaping a national identity. Newly independent states emerging from colonial rule, such as the republics of Indonesia and Algeria and the Islamic republics of Malaysia and Pakistan, are prime examples of countries in which the idea of a state mosque, as opposed to that of the mosque of a ruler, has been introduced. Just as the leaders of the new political entities attempted to define their state in both modern and Islamic terms, so too did they and their architects seek to embody the state in a monumental building which would express both these characteristics.

The state mosque is a building initiated by the central government and paid for by public funds. It is inevitably conceptualized by a committee with an insistence upon a clearly recognizable image, that is to say explicit in terms of regional, modernist and Islamic references. The earliest state mosques were also often planned as symbolic monuments to independence and individual examples were generally seen as representing the projection of a country's Islamic and national identity and the legitimization of its regime in the eyes of the world. Further, this essentially contemporary phenomenon was also driven by the necessity to implant and to develop a national identity distinct from that of a similar but often unfriendly neighbour.

Scale is an important factor in these new buildings: they are large complexes with a capacity ranging from 5,000 to 25,000 worshippers in a single covered space, and provision for between 50,000 and 200,000 in the courts and open areas during major Muslim festivals such as Eid al-Adha. The state mosque complex usually also includes a madrasa and sometimes an Islamic university, a library and spaces for social gathering. The emphasis on the multiple use of space can be seen as a rebirth in mosque design consciously harking back to the earliest mosques which tended to be multi-functional buildings.

Unlike local community mosques which were usually integrated into the urban fabric, state mosques have been treated as isolated monuments to be as highly visible as possible. They share this landmark aspect with many historic

(Above) View of Islamabad, capital of Pakistan, showing the King Faisal Masjid (1970–86), designed by the Turkish architect Vedat Dalokay. Resembling a massive tent, the concrete structure and its four minarets dominate the city (see p. 76).

(Opposite) The exposed concrete ceiling of the prayer hall in the Sher-e-Bangla Nagar Capitol Complex Mosque (1962–83), Dhaka, by Louis Kahn. A series of sculptural cutouts allow the interior to be flooded with natural light (see p. 98).

large-scale buildings, such as the dynastic mosques of Istanbul, Isfahan, Delhi or Cairo. Congregational mosques were traditionally the largest buildings in any city, and their monumentality was mediated through the structure of their dependencies. By virtue of their scale and functions they merged easily into the general urban matrix. By contrast, the state mosque is a type that was perhaps never intended to be integrated into a densely built urban fabric, but rather to stand apart from it.

Quite often, for reasons ranging from changes in the programme to funding difficulties, the completion of a state mosque may occur only decades after the decision to build it was first taken. Nonetheless, the visual identity of the state mosque as an expression of nationhood and political will is anchored in the prevailing social and political climate of the time in which the idea took shape. It is for this reason that the state mosques discussed below are presented in the order in which the projects were conceived, regardless of when they were eventually realized or, in a few cases, have not proceeded beyond the project stage.

Istiqlal Mosque, Jakarta, Indonesia

Indonesia, a nation which has a population of around 90 million and also the largest number of Muslim inhabitants in the world, appears to have been the country in which the concept of the state mosque was introduced, coming ten years after independence from Dutch colonial rule was achieved in 1945. A competition was organized and sponsored by the Indonesian government for the design of the Istiqlal (Freedom) Mosque to be sited in the centre of the capital, Jakarta. A requirement of the competition was that the mosque should accommodate at least 20,000 people, a figure considered enormous in 1955, but which had been

The Istiqlal Mosque (1955–84), Jakarta, by F. Silaban.

(Left) Aerial view from the south: in addition to the main prayer hall, the complex contains spaces for classrooms, meetings and offices. A major festival of Islamic arts is also held in the courtyards and lower level of the complex.

(Above) The tall minaret, a modernized version of the pencil-like Ottoman type, is a prominent feature of the burgeoning metropolis.

(Opposite) Site plan showing the mosque surrounded by gardens and a canal; and exterior view seen from the rectangular courtyard, showing the main prayer hall on the left and the entrance pavilion on the right.

expanded to 100,000 (including worshippers using the courtyard spaces) by the time of completion in 1984.[1]

The participants in the competition were specifically asked to use materials that were long-lasting, maintenance-free and, wherever possible, locally manufactured. That all the architects were Indonesian clearly projects nationalist concerns.[2] The winning design was by F. Silaban (who died in 1986).[3] Silaban chose to express the image of a modern nation not in a regional style but rather through imported idioms, specifically the use of such Ottoman references as the landmark minaret and, more generally, the monumental socialist-realist architecture of the Soviet Union, if not the earlier secular architecture of Atatürk's Turkey. The idea of adopting a regional image does not appear to have occurred to him.

References to Ottoman architecture are not unusual in state mosques and are also found in those of Malaysia and Pakistan. The influence of socialist realism is apparent in the many manifestations of buildings and monuments in Indonesia commemorating the war of independence under Sukarno. The influence of the Soviet and Chinese Communist parties on Indonesia was at its zenith in 1961 and the expressions of heroic monumentality inherent in the architecture of those states were regarded both as reflections of liberation and as populist nationalist gestures.[4] It thus seems plausible that Soviet advisors probably played a role, directly or indirectly, in the elaboration of this new national image, characterized by the combining of an imported secular architecture with an Islamic religious building type. As Sukarno has stated in his autobiography: 'The Communist Bloc gave Indonesia a monument commemorating her struggles. The so-called free world didn't. Why not? We're a people who thrive on symbols.'[5]

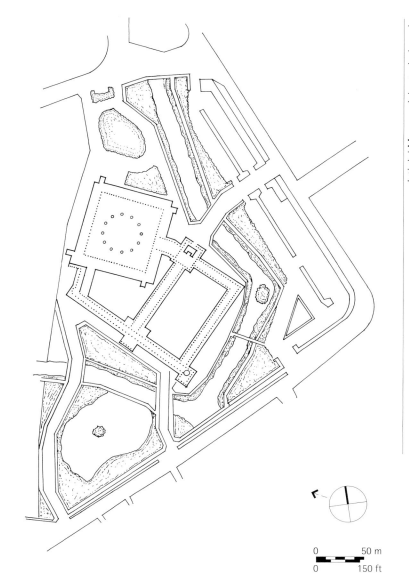

0   50 m
0   150 ft

As the first step, a management committee made up of private individuals was formed; however, work did not begin until 1961, when a presidential decree was issued to establish a new committee to oversee the construction of the mosque. At a ceremony held in August (on 12 Rabi' al-Awwal – the date on which the birth of the Prophet Muhammad is commemorated – in the Muslim year 1381) the first pile of the mosque was driven into the ground by President Sukarno. Over the following years, funding for the mosque was obtained through voluntary contributions from the general public, proceeds from exhibitions and shows and a philanthropic foundation, Yayasan Dana Bantuan. By 1966, it became apparent that the donations received would be insufficient, and in 1969 the project was placed under the aegis of President Sukarno and publicly funded by the Bank of Indonesia and by the Ministry of Finance through the State Secretariat. Subsequently, until its completion in 1984, the mosque was funded incrementally through a series of five-year development plans. Consequently, though this was the first building conceived as a state mosque, its eventual completion occurred at about the same time as other similar projects begun later were being realized.

The site chosen by the government was the Wijaja Kusima Park, in an area partially bounded by a canal linked to the Ciliwung river in central Jakarta. The choice was doubly symbolic for the establishment of a monument to national independence, for not only was it the site of a ruined former Dutch fortress but it was close to the country's national monument, known as 'Monas' (the Indonesian abbreviation for 'Monument Nasional').[6]

The Master Plan for the Istiqlal Mosque comprised a five-storey domed prayer hall with an area of 36,980 sq. m (398,000 sq. ft), a domed entrance pavilion of 5,000 sq. m

(53,800 sq. ft) with connecting galleries, a large courtyard of 29,000 sq. m (312,000 sq. ft) separated into two parts, a minaret, landscaped gardens and parking for 800 cars on site. After the competition, Silaban was asked to submit additional plans for a fountain garden, landscaping and parking facilities. Bridges permit access to the mosque by pedestrians and vehicular traffic from all directions. A basement area under the courtyard houses office space, as well as sanitary and ablutions facilities. Space for diverse activities such as lectures, exhibitions, conferences, bazaars, and social and cultural programmes for women and children was also provided, as well as a slaughterhouse for offerings on Eid al-Adha.

The general layout was dictated by three main axes. The vertical axis was expressed by the presence of the dome over the prayer hall. The two horizontal axes are the east-west prayer hall with the *qibla* wall facing west, and the southeast-northwest axis of the courtyard oriented on the national monument. The symbolic significance of the courtyard orientation towards the Monas underlines the intention to relate the two structures, and emphasizes the identification of the mosque itself as a national monument. A further dimension of meaning might be inferred from a statement made by Sukarno, in which he referred to the Monas as 'the navel of the earth'.[7]

In Indonesia, the simple east-west orientation of the mosque was traditionally the rule (with some exceptions), following the model of the early mosques like Demak Jami in which the indigenous Javanese Hindu temple forms and spatial concepts were adapted to Muslim use.[8] Another aspect of the design derived from Hindu-Javanese spatial organization was the progression from secular to sacred space. In the Hindu temples of Indonesia, this transition was formalized in a series of two or three courts. The layout of the Istiqlal Mosque recalls this tradition in the treatment of the courtyard, where a notional space of two transitional courts is implied by the line of a median arcade connecting the south arcade to the main entrance building.

The main access to the prayer hall leads from an entrance pavilion with a tower topped by an Indian *chhatri*-like dome. This pavilion sits on the axis of the *mihrab*, is connected to tall arcades surrounding the courtyard, and gives access to all floors in the prayer hall. Additional access was provided to all floors by staircases placed at each of the four corners of the building. The entrance pavilion tower is also used as the location from which the drum (*bedug*) used for the call to prayer is struck. Thus, the role of the single Ottoman-style minaret is purely that of a landmark.

Contemporary materials such as concrete and steel were used to create an image of modernity. Concrete cast *in situ* and pre-stressed reinforced elements were the principal materials used throughout the building. The façades of the prayer hall were all treated identically: unadorned concrete piers rising to the height of a flat roof with a simple cornice. The arcades and their entrances are post-and-lintel concrete structures with flat roofs.

The prayer hall, five storeys high, is square in plan. The central dome measuring 45 m (147 ft) in diameter rests on twelve fluted steel columns arranged in a circle. The outer edges of the hall are lined with rectangular piers supporting the cantilevered balconies on each of the upper floors. The *mihrab* is conceived as a triptych of openings through which natural light filters into the interior; the *minbar* stands in the opening to the right, and inscriptions in copper line the walls. The internal space reflects the unadorned exterior. There are no arches and ornament is restrained. The hall is well lit by both natural and artificial light, and the interior finishes – steel, marble and ceramic tiles – are highly polished to provide reflective surfaces.

(Opposite) The interior of the prayer hall, five storeys in height, showing massive steel-sheathed columns and part of the *mihrab* wall decorated with huge calligraphic panels bearing the names Allah and Muhammad. The marble-clad columns and the perforated screen walls of the exterior walkways (below) overlook pools in the courtyard.

(Below) The interior of the central dome, 45 m (145 ft) in diameter, lined with delicately coloured steel panels, and plan of the prayer hall at second-storey level showing the gallery and the circular arrangement of the columns supporting the dome.

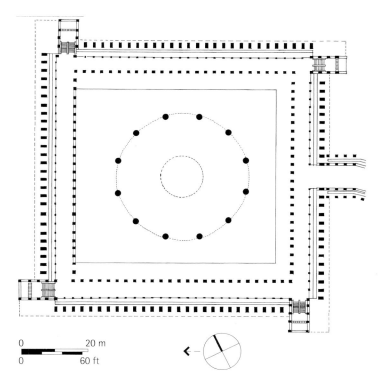

0   20 m
0   60 ft

Both inside and out, the mosque complex is a powerful architectural statement. Its massive scale, multi-storeyed prayer hall and the use of marble and steel combine to give the impression of solidity and lend weight to the importance of the state mosque. Such a strong statement is in sharp contrast to the architectural and design traditions of the Indonesian archipelago, where softer materials such as wood and thatch, and construction on a smaller scale (even in public buildings) had been the norm.[9] As a statement of modernity and nationalism, based on the principles of the *pancasila*,[10] the Istiqlal Mosque does what it was supposed to do – herald a new heroic era in the country's history.

Masjid Negara, Kuala Lumpur, Malaysia

Although about 90% of the population of Indonesia is Muslim, the newly independent secular state seems to have been less concerned with conveying an Islamic image than was the case in the neighbouring Republic of Malaysia. There, the Malay Muslims (constituting roughly half the population) used their political supremacy to express a national identity in Muslim terms precisely in order to assert their cultural and demographic predominance. They sought also to broadcast this status to the country's sizable Chinese and Indian minorities, as well as to the outside world.[11]

The Federation of Malaysia comprises thirteen individual states, each with its own ruler and parliament. The states also elect members to the central parliament which has in recent years been the government decision-making body. In the years following independence in 1957 at least three state mosques were built, in Kuala Lumpur, Seramban and Selangor, respectively. The most important of these was the National Mosque in Kuala Lumpur, opened in 1965 on the eve of the anniversary of the granting of independence. At that time it was the largest new mosque in Southeast Asia, with accommodation for about 3,000 worshippers in the prayer hall, and another 5,000 on verandahs that border it on three sides. Conceived as a national monument, the building was differentiated from the state mosques of the individual entities within the federation. The purpose of each state mosque was to project the identity of the individual state and to proclaim the importance of Islam. It is not surprising that the construction of a truly National Mosque in the capital city was intended to express the unity of the states within the federation. The situation in Malaysia reflects what the anthropologist Clifford Geertz has called 'nationalism within nationalism' formed by joining ethnic and local groups to create an 'artificial' union of a state.[12]

Plans for a national mosque were already taking shape about a month before independence, when the Federal Executive Council decided that a mosque should be built and named after the Prime Minister, Tunku Abdul Rahman, as a token of popular appreciation of his role in bringing the country peacefully towards independence. After independence, the Conference of Rulers was consulted,

The Masjid Negara (National Mosque; 1957–65), Kuala Lumpur, capital of the Malaysian Federation. Designed by Baharuddin Abu Kassim, this was the first example of a state mosque to be completed in a newly independent Muslim nation. The building is notable for its Ottoman-like minaret set in a pool (above) and its tile-covered folded concrete-plate roof (right), recalling the parasol, a traditional emblem of Malay royalty.

and with their agreement a committee was appointed for the mosque project, which was now renamed Masjid Negara (National Mosque) by the Prime Minister, who declined the honour of having it named after himself.[13]

The tasks of finding possible sites and of administering funds for the construction of the mosque fell to the Central Organizing Committee.[14] The Committee also appointed a nine-man working party to oversee construction and fund-raising. The cost of construction was initially estimated at 5 million Malaysian dollars, but it became clear that this figure would have to be doubled if a mosque 'of sufficient size befitting a sovereign nation' were to be built.[15] The federal government agreed to contribute 4.5 million dollars, while the state governments donated amounts totalling 2.5 million dollars. A further 3 million dollars was raised from public donations.[16]

The Prime Minister was personally responsible for the final choice of the site (from several put forward by the Committee for consideration), which had the advantage of being close to the railway station and the Negara (National) and Merdeka (Freedom) Stadiums, where ceremonies of national importance were frequently held. At the time, the chosen location was on the edge of Kuala Lumpur in an area that had been earmarked for future development and which now forms the central part of the city. However, since the amount of state-owned land then available was found to be inadequate, it was necessary to extend the proposed site through the acquisition of adjacent land. The owners of the land in question agreed to the terms offered and were duly compensated. Special attention was paid to the manner in which this land was acquired, for in accordance with Islamic law and tradition no mosque can be built on land that has been obtained through a forced sale or confiscation.

The original design brief was given by Tunku Abdul Rahman and refined by R. Honey, senior architect at the Public Works Department (PWD) and its Deputy Director until 1962. The Central Organizing Committee's first task was to choose an architect. The possibility of holding an international competition, later modified to a national competition, was considered but was eventually rejected. The reasons behind this decision included the expense and delay arising from such a process, as well as the competition rules which would have limited the Committee's input, as the sponsoring authority, in choosing the winning design.[17] The Public Works Department was thus assigned the task of designing the mosque and supervising its construction.

There are several claims as to who was the architect for the project. Records show that Ivor A. Shipley was in overall charge of the architects' group in the PWD. However, it is generally accepted that Baharuddin Abu Kassim, at that time Senior Architect in the PWD, was the principal designer and saw the project to completion. Indeed, he is the person mentioned by the Prime Minister in his opening address in August 1965. (In 1987, Baharuddin, who had become a senior partner of Jurubena Bertiga International, was officially commissioned to carry out the extension to the

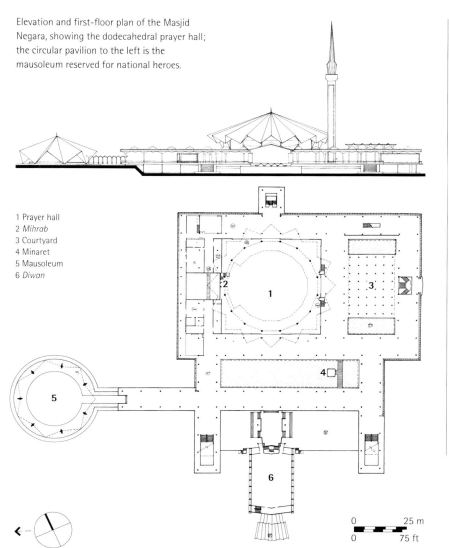

Elevation and first-floor plan of the Masjid Negara, showing the dodecahedral prayer hall; the circular pavilion to the left is the mausoleum reserved for national heroes.

1 Prayer hall
2 *Mihrab*
3 Courtyard
4 Minaret
5 Mausoleum
6 *Diwan*

0   25 m
0   75 ft

mosque.) Two other architects, Howard Ashley and Hisham Albakri, also seem to have played important roles in designing the building.[18]

It is in this context that the project brief prepared for the architect about the nature and scope of the undertaking should be examined. Baharuddin, trained at the University of Manchester, was faced with the formidable problem of developing a cognitive and symbolic language on a scale without precedent in the native architecture of Malaysia. His local references were mixed. Mosques had been mostly small wooden structures with a mélange of elements derived from Chinese, Malay or Anglo-Indian colonial models, such as the town mosque in Seremban or the old minaret in Singapore. The largest scale previously employed was seen in buildings dating from the period of British rule and characterized by the pervasive Anglo-Indian colonial style – an architectural language which was clearly not acceptable, mainly for ideological, but also for formal reasons. Now, a regional idiom was achieved by turning to the domestic vernacular and to rural architecture. In this case, the high pitched roof of the typical house was monumentalized and multiplied to become a new icon. The expression of modernity was made possible through the use of concrete, so permitting larger structural spans and greater plasticity.

(Below) The covered pavilion used as overflow prayer space, for informal classes and meetings, or just for repose, represents a modified form of the parasol structure, each bay being clearly expressed and reflected by panels of glass.

(Bottom) The well-proportioned prayer hall is an almost multi-directional space with a women's gallery above. Its columns are detailed with *muqarnas* plaster capitals, one of the conscious historicist quotations inserted into an otherwise overwhelmingly modernist design.

(Opposite) The rosette in the roof of the prayer hall is a replica of the centrepiece in the principal dome of the seventeenth-century Sultan Ahmet (Blue) Mosque in Istanbul. Concrete grillework screens around the prayer hall provide an effective light filter while allowing air to circulate freely.

Before beginning work on the design, Baharuddin and his colleagues at the PWD made a study of congregational mosques throughout the Muslim world and travelled to visit many of them. The Malaysian government also solicited the advice of the government of the United Arab Republic (Egypt) in the form of suggestions and potential designs based on Egyptian mosques. In addition, the architects visited Brunei to study the Bandar Abbas Mosque (1958; see p. 93), which is based on Mughal Indian models. The definitive design was approved by the Central Organizing Mosque Committee in 1960.

The project included a women's prayer hall, a conference hall (*dewan*) for 500 with kitchen, a royal antechamber, a room for the *imam* and ablutions facilities. A mausoleum for national heroes was also included, separate from the rest of the complex but connected to it by a long covered walkway. The rest of the 13-acre (5.3-hectare) site was landscaped. The initial choice of marble as the primary decorative finish for the whole complex had to be reconsidered when it became clear that its use would be too costly, and it was agreed that terrazzo should be substituted in most areas.

In plan, the complex is divided into two parts. The courtyard and the prayer hall together form one part and are separated from the conference hall to the south by a large rectangular pool in which stands the minaret, connected to land by a footbridge. A defining aspect of the design is the use of water which plays more than a purely ornamental role. It divides spaces, demarcates areas used for prayer from those having social functions, and externally it signals the presence of the *mihrab*. The white, vast plaza holds, as if on a tray, a hall into which has been inserted a circular structure covered with a roof of folded concrete plates, a pencil of a minaret, and a smaller echo of the large circular structure, which is a memorial building.

From the main entrance the complex is accessible through a courtyard covered with 48 concrete parasols joined by strips of anodized gold aluminum. On three sides of the prayer hall the verandahs are covered by a series of

domes sheathed in blue tiles placed at regular intervals. The verandahs are screened from the outside by terrazzo grillwork which is said to have been modelled on patterned openwork screens found in India, notably those seen in the mosques of Agra and Fatehpur Sikri.[19] The dominant motif in the design is the use of folded concrete plates in the pointed roof over the prayer hall to create a monumental version of the pitched roofs of Malay longhouses, but even more to echo the shape of a parasol – the traditional emblem of Malay royalty.

The prayer hall is square in plan, surrounded by walls of reinforced concrete faced in marble with openings on three sides and a total of nine wide aluminum sliding doors. The roof resembles an unfurled parasol 200 ft (61 m) in diameter supported on sixteen columns, each 3 ft (1 m) in diameter. The interior is lit by sixteen chandeliers and by natural light filtered through the terrazzo screens and the coloured glass windows in the clerestory. The *mihrab* in the west wall is

decorated with calligraphic inscriptions and blue tile mosaic; framed by a rectangular band of inscriptions, it forms a deep screened niche.[20] The *minbar* is cantilevered in reinforced concrete and faced in white marble. The gallery in which the women's prayer area is situated is in the form of a cantilevered mezzanine, sheltered from view by terrazzo screens. An unusual feature at that time (although now common) was the inclusion of a radio-TV broadcasting booth, situated directly opposite the *mihrab*.

Although the roof of the Masjid Negara derives its inspiration from the traditional Malay type and was intended to invest this new symbol of national (pan-ethnic Islamic) identity with local traditional forms, the influence of Ottoman architecture is unmistakable in the minaret. Other historicist references include the aluminium rosette at the apex of the roof, which is an exact replica of the centrepiece in the dome of the Sultan Ahmet Mosque (Blue Mosque) in Istanbul. In a country where the Ottoman Empire has played no particular role historically and where there is no Turkish community, such references are probably best understood on the one hand in the context of the enduring image of Ottoman mosque architecture in general, and on the other in terms of Turkey's importance as the first modern state in the Islamic world.

In terms of function and design the complex works well. Its scale is pleasing as it is not overwhelming in the way that many state mosques are, and the building retains a direct relationship to the environment. The use of water and landscaping lends the mosque a more humane aspect, and the modulation of light, shade and reflections enliven its masses. Materials and finishes are unpretentious, and surfaces and detailing are simple and easy to maintain. All in all, the result is a tangible symbol of the spirit of the nation, and for its time and within its region the complex remains a significant architectural work. Assertions that this is a building for a modern state are displayed in the white surfaces, the fenestration and a frankly 'high-tech' look. Yet, this very feel of modernity is, at the same time, tempered by historicism. In carrying out the wishes of the commission, the architect felt compelled to create monumental forms, to develop a dome-like structure, and to include ornament and a minaret. These features are very much part of a modern approach because the typical Malay mosques were considerably smaller and built of softer materials, as were the larger Anglo-Indian pastiches of the colonial era. Local architectural character was provided by superimposing two symbolic meanings onto the folded concrete roofs constructed from imported materials and by means of contemporary technology.

The paradoxes perceived today in of the mixture of the modern and the historic seem not to have been articulated or recognized as such at the time of construction. At least there appears to have been no criticism of this building from any standpoint, but rather a sense of self-congratulation based on the nation's ability to design and finance a major building that is unique to its place in spite of being modern.

(Opposite) The design of the Al-Mukminin Mosque (1987) in Singapore utilizes the parasol structure first employed in the Masjid Negara, Kuala Lumpur. The older Anglo-Indian styles of mosques such as that of the Sultan Mosque remain common features and an alternative expression in the recent architecture of the Malay Peninsula.

That the Masjid Negara was successful in creating a powerful new symbol of national identity is confirmed by the small-scale replication of its roof form in village mosques, as well as its use in other buildings such as the Al-Mukminin Mosque in Singapore (1987) and in another contemporaneous project for a state mosque in Malaysia – that of Seremban – in which a variation of the typical Malay pitched roof is once again multiplied into a new iconic form.

Negeri Sembilan State Mosque, Seremban, Malaysia

A competition for the Negeri Sembilan State Mosque (1967) in Seremban, one of the thirteen states in the Federation of Malaysia, was launched in 1962 by the State Committee established for this purpose and presided over by Dato Mohamed Said bin Mohamed. The official assessors of the competition were two members of the Federation of Malaya Society of Architects, Howard I. Ashley (Edinburgh) and, notably, Baharuddin Abu Kassim himself while he was still with the Public Works Department. Of the eleven designs submitted, the winners were those by Datuk Lim Chong Keat and Chen Voon Fee of Malayan Architects Co-Partnership.[21] The building was completed, however, by Jurubena Bertiga International, the firm which Baharuddin joined as soon as construction of the Masjid Negara was completed, and while the Negeri Sembilan State Mosque was still in the final design stages. Predictably, he took over the project as the partner-in-charge at that time.[22]

The 5-acre (2-hectare) hill site on which the mosque stands is state-owned land, situated between the State Assembly Hall and the General Post Office, and overlooking the state lake gardens to the east and Bathurst Road to the west. The brief called for a prayer hall with a capacity of 2,000 worshippers (approximately 10 sq. ft or 0.9 sq. m per person), a *mihrab* and a *minbar*, ablutions and sanitary facilities for men and women, a conference room of about 850 sq. ft (80 sq. m), a room for the *imam* of 400 sq. ft (37 sq. m), carpet storage, an open area with shelter for cooking and attached storage space, and a covered eating area for 100 people, a built-in amplification system, a boundary with gates, landscaping with pools and a VIP car park on site with a garage for the *imam*.[23]

The nine-sided Negeri Sembilan State Mosque (1967) also features the use of the parasol form; the regular polygon has a roof comprising nine sections and has a minaret at each corner. The building is placed on a raised podium, as seen in the east elevation (right).

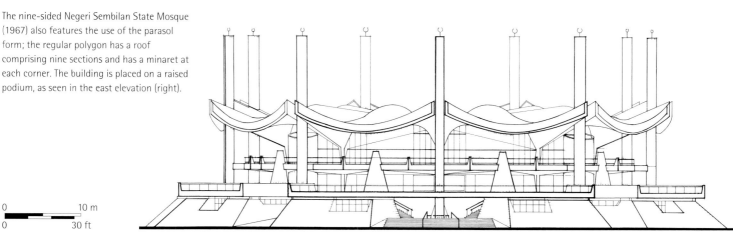

0   10 m

0   30 ft

In plan, the mosque is a nine-sided polygon, each side representing one of the nine districts of the State, under a royal parasol. It is a two-storey building, principally of concrete but with large areas of curved glass walls. In the basement are the meeting rooms, men's and women's dining halls, and the sanitary and ablutions facilities. The most significant formal and image-making features of the mosque are also those of its structure. Its parasol roof is a hyperbolic concave concrete shell anchored by nine towers. These towers are in effect minarets, each topped with a star-and-crescent finial, symbolic of Islam. A ring of first-floor terraces is supported by nine conical buttresses rising from ground level. The building has two entrances, one from the car park on the north side with a ramp, while the main entrance is on the east façade.

In comparison to the Masjid Negara, Negeri Sembilan is much smaller, with a capacity for only 1,500 worshippers (fewer than the number stipulated in the project brief). The interior is a large open polygonal space with a *mihrab* shaped like an inverted conical buttress. The *mihrab* is slit in the centre by a narrow panel of glass to allow light to filter in, and is surmounted by two rows of Qur'anic inscriptions in gold mosaic. The *mihrab* structure rises vertically and pierces the gallery. Its bold, sculptural shape is further accentuated by the window wall behind it. For all that, however, it is not expressed as strongly on the exterior, a deficiency that was subsequently criticized in an article from the Federation of Malaya Society of Architects.[24] The atmosphere of the interior, which is generously illuminated thanks to the glass walls, is partially modulated by means of carved timber screens that cast pleasing patterns of dark and light into the hall and are also used as partitions to provide privacy. Thus

(Below) Negeri Sembilan: floor plan of the mosque and a view of the interior of the prayer hall which is enclosed by full-height glass walls with wooden screens; within this space the *mihrab* and *minbar* form a sculptural unit.

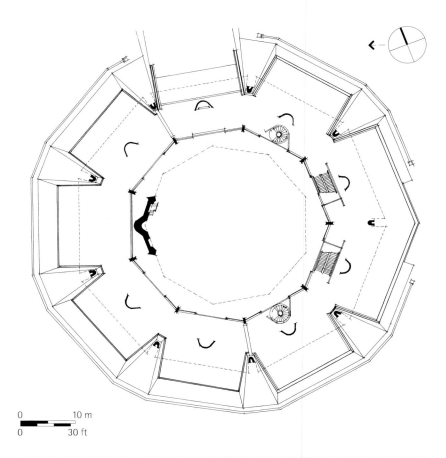

0   10 m

0   30 ft

(Left) The State Mosque of Selangor (1988), designed by Baharuddin Abu Kassim; set in a 36-acre (15-hectare) park, this is probably the most monumental mosque in Malaysia. The enamelled dome and the four slender Ottoman-style minarets which frame the mosque are visible from a great distance.

(Below) The Sarawak State Mosque (1990) by Sami Moussawi has a complex interior which hides the simplicity of its square plan. The building is reminiscent in layout and detailing to the mosque in Rome (see p. 243), but is less architectonic and more intricately decorative.

screened from the open interior space, the women's galleries give directly onto the surrounding terraces.

Negeri Sembilan represents a contained solution in which all activities are housed in a single structure. The folded concrete roof of Baharuddin's Masjid Negara served as its point of departure, but here the architects have dispensed with references to other cultures, preferring instead an interpretation of a regionalist model. Thus, the upturned pitched roof as adapted in Chinese Malay buildings from the typical Malay roof appears to be the essential point of reference. This choice may perhaps be better understood in the light of the heated debate which took place in Malaysia during the 1960s and 1970s concerning methods of forging a national identity in the context of a multi-ethnic society – a problem yet to be fully resolved.[25] Like the Masjid Negara, this building represents the outcome of a conscious attempt to produce a synthesis of modernity and traditional design, and is an example of a reinterpretation of a historic Malay architectural form executed with the use of contemporary concrete technology.

State Mosques of Selangor and Sarawak, Malaysia

Later state mosques, such as the Masjid Sultan Salahuddin Abdul Aziz Shah Mosque in Shah Alam, Selangor (completed in 1988), and the Sarawak State Mosque in Kuching (1990), do not continue the earlier experiments, but reflect the more global pan-Islamic formal language. The Selangor Mosque by Baharuddin Abu Kassim of Jurubena Bertiga International boasts four of the tallest minarets in the world, 137.40 m (450 ft) in height.[26] Its prayer hall, almost square in plan, can accommodate over 10,000 worshippers under an immense dome, 51 m (167 ft) in diameter, which rises to a height of 90 m (295 ft). The double-skinned aluminium dome was fabricated in sections in the UK and is covered by vitreous enamel panels in deep azure decorated with Islamic-inspired geometric patterns. The materials were

obtained from various countries: the walls are faced with Malaysian granite and the floors are of local marble; the coloured glass was produced in the USA, the chandeliers in Germany, while the wood latticework was imported from Korea and the carpet from Belgium. No expense was spared in the effort to produce a high-quality building.[27]

The Sarawak Mosque was designed by Sami Moussawi (joint architect of the Rome Mosque – see Chapter 6), with the local architects Perunding Utama. It is simpler on the exterior and features an intricate hypostyle interior derived from the design for the Rome Mosque. As Ken Yeang has noted, 'The main dome and other parts are covered with coloured mosaic tiles and plaster work. Forty smaller domes surround the main dome, and are supported by pillars that consist of four shafts that open towards the top, resembling hands during the act of prayer.'[28]

King Faisal Masjid, Islamabad, Pakistan

A solution for a state mosque which introduces another radical reinterpretation of the dome is found in the King Faisal Masjid (originally called the Grand National Mosque) built in the specially created post-independence capital of Pakistan. Though the building was completed only in 1986, the idea and the location for a national mosque had been projected as early as 1960 by Constantinos Doxiadis in his Master Plan for the city.

When Pakistan came into being following the partition of India in 1947, Karachi was the capital. A military régime soon decided to move the seat of government away from the influences of a large, sprawling commercial port city to a place from where the country could be more effectively controlled. The site for the new capital was chosen in 1959 by a Commission headed by General Mohammad Yahya Khan, then Chief of Staff of the Army, and advised by Doxiadis and Sir Robert Matthew, the chief co-ordinating architect.[29] The capital was to be developed at the foot of the Margalla Hills, on the Potwar plateau near Rawalpindi. The 44-acre (17.5-hectare) site of the proposed Grand National Mosque was set against the background of the Margalla Hills and on an axis with the main approach road (Shahrah-e Islamabad); thus it would be visible from miles away, a vertical landmark in the new capital city.

The impetus to begin the mosque came in 1966, when King Faisal of Saudi Arabia made an official visit to Pakistan and agreed to finance the project. Because of the king's role in financing and encouraging the building of the mosque and the Pakistani government's close ties to the Kingdom of Saudi Arabia, the mosque was given the name King Faisal Masjid and is usually not referred to as the national or state mosque. In 1968, an international competition (restricted to Muslim architects) for the King Faisal Masjid was held under the aegis of the Capital Development Authority and sponsored by the International Union of Architects (UIA) based in France.[30] The winning design, submitted by the Turkish architect Vedat Dalokay (1927–81), proposed an original tent-like structure.[31] Indeed, Dalokay's design was among the first in Pakistan to depart from the conventional arch-and-dome type. It was in fact a variation of the one he had submitted as a winning entry for the Kocatepe Mosque Competition in Ankara in 1957, where he had proposed a

The King Faisal Masjid (1970–86), Islamabad, was designed by its Turkish architect Vedat Dalokay as a tented concrete structure echoing its hillside backdrop, while the placement and the form of the tall minarets reveal their Ottoman antecedents.

(Opposite) Site plan of the King Faisal Masjid and Islamic University: the mosque lies to the left of the raised entrance plaza.

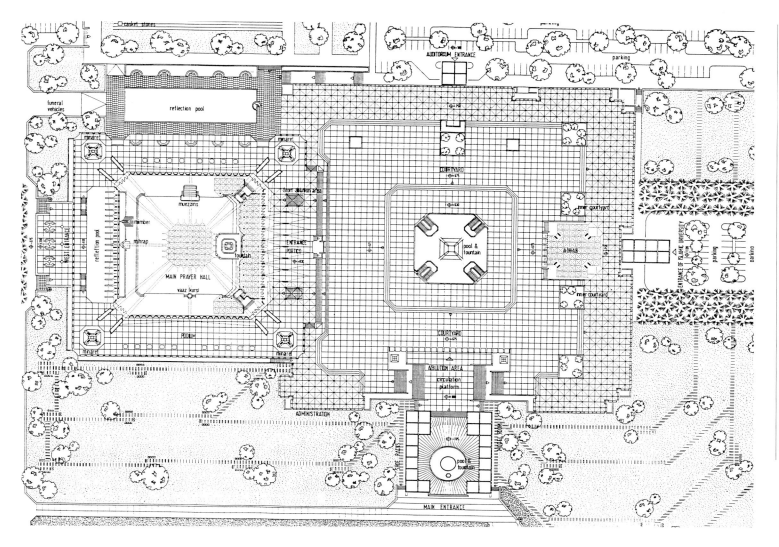

King Faisal Masjid, Islamabad, Pakistan

concrete shell in dome form (as noted below). For Islamabad, the shell became a giant tent.

The initial brief called for a prayer hall alone, but in 1970 it was decided to incorporate the Islamic Research Institute offices and, in 1982, to add sufficient space for the faculties of the International Islamic University; these additions more than doubled the area originally allocated to the project and quadrupled the overall cost to US$40 million,[32] but did not affect the basic design of the prayer hall itself since they were all external to it.

Set against the hills, the building can be seen from a considerable distance on the two main axial approaches to the city. The master plan for Islamabad put the mosque at the north, or 'head' of the city's main approach road, the Shahrah-e Islamabad, and angled to it as dictated by orientation requirements. The land around it is open and the complex is conceived as a monument to be viewed from and reached by highways terminating at a bus stop and parking area. It is seen as a point of destination and as an object, not as a central integrated feature of the urban fabric and in this respect is similar to most other national or state mosques.

Seen against the hills, the mosque resembles a small mountain or an enormous white tent framed by four slender fluted minarets, one at each corner. The physical environment alone is the main contextual aspect here. The mosque was described by the architect as a 'modern structure . . . perfectly in harmony with the eternal image of a tent which is behind any large single-vaulted space. I would describe it as the last tent of the Margalla hills, an extension of the hills – on the plains'.[33] The grandiose scale of the project can be more easily appreciated if one considers the following breakdown: a main prayer hall for 10,000 men; a women's prayer gallery for 1,500 worshippers placed directly above the main entrance; additional spaces in a courtyard for 40,000, a podium with a north platform for 27,000 and porticoes which can accommodate 22,000; and green areas which can be used as open-air prayer areas by up to 200,000 people. A large fountain precedes the entrance to the mosque which stands on a raised platform reached by stairways.

Based on a 200-ft (61-m) square plan, the prayer hall is spanned by a space-frame structure of triangular folded concrete plates that meet at the summit, 132 ft (40 m) above floor level. The roof was a feat of carefully calculated engineering: the plates were constructed simultaneously so as to meet exactly at the apex. The glazed intervals between the plates admit natural light to the prayer hall and help to lend an ethereal quality to the structure. Monumentality and modernity, two of the prerequisites in the project brief,

are provided by the virtuoso-like display of the very latest in contemporary structural techniques, especially in the folded concrete plates, and by the absence of more readily available local materials, such as stone and brick.

Inside the main prayer hall, the most striking aspect is that of the vertical emphasis. The vertical axis, a feature usually equated with Ottoman architecture, is thus favoured in preference to the horizontal extension of space inherent in the orientation towards Mecca. The sheer size of the interior all but overpowers the *mihrab* and *minbar*; this was no doubt a conscious choice on Dalokay's part, as was the clearly differentiated *qibla* wall. The restrained decorative treatment of the interior is limited to calligraphy and a profusion of Iznik blue-and-gold calligraphic decorative tiles (the work of Menga Ertel, a Turkish tile designer) covering the *qibla* wall. In front of the wall stand the *mihrab* and *minbar*, both designed by the prominent Pakistani artist Gulgee. The unusual and tall *mihrab* is a freestanding sculptural element in the form of a vertical open Qur'an, the spine of which bears the word Allah repeated in mirror-image and the pages of which display Qur'anic verses. The *minbar* is a more conventional arrangement of steps. The *qibla* wall has a narrow glass band along its length and is additionally enlivened by shimmering indirect light reflecting off the large pool outside and parallel to the wall. The *dikka* (rostrum) for Qur'an reading competitions (especially on Milad al-Nabi, the Prophet's birthday) along the north wall is a large raised platform decorated with calligraphy by the prominent modern Pakistani artist Sadequain (1930–87), executed in a painterly style rather than by a trained calligrapher. The concrete structure is exposed and painted white, and the floors are of polished granite. The women's mezzanine with its own entrance is approached through an archway inscribed with an excerpt from a *Hadith*: 'Heaven is under the feet of mothers.' The non-loadbearing concrete walls are treated as screens. The architect seems to be suggesting that the worshipper

(Opposite) The dramatic volume of the prayer hall with its central chandelier emphasizes a unified single space in the manner of Sinan's sixteenth-century Ottoman mosques in Istanbul.

(Below) The unusual *mihrab*, designed by the artist Gulgee in the form of an open Qur'an, stands in front of the *qibla* wall decorated with calligraphic tile work.

(Bottom) The large *dikka*, occasionally used for Qur'an-reading competitions, and to the right part of the women's mezzanine.

contemplate the space itself, achieved through the use of modern technology, as a way of communing with God.

Dalokay was an architect who had the ability to use materials with great skill and create desired effects. In the King Faisal Masjid he designed a building that has come to be regarded as a symbol of the city in much the same way as the Opera House has done in Sydney and as, in an earlier *tour de force* of engineering, the Eiffel Tower did in Paris.

The result can be parsed in several ways. The four minarets, each almost 300 ft (90 m) high, and the folded carapace of the central space are reminiscent of Ottoman and, more specifically, of Stambuli emblems of power; however, they are rendered in modernist terms that, in the end, were not considered acceptable in the case of the Kocatepe Mosque in Ankara. It is all the more significant that such a design should have been acceptable in Pakistan. The vernacular was not an issue here because for the state its identity and authenticity is derived directly from the building's modernity and the overt proclamation of its Islamic character. While one can perhaps see in the giant raised platform of the mosque an Eidgah-like space reminiscent of the Badshahi Mosque in Lahore, more specific allusions were apparently not to be evoked. One can even posit an ambivalent attitude to the Mughal past, Indian and not Indian; theirs and ours; lost and remembered. Better to make the leap into the future and refer to Islam only in its most victorious terms: the undefeated, untouched Ottoman symbol. It is also conceivable that these formal elements were all the more acceptable in an Islamic state since the remembered form of the shrines at Mecca and Medina was also an Ottoman one. The very scale of the work, its magnificent setting against the hills, its strong formal statement and modernity make the King Faisal Masjid a milestone in the contemporary architecture of the Islamic world.[34]

(Above and left) The monumentality of the Kuwait Great Mosque (1976–84) by Mohamed Makiya is matched by the architect's use of rich materials and easily identifiable pan-Islamic elements such as arches, dome and tall minaret. The structure incorporates many modular elements.

(Opposite) Ground-level plan, sectional perspective of the prayer hall, and a view into the huge dome which rests on a drum with 96 lancet windows, allowing natural light to enter the prayer hall from above.

Great Mosque, Kuwait City, Kuwait

A different approach to the one adopted in Islamabad is manifested in the Great Mosque in Kuwait City (1984), designed by Mohamed Makiya of Makiya Associates.[35] The project was bolstered by a growing regional confidence, much enhanced by new wealth from oil revenues. The insistence on modernity was diluted by a demand for regional authenticity made by the client (the Ministry of Public Works), which expressly stipulated that the design should 'follow the Arab-Islamic style'.[36] This was realized, in the main, through a rich and extensive programme of decoration, inscriptions in particular (generally minimal in the examples discussed above), and by the use of arches serving as emblematic elements.

The idea of building a state mosque in Kuwait dates back to the early 1960s, coinciding with the end of the British protectorate in 1961. At the time, an unidentified architect was commissioned to design a state mosque to replace an older mud-brick one. The project never went further than the drawing board and it was only in 1976 that the government revived the idea, organizing an international design competition through the Major Works Department of the Ministry of Public Works. An initial list of sixteen international firms were invited to design a mosque that would stand forth as a statement of unity and national identity, using the regional architectural and decorative traditions of Kuwait and the Gulf States as a springboard. The new mosque was to be located on a vast 4.5-hectare (11-acre) site close to the seashore, in the vicinity of the Seif Palace and the central business district of Kuwait. It was also conceived by the authorities as the focal point of an urban renewal project in the Sharq area to the northeast of the mosque site, which would be treated as a preservation zone with limited low-rise development.

The brief called for a main prayer hall with an area of 5,000 sq. m (53,800 sq. ft) to accommodate some 7,000 male worshippers, a gallery for women occupying 200 sq. m (2,150 sq. ft), a separate entrance and reception area for the Emir, a library and conference centre, administrative offices, a minaret, and parking for 700 vehicles. A daily prayer hall for up to 500 worshippers was added to the programme later. Beyond the functional requirements, the client also requested that the competing architects provide detailed drawings of the structure's proposed decorative scheme.[37]

From the eight firms that were short-listed two finalists were chosen, Makiya Associates (architects of Khulafa Mosque in Baghdad and the Siddique Mosque in Doha, Qatar) and Sir Frederick Gibberd of London (the British firm responsible for the design of the Regent's Park Mosque). The winner, Makiya Associates, was awarded a consultant's contract in 1977, and the construction contract in 1979. Probably the most distinguished Iraqi practitioner of the day, Mohamed Makiya had trained in England, first in Liverpool as an architect and planner and later at Cambridge University. He set up his practice in Baghdad in 1946 (and also taught there) and in the 1960s and 1970s had offices

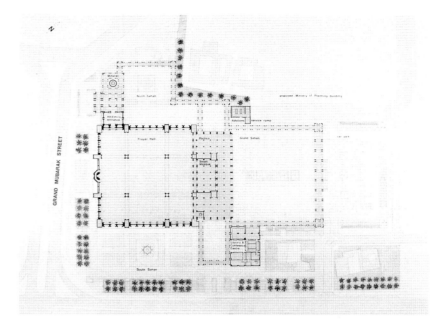

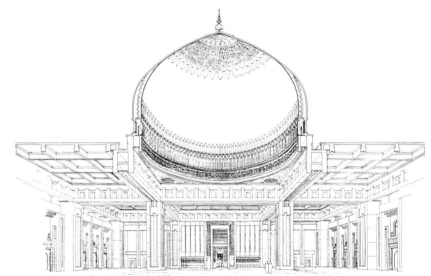

elsewhere in the Gulf region. In 1975 he based himself in London. Having built extensively in the Arab world, including a number of mosques, and won a number of important competitions, he was extremely well regarded in the region.

The site's urban context, featuring wide avenues and low-density construction in a city dominated by the use of the automobile, played a role of capital importance in the design conceptualization similar to that of the King Faisal Masjid in Islamabad: 'The design of the mosque, consciously or unconsciously, acknowledges the . . . characteristics of an urban centre such as Kuwait. Therefore, there is an attempt aimed at taking advantage of the site's high visibility. As a result, the monument is surrounded by landscaped areas providing additional surrounding open spaces, and further emphasizing it as a monument which can be viewed from all sides. . . . Very few worshippers will approach the mosque exclusively as pedestrians. For most, the exterior formal arrangement of the mosque will be experienced mainly through the windows of a moving vehicle. . . . In general, Makiya's design is an extroverted one which capitalizes on the visibility provided by its location.'[38]

The mosque complex consists of a series of connected rectangular courtyards around the main prayer hall, which measures 72 x 72 m (235 x 235 ft).[39] The women's gallery is situated above the entrance and is preceded by a portico six bays deep which also incorporates the daily prayer hall occupying 400 sq. m (4,300 sq. ft). The large forecourt (*sahn*) to the northeast echoes the dimensions of the main prayer hall. Ablutions facilities are housed in a building to the north and in the cultural centre located on the southeast side of the complex. The minaret, with its own smaller *sahn*, stands close to the Emir's private entrance and reception area in

the northwest corner. Flat-arched arcades with a total area of 2,000 sq. m (21,500 sq. ft) connect the different parts of the complex. The parking area is situated at the main public entrance to the complex on the northeast side and extends roughly halfway under the forecourt. The core of the entire complex – a large central dome and single minaret – may in some sense be a general stylistic reference to the mosques of Cairo, yet the new profile of the dome and the very scale of the core make such a comparison difficult. Rather, one thinks of the Khulafa Mosque itself and its own background in the great domed shrines of Iraq (Kerbala, Najaf, Samarra and Al-Gailani) with their Iranian Safavid-period domes and minarets. However, to have pointed out such a connection at the time of the mosque design would have extended the Arab-Islamic limits of the brief into a truer reflection, albeit unacceptable to the client, of the historic precedents of these architectural forms.

The elevations of the prayer hall are composed of a series of wall bay units and windows in the gallery and on the first floor, except for the *qibla* wall which is a blank façade distinguished by the massive projecting *mihrab* niche. The parapet is topped by crenellated pointed arches. The central dome over the main prayer hall rises to a height of 43 m (140 ft) with 96 lancet windows around its base. It is supported on four piers with massive girders spanning the intervening spaces. In his original scheme, the architect intended to set the dome at the centre of a hypostyle hall with domed bays, but at the client's request he later developed the main hall into a centralized cruciform (Ottoman) model by suppressing the multiple columns and domed bays. The great dome is clad in glazed white tiles on the exterior.

The interior of the main prayer hall is divided into nine bays of varying sizes defined by the central piers. It is separated from the portico by a partition wall of coloured glass blocks. Shaded windows in coloured glass admit diffused natural light. The interior surface is ordered by a decoration of geometric ornament and bands of calligraphy in Kufic script. A calligraphic band in turquoise and blue tile girds the drum of the dome, while geometric patterns and bands of calligraphy define the apex and the base of the dome, the interior wall bay units and the ceilings. The *mihrab* and *minbar* are placed within a large rectangular frame richly decorated with Qur'anic verses in Kufic script.

The extensive employment of modern pre-cast concrete manufacturing and assembly techniques has given a new interpretation to the chosen vocabulary of design elements. In the design concept, Makiya sought to draw 'a distinction between elements which have a structural integrity and elements which are volumetric and have a space creating function'.[40] In order to achieve this aim he developed a repeatable wall bay unit, 6 m (20 ft) deep, the façade of which was composed of a pointed arch encompassed by a freestanding flat arch and constructed in pre-cast concrete panels combined with natural stone finishes. It was felt that this element regenerated the idea of 'the traditional niche [*mihrab*] in a new way, recreating a quality of space and light which is fundamentally Islamic'.[41] Moreover, its use permitted the architect to relieve the external walls and the arches themselves of their usual structural function. Another interesting feature is the careful attention paid to joints in materials which are 'expressed as an architectonic version of calligraphy in traditional usage'.[42]

The architect designed a decorative scheme intended to be in keeping with the powerful formal language of the complex, but this scheme was not realized. Instead, the client undertook to finish the mosque by employing craftsmen from abroad, with specialists coming from Morocco (plaster and tile work *zellij*), Egypt (calligraphy), Pakistan (stone carving) and India (wood carving) to execute the ornament. In the final construction stage, the client requested that even more ornamentation be added to the interior surfaces of the mosque and to the Emir's reception area. The supervising engineer at the Ministry of Public Works recommended that some of the exposed concrete surfaces be covered in travertine and that travertine frames be placed around some of the concrete panels in the Emir's reception area. The additional ornamentation – painted plaster work and tile mosaic *zellij* inspired by North African examples – was carried out without consulting the architect, who subsequently considered the colours and decoration excessive and unsympathetic to their context.[43]

From the client's perspective, there appears to have been no motivation to create, or intrinsic interest in seeking, a modernist display. There seemed to be no necessity to demonstrate a sense of modernity in the Kuwait of the 1970s. Rather, it was the architect who intended to wrap his already stylized architectural modernism in a decorative

(Opposite) The interior of the massive prayer hall, which can be entered from three sides, looking towards the *mihrab* set in the *qibla* wall.

(Below) Architect's drawing of details of a wall section consisting of assembled modular elements that lend the building a sense of scale

and texture and also carry the mechanical services: external elevation; section; and internal elevation.

(Bottom) The *mihrab*, placed at the centre of the *qibla* wall, has an ornamented surface accented by light from above.

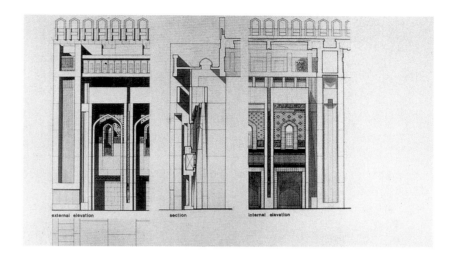

external elevation   section   internal elevation

scheme that sought to reinvent a language of ornament, only to have it swamped by massive applications of newly revived and expanded craft traditions.

Built at a total cost in excess of US$50 million, the mosque was apparently used only periodically throughout the 1980s: the main prayer hall is only open for Friday prayers and on special occasions, the smaller hall being used for daily prayers. On the one hand, there is no local community nearby to use the mosque on a regular basis, and on the other, as Al-Asad has suggested, the outbreak of hostilities between Iran and Iraq in 1980, together with an assassination attempt against the Emir, led the authorities to discourage crowds in the vicinity of the Seif Palace.[44] 'While this mosque may not have been meant as a public gathering centre, it does seem to have been intended as a massive and dominating visual symbol. On that level, it proves to be quite effective [. . .] It has been given an aura of grandeur, if not sanctity, to the extent that any activity beyond that of performing the prayers (which also has been limited) is not encouraged [. . .] It has provided the newly evolving metropolis of Kuwait [with] a distinctive architectural monument with which it is becoming identified. In that sense it will function as the religious counterpart to the celebrated [Water] Towers of Kuwait. . . . With over 8,500 sq. m [91,500 sq. ft] of built up area . . . , it is difficult for such a monument to pass unnoticed. All in all, the structure possesses the presence, elaboration and assertiveness anticipated of a state or official mosque.'[45]

State Mosque (Competition), Baghdad, Iraq

The international competition for a State Mosque in Baghdad, initiated in 1982, was a major event in mosque design, indeed, in architecture generally. It provoked a great deal of interest and debate at the time among architects, historians and critics from both the Islamic world and the West. The project was intended to provide a major new monument for the Iraqi nation, situated in the capital city.[46] As Rifat Chadirji, the convenor of the competition, noted, 'The religious and political importance of the Mosque, together with its monumental scale, offered an opportunity to make a significant contribution to architectural design. Regardless of whether it would ever be achieved or not, this consideration became a major objective. In fact, the authorities considered the project as an important cultural event of the present time and one that would remain significant in the future'.[47] The competition was particularly significant in terms of scale: the brief called for a mosque to accommodate 40,000 worshippers; the building would be the largest contemporary mosque complex in the world and, as such, raised new design issues and problems for architects.[48] Although the mosque has not been built,[49] the concept remains important because it initiated an international dialogue and involved the participation of several 'signature' architects.

Unlike many of the historic urban centres in the Islamic world, the city of Baghdad had not retained its original great/congregational mosque. The idea of building a central or state mosque (as well as other mosques in each of the provincial capitals of Iraq) was first proposed in 1979, in the heat of preparations for the Conference of Non-Aligned Nations planned to take place in Baghdad in 1982.[50] The conference never came about; but many of the architectural and planning schemes which formed part of the effort to ameliorate and beautify the city of Baghdad were at a quite advanced stage as designs and some were built. As part of this building campaign, and despite the outbreak of the Iran-Iraq hostilities, or perhaps because of them, a state mosque was required. For a socialist country like Iraq this late formulation of the need for a state mosque can be seen in terms of a programme of nation-building expressed through several works on a monumental scale.

In the spring of 1982, consideration was given to the preliminary programme brief and the selection of a site for the mosque, and the idea of staging an international competition was put forward by the architect Rifat Chadirji (who was also put in charge of the competition), in his capacity as counsellor to the Mayor of Baghdad, Samir Abdul Wahhab. The site proposed was in a peripheral district of Baghdad, not far from the western gate of the celebrated circular city of Al-Mansur (founded in 762). It was flat, trapezoidal in shape and its only interesting topographical feature was an existing canal, which was integrated into most of the designs submitted with varying degrees of effectiveness. The Ministry of Awqaf and Religious Affairs in conjunction with the Mayoralty of Baghdad initiated a study to determine the most appropriate size for the mosque complex and the extent of the activities to be contained within it. Alternative capacities of 15,000 and 40,000 worshippers were analyzed in terms of atmosphere and function of prayer and ritual, facilities for ablutions and access, acoustics, pedestrian and vehicular circulation, etc. An air-conditioned space to accommodate 30,000 men was finally decided upon (supplemented by a prayer hall for 3,000 women and a prayer hall for daily use by up to 1,000 worshippers) with additional prayer space for at least 4,000 people outside. Facilities were also to be provided for religious education, including a library, meeting rooms, and temporary and permanent accommodations for visiting religious officials and personnel.[51]

In July 1982, President Saddam Hussein, acting on the recommendation of the Mayor of Baghdad, appointed the Committee for the State Mosque Competition, consisting of: Rifat Chadirji (Chairman);[52] Dr J. Kettaneh, Ministry of Awqaf and Religious Affairs; Halim Witwit, Ministry of Public Works and Housing; Dr Sabah Azzawi, Mayoralty of Baghdad Design Department; and George A. Dudley (best known for his activities as architectural advisor to Governor Nelson Rockefeller of New York State) as professional advisor and co-ordinator. Participation in the competition was to be by invitation only, and in September twenty-two architectural firms were invited to submit designs in the pre-qualification stage of the competition. The competition brief, prepared by

J. Kettaneh and George A. Dudley, was distributed to the competitors at the end of September and the deadline for submissions was set for 19 January 1983. The brief insisted, among other things, on monumentality, a strong identity and a synthesis of past and present. It stipulated that the mosque was to be 'the highest expression in creative and physical terms of the religious, state and national beliefs and aspirations of the people of Iraq and their leadership . . . The heritage of historical settings and styles as well as contemporary design qualities must all be integral to the final architectural creation. The State Mosque is of such magnitude and importance that it should reflect in certain spaces to be selected by the competitor, and confined to those spaces, certain stylistic features from such Islamic countries as Egypt, Morocco, Syria, etc.'[53] After the individual schemes had been evaluated by the selection committee appointed by Rifat Chadirji, the Competition Committee selected seven designs submitted by: Test/Ma'ath Alousi of Iraq Consult (Iraq); Kahtan Al-Madfai (Iraq); Mohamed Makiya of Makiya Associates (London); Robert Venturi of Venturi, Rausch & Scott-Brown (USA); Minoru Takeyama of United Actions (Japan); Rasem Badran of Shubeilat, Badran & Kailani (Jordan); and Ricardo Bofill of Taller de Arquitectura (Spain).[54]

The architects were selected to represent a wide range of cultural and geographical backgrounds, Muslim and non-Muslim alike, reflecting a desire to mark the importance and scale of the competition. Among the three Iraqi entrants Mohamed Makiya was the architect of the Kuwait Great Mosque and of the Khulafa Mosque in Baghdad. Makiya's inclusion among the finalists was not surprising as, together with Chadirji, he had been a founder of the School of Architecture at the University of Baghdad in 1959. He had participated in several major mosque competitions, among them the Islamic Cultural Centre in Rome and the King Faisal Masjid in Islamabad, and at that very time the Kuwait Great Mosque was under construction. This was the second major project in Iraq in which he had been involved after eight years of exile – a project that he saw as 'the mosque he had trained for his whole life.'[55]

The other two Iraqi architects were Kahtan Al-Madfai, a contemporary of Makiya and Chadirji and their colleague at the Baghdad School of Architecture, and Ma'ath Alousi, a member of the younger generation of architects, who had trained at the Middle East Technical University (METU) in Ankara, founded the firm Iraq Consult, and who had been responsible for numerous projects in the Gulf States and Sudan.

Of the non-Iraqi architects, the Jordanian Rasem Badran was trained in Germany and had worked there for three years before returning to Jordan as co-founder of the firm Shubeilat Badran Associates; he had won second prize in the 1979 competition for the King 'Abd Allah Mosque in Amman, Jordan. Participating architects from outside the Arab world included Minoru Takeyama, trained in his native Japan and the United States, who has worked for several internationally recognized firms and received an honourable mention in the Madrid Islamic Cultural Centre Competition of 1980 (in the event, however, it appears that Takeyama did not submit a scheme). Several other internationally known architects were considered by Chadirji for inclusion in the competition,[56] and those finally chosen were: the American Robert Venturi, the influential theoretician and practitioner who was already building a project in Baghdad; and the Spaniard Ricardo Bofill whose built work was mostly in Europe, but who had some experience in Algeria.

The jury was made up of Rifat Chadirji (Chairman), a representative from the Ministry of Waqf and Religious Affairs, George A. Dudley (Secretary), Stefano Bianca of the Swiss Federal Institute of Technology, Professor Dogan Kuban of the Istanbul Technical University, and William Porter of the Massachusetts Institute of Technology who was, however, unable to attend. Their role was to review the entries and recommend the first and second places, though the Iraqi government reserved the right to make the final decision. The jury studied the projects according to four criteria, those of function, form, cultural continuity and architectural quality, while also addressing the question of style. The huge scale of the proposed building implied that the mosque should relate to the historic architecture of the Islamic world in its widest sense, not just to local Iraqi styles. Furthermore, the brief specified that each entrant provide a written statement explaining the design conceptualization, including its technical and functional aspects, and that he be assisted by an advisor versed in Islamic history and in Islamic architecture and decoration.[57] As Mohammad Al-Asad has remarked, 'It is obvious from the choice of architects, jury members and the wording of the competition programme, that the intention of such a project was not only that of creating a specific monument, but also of an architectural event. Here, the abilities of a few gifted architects were put to use not only to come up with an appropriate design for a particular mosque but also to attempt devising vocabularies suitable for a non-western, Arab-Islamic twentieth century setting.'[58]

By unanimous vote, the jury recommended the project design submitted by Rasem Badran, and the joint runners-up, Ricardo Bofill and Test/Alousi, were invited to assist the winner. The results were made public at the end of an official symposium held at the National Assembly in Baghdad in October 1983, presided over by President Saddam Hussein and attended by over 300 participants representing the international architectural community. Very soon afterwards, however, it became clear that the recommendation of the jury was not going to be accepted by the government. In subsequent discussions other projects were put forward by Chadirji, by the Mayor and by President Saddam Hussein himself. An attempt was made to bring together the designers of the favoured projects, Bofill and Venturi respectively, but this initiative was rejected by the representatives of Venturi,[59] and Badran was generally recognized as the winner of the competition.

The project designs

Rasem Badran's prize-winning entry proposed a structure built almost exclusively in brick, based on the prototypical plan of a rectangular hypostyle prayer hall with a courtyard and surrounding porticoes. In this instance, the architect acknowledged his historical sources as being those of the early congregational mosques in Kufa and Samarra, and later mosques in Kairouan and Cairo. More precisely, the plan of the complex appears to be based predominantly on the mosque at Kufa (AD 637, rebuilt 670), while the outer walls recall those of the mosques at Samarra. The mosque complex is square in plan (225 x 225 m / 738 x 738 ft); the scheme is based on a 15-m (49-ft) module and features a wide rectangular courtyard. The mosque is raised up on a 'protective' earth-mound that 'acts visually like a base of an ancient *ziggurat* (Agar Quf)'.[60] Within the mound transitional spaces would be provided for the performance of ablutions.

The prayer hall is covered by a large central dome with two subsidiary domes, one identifying the location of the daily prayer hall and another over the passage leading from the housing complex; all three domes were to be clad in turquoise ceramic tiles. The principal dome is distinguished by a golden band creating a clear visual separation from the brick drum, and serves to identify the complex as a mosque when seen from a distance. The form of the domes and their tile revetment seem to be frank quotations of domes in Isfahan dating from the Safavid period, specifically those examples associated with the major shrines in Iraq. The supposedly casual location of the three domes of different sizes and of the two unpaired minarets seems to have represented an attempt to hark back to the same kind of juxtaposition of forms seen in earlier complexes.

The existing canal and a newly created lake would provide the irrigation base for an extensive landscaping programme

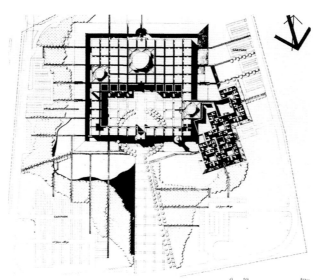

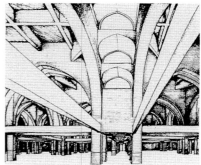

The winning scheme by Rasem Badran consists of a brick structure comprising a traditional rectangular hypostyle hall, domes and minarets, and courtyard with surrounding porticoes. The buildings stand on a raised platform, beneath which all the ancillary services are located.

comprising groves of date palms and orange trees. Trees were to be planted around the outer walls so as to provide a buffer between the mosque and the car-parking areas on the northern and eastern sides of the complex. The main approach was defined by two axes, one an existing avenue of trees which follows the building line, and the other corresponding to the *qibla* axis. This takes into account both the sacred aspect and a secular consideration – the axis of the housing complex situated close to the northwestern corner of the mosque, also oriented according to the boundary of the site. A row of fountains inspired by those at the Taj Mahal and placed on the edge of a platform to be built in the artificial lake would be located along the main approach on the *qibla* axis. An existing circle of trees was also retained and integrated into the design of the proposed main gateway, which was described by the architect as a 'defensive'-looking structure, derived from Ayyubid and Mamluk portals of Cairo, Damascus and Jerusalem, with flanking towers reminiscent of the palaces at Ukhaidir and Atshan (both in Iraq).

The interior of the proposed prayer hall has a non-directional quality. It is characterized by clusters of four columns in lieu of massive piers, evoking the rows of brick piers in the Great Mosque of Samarra or the Mosque of Ibn Tulun in Cairo. Tie-beams and a system of paired four-centred arches running perpendicular and parallel to the *qibla* wall recall early mosques such as that of Amr Ibn al-'As in Fustat. Stepped windows between the pairs of arches, inspired by the fourteenth-century Khan Marjan in Baghdad, allow natural light to filter into the prayer hall. The main dome covering the nine central bays of the prayer hall rests on a brick drum supported on a square base which distributes the weight to four corner piers, themselves resting on pillars, allowing an unobstructed view of the *mihrab*. Ornamentation is noticeably minimal, though the interior of the dome was to be decorated with a band of Qur'anic inscriptions.

On the whole, the mosque design presents an eclectic mix of elements that are combined to achieve an easily recognizable and traditional composition. In his statement to the jury, Badran describes the aim of the scheme as the creation of 'an Arab-Islamic complex: unmistakably Iraqi, unmistakably contemporary, and understandable to everyone, educated and unsophisticated alike, from whatever part of the world he may come'.[61] Indeed, the major design elements proposed by him are derived in the main from Abbasid architecture in its widest geographical manifestation. Interestingly enough, however, echoes of other periods and types are evident, whether it be the skyline reminiscent of Safavid-period architecture, the fortified aspect of palaces and portals or even *ziggurats*. While the intention of the design is to retain the traditional Iraqi architectural language based on the use of brick, Badran has succeeded for the most part in reinterpreting and integrating a variety of historical forms and structural techniques in a contemporary way.

Test and Ma'ath Alousi cited Iraqi Abbasid architecture in general as their principal source of inspiration. They sought to integrate the mosque complex within a hypothetical urban context in order to recreate the relationship that formerly existed between historical great mosques and their urban environment. This was the only project that treated the mosque as a potential focus of urban development, as part of a neighbourhood. This relationship was recreated in microcosm in the spatial arrangement within the complex itself, with its network of alleys and small courts on the north side, and in the adjacent housing complex.

The design criteria, as perceived by the architects, were based on: formal and structural unity; balance between the various components and parts; and the repetition of basic architectural features and elements. 'While the balance of the various parts signifies the equality . . . of all worshippers, the repetition of basic architectural features emphasizes the recurrence of worshipping the One God. The solidity of brick walls symbolizes the solidarity of the praying community.'[62]

The brick complex is accessible on three sides, the main entrance on the east side being articulated by a large domed building. The plan is rigorously symmetrical. The prayer hall is surrounded on three sides by five rectangular courtyards, the largest preceding the prayer hall. The housing complex, based on the courtyard-house type, is on the west side, and the whole would be unified by an interconnecting grid of porticoed arcades. These transitional areas and the open spaces of the courtyards are further bound together by the geometric patterns of their forms. Doubled arcades on piers running parallel and perpendicular to the *qibla* wall fill the interior of the hypostyle prayer hall. The space in front of the *mihrab* is surmounted by a small dome.

Ricardo Bofill's project also emphasized regularity and symmetry, but in another vein. He set the great rectangular mass of prayer hall and courtyard in a grid of gardens. The point at which the prayer hall and courtyard adjoin also corresponds with the line of an overlapping great forecourt which embraces all other elements of the complex within its rectangular walls. These include the identical towers of the facilities buildings which are separated by a large rectangular pool. Rising in a pyramidal tower shape at the inception of the central organizing axis for the complex is the minaret, the landmark feature of the mosque, the technical function of which is to serve as a water tower (echoing in some way the well-known Kuwait Water Towers). Other tall structures are massed along the same northwest boundary. Flanking the minaret are two towers, forming a monumental gateway. One of these houses the library facilities, classrooms and meeting rooms, while the other provides temporary living accommodation for visiting dignitaries, some apartments for permanent staff, a dining hall and kitchens.

Access to the mosque's outer courtyard is through a massive triple doorway. The open space is surrounded by double-bayed arcades along which the ablutions fountains

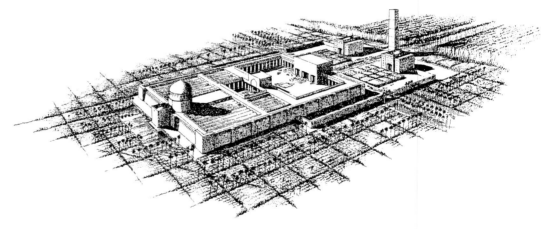

Ricardo Bofill's entry emphasizes regularity and symmetry; the vast prayer hall is set within gardens laid out in grid form. The single tall minaret, set on the main axis, acts as a marker for the mosque site. The prayer hall with massive columns consists of uniform bays lit by small openings in the roof.

are located, as well as shops, toilets and offices on the north side. The mosque proper is divided into four spaces: the main prayer hall for special occasions, an open-air prayer court, and a daily prayer hall and a women's prayer hall flanking the prayer court. The dimensions, including the prayer court, are roughly 160 x 240 m (525 x 787 ft).

The main prayer space is a rectangular hypostyle hall based on a T-plan (like the mosque of Abu Dulaf in Samarra or the Great Mosque of Kairouan). The regular, arcaded bays run perpendicular to the *qibla* wall but stop short, leaving an aisle immediately parallel to it. The central axial aisle is slightly wider. The architect has taken advantage of this arrangement to introduce a variation of light and volumes into what would otherwise have been an undifferentiated forest of vertical supports. While the individual bays are uniformly and evenly lit by small openings in the roof, the *qibla* wall and central aisle are highlighted by a variety of dramatic effects: the entire length of the *qibla* wall is lit by a clerestory which is also carried over the central aisle. The main dome punctuates the space at the crossing. The extruded niche of the *mihrab*, in an echo of the Great Mosque of Cordoba, is subdued and unlit, an 'infinite space'

as the architect calls it. The effect of this spatial and volumetric organization is to create a powerful and sober monumentality with a strong directional aspect. The latter is further emphasized by the decision to draw attention to the *qibla* wall by inserting a continuous carved band of Qur'anic inscriptions at a height where the light reveals it to best advantage. On the exterior, running the entire length of the *qibla* wall, is a large pool set into the grid of the garden.

For the vocabulary of architectural elements, Bofill chose to emphasize the classical heritage within the Islamic architectural tradition. This strategy allowed him scope to introduce expressions and variations of the classical idiom, elaborating Roman or even neo-classical examples. Additional references to the Mesopotamian, ancient Egyptian, and Romanesque traditions have been pointed out by commentators.[63]

The project by Mohamed Makiya features a landmark minaret and dome, combined with a strong axial plan. According to him, the element of innovation lay in the flexibility of the spatial organization, provided by a geometric composition based on modular spatial units.

The general layout is organized around three principal foci: the mosque itself, the cultural centre, and the minaret rising to a height of 240 m (785 ft) above ground level and also serving as an observation tower for visitors. (If this had been built, it would have been the tallest minaret in the world by far.) The residential area, a public amenities area and parking at ground level and underground are situated on the north side of the complex. The whole is encompassed by gardens. Lateral entrances lead to porticoed arcades running parallel to the *qibla* axis, so defining the north and south sides of the courtyard. Makiya repeats the distinctive arches seen in his previous designs (such as those for the Khulafa and Kuwait mosques) employing them here in the freestanding structure that forms the entrance gateway to the complex located on the *qibla* axis. Attached to the prayer hall are four satellite cultural pavilions, each of them covered by four small domes, based on the prayer hall module. Two other structures, a daily prayer hall and the Jerusalem Pavilion, the latter inspired by the Dome of the Rock, flank the entrance to the main prayer hall. Both are based on the same module and serve, in Makiya's words, as 'joints' connecting the three main foci of the scheme.

The main prayer hall is a hypostyle space with an area of 26,000 sq. m (280,000 sq. ft). It is composed of square modular units, each topped with a small dome, above which towers the mass of the principal dome over the *mihrab*. Makiya has used the opportunity of this project to elaborate on his earlier experiments with large domes, such as at Khulafa and the Kuwait Mosque, while still maintaining the profile of a Safavid dome. Much has changed, however, for the base of the dome now breaks the line of the *qibla* wall, so monumentalizing the *mihrab* on the exterior. Outside, an artificial lake from which the *qibla* wall rises reflects the high drama of the extruded *mihrab* and the dome above it, rising to a height of 95 m (310 ft).

The scheme proposed by Kahtan Al-Madfai was inspired by the desert environment, which is evoked by the use of repeated elements such as palm-tree motifs. He has stated that Islamic numerology was also a source of inspiration in determining the proportions.

The complex is divided into two sections which in plan almost form a mirror image. They are separated in part by a triple-bayed arcade giving access from the east and west sides, and in part by courtyard spaces. The ceremonial entrance is located on the *mihrab* axis. The layout is based on a 40 x 40 m (130 x 130 ft) grid with avenues 8 m (26 ft) wide flanking the grid. These dimensions determined the span of the arches which rise to a height of 10 m (33 ft). The main prayer hall is kept distinctly separate from the daily prayer halls, the tall cylindrical minaret and the other facilities called for in the programme. The main prayer hall is E-shaped (with the long side constituting the *qibla* wall), embracing two courtyards. Two large domes, the principal one over the *mihrab* on an octagonal drum of arches and *muqarnas*, and the other over the entrance to the main prayer hall, are apparent variations on the form used in the Dome of the Rock. According to the architect, 'the great dome over the *mihrab* represents a purely religious function while the second dome dominating the *sahn* symbolizes the transition from sacred to secular worlds.'[64]

Robert Venturi's design for the Baghdad competition was at once the most audacious and the most controversial. In the project description, he summarizes the design guidelines as being 'to develop a building in which scale and elements

Mohamed Makiya's design features the tallest minaret (intended to serve as an observation tower) and a prayer hall surmounted by the grandest Safavid-style dome, all set within a scheme of modular units in formal gardens.

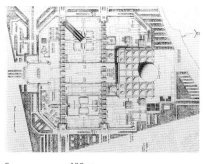

0   100 m

0   300 ft

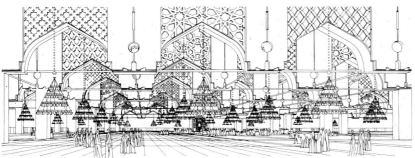

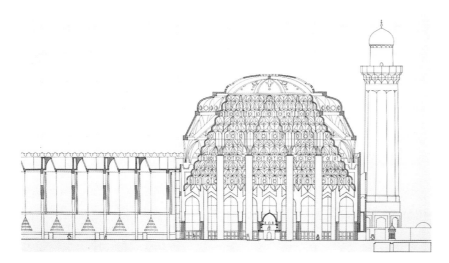

Robert Venturi's design is also based on a scheme inspired by the traditional hypostyle hall; here the interior space is measured in bays which no longer need support from below but hang as decorated screens parallel to the *qibla* wall. The courtyard with its small domed pavilion is shaded by a giant *muqarnas* parasol. The overall project, featuring a single freestanding minaret, has been carefully detailed to be read on an urban scale and then on a much reduced human scale within the complex itself.

PERSPECTIVE FROM APPROACH - ESPLANADE AND MINARET

express monumentality in architecture as well as human scale; in which the spatial layout is unequivocally egalitarian; and where symbolic elements such as arcades, ornament, dome, *muqarnas*, crenellations and minaret have clear and acceptable referents'.[65] From these basic premises, he has developed a design programme in which form and ornamentation operate on two levels: thus, the design seeks to produce easily recognizable and readable symbols, while toying with expectations and illusion in a provocative manner. This tendency is evident in his treatment of the hypostyle hall, the domes and the inscription programme.

For his development of the main hypostyle hall, Venturi focused on the same key historical models as those used by the other architects, but chose the Mosque of Ibn Tulun in Cairo as his inspiration for ordering the vast interior space. The repetition of the long screens of arches, each one with a band of calligraphic inscriptions, was the compelling image he transformed and elaborated on the necessarily vast scale of the new mosque. No longer constrained by structural limitations such as the need to support the arches with piers, he chooses to suspend the screens from the ceiling and thus free the floor. In order to relieve the vastness of the resulting open space, rows of low candelabras were planned. The bright colour and oversized scale of the calligraphy are revealed in their essence on the *mihrab*, which is treated as a flat-framed arch. A fenestrated dome of modest proportions admits light to the space in front of the *mihrab*, and marks its location in the *qibla* wall when viewed from outside.[66]

The specifications for a separate daily prayer hall and a hall for women allowed the architect to place them on either side of a great court which would also accommodate the overflow of worshippers on special holidays. It was the size of the resulting court and the fact that it would become a completely open, sun-lit space that engendered the idea of providing a shade or parasol for it. This, in turn, was a pretext for the inclusion in the complex of a design feature unique to the architecture of Islam – the *muqarnas*. The model for the proposed *muqarnas* parasol was not a single example, but a number of stone and plaster portals and domes, ranging from the Iman Dur mausoleum near Samarra in Iraq to the reconstructed *muqarnas* dome from Takht-i-Suleiman in Iran. The moulded and pierced double-shell canopy was to be raised on eight supports above the open space; it is important to note that while its circumference covered only the width of the rectangular courtyard, the ends of the longer sides were left open to the sky – another indication of the parasol nature of the 'dome'.[67]

Considering the prospect of the entrance façade seen from close up and from a distance helped to determine the height and exterior colour of the canopy. The chosen colour, blue, is echoed on the monumental front wall in a tiled band with an inscription in white Kufic script, lending a sense of sobriety to the ensemble. The landmark minaret, placed at the end of this wall, completes the exterior.

The housing and other facilities called for in the brief are treated by Venturi as urban appendages which depend and

devolve from the mass of the mosque but are not ordered by it in terms of orientation and layout. A lower, square tower serves to reduce the visual impact of the block by providing a vertical focus related to the height of the lower dependencies.

While all the designs submitted for the State Mosque in Baghdad cite the past, they do so in different ways, and some more literally than others. Recurring elements in the projects are the use of domes and minaret on a grandiose scale as prominent landmarks signalling the presence of the mosque, and the use of a hypostyle plan for the prayer hall, which may be largely due to the functional requirements of size. Forms and ornamentation from diverse historical sources are adopted without deliberate literal borrowing with regard to scale, context or materials, since all the architects involved felt that designs for contemporary mosques should be unambiguous in their attempt to reinterpret old meanings.

Al Umma, Tripoli, Libya (project)

The interpretation of past models as a historicist gesture, for example in the case of the Kuwait Great Mosque and in some of the Baghdad mosque competition entries, has been repeated frequently elsewhere in other state mosques. The

The competition-winning entry for Al-Umma Mosque (1981), Tripoli, by the Canadian firm Arcop Associates features Ottoman (and Safavid) elements of a single prayer hall space, preceded by a gigantic screen portal. The site plan (below) shows the relationship of the proposed mosque to the city grid and the waterfront.

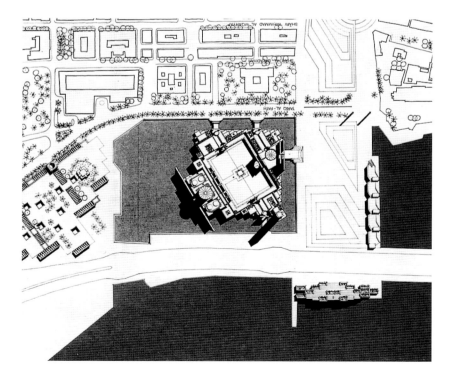

(Below) Model of the prayer hall of the Tripoli project; the intended pre-cast concrete structure features a central dome on a polygonal base supported by piers.

(Bottom) Section along the main axis.

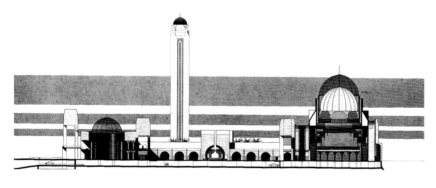

(Opposite) The Sultan Omar Ali Saifuddin Mosque (1958) in Bandar Seri Begawan, Brunei, is a monumental building in the Mughal/Anglo-Indian manner surrounded on three sides by an artificial lagoon, at the centre of which is moored a copy of a sixteenth-century royal barge (*mahligai*), used for special occasions.

Ottoman precedent is used almost literally in the proposal for such a project in Tripoli made by Ramesh Khosla of the Canadian firm Arcop Associates, well-known for designing modern commercial buildings in Canada and hotels that relate to the local vernacular in India and Pakistan. Arcop's project for Al-Umma, the Nation's Mosque, was the winning scheme of a limited competition sponsored by the Libyan Ministry of Housing in 1979. The design was developed through several stages before the final version was approved in 1981.

The project brief asked that 'importance and distinction be achieved . . . that would present the characteristics of Libyan Islamic architecture . . . noticeable in the old Libyan "Morabitia" (architecture)', and went on to specify an internal courtyard or patio surrounded by a simple structure to 'give a feeling of solemnity' and to call for use of '"Mass" as an architectural method without dissipating this intention by trying to make decorative architectural units. The design should not be imitative or repetitive of previous works . . . [and] should harmonize the proposed mosque with the redevelopment of the corniche area and give space for pedestrians on the Green Square.'[68]

The programme stitipulated that the prayer area should accommodate 2,700 men, with a separate space for 300 women on another level; the forecourt had to be large enough for a further 6,000 men – making a total of 9,000 worshippers. It was stated that the mosque should have a dome about 50 m (165 ft) in height, while that of the minaret was to be some 70 m (230 ft). In addition, adequate ablutions facilities, a *madrasa*, a library, museum and living quarters, all within a landscaped area, were to be provided. Overlooking the plaza and 'Green Space' there was also to be a balcony from which the public could be addressed. These aspects of the mosque are consistent with its national role. The proposed form of the main mosque structure is essentially a dome resting on the frustum of a pyramid. The dome would be supported on a circular beam (as in the Regent's Park Centre) resting on five pylons. The building was to be constructed in pre-cast concrete with patterned infill panels.

In most cases the architect's response to place and culture is clearly perceivable, but in this instance the choice of an Ottoman model is again an evocation of the period during which a considerable part of present-day Libya was a province of the Ottoman Empire. The wealth of North African precedent is accorded only passing reference in points of detail.

Another important model, the Indian Mughal mosque, has been used in a number of schemes, notably in the Sultan Omar Ali Saifuddin Mosque in Bandar Seri Begawan, Brunei, and in the Maldive Islands.

The mosque in Brunei,[69] completed in 1958, has a dome (the surface of which is covered with 3.3 million pieces of gold mosaic) that reaches a height of 165 ft (50 m). The

(Above) Exterior and interior views of the
Al-Aa'zam Mosque and Islamic Centre (1984),
designed by Hajeedar & Associates, which
serves as the National Mosque of the Republic
of the Maldives. Its style reflects a simplified
version of Mughal and Anglo-Indian features
made possible by the use of modern
construction materials.

walls are faced with Venetian marble, and many of the
windows feature stained glass. The forms of the dome and
the arched openings make clear reference to late-Mughal
architecture.[70] The mosque is surrounded on three sides by
a lagoon, at the centre of which is a copy of a sixteenth-
century royal barge (*mahligai*) which is used occasionally
for religious ceremonies such as the annual Qur'an reading
competition.

The Al-Aa'zam Mosque and Islamic Centre, by the
Malaysian architect Hajeedar & Associates, stands in Malé
on the capital island of the Islamic Republic of the Maldives.
Completed in November 1984, the building serves as the
republic's National Mosque, having a congregational
capacity of 4,500 people. Its design is similar to that of
Hajeedar's earlier mosque, Abu Bakar as-Siddiq, near Kuala
Lumpur (see Chapter 3) and is modelled on it. Here, the
Mughal style is reinterpreted by using contemporary
materials and technology, and is transformed to produce
a hybrid modern building.

Capitol Complex Mosque, Dhaka, Bangladesh

Although in most instances state mosques have been
commissioned as independent projects, some examples were
conceived as an integral part of a new complex, such as the
Capitol in Dhaka, or as an addition to an existing mosque,
as in the case of the parliament building in Ankara. It can
be argued that these buildings do not necessarily qualify
as state mosques in the same sense as those discussed
above, for the process of commissioning these buildings
does not seem to have been imbued with the same purpose
of creating a national symbol through modernity and the
clear statement of an Islamic identity. Despite this, however,
the examples in Dhaka and Ankara – if viewed individually as
part of a building that is symbolic of nationalist and Muslim
identities, and in the absence of a designated state mosque,
serve the same fundamental purpose and form an important
postscript to the discussion concerning the manifestation of
the state as client.

The Dhaka example is particularly interesting, both for its
architecture and for its symbolic significance. The project
started in 1962, when present-day Bangladesh was still East
Pakistan as part of the design for a second capital. The
establishment of this eastern seat of government (to be
named Ayub Nagar after the then President Ayub Khan) was
a move intended to counter growing nationalist sentiment
in the area; the commission for the project was given to
Louis Kahn, who had worked in India and was considered
as a master of twentieth-century architecture. The plan
was seen as a gesture of recognition of the status of East
Pakistan and as a symbol of national unity and a sign of
modern development. A brief for the work was quickly
drawn up, but much of the detail was left to the architect to
interpret and indeed to redefine. Kahn saw this project as a
grand spiritual mission and sought to produce 'a recognized
symbol that would be universal and transcend cultural

differences' in the context of 'representational democracy' (the government's phrase).[71]

By March 1963, Kahn had designed a grand scheme that was divided into two 'citadels': the Citadel of Assembly (the National Assembly building, the Supreme Court and a large mosque); and the Citadel of the Institutions of Man (other civic and institutional buildings). The layout was axial, governed by strong geometric forms. The ideograms that he developed underwent changes as the plan was refined.[72] It is beyond the scope of this work to describe the design except insofar as it concerns the mosque. Construction of the National Assembly began in 1965, but various aspects continued to evolve and change until 1971, when the roof design for the Assembly Hall and prayer hall were completed. Civil war broke out that year and in 1972 Kahn renewed his contract with the newly formed Bangladeshi government; he then worked on a new plan which was unveiled in 1973. Following Kahn's death in 1974, it fell to David Wisdom & Associates (comprising Kahn's long-time colleagues Wisdom, Henry Wilcots and Reyham T. Larimer) to oversee the construction work, including the prayer hall, which was largely completed by mid-1983. Six years later, the National Assembly building was the recipient of an Aga Khan Award for Architecture.

The original brief called for the inclusion of a prayer room with an area of approximately 3,000 sq. ft (280 sq. m) within the complex. In his scheme Kahn went much further, producing a design for a large mosque that was to be the

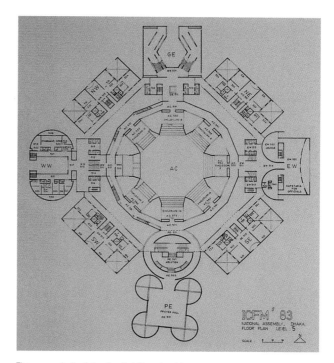

The prayer hall of the Capitol Complex Mosque (1983) designed by Louis Kahn is located above the bastion-like entrance to the National Assembly complex in Dhaka (below). It is turned at a slight angle to the main building in order to conform with the *qibla* requirement. (Overleaf) The *qibla* wall of the starkly dramatic prayer hall with corner windows has a teak-panelled dado rising into a vertical *mihrab*.

focus of the Citadel of Assembly or, as he put it, 'the pivotal centre of the plan, the centre of life'.[73] The mosque occupied some 30,000 sq. ft (2,850 sq. m) and was distinguished by four tall minarets. Commenting on the central role accorded to the mosque in his overall scheme, Kahn wrote: 'Observing the way of religion in the life of Pakistan, I thought that a mosque woven into the space fabric of the assembly would express this feeling. It was presumptuous to assume this right. How did I know it would fit their way of life? But this assumption took possession.'[74] The overt inclusion of such a gesture caused controversy amongst the authorities, who wanted diversity reflected and did not wish to see religion used as the basis for development.[75] It was eventually agreed that the mosque should not be a separate building and that it should not have the appearance of a 'typical' mosque, thus reverting to the original idea of incorporating a prayer room. As the mosque was intended to serve only govern-ment officials working in the complex, this decision was an appropriate one. (One can only speculate how a large mosque might have been used in Dhaka in the years since the 1980s, when Islamic sentiment began to be expressed more openly.)

By May 1964, Kahn had incorporated the prayer room into the Assembly, although he still referred to it as 'the mosque' until later, and it also continued to assume an important symbolic function as the space above the gateway to the monumental octagonal building. The gateway itself consists of a square with four circular corner 'turrets'; within the entrance block the axis is shifted to reflect the direction towards Mecca.[76] 'As such, it is but a vestige of Kahn's initial epiphany, although the revised mosque entrance remains strongly articulated.'[77] Kahn could have eliminated this angle by altering the axis of the whole building, but he deliberately retained this to give the prayer hall its own identity: as he said, 'I made it different that way so that you could in fact express it differently.'[78]

The exterior of the mosque is identical to the rest of the building in its finish of exposed grey reinforced-concrete panels with bands of white marble. It is the interior that captures the importance of Kahn's expression of the

spiritual. The simplicity of the interior matches that of the exterior. The cubical prayer hall is an imposing space, stark and unadorned except for the ornate teak *mihrab* niche and shoulder-height panelling. The corners of the cube have circular cut-outs bounded by vertical cylindrical light shafts. The light enters the hall indirectly through these filters, giving the space a glow and casting shadows as external conditions change. Through the modulation of light and the articulation of a 'silent space', Kahn has created a fitting atmosphere and place for prayer, powerfully expressed.

The Assembly building, begun in 1965, was completed after East Pakistan had become Bangladesh, changing its role from that of a symbol of unity and integration into one of independence. The official name for the capital, Ayub Nagar, became Sher-e-Bangla Nagar – the City of the Bengal Tiger – a reference to the *nom-de-guerre* of the Bengali nationalist leader Fazlul Haq. It is a testimony to the architect's abstraction of place and of Bengali architecture that his design could accommodate these changes of meaning. Kahn's understanding of the spiritual has not only given Bangladesh a major architectural work, but also the Islamic world a significant place of prayer.

It is perhaps fitting that this chapter should end with an example from Turkey which, as a modern secular state and the never-colonized inheritor of Ottoman architecture, served as the major inspiration for the earlier Indonesian, Malaysian and Pakistani mosques, if not for the later designs for Kuwait and Baghdad.

Ironically, plans for the construction of a large modern mosque in Ankara referred to as the Kocatepe Mosque – the great concrete shell project by Vedat Dalokay and Nejat Tekelioglu that won in the 1957 competition – were stopped after the foundations had been laid in 1963.[79] Dalokay would later see his experimentation with concrete shells realized in Pakistan. In Ankara a copy of a generic grand Ottoman mosque was proposed by Hüsrer Tayler and Fatim Uluengin in 1967, constructed, and finally

(Opposite) The cut-outs at the corners of the prayer hall contrast with the concrete walls banded in marble stripes, and the ablutions area (below) has perimeter seating placed next to a water channel.

(Right) The winning entry by Vedat Dalokay in the competition for the Kocatepe Mosque in Ankara was not built because of its overtly modern look; instead, an Ottomanesque structure (overleaf) was built in 1987 on foundations already laid for Dalokay's project.

(Right) The Mosque of the Grand National Assembly (1987–9), Ankara, by Altug, Behruz & Can Çiniçi, was inserted into the existing parliamentary complex. The elegant plan places the mosque at an angle to the assembly building, creating a discreet religious counterpoint to an otherwise secular symbol; to the left is a small library.

(Below) The Kocatepe Mosque, Ankara, as finally built in Ottomanesque style.

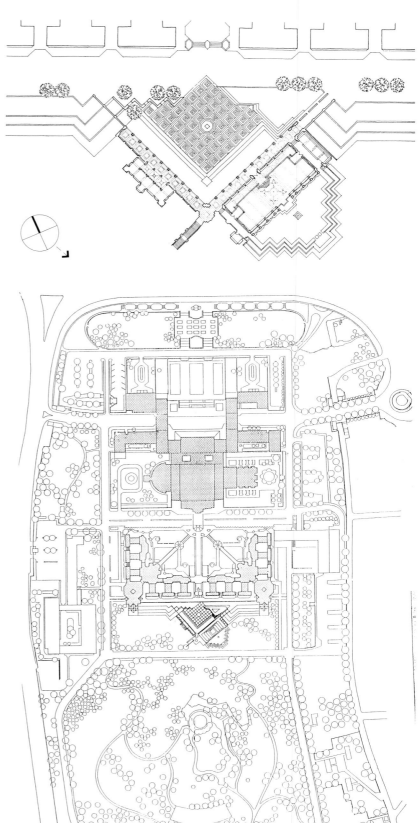

inaugurated in 1987. Despite the fact that the Kocatepe Mosque dominates the skyline of Ankara, the building is not loaded with the same sense of purpose associated with forging a national image. That task had already been achieved earlier through Atatürk's decision in 1923 to make Ankara the capital of the new republic, far from the imperial connotations of Istanbul, and the subsequent construction of the main government buildings, including the Parliament, and of the mausoleum of Atatürk.[80] Here, in the Kocatepe Mosque conservative taste and, perhaps, a popular longing for easily recognizable, familiar forms have surfaced. Through this massive building, Ankara has been deprived of its modern republican image and has acquired an Ottoman, Istanbul-like quotation.

Grand National Assembly Mosque, Ankara, Turkey

Since 1989 the modernist, republican image has been re-asserted with the completion of a mosque for the parliament building, though the inclusion of a mosque in the parliament complex was an initiative that ran counter to the secularist nature of the Turkish state. The initiative was, however, not implemented without public protest.[81] It addressed a perceived need in Turkey to modulate the secularist image of the state by including a mosque within the confines of the very buildings which symbolize that image.

The Turkish Parliament wanted to build a mosque as part of the Public Relations building designed by Behruz Çiniçi. The team of Altug, Behruz and Can Çiniçi was commissioned in 1985 to design a building to be known as the Grand National Assembly Mosque.[82] The only functional stipulation made by the client was a prayer hall with a capacity for

500 worshippers. The rest of the programme was left to the architects' discretion.[83] In their search for a solution that would respect the integrity of the existing complex (originally designed by Holtzmeister in the 1930s), they opted for the Ottoman *külliye* as an organizational device. This consisted of a large courtyard defined by two buildings that would accommodate respectively the mosque and a library which they added to the outline programme. Construction began in April 1987 and was completed in 1989 at a cost equivalent to US$1.7 million.[84]

The 2.5-hectare (approx. 6-acre) site is surrounded by a sloping park area. The mosque is approached by a pathway which begins in front of the Public Relations building and terminates behind it in a triangular plaza with the mosque on the southeast side and the library on the southwest side. The inward focus of the *külliye* composition was important, as the architects wanted the mosque to be in a private and secluded setting. The natural slope of the site enabled the architects to conceal the building from public view on two of its sides, which would otherwise have faced onto the adjacent street, and to leave open the side facing the plaza.

Both the library and the mosque have a canopy running the full length of each building. They share a corner angle which is defined by two-stepped, superimposed balconies forming a square prism. This element is intended to function as a symbolic minaret. The mosque itself is distinguished from the library by its stepped, almost pyramidal, roof. On the interior, the steps correspond to a rising series of beams which support a small dome resting on stylized squinches. Low rectangular apertures in the space between the beams of the roof structure admit natural light.

(Below) A raised platform serves as a substitute for a conventional minaret. It stands at one corner of the triangular plaza, adjacent to the façade of the mosque.

(Overleaf) The unusual transparent *mihrab* provides a direct view onto a sunken garden, a large area of which is occupied by a pool.

(Below) The prayer hall has an interior in the modernist/brutalist manner with a stepped pyramidal roof. The *qibla* wall incorporates a transparent band of windows with a full-length glazed *mihrab* niche at the centre. Exposed concrete walls are softened by decorative ceramic panels and by the marble-paved floors.

(Right) The proximity of water and greenery create a peaceful outlook from the prayer hall without unwanted visual distractions.

The prayer hall, with an area of 500 sq. m (5,380 sq. ft), is organized on two levels. The entrance is raised above the main floor and there is a view across it towards a large, transparent, and innovative *mihrab* in Plexiglas, through which can be discerned a sunken garden and a cascade pool. The *mihrab*, similar in its transparency to the *qibla* wall in the King Faisal Masjid in Islamabad, does not distract the worshipper since the sunken garden creates a closed vista. The rectangular form of the prayer hall aligned with the *qibla* wall is less usual today in Turkey, where new mosques tend more often than not to be based on the Ottoman single-dome model. One may interpret this as an attempt to return to the basic original definition of the mosque and render it in a new visual language. The prayer hall is separated from the entrance and the women's prayer area by translucent screens which rise to a height just above eye-level. The entrance level is connected to two outdoor corridors, one of which leads to the ablutions facilities, and the other to the *imam's* room. Both corridors provide access to the sunken garden.

The mosque was constructed in reinforced concrete.[85] On exterior surfaces, it is totally exposed and rough-textured, showing the pattern of the timber shuttering. Inside, the structural members are in exposed concrete with a smooth finish. Other elements are covered with timber screens framed with marble. However, epigraphy is limited to a symbolic minimum and there is very little use of traditional blue Turkish tiles. In her review of the mosque, Jale Erzen has commented that while 'the tectonic character of the building conveys a distinctly modern language, details and ornaments speak of a classical inspiration. Particularly the pavement of the courtyard and the profiled plinth of the building, both in local stone, give the outdoors a classical sense of detailing.'[86] The architects emphasize that 'The building design focuses its aim at creating a space for the individual believer. It is free of traditional architectural clichés . . . the focus of the design is on the iconoclastic nature of Islam.'[87] They have succeeded in achieving this stated objective.

The mosque is remarkable for the clever way in which the architects dealt with an existing architectural context.[88] They skilfully addressed issues relating to contemporary mosque design in Turkey through the use of a traditional organizational device, the *külliye*, while at the same time opting for innovation in terms of the spatial treatment of the prayer hall and the abstraction of the generic elements, such as the *mihrab* and minaret.

The majority of state mosques date from the years between the 1960s and the 1980s, and more recent examples are relatively few in number. The need for expressing a national identity has been tempered by a desire to recognize diversity of populations within each country. Given the facts that such grandiose gestures are now becoming prohibitively expensive and that the Islamic countries that gained their independence before the 1980s have already made such architectural statements, the need for such buildings may now be diminishing. It remains to be seen whether those Central Asian republics (formerly part of the USSR) with Muslim majorities, as well as other countries in transition will attempt to build state mosques. Decentralization has begun to devolve the active patronage of new mosques to provincial authorities, municipalities and institutions. Their roles often – though not always – tend to reflect local taste on a smaller scale.

Interior of the National Assembly Mosque: the multi-level entrance area preceding the prayer hall.

Commissions by local government bodies

As state controls have been expanded and consolidated in Muslim nations, the building of mosques for local communities has been overseen by regional and local authorities, much in the same way as they have been made responsible for the provision of schools, hospitals and housing. Physical development plans and master plans for urban and rural settlements were the vehicles through which the very fabric of the nation was imagined, projected and built.

Government, developed from a single centre – be it a national leader/party/family dynasty – has been at once the agent of change, the executive responsible for administration and the guardian of national identity. From the political concept of 'guided democracy' is also derived the structure of local administration which connects everything, through tightly controlled bureaucratic links, to the centre of government. Throughout the Islamic world, even in those states which were not formerly colonial territories, a centralized system of government has been the norm.[1] Thus, the state as client is represented at the local level through its branches, whether the Ministry of Housing and Development, the Ministry of Awqaf or Religious Affairs, the city development authorities or individual municipalities. None of these branches, even the municipalities, can raise any of their own revenues; they simply disburse funds allocated to them by the central government.[2] In this context, programmes for the building of mosques controlled by these various agencies deserve attention, for the plans proposed are to a large extent also centrally conceived, though they may differ considerably in the manner of their realizations.

Since the 1950s, local authorities in the Islamic world have probably been responsible for the construction of more mosques than have individual patrons or even local communities. They are essentially confronted with the task of building mosques either as part of new urban communities, usually in new towns or suburbs, or less frequently within an existing urban fabric. Local government interventions take one of two forms: they may create either a mosque which is individual and special or a mosque type which is capable of being repeated in similar contexts and situations. In the latter case, the mosque is usually related to a new

(Above) The underside of the bronze chandelier suspended from the dome of the Island Mosque (1986) on the Jeddah corniche, designed by Abdel Wahed El-Wakil (see p. 134).

(Opposite) The courtyard of Al-Kindi Plaza Jami (1986), the mosque commissioned by the Riyadh Development Authority as part of its development of the city's Diplomatic Quarter (see p. 128).

(Below) Floor plan of the New Gourna village mosque (1945–8) and general plan of the overall scheme by Hassan Fathy showing the mosque to the north, the theatre to the west, and the main market to the east.

(Bottom) The mosque courtyard shaded by trees, looking towards the barrel-vaulted *iwan*.

(Opposite above) The cupola of the mosque, built by Nubian masons using traditional baked-brick construction methods.

(Opposite below) The mosque as seen from the main square of New Gourna: the staircase minaret, built of mud brick, frames the entrance and balances the mass of the dome.

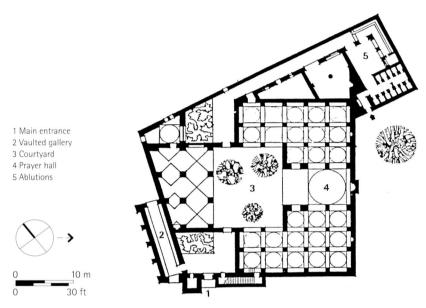

1 Main entrance
2 Vaulted gallery
3 Courtyard
4 Prayer hall
5 Ablutions

0   10 m
0   30 ft

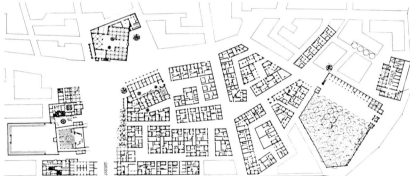

settlement. In the case of the implantation of new mosques in urban contexts, such buildings are included in response to demand from local inhabitants or because they fit into a local authority's plan which calls for a ratio of one mosque per so many hundred people – the figure being determined by the planning authority itself. Though local authorities are primarily active in urban situations, large-scale rural interventions have also been a feature of the recent past.

Village Mosque, New Gourna, Egypt

One of the earliest examples of a planned community with a mosque was Hassan Fathy's New Gourna Village (1945–8). Although, strictly speaking, this mosque is outside the period covered by this study, it deserves mention because the project was widely published and disseminated, and for later architects has become a paradigm that counts very much as an alternative to centrally planned and replicated models. It was an idealized vision of an arts and crafts ideology involving a rural community in which villagers were encouraged to participate in the process of planning and building. That such a mosque could be built within the framework of a state bureaucracy is perhaps more indicative of the incomplete centralized control in Egypt at the time than of any active governmental decision to espouse a visionary concept.

New Gourna was a project undertaken by the Egyptian Department of Antiquities in an effort to stop tomb-robbing and the destruction of ancient artifacts in the Tombs of the Nobles at Luxor, just behind the old village, by moving the local population to a newly developed site. It was largely thanks to two individuals in the Department who admired the work of Fathy, Osman Rustum, the Head of Engineering and Excavation, and Dr Alexander Stopplaere, the Chief Restorer, that he became the architect for the new project in 1945.

The original master plan for the village was drawn up between August and October of 1945. It comprised housing for the 7,000 inhabitants of Gourna, and an extensive array of public facilities: a mosque, Coptic church, village hall, theatre, sporting club, village crafts exhibition hall and school, market place, police station, dispensary and women's social centre, separate primary schools for boys and girls, a *khan* and an artificial lake. The master plan for the village was never fully realized, and the final product represents only partly what Fathy intended. The layout of the village was organized around the existence of family and tribal groups: in the development of the master plan the four tribes of Old Gourna, each led by a sheikh or *imam*, were considered as unified yet separate.[3] The resulting four districts were disposed around a square with the mosque as its focal point, directly facing the main entrance to the village. The four-part division was reflected in the mosque design, in which Fathy provides four separate *iwans* within a single structure.

The mosque design is generated out of Nubian traditions in respect of the disposition of its horizontal and vertical masses, and it was the first building on the new site.[4] As

(Below) The interior of the dome, which rests on articulated squinches. Openings in the octagonal base and in the dome itself create patterns of light and provide ventilation.

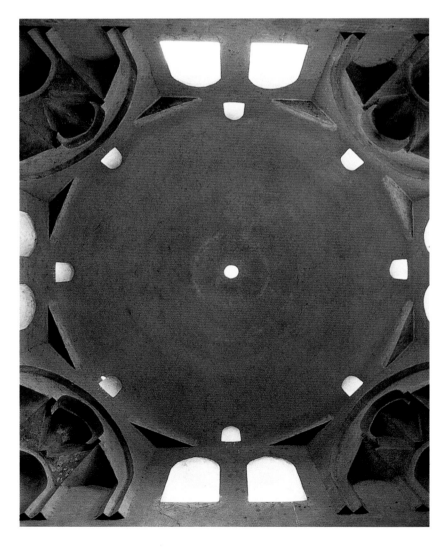

with the entire development of New Gourna, the mosque is constructed of mud brick, except for the main dome, the larger dimensions of which demanded the use of baked brick. The external features of the mosque are a vaulted gallery on the western façade which provides a shaded area where passers-by and visitors can sit and rest, a large dome with arched apertures above the *mihrab* area, and a striking exterior staircase leading to the minaret. The staircase, a typical element of mosques in Upper Egypt, was a deliberate choice on Fathy's part as an expression of a local tradition, important because 'the religious architecture of the locality will have grown to represent its people's idea of the holy, [...] I think it right to respect and keep the local forms and character – as I kept the Upper Egyptian tradition of a bold, straight outside staircase to the minaret, which stood up like a high pulpit above the mosque'.[5] Around the sides of the courtyard are the rectangular prayer hall and the *iwans*. One of these prayer areas, called the 'main *iwan*' by Fathy, is covered by a transversal barrel vault, directly preceding the large dome over the *mihrab*. The prayer hall consists of small square bays covered by shallow domes resting on square columns, and by the large dome supported on square columns and resting on squinches.

Two entrances to the mosque, under the minaret or through the ablutions area, are used by worshippers according to whether they are washed or not on arrival. In both cases, the courtyard only becomes visible by turning a corner. The ablutions facilities provided small blocks on which individual worshippers can sit in comfort while washing. Arched openings varying in size surround the courtyard: the largest of these is the *iwan* leading to the main dome. The north wall of the mosque was extended considerably beyond the main mass of the building, thus creating extra space to contain the ablutions facilities. The rest of the structures, such as the minaret, a vaulted arcade serving also as guest quarters (*madyafa*), a study for the *imam*, a small room for private prayer and a store room are formed organically out of the main structure, which explains the irregular and trapezoidal forms of some of the interior spaces, at times devoid of right angles. There appears to have been no designated prayer space provided for women, though in recent practice they have often used the rear (west) *iwan*, since the four tribal groups are no longer strictly differentiated.

The question of light was important for the atmosphere that the architect wished to create: how the interior spaces would be lit and how the walls would be modulated were major considerations in the design.[6] The main prayer hall is lit by means of the windows in the dome and by diffused light from the courtyard. The dappled, multi-patterned effect, at times restrained, at times alternating with deep shadows, was surely an aesthetic move. The subtle and controlled use of natural light gives rise to a sheltered environment that is conducive to meditation and prayer.[7] The overall design is of the utmost simplicity, using only what is considered essential and intended in every way

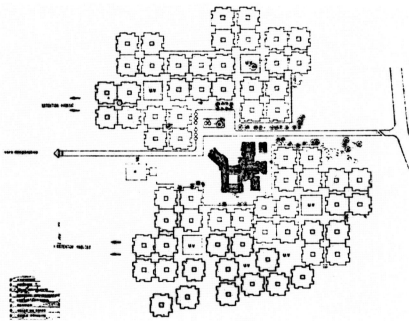

(Top) General view of Ma'ader Village (1975–80), by the El-Miniawy brothers; the mosque is the taller building seen in the background.

(Above) Plan of the village; the mosque was designed to be the focal point and the physical centre of Ma'ader, through which a main road passes.

to be in harmony with the needs of the community and compatible with their way of life. The building exudes calm and serenity, providing an oasis of shade away from the harsh glare of the sun, and remains one of the most successful environments for prayer.

New Gourna created an idealized vision and layout of a village which became for other architects an icon of a validated rural design. It also represented an affirmation of the use of natural or low-technology building materials in new or revisited architectural forms. The example it set has since been adopted worldwide through the development network comprising Non-Governmental Organizations and international agencies.[8] Although New Gourna was conceived and built in the late 1940s, the influence of its plan and the building system employed there can be detected only from the mid-1960s and early 1970s, when Fathy was able to publish the story of New Gourna and to gather around him a fluid and informed circle of students and apprentices.[9]

Village Mosque, Ma'ader, Algeria

From this circle of followers of Hassan Fathy came the Egyptian brothers, Hany and Abdel Rahman El-Miniawy, though it is not clear how long they were part of it. The brothers were members of a larger team that included Hamdi Diab (1945–76) and Hammam El-Miztikawi. They have been active in Algeria since 1969.

The design for the village and the village mosque of Ma'ader in the M'sila region of Algeria is based directly on

Village roofscape. The two-stage minaret rises above the vaults of the surrounding houses, providing a landmark when seen from a distance and identifying the mosque in the village itself.

(Right) Plan of the Ma'ader mosque complex, showing the mosque itself, a school and the public bath house (*hammam*).

(Below) The square minaret, reached by an external staircase, simultaneously harks back to a very old tradition of minaret design and recalls Hassan Fathy's more recent New Gourna minaret.

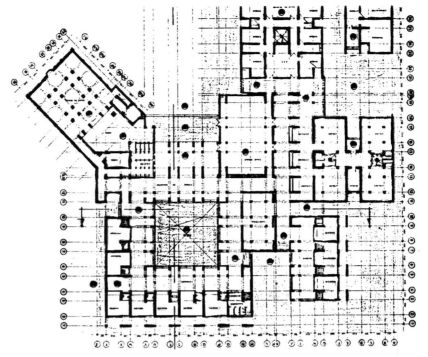

the New Gourna example. The *wilaya* of M'sila acted as the client and the village was begun in 1975 and completed in 1980. The layout of the mosque, the domed bays of the prayer hall, and the staircase minaret are all governed by the use of a system of Nubian-style vaults and rendering. Strictly speaking, this project cannot be called a version of the local architectural idiom, for vaults do not feature in the traditional architecture of M'sila, where flat roofs and *pisé* (rammed earth) construction are the norm. Yet within the vast resettlement and building programme of the agrarian reform undertaken in the 1960s and 1970s by the socialist government of Algeria, where the typical 'socialist village' consisted of nothing more than rows of cement-block or concrete buildings along a single street, the mosque itself and the surrounding village represented a major new departure.[10] The El-Miniawy brothers created an alternative approach using the New Gourna template – a socialist village with a mosque as its focal point.

Boumedienne Village Mosque, near Abdala, Algeria

Within the same vast programme of resettlement a new agrarian village was built in the northwest of the country near Abdala (Bechar) for a semi-nomadic population and named after President Houari Boumedienne.[11] Ricardo Bofill of the Atelier d'Architecture et d'Urbanisme in Paris received the commission. Among Bofill's design objectives was the development of a simplified construction system employing only locally available building materials, while adapting the project to the desert climate. The design commenced in December 1977; construction began in early 1978 and was completed in 1980.

Bofill used the opportunity offered by this commission to work with the basic geometries of circle and square. The circular plan of the village is articulated by five inscribed squares, with all the public, communal services being

(Above) Ricardo Bofill designed the mosque (1977–80) as part of a new village in the Bechar province of Algeria. The design for both village and mosque employs the circle and square as a means of establishing a new architectural language not derived from indigenous building styles but based on abstractions of Middle Eastern references.

(Below) Conjectural plan (based on literary sources) of the circular city of Al-Mansur, Baghdad, founded in 762. The mosque (A) and palace (B) are shown as the focal point of the layout, the overall diameter of which was over 2.5 km (1¹/₂ miles).

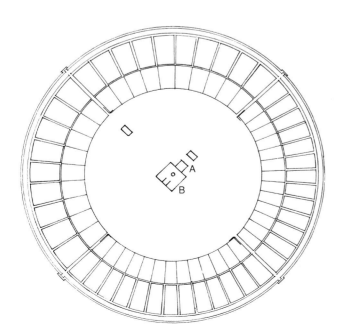

concentrated in a single monumental complex in the central square. The mosque and its minaret provide the focus of this square. The overall exercise clearly provided the architect with an opportunity to explore historic and cultural references, not so much in terms of the design of mosques as in the layout of settlements. In this case, however, his inspiration was the monumental (and vanished) circular city of Al-Mansur, Baghdad – a reference which he and his clients, if not the resettled population, would appreciate.

Baked brick was the principal building material employed, and the loadbearing walls were doubled in thickness; the foundations consisted of lightweight concrete slabs with hollow-brick infill; roofs were covered with brick panels set in a reinforced-concrete frame; façades were given a limestone-cement finish and then brightly painted. Spanish construction workers were brought to Algeria to train Algerian army personnel who completed the work.

The installation of mosques in totally designed and controlled rural (and urban) entities was connected in the Algeria of the time with a programme of expanded state ownership and control of mosques as socio-religious and political centres. The intrusion of the state into mosque building in this instance lies in the official recognition of the fact that the mosque remains a continuing locus of each community with a potential for exploitation by those seeking to express anti-government political opinions.[12] In the end, as subsequent events in Algeria have revealed,

115

it proved impossible to impose such control, and the intervention of the state in mosque building did not lead to the results that the government desired.

The espousal of government mosque-building programmes may also come about without the vast experiment in social engineering upon which Algeria embarked from the 1960s to the 1980s. It may be adopted as a means of establishing a fundamental image and identity.[13] Programmes may be promulgated through the Ministry of Religious Affairs, other ministries or provincial/state governments in an attempt to intervene in or to change the course of the visual/design nature of current mosque-building practice. Such is the case of Pahang State in Malaysia.

Mosque Programme for Pahang State, Malaysia

The client for a set of new mosques, the Amanah Saham Pahang Berhad (ASPA) – which may be translated as the Investment Trust for Pahang – was a foundation formed to develop the vast timber resources of the state. In this sense, ASPA is more akin to a *waqf* controlled by the state government. The Pahang State authorities requested the development of rural areas and small towns, and in response

A typical C-type mosque (1986) in Pahang State, Malaysia, the design of which was inspired by that of traditional timber buildings in the region; the exposed timber structure, roof openings and side screens form part of the simple aesthetic of the design. The use of painted galvanized-metal sheeting as the roof covering, though controversial at first, soon won acceptance among the local people for whom the mosque was provided.

ASPA developed a typology of regional mosques to be built using local timber and construction methods, thus keeping the budget low. The client stipulated that to facilitate ease of construction and replicability the mosques should be made of prefabricated sections, mainly of timber, and that the design should project a 'Pahang theme'.[14]

The architect chosen was CSL Associates of Kuala Lumpur; the firm's principal, Jimmy C. Lim, was already well known as a 'timber guru' and had over the years undertaken wooden constructions using regional and Malay traditions as his source of inspiration – mainly evident in elegant houses designed for wealthy clients and in vacation hotels. Lim's main reference for the design was to local environmental conditions, with particular attention to climate.[15] His quest for a 'Pahang style' was to find its cultural roots in the Bugis, a seafaring people, who had originally migrated from Makasar or Ujung Pandang on Sulawesi in Indonesia. The major source of inspiration for the mosques was the Kampung Laut Masjid in Kelantan, the oldest extant timber mosque in Malaysia (built in the seventeenth century), and another source was the old Masjid Ende, a masonry structure combined with a *bumbung limas*, or pitched pyramidal *meru* (layered) hardwood roof, and surrounding timber verandahs.[16]

A number of designs were developed – designated types A to E – with a capacity of either around 300 to 350, or 500 to 600 worshippers. Thirteen mosques were built as part of the original contract.[17] In conjunction with his structural engineer, Warwick Colefax, the architect developed a construction system involving the use of timber stilts on reinforced-concrete footings. An additional storey at lower ground-floor level can be accommodated to provide space for activities other than prayer. In general, the structural grid for the square prayer hall is based on an 8 ft 9 in. (2.67 m) module, with verandahs 8 ft (2.44 m) wide on three sides and the *mihrab* recess and storage space along the fourth side. Construction is based on a simple timber post-and-beam prefabrication system which can be adapted to the different plan types and to local conditions. The floor of the building is raised above ground level so that on an undulating site erection does not involve additional earthwork; this method also overcomes the risk of storm-water flooding and provides cross-ventilation, making costing a predictable exercise. The roof support consists of two types of truss: one for the upper part and the other for the lower part. Basic services include a simple electrical circuit, septic tanks for sewerage and a water tank located above the false ceiling in a separate ablutions pavilion.

By way of example, the 'B2' type mosque, measuring 68 ft 6 in. x 68 ft 6 in. / 20.88 x 20.88 m overall, has a capacity for 300 worshippers. The prayer hall can be entered on three sides from the verandahs, the fourth side being that of the *qibla* (with the *mihrab* articulated in the interior but not externally) and the storage spaces. The structure has a two-tiered roof. The 'C' type mosque, with an area of 86 x 86 ft / 26.21 x 26.21 m) accommodates up to 500 worshippers and

(Right) Roof detail showing the elegant and economical nature of the structure.

(Below) Generic section of a C-type mosque and plan of a B2-type mosque; the design is based on a module 8 ft 9 in. (2.67 m) square, with the use of prefabricated elements. The actual orientation of each individual building is determined on site.

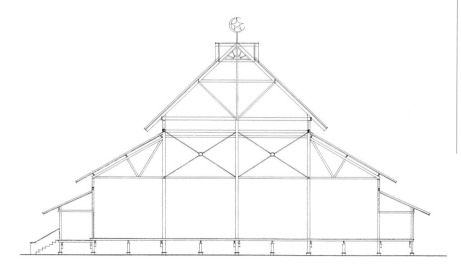

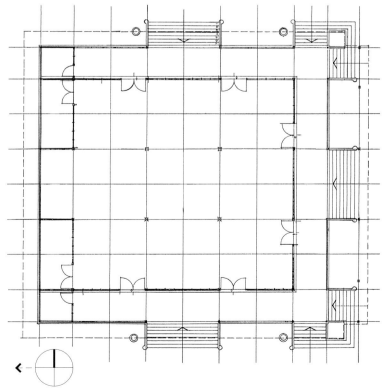

The Darul Aman Mosque (1986) in Gelang Town, Singapore, one of a number designed and built by the Housing and Development Board as part of the basic provision of religious, educational and social facilities included in recent housing schemes.

(Below) General view from the southwest and site plan.

(Opposite) Interior view of the prayer hall. The pitched roofs of the covered extension and the main prayer hall hark back to local pre-Islamic architecture. The screened mezzanine level with the women's gallery is clearly discernible.

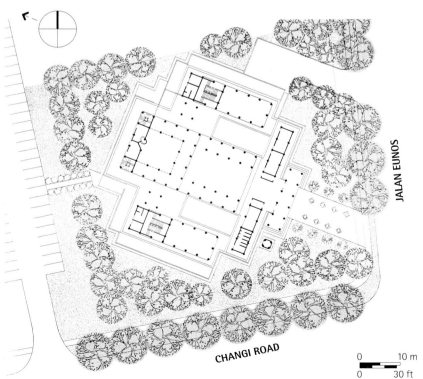

JALAN EUNOS

CHANGI ROAD

0   10 m
0   30 ft

is based on the same modular grid as all the other designs. Due to its greater size, it also has eight columnar supports for a three-tiered roof structure which, according to Lim, 'provokes an imagery of ascendancy to spiritual heights'.[18]

Construction of the thirteen mosques began in January 1985, each taking about three to four months, and all were completed within budget by the following November.[19] The architect has responded well to his client's brief, producing a series of mosques with designs that are economical, simple and elegant; the buildings also reflect historical and local stylistic traditions and forms, which have been intelligently translated into a timeless idiom. The solution thus realized in rural areas is a good one and represents an approach that could also be applied successfully in urban situations.

Housing and Development Board Mosques, Singapore

In the tightly controlled urban setting of Singapore, the programme of mosque building in the new townships is the responsibility of the Housing and Development Board (HDB).[20] In a modern state which is multi-ethnic and multi-confessional, the mosque-building programme forms part of a larger initiative that provides the professionals, technical expertise and subsidies to build a variety of religious centres – churches, temples and mosques. The policy of the HDB has been to 'reflect the architectural flavour of the South-east Asian region', while at the same time 'introducing hi-tech materials into the construction of mosques to reflect a progressive image within the traditional design'.[21] In a programme begun in 1975 and intended to produce a 'new generation' of mosques, the HDB chose to prepare an individual mosque design for each community rather than provide a single repeatable model. The Muslim Religious Council of Singapore (MUIS) established a Mosque Building Fund to which Muslim residents each contributed 46 cents (approx. US$0.30) a month towards the cost of constructing 'new-generation' mosques within the new public housing estates where they lived.[22] For instance, in Gelang Town, an estate of 200,000 people (of whom Muslims constitute a minority of around 20,000), finance for the mosque also came from individual patrons and from the compensation paid to the community by the government for the loss of the earlier and smaller Amina Mosque, demolished as part of the redevelopment scheme. The new mosque stands on a prominent site with an area of 3,561 sq. m (38,300 sq. ft) within the high-rise housing development.

In contrast to the older mosques in Singapore, which tend to be smaller and devoted exclusively to prayer spaces, these new buildings were conceived and designed as multi-functional complexes as much for educational and welfare programmes as for religious activities, thereby giving the buildings a prominent social focus.[23] The authorities felt that this socio-religious approach was particularly important in the sense that it harked back to the 'golden era' of Islam and the concept of the mosque as both a spiritual centre and an educational institution. By 1986, eight of the fifteen mosques projected had been built. The Darul Aman Mosque

in Gelang Town was designed by Mohamed Asaduz Zaman of the HDB and completed in August 1986. The site was selected by the HDB after discussion with the MUIS, which provided the land at a subsidized price.

The design is based on local Malay architectural forms, featuring pitched *meru* roofs and timber construction.[24] The mosque, which is laid out symmetrically along an axis determined by the *qibla* wall, consists of a main prayer hall surmounted by a double roof (a large-scale variation of the *meru* roof) preceded by the principal courtyard.[25] The latter is flanked by two smaller courtyards, classrooms for Qur'anic instruction and extended prayer halls. Traditional Malay motifs and geometric patterns were employed to decorate the mosque, while a simple rhomboid motif, used as a repetitive structural and decorative element, recalls earlier buildings in Neo-Tudor style erected under British colonial rule, such as the Selangor Country Club (1890). This motif lends a visual unity to the entire mosque complex.

The structural method employed is a reinforced-concrete post-and-lintel system combined with steel box-section roof trusses. The rhombic frame of the roof structure was assembled on site and put in place with the aid of cranes; the roof tiles imported from Italy were chosen especially to match the colour of the traditional Malay roof.[26] The project cost was equivalent to around US $1.5 million, which was below the prevailing construction costs for timber buildings at the time.

Darul Aman represents one of the more successful designs in the overall programme. It veers away from the

Unlike the Darul Aman Mosque, most recent examples built in Singapore by the HDB, such as the Masjid an-Nur in Woodlands New Town (above) and the Masjid Jurong (left), reveal a blend of Anglo-Indian and contemporary architectural expression.

(Opposite) The Ahle Hadith Mosque (1969–73), Islamabad, built by the Capital Development Authority for a neighbourhood with 6,000 inhabitants.

(Above) Floor plan and roof plan.

1 Entrances
2 Classrooms
3 Ablutions
4 Prayer hall
5 *Mihrab*
6 Courtyard
7 Minaret
8 *Imam's* living
  quarters

(Below) A view of the entrance leading to the courtyard shows the use of repeatable pre-cast vaulted elements which are interpreted in a modernist style.

very popular and populist version of the mosque which is derived from the Anglo-Indian vocabulary; instead, its design embraces aspects of a local profile. It is difficult to ascertain with any degree of certainty whether the choice of this version featuring regional characteristics was entirely attributable to the somewhat more traditionalist nature of the Gelang Town community. However, this building differs sufficiently from the other seven mosques forming part of this programme to suggest that there was another, quite different voice involved in the decisions about the form it should take.[27]

The reconstruction and urban planning of the city-state of Singapore was reimagined for the late twentieth century and beyond, resulting in high-rise subdivisions into which were incorporated various community facilities, including mosques. It is worthy of note that the HDB should have opted for individualized designs in this context – driven perhaps to create recognizably different landmarks in a city that has become more and more uniform in appearance. The rebuilding of Singapore has continued in its own individual manner the era of building newly created capitals – Brasilia and Islamabad come to mind.[28]

Capital Development Authority Mosques, Islamabad

Islamabad, with its extensive grid laid out by Constantinos Doxiadis on the principles of Ekistics, was part of this era of physical planning and thinking about new urban entities,[29] and it was in this context that the districts within the new capital were developed.[30] With it came also the programme of mosque building, overseen by the Capital Development

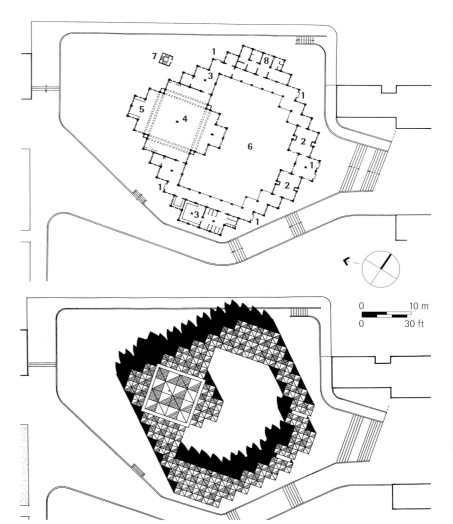

Authority (CDA). In contrast to the later Singapore examples featuring a more individualized design choice, this building programme in the 1960s generated the five types of basic repeatable mosque designs, intended to be implanted wherever a mosque might be needed. Doxiadis's plan divided the city into a number of sectors, each being theoretically self-contained and having its own housing, bus depot, shopping centre and mosque. Within this framework the CDA's designs for the neighbourhood mosques were of a pan-Islamic nature, and local form and character were not brought into play.

The Ministry of Awqaf commissioned Anwar Saeed of the CDA to design several mosque types as neighbourhood or sector mosques for Islamabad. The architect, who was trained in the USA in the 1950s and very much formed by the Modern Movement, wanted to develop an economical mosque design in a modern idiom by the repetitive use of easily identifiable Islamic motifs. His hope was that the principles underlying his design would provide inspiration for future mosque projects of this kind. He also felt that this project was of particular significance to the Islamic world in general, given the growing demand for simpler and cheaper mosques to be built in close proximity to worshippers, so making acts of daily prayer more convenient.[31]

The Ahle Hadith Mosque, a C-type mosque, for example, was built for a community of 6,000 people on a flat open site in a residential area of Islamabad. It accommodates 280 worshippers in the prayer hall and about 650 in the court and on the verandahs. The project was begun in 1969 and construction, which took two years, was completed in 1973. The mosque represents a departure from the conventional designs that had been prevalent on the Indian subcontinent; it is rather an attempt to use traditional design elements in combination with a bold new structural method. The design is based on a grid of 8 ft or 2.44 m. The form relating to this grid is a concrete groin vault supported by four reinforced-concrete columns. This basic element was repeated

throughout the building, consisting of a courtyard, prayer hall and other communal rooms, together with an ablutions area and quarters for the *imam*. No provision was made for the inclusion of separate prayer space for women, given the fact that in everyday practice Pakistani women have seldom prayed in mosques.

In this example, the vaulted elements were staggered diagonally to fit the irregular site and blend in with the surroundings. The plan of the whole complex thus resembles a truncated lozenge in shape. The entrance to the mosque is through a square hall on the east side. On either side are rooms used for Qur'anic instruction. High vaulted arcades follow the perimeter of the large paved central courtyard leading to the *imam's* quarters and women's ablutions area on the north side and the men's ablutions facilities on the south side. The entrance hall is on an axis with the square prayer hall, with the latter constituting the focal point of the complex. Its height exceeds that of all other rooms, and its plan comprises four equal units (each equivalent to four modules), the whole being surrounded by quadripartite vaults which converge on a single column at the centre of the hall. The arched openings of the exterior walls are filled with open screens.

Anwar Saeed's approach to repeatable mosque designs remains constant in his other types. Thus, for example, Type B features the same courtyard-based plan combined with a concrete-shell modular structure – the notable difference in this instance being the use of brick walls to enclose the building. The fact that he was working with the Capital Development Authority and not directly for a particular client, and that the development of these mosques was not subject to formal constraints, gave him a freer hand. The results are very much part of the modernist ethos which pervaded the planning and architecture of Islamabad as a whole, and which was encouraged by leading architects such as Zaheer Uddin Khwaja and Habib Fida Ali. This remains true despite the insistence of some foreign and

(Opposite) The Ahle Hadith Mosque complex is composed around a courtyard with arcades on three sides and the taller prayer hall (visible in the background) on the fourth.

(Left and above) The prayer hall, showing the screened openings of pre-cast concrete which admit natural light and provide ventilation, and detail of arcades surrounding the courtyard.

The Nilein Mosque (1984), Khartoum, by Gamal El-Dowla Abdel Gadir.

(Below) Section of the modern folded concrete-slab structure and an interior view of the circular prayer hall, showing the massive dome supported by a ring beam.

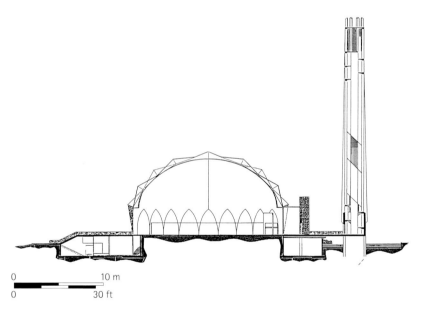

```
0          10 m
0          30 ft
```

local architects on designing and building a number of awkwardly parsed 'Mughal inspired' buildings.[32] In terms of size and scale, the Ahle Hadith Mosque is as large as many congregational mosques., but what makes the building significant for any designer of mosques is the fact that Saeed understood that roof spans no longer needed to be covered by domes and therefore went on to experiment with a variety of concrete shells in creating the type of shaded prayer hall required by the climate. This structural freedom has, of course, been recognized by other architects and is illustrated elsewhere in the Defence Officers' Housing Society Mosque in Karachi (Masjid-i Tooba; Chapter 5), and the Nilein Mosque on the periphery of Khartoum, Sudan.

Nilein Mosque, Khartoum, Sudan

The genesis of the concrete-and-aluminium domical structure of the Nilein Mosque dates from 1974, when the original design was prepared by Gamal El-Dowla Abdel Gadir as his graduate student project at the University of Khartoum. The project was presented to the President of Sudan, who was impressed by the design and proposed its implementation at a prominent site near the confluence of the White Nile and the Blue Nile.

The client of record was the Government of Sudan, essentially represented by the design team and overseen by officials in the President's office.[33] Gadir, being young and inexperienced, worked in collaboration with the Hamdi Group and a local team of architects and engineers.[34] The design was finalized by October 1976, when construction commenced. After several interruptions the project was finally completed in 1984. The cost – equivalent to US$7 million – was met mainly from public funds.[35]

The mosque complex consists of a circular prayer hall and adjacent annexe pavilions set in a garden. The prayer hall, with an area of some 1,900 sq. m (20,450 sq. ft), stands at the centre of a raised terrace approached by flights of steps on three sides, the main one being opposite the *mihrab*. The Centre for Islamic Studies, offices, a lounge, ablutions facilities, and a women's prayer hall are housed at ground level below the terrace. The mosque is ringed by reinforced-concrete supports joined at the apex to form pointed arches, on which rests the concrete ring beam supporting the dome. Developed as an aluminium space-frame, the dome itself is faceted with rhomboid forms – a distant echo of *muqarnas* vault construction.

The ornamentation programme of the interior was paid for by King Hassan II of Morocco, who provided a team of craftsmen from Fez headed by Mohamed Ben Hassan Baso. The *mihrab* and *minbar* form an independent unit of carved plaster work. Carved and painted plaster decoration on the interior of the dome completed the scheme.

A freestanding minaret, 27 m (88 ft) in height and placed behind the *mihrab*, is constructed from eight vertical ribs on an octagonal base. A short distance beyond it stand twelve symmetrically arranged small pavilions housing the library and the Arabic language school. The main building

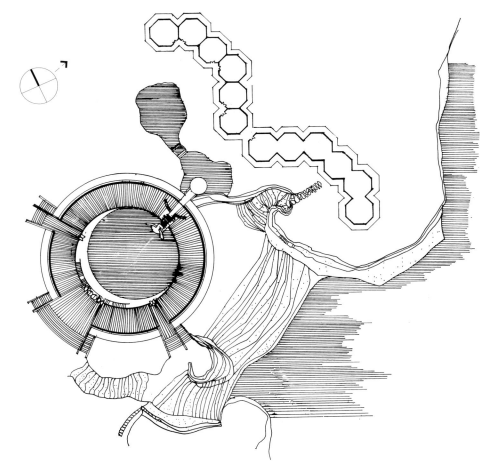

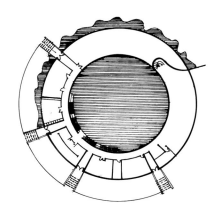

(Above) General view of the Nilein Mosque, sited at the confluence of the Blue Nile and the White Nile; its minaret is visible from both Khartoum and Omdurman. The adjacent library and school pavilions overlook the river; administration and cultural buildings can be seen in the foreground, at the entrance to the complex.

(Left and below) Site plan and main-level plan of the mosque. The prayer hall is approached by a flight of ceremonial stairs directly opposite the *mihrab* and the freestanding minaret. Standing on a circular podium, the mosque is surrounded by a reflecting pool.

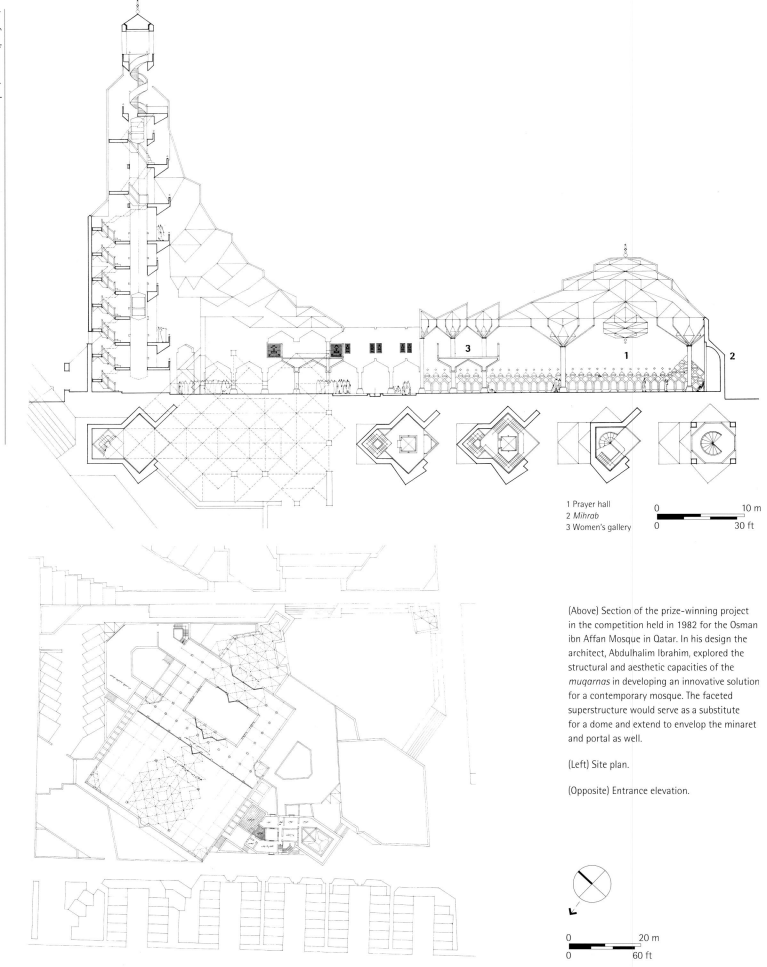

1 Prayer hall
2 *Mihrab*
3 Women's gallery

0   10 m
0   30 ft

(Above) Section of the prize-winning project in the competition held in 1982 for the Osman ibn Affan Mosque in Qatar. In his design the architect, Abdulhalim Ibrahim, explored the structural and aesthetic capacities of the *muqarnas* in developing an innovative solution for a contemporary mosque. The faceted superstructure would serve as a substitute for a dome and extend to envelop the minaret and portal as well.

(Left) Site plan.

(Opposite) Entrance elevation.

0   20 m
0   60 ft

is surrounded by a reflecting pool which, according to the architect, was inspired by the Qur'anic verse (XXI:30), 'We created from water all living things.'[36]

The non-directional design of the mosque allows it to be opened on all sides – a vital consideration in a very hot climate. Its location at the water's edge makes the building feel cooler. The client regarded the building as a very radical rupture with conventional mosque design and was concerned that it might be considered a bad innovation (bid'a)[37] because 'for the very first time in the country the introverted space, private and sacred, of the mosque is completely changed.' However, it was recognized that 'on the other hand, it is in harmony with nature and is part of the country . . . and [the design] reinforces known forms of the dome, mathematics, and is a symbol of Islam.'[38]

The inclusion of a dome in contemporary mosque design was to create problems for many an architect. Not forced by structural necessity to understand its properties and limitations, architects have struggled to determine the correct proportions and place for a dome within a new building. An added difficulty has been that for decades the design of vaults, and of domes in particular, has had little place in the curriculum of architectural schools. As often as not, however, an individual architect is forced by the client to introduce a dome into the roof line as a characteristic feature symbolic of the mosque. Particular circumstances have allowed some architects to take up the challenge of the apparent contradictions of structure and outward symbol to propose alternative forms which would still be readily identifiable as landmarks designating a mosque in the cityscape. Often such a course has in fact been possible within what might seem the particularly constraining circumstances of commissions by governmental authority or its branches.

Osman ibn Affan Mosque, Qatar (project)

Developed for a competition organized by a local authority in Qatar, Abdulhalim Ibrahim's design for the Osman ibn Affan Mosque won first prize. Oleg Grabar noted, 'By giving it the name of one of the Orthodox Caliphs of Islam . . . the ruler of Qatar clearly wished to endow it with a greater importance than that of a place for community worship.'[39] The mosque was envisaged as the future centre of a new

subdivision of the city which was being developed in the 1970s. The architect confronted the question of the nature of the roof for the mosque head on. Bound as he was by the brief which specified the facilities and sizes of the spaces, and being unwilling to copy a dome, he undertook to explore the structural and aesthetic possibilities of the *muqarnas*, given that the brief did not specify the nature of the mosque's roof covering. He therefore enlarged the individual elements of its intrinsic geometric pattern and used them in developing the plan for the prayer hall and subsidiary spaces. Most significantly, he used the enlarged elements as the basis for the roof structure and treated this new assembly as an external symbol of the mosque. The resulting faceted superstructure serves as stand-in for a dome and envelops the minaret-portal complex as well. By opting to avoid the domical profile, the architect acknowledged the structural source of dome-building, and attempted to transfer the symbolic meanings of a dome to a *muqarnas* structure: this bold move has also fathomed the primordial nature of the *muqarnas* as a form having connotations of the heavens.[40]

Other features of the design include a women's gallery, ablutions area, offices and classroom areas. The fact that it will not be realized (another scheme was subsequently chosen) should not detract from a proper appreciation of the architect's innovative manipulation of the standard architectural features of the mosque.

The problem of developing an appropriate architectural language for the contemporary mosque has been acute in some Arab lands at the centre of the Muslim world, encumbered as they are with the heavy baggage of Islamic history. For instance, in Saudi Arabia the dome form still possesses a narrow range of connotations for the client, whereby for example in the very conservative Wahhabi milieu the presence of a dome would connote a shrine or mausoleum and would thus be considered inappropriate in the context of a mosque.[41] The use of the dome only began to reappear there as recently as the 1970s, so it is hardly surprising that architects building in that country since the 1960s, in a period of rapid expansion made possible by oil revenues, looked elsewhere for inspiration. For the purposes

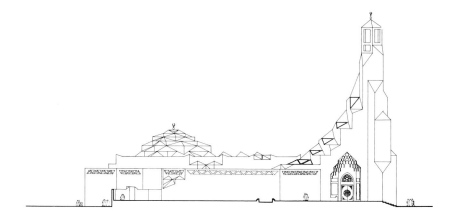

(Opposite) Al-Kindi Plaza Jami (1983–6), Riyadh, designed by BEEAH, overlooks a public square raised on a podium. Arcades of varying heights are punctuated by passageways and entrances, such as that of the mosque seen on the left. The twin minarets of the mosque dominate the triangular plaza of the complex.

(Below) Cutaway axonometric projection of the complex, comprising a large mosque to the west and commercial and administrative

facilities to the east, and a section through the complex showing the mosque interior, the location of the minaret and gateways, the plaza and adjacent shops and offices, with parking space below.

(Overleaf) Interior of the prayer hall of the Al-Kindi Plaza Jami and a detail of one of the arcades in a small shaded court, the style of which echoes the characteristic architecture of the Najd region.

of creating a new national vocabulary of forms, the Saudi Arabian decision-makers and architects also looked to their own regional style of architecture. Najdi vernacular architecture, featuring solid crenellated walls with small openings and the use of rammed-earth forms, began to be widely adopted as the image for new Saudi architecture, albeit using concrete and steel structures instead of earth, and incorporating all the comforts made available by modern technology, including artificial climate control.[42]

Al-Kindi Plaza Jami, Riyadh, Saudi Arabia

The Al-Kindi Plaza development in the central area of Hayy Assafarat (the Diplomatic Quarter) comes under the aegis of the Riyadh Development Authority. The project as a whole comprises the basic administrative and commercial facilities for the community and includes a large mosque. The total site occupies about 20,000 sq. m (215,300 sq. ft), with a floor area of c. 50,000 sq. m (538,200 sq. ft). In 1983, the project was given to the Saudi firm BEEAH (standing for 'total environment' in Arabic), its partners being Ali Shuaibi and Abdul-Rahman Hussaini. The work was completed in November 1986 and received an Aga Khan Award in 1989. The architects organized the mosque around the almost obligatory open square (*maidan*); they incorporated two complex gateways that link the building to the adjacent streets at ground level for pedestrian access and below ground for vehicles and parking.

The architecture of the Najd region is used as the basic vocabulary, while the structure consists of a reinforced-concrete frame system and hollow concrete blocks with a finish of earth-coloured stucco sprayed on the surface to approximate to the appearance of traditional mud plaster.[43] Two tall, square minarets mark the gateways to the mosque which dominates the triangular *maidan*, forming its west side. The marble-paved *maidan* permits very little shade before late afternoon, a fact which limits its use to evening prayers on Friday. The mosque itself covers some 6,600 sq. m

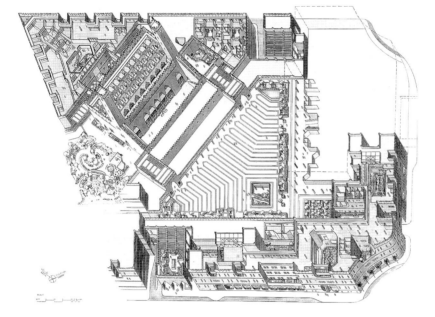

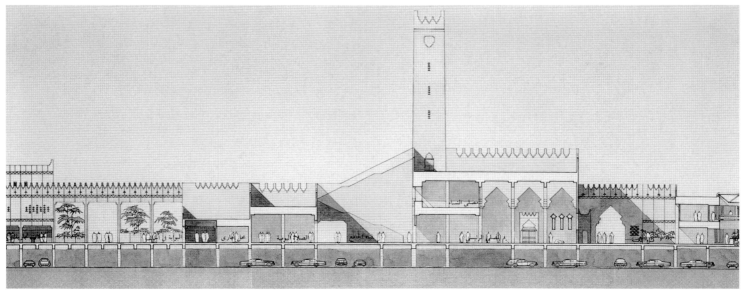

(71,000 sq. ft) and accommodates about 6,000 worshippers. The square hypostyle hall with double-height ceiling and mezzanine is incorporated into a triangular building which also houses the administrative offices. The architectural language and vocabulary employed in both this project and the mosque for the Qasr Al-Hokm (also for the Riyadh Development Authority), designed by Rasem Badran two years after the completion of the Al-Kindi project, are strikingly similar.

Imam Turki bin Abdullah Jami, Riyadh, Saudi Arabia

In designing the mosque for the Qasr Al-Hokm (Justice Palace District), the Jordanian architect Rasem Badran used the commission as an opportunity to revisit his winning project for the Baghdad Competition in 1983 (see Chapter 2) and to study and further develop his ideas for a hypostyle hall mosque without dome.[44] Here, with the dome omitted and reduced in scale, the plan of the Baghdad mosque has been transformed into a prayer hall seven bays deep and thirteen bays wide. Its proportions have evolved to present a solid fortress-like aspect (inspired by Najdi vocabulary) when seen from the busy streets surrounding it.[45]

The Qasr Al-Hokm District has been the historical core of Riyadh, the educational centre and the seat of government since the establishment of the unified kingdom of Saudi Arabia in 1932. New work on the district was initiated in 1976, and in 1983 the first phase of construction, consisting of the Governorate, Municipality and Police Headquarters, was begun. Following its completion in 1988, work on Phase II started; the projects comprised the Imam Turki bin Abdullah Jami, Qasr Al-Hokm, together with several other major squares, gates, a tower and parts of the old wall of the city, as well as roads, public utilities, and some commercial and office buildings. This phase, which included Badran's mosque, was completed in 1992, and the third and final phase commenced in 1994.[46]

Badran's project lies at the centre of the revitalization programme for the old city of Riyadh. The intention of the planners has been to recreate a sense of the old urban morphology of the city.[47] Previously, the old Justice Palace and Jami had been linked by a bridge. Badran's new project replaces these two traditional elements, with the new Justice Palace and the main mosque occupying sites on two sides of al-Adl Square. Surrounding them are other cultural, educational and public buildings. Badran cites three main factors that characterize his design: the relationship of the building to the street where 'the street and walls were rather simple and domestic in scale [and intended] to resemble walls of the city of Riyadh; the building masses on the second level resembled the evocative residential system; and the climax of those levels was the main building in which the ruler meets his people. It was realized as one dominant mass resembling the old four-towered fortress – Al Masmaq.'[48] The Imam Turki bin Abdullah Jami, rebuilt at its original location, has an area of 16,800 sq. m (181,000 sq. ft). It is comparable in scale to most state mosques and is often referred to locally simply as the Grand Mosque. The building has entrances on al-Adl and Assafat Squares, as well as on the street whose name it bears. Nearly 4,800 sq. m (51,500 sq. ft) of shaded arcades are provided adjacent to its entrances. The entrance gates open on a 6,320 sq. m (68,000 sq. ft) courtyard, the walls of which are 14.80 m (48 ft) high. The mosque interior can accommodate around 17,000 worshippers and additional space can be made available in the courtyard for further 5,000 worshippers. There is a

A general view of the main square and the old mosque in Riyadh c. 1920 before the area was redeveloped, and (below) the new Imam Turki bin Abdullah Jami (1992), designed by Rasem Badran, built as part of the newly reconstructed administrative district in the capital.

separate hall for women with its own entrance. At the rear of the courtyard are wooden beamed ceilings, to which are attached the lighting units and sound amplifiers. On the north and south sides of the building adjacent to the courtyard stand the two minarets, each with traditional square plan, rising to a height of 50 m (164 ft). Badran has capitalized on the shift out of the street grid by siting the two minarets framing the prayer hall so as to indicate the *qibla* direction in the urban context.

The use of a dome and of all arched and vaulted forms has been avoided, and the construction materials employed allow for clear spans, thus distancing the design from the pan-Islamic style with its familiar multiplicity of arches and moulded arched elements. The architect introduces (or reinterprets on this larger scale) the stepped openings of Najdi building traditions and the standard features found in mosques of the region – the *sahn* (courtyard), *riwaq* (arcade), and hypostyle prayer hall. His development of the concept of the multi-columnar hall has played a major role in the design.

The primary elements used in construction consist of prefabricated concrete units. The exterior walls and upper portions of the interior walls are faced with local limestone and, in keeping with local tradition, have only a limited number of openings in sizes intended to limit the effects of the harsh desert climate. The lower portions of the interior walls and columns are lined with white marble. Triangular pre-cast beams and textured ceiling slabs create an effect similar in appearance to that of the wooden ceiling of the earlier mosque on this site. Badran has sought to retain such visual precedents through the introduction of specific earth-toned colours and patterns. The pre-cast elements,

(Below left) The monumental interior of the prayer hall of the Imam Turki bin Abdullah Jami, which features a limited ornamental programme and a stepped superstructure that also carries all the mechanical services.

(Right) Architect's sketch of visual elements used in composing both the mosque and the entire urban complex.

(Below right) Plan of the mosque and adjacent buildings; the mosque has no dome and features a hypostyle layout with columns arranged in rows parallel to the *qibla* wall.

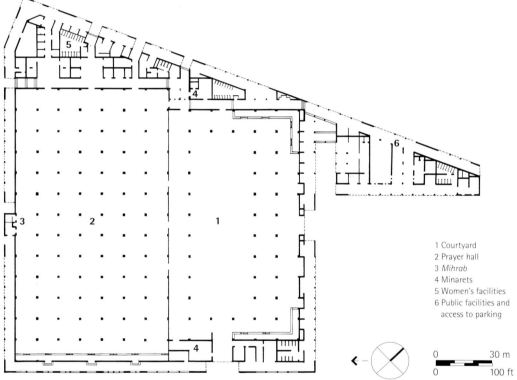

1 Courtyard
2 Prayer hall
3 *Mihrab*
4 Minarets
5 Women's facilities
6 Public facilities and access to parking

0   30 m
0   100 ft

into which are integrated air-conditioning and lighting elements, are supported by round columns which also incorporate services, thus allowing the roof structure to be exposed and avoiding the use of suspended ceilings. This method of resolving lighting and air-conditioning requirements has been adopted by other architects such as Bofill in his entry for the Iraq State Mosque Competition (see Chapter 2), and is also used in the Islamic Centre in Rome (see Chapter 6).

Other facilities include two libraries, each with an area of 325 sq. m (3,500 sq. ft), for men and women respectively. There are also residences for the *imam* and the *muezzin*, as well as some government offices and commercial space at ground-floor level. The mosque is equipped with modern television and radio broadcasting facilities, including the use of television cameras operated by remote control. Both the mosque and the Justice Palace are protected by electronic security devices.

Of particular interest are Badran's graphic studies for his projects, which he uses to articulate and to discuss his ideas with clients. Anecdotal evidence illustrates how Badran was able to ensure his selection as the architect for Qasr Al-Hokm and the mosque: the architects who had been invited to submit entries for the project competition were asked to present their proposals to the client in person. Badran did so by preparing marvellous sketches to convey his ideas. (Verbal skills do not appear to be his forte.) By the end of the presentation, he had left all his fellow-competitors behind, secured the mosque project for himself, and indeed had extended it into an urban design scheme.[49] Although he pays some attention to historical analysis, his work is based on an intuitive and visual understanding, and on observation of the built environment. Through these strategies he has produced a strong, sober building that is in keeping with its specific site and with a restrained formal language.

The Seafront Mosques, Jeddah, Saudi Arabia

In contrast to the sobriety of the Najdi capital Riyadh, set in desert surroundings, Jeddah in the Hijaz region is open to the Red Sea and to polyglot external influences.[50] Here, three small mosques (*zawiyas*) – the Corniche and Island Mosques, and the Al-Ruwais Mosque – designed by the then London-based Egyptian architect Abdel Wahed El-Wakil attempt ' to integrate the continuity of an Islamic tradition within a new context'.[51] In general, newly developed city plans in the Middle East and Asia have sought to bring the seashore into the city and exploit it as an opportunity for providing parks and places of recreation.[52] These compact buildings, forming part of a series of small mosques sited at intervals along the coast, were conceived as places of worship for use by visitors to a popular recreational area of the city, and intended to provide sculptural features that would enhance the urban landscape.

The mayor of Jeddah, Mohammad Said Al-Farsi, himself an architect, instituted a programme of public sculptures to serve as landmarks in the expanding city. The coastal sites for both the Island and Corniche Mosques were donated by the Municipality, having been chosen by the mayor for their striking visual impact. The corniche, which consists essentially of reclaimed land, has become popular as a recreation area frequented by families living in the city and by visitors from various parts of the Arabian Peninsula. The area abounds with parks, restaurants and non-figural sculptures (abstract geometric arrangements and sometimes bizarre representations such as oversize Mamluk lamps, as well as real cars mounted in blocks of concrete). These new buildings and decorative displays were to be financed by wealthy individuals as gifts to the city. Among those who were approached by the mayor with the idea of placing a commission was El-Wakil, who in turn suggested that a series of small mosques be built. It was thus in the context

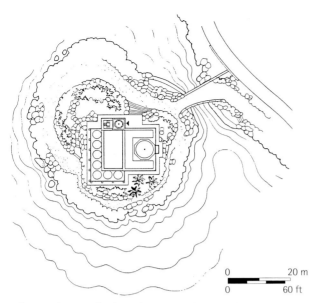

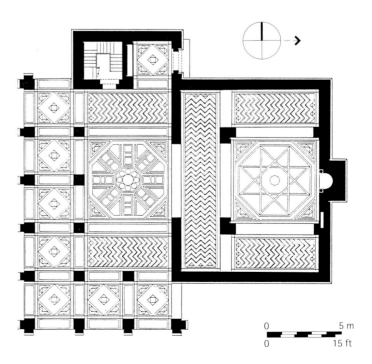

The Island Mosque (1986), Jeddah, the first of a series of mosques designed by El-Wakil to be built along the Red Sea coast.

(Opposite above) Exterior with portico open to the sea.

(Opposite below) The central domed area of the mosque, showing the restrained decoration of the *mihrab* in grey granite and of the dado in carved wood.

(Left) Site plan of the Island Mosque showing its open aspect on the west side overlooking the sea and the closed east side facing the city and Mecca.

(Below) Section (west–east) of the Island Mosque and floor plan showing the entrance hall adjacent to the minaret and use of patterned stone flooring throughout.

of an exuberant display of consumerism that El-Wakil introduced his mosque designs.[53]

While the construction of the mosques has been financed through the municipal authorities and formed part of a larger scheme undertaken in 1980 by the Ministry of Hajj and Awqaf and its Deputy Minister Husam Khashoggi to develop contemporary and traditional architecture in Saudi Arabia, the buildings might also be considered products of individual patronage in that they were motivated by one man in particular, Mohammad Said Al-Farsi, who not only sponsored the idea, but selected the sites and proposed El-Wakil as the architect.[54] (Curiously, the mayor personally commissioned a mosque from Raouf Mohammed Helmi, in which the architect has demonstrated a similar design approach.[55]) The Island and Corniche Mosques were financed by the Ministry of Hajj and Awqaf and the Municipality of Jeddah, while Al-Ruwais was financed by the Municipality and Sharbatly Abdel Rahman, a businessman in Jeddah. Construction of all three was supervised by Concenter (Deputy Minister Khashoggi's firm), which also acted as project manager for the Corniche Mosque.[56] In selecting El-Wakil, the client knew that his buildings would be a counterpoint to other modern mosques on the corniche.

The Island Mosque – the first to be commissioned – was designed in 1983 and completed in 1986.[57] As its name implies, it is located on a small artificial island with an area of 2,500 sq. m (27,000 sq. ft) off the northern corniche, and can be reached on foot by a narrow bridge. Worshippers park their cars in the area provided near the bridge and proceed from there to the mosque. The approach area was to have been landscaped and other facilities included in the programme, such as ablutions, were also not executed. The mosque, which occupies 400 sq. m (4,300 sq. ft), comprises a rectangular prayer chamber, a porticoed courtyard and a minaret on the north side. The *qibla* wall with projecting *mihrab* presents a blank face to the mainland, while the courtyard (west) side of the mosque is open towards the sea, offering a splendid view through the arcades. Above the prayer chamber is a dome 6 m (20 ft) in diameter resting on

squinches on an octagonal drum. Suspended from the dome is an imposing circular bronze chandelier. The surrounding roof areas on three sides are covered by vaults 3 m (10 ft) in width. The square minaret with internal staircase on the north side is surmounted by a small dome echoing the shape of the main dome; it also features a narrow balcony with patterned wooden railings. The entrance, adjacent to the minaret, leads directly to the courtyard, and worshippers have to make a 180° turn to enter the prayer hall.

Decoration is restricted to specific areas of the mosque. The heavy entrance door is decorated with ornamental bronzework and has above it a lintel supporting an arch in carved plaster relief; the door opens into an antechamber preceding the prayer hall. The floors of the courtyard and of the prayer hall, as well as the *mihrab* niche, are finished in patterns created by the use of grey granite of contrasting tones, while the interior walls are simply rendered in white-painted plaster.

The Corniche Mosque of 1986 is the smallest of the Jeddah mosques, with an area of only 195 sq. m (2,100 sq. ft).[58] Its site is 1,200 sq. m (13,000 sq. ft) of reclaimed land at the northern end of the corniche. The building presents a compact, sculptured formal arrangement: a small domed prayer hall with an antechamber covered by a barrel vault, an open court, a two-bayed portico facing west towards the sea, and a minaret. The main dome over the square prayer chamber and the two smaller domes over the portico rest on squinches. On the south side of the prayer chamber an external staircase leads to the minaret, which consists of a short octagonal shaft set above a tall square base and featuring a balcony resting on two rows of *muqarnas* vaults. Both the main dome and the minaret are surmounted by pointed finials. The *qibla* wall is defined by crenellated corner pylons and the external expression of the *mihrab*. After entering the building from the *qibla* side through an antechamber, worshippers then proceed through the inner court to the prayer chamber and, as in the case of the Island Mosque, they are thus obliged to make a 180° turn in order to face the *mihrab*. A brass chandelier is suspended from the centre of the unadorned *mihrab* niche, which is finished in white plaster and has a circular aperture above it. As in the Island Mosque, the patterned floor surfaces are in granite of contrasting shades.

The third mosque, Al-Ruwais, which was built in 1989, differs significantly from the earlier examples in terms of its formal arrangement. Situated to the south of the other two structures and set back from the corniche, the building covers 216 sq. m (2,325 sq. ft). Here, three domes (supported by externalized stepped drums in the manner of Cairene Mamluk monuments) line the *qibla* wall and are preceded by two series of stepped bays covered by barrel vaults. The domes and the short square minaret at the southeast corner create a pleasing rhythmic composition; in the opinion of Chris Abel, they 'confirm the movement away from the strict traditions with which El-Wakil is usually associated, as well as echo the sea against which the mosque stands. Only the

The Corniche Mosque (1986), the smallest of the seafront mosques, is a compact sculptural arrangement of dome, vaults and tower.

General view from the southeast (opposite above) showing the *mihrab* projection on the *qibla* side, and detail at roof level (opposite below) revealing a rich and varied composition of volumes.

(Below) East-west section through the prayer hall and the domed portico of the Corniche Mosque.

(Bottom) Al-Ruwais Mosque (1989), shown in an axonometric projection from the west, differs from the two earlier buildings by El-Wakil in its elaboration of vaulted structures and in having a square minaret.

0   5 m
0   15 ft

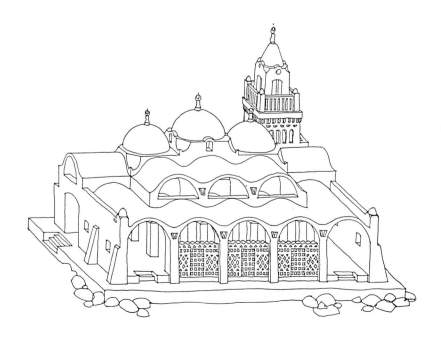

137

orthodox forms of the minaret and the three domes over the prayer room qualify what is otherwise El-Wakil's most modern exercise in mosque design'.[59]

All three mosques are built on concrete foundations using loadbearing red terracotta brick covered in white plaster. They are all open to the elements, and while in theory this feature represents a logical and sympathetic response to the coastal sites, in practice it has inevitably given rise to maintenance problems.

In a city where daily use of the automobile plays an important role, the mosques are not sited within residential neighbourhoods and thus have a 'drive-in' quality to them (especially since many of them do not incorporate ablutions facilities, so obliging worshippers to be cleansed and ready for prayer upon their arrival). Though each design is unique, all three display a combination of historical references to various traditions, notably the vernacular and monumental architectural language of Egypt and the whitewashed walls of the Mediterranean region. Indeed, El-Wakil has himself cited the Paraportiani Church on Mykonos as a source of inspiration for the Corniche Mosque.[60] The Hijaz region in which Jeddah is located has had a longstanding historical connection with Egypt. From the Mamluk period onward, the architecture of Jeddah has been influenced by imported styles, and particularly by those of Egypt.

While the idyllic settings of the sites presented an opportunity to concentrate almost entirely on the sculptural form, El-Wakil stayed well within his self-imposed limits of traditional architectural forms. As he said in an interview, 'I believe the notion of innovation is meaningless in sacred architecture. Architecture is a collective art and its buildings have been established through universal symbols, and with the skills and techniques of craftsmen preserved and handed down through generations. [It is] a language of forms embedded with meaning, symbols and signs – an established vocabulary by which the architect, with legitimate form, is similar to the poet, whose mere juxtaposition of common words expands the heart without seeking new words or changing the grammar.'[62] El-Wakil's buildings are conceived to stand on their own in the landscape. Unlike many urban mosques that were, often of necessity, skilfully integrated into their surroundings, these buildings are best appreciated when viewed as detached objects.

'Mimar' Mosque Competition

Concurrent with the design of El-Wakil's mosques in Jeddah, and an interesting footnote to the concept of the mosque as object along the Jeddah corniche, was the architectural journal *Mimar*'s Design Competition, sponsored by the Mayor of Jeddah, Mohammad Said Al-Farsi, and with the same brief. The jury, which met in January 1985 in Jeddah, consisted of four members: Abdel Wahed El-Wakil; Kamel Abdullah Komsany, deputy mayor of Jeddah and a practising architect; Leon Krier, architectural theoretician and planner; and Hasan-Uddin Khan, editor-in-chief of *Mimar*.

The competition was open to anyone up to 35 years of age. Over 240 entries were received from students and practising architects from some twenty countries, and the responses to the brief were understandably diverse.[63] In reviewing the entries, the jury adopted a somewhat conservative stance, favouring designs that would be readable and understandable to most people, as well as those in which the emphasis was placed on creating an appropriate atmosphere of peace and tranquillity necessary in a place of prayer; they therefore shunned designs that were 'clever' or astonishing, or that exhibited pronounced individualistic expressions.[64]

Certain recurring themes that can be identified in the projects submitted include: the metaphor of a sailing boat; shell structures or sculptures; desert imagery and shade-producing features; the idea of transition and sequence in the bridge and promenade; and the use of a landmark minaret as a beacon or lighthouse by the sea. In some instances there was an exploration of indigenous technologies evident in the design of windcatchers and the use of water as a cooling device, and of modern construction technologies using space-frames, concrete shells and sometimes folded-plate structures. However wide-ranging the submissions may have been in their use of imagery, three mainstream design approaches are identifiable. One is the traditional approach in which use is generally made of the Egyptian vernacular, drawing on the work of contemporary architects like Fathy and El-Wakil. Another approach also draws on 'traditional' vocabularies which, on closer inspection, seem to be fragmented in the design, the innovative aspect of which strikes the observer only secondarily. The third approach is a contemporary one in which the design makes use of technologically inspired or post-modern imagery.

The jury finally selected two winning projects. The first prize was awarded to M. N. Ahari and F. Firouz, architects practising in New York City. Their design illustrates the adaptive traditional approach, being characterized by the rich juxtaposition of mosque components, strong geometry and an unusual minaret. Here, the minaret stairway of Hasan Fathy's New Gourna Village Mosque is transformed by giving it a more modern character and a dramatic angle. The second prize went to Rami El-Dahan and Soheir Farid, a husband-and-wife team working in Cairo. Their scheme illustrates the vernacular approach, employing traditional vocabularies in a straightforward and elegant manner. Both the winning projects are based on traditional layouts and make play mainly with geometry and the juxtaposition of various elements. Although some of the entries submitted took account of the site's context, a large majority of them ignore this factor, including the project awarded second prize, in which the building is turned to face away from the sea. Nevertheless, several proposed designs were encouraging in their attempt to furnish solutions to the difficult issues presented by the requirements of the contemporary mosque.

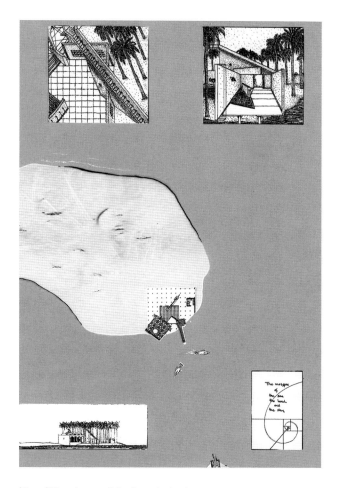

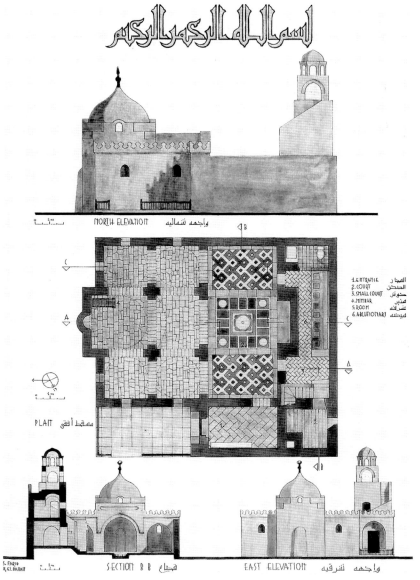

الرحمن الرحيم الله بسم

NORTH ELEVATION وأجهه شماليه

1. ENTRANCE الصبار
2. COURT الصحن
3. SMALL COURT حوش
4. MINBAR منبر
5. ROOM غرفه
6. ABLUTIONARY ميضه

PLAN مسقط أفقي

S. FARID
R. EL-DAHAB

SECTION B B قطاع

EAST ELEVATION وأجهه شرقيه

(Above) The winners of the first prize in the *Mimar* competition, M.N. Ahari and F. Firouz, produced an elegant and almost traditional solution. Their presentation illustrated the salient design features with an economy of expression.

(Above right) The second prize was awarded to Rami El-Dahan and Soheir Farid for their traditional scheme revealing careful design and a clear understanding of the problem: this was one of the few entries that could have been built as presented.

(Right) One of the projects commended by the jury, as submitted by Hasan Özbay, explored the idea of a shaded and tented oasis enclosed partially by radiating walls, all in a landscaped island setting.

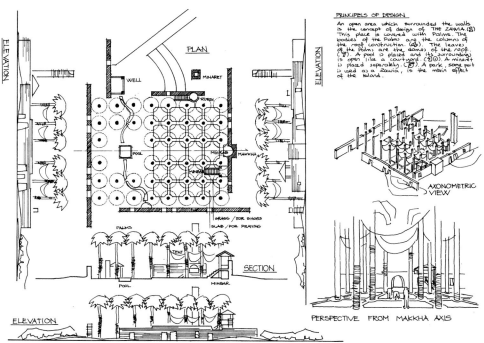

ELEVATION

PLAN

WELL

MINARET

POOL

MIHRAB

MAKKHA

GRASS / FOR SHOES
SLAB / FOR PRAYING

PALMS

TENT

SECTION

POOL

MINBAR

ELEVATION

PRINCIPELS OF DESIGN

An open area which surrounded the walls is the concept of design of THE ZAWIA (1). This place is covered with Palms. The bodies of the Palm are the columns of the roof construction (2). The leaves of the Palm are the domes of the roof (3). A pool is placed and its surrounding is open like a courtyard (4). A minaret is placed seperately (5). A park, some part is used as a Zawia, is the main object of the Island.

AXONOMETRIC VIEW

PERSPECTIVE FROM MAKKHA AXIS

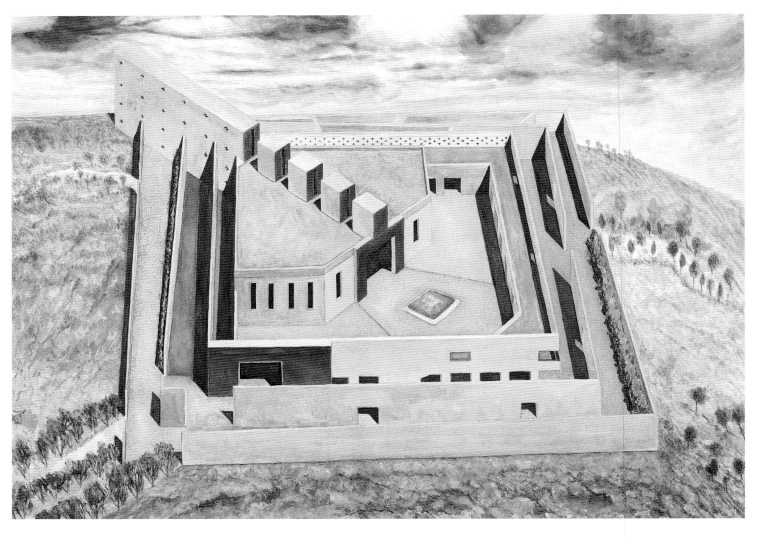

Mosques in Shushtar New Town, Khuzestan, Iran

An opportunity for addressing the problems associated with designs for mosques to be inserted into a new urban context was presented by the development of Shushtar New Town in Iran. Kamran Diba of DAZ Architects,[65] fresh from building the University Mosque at Jondishapur (see Chapter 4), responded to a commission from the Iranian Housing Company (Sazeman Khaneh Sazi) and the Karoun Agro-Industry by proposing two mosque designs. This new town in Khuzestan was intended to provide housing for around 30,000 workers and employees of the Karoun Agro-Industry and was located across the river from historic Shushtar. The client's interest was limited to the provision of housing, and did not extend to include any social or cultural facilities. Accordingly, the project was planned and designed by the architects alone, and was only partially completed by 1978. After the Iranian Revolution of 1979 work on the development was interrupted and reportedly not resumed.

The choice of Kamran Diba to design the new town was a good one, for he is a talented architect who has worked extensively in the public realm. Coming out of a modernist tradition, he regards himself as a problem-solver and a contextualist. Diba is also a painter and sculptor: this background, combined with his architectural training in the United States at Howard University, Washington, DC,

imbued his work in Iran with a sense of the modern and the contemporary, making him wary of using historicist or traditional vocabulary directly. His starting point is a feeling for space, for the flow of movement, light and shade, as well as for the textures and materials (especially brick) used in historic monuments and vernacular buildings. He is very aware of the urban context and of what he has referred to as 'the strange interwoven monolithic tissue of mud brick vernacular towns and villages'; he also stressed that 'one of my endeavours was the attempt to understand and reveal the secrets of Persian vernacular architecture'.[66] Diba's project for the new Shushtar settlement reflects both his concerns with urban design and his love for monolithic and monochromatic structures.[67]

The limited brief of the commission, while not specifically calling for the inclusion of a congregational mosque, did allow the architect to develop what he perceived to be the need for a religious-social space in the community. Thus, the inclusion of the *jami*, or Friday mosque, was the architect's own idea. Assisted by M.T. Behrouzian, Diba conceived the idea of building a mosque on a prominent site near the edge of the cliff over looking the Old Town, river and the centre of the new town. It also furnished him with the opportunity to propose a series of alternative designs for the dome and minaret. The mosque, which was to be constructed on a site

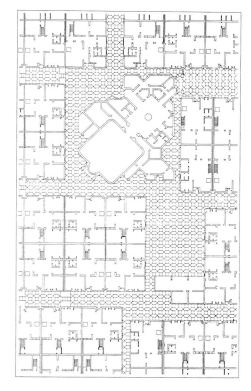

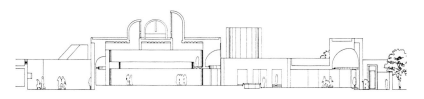

occupying 2.5 hectares (6 acres), was commissioned in 1977 but never built. The location of the mosque was at the mid-point of the long pedestrian boulevard linking the upper eastern portion of the town to the lower western section, thus marking the open space at the edge of the ravine which divides the town into two distinct levels. Pedestrians crossing from one section to the other would have had to pass through the mosque complex. A series of passages around the mosque was designed to provide space for street vendors and shade for pedestrians.

The mosque itself, however, was protected from casual everyday intrusions by three separate layers of walls. While the courtyard would be easily accessible, entering the prayer space would require an extra effort in order to penetrate further into the core of the complex. The repetition of walls also allowed the architect to adjust the orientation of the inner courtyard space gradually towards the *qibla*; a deep, tall interior space was therefore devised to give added emphasis to this orientation. Small cavities in the walls allow some natural light to penetrate into the otherwise dark central space. The *mihrab* rises within its own *pishtaq* frame above the height of the walls of the prayer hall. If the mosque had been built, it would have been a prominent landmark and its bulk and tiled surface would have dominated the horizon of the ravine.

A second mosque – a neighbourhood *masjid* – was to be located within one of the residential districts. In order to break the monotony of the horizontal grid and give individual character to each block, the architect employed various means: north-south alleyways, open play areas, a bath house, a central plaza, and a neighbourhood mosque. The *masjid* (built 1974–6) occupies a site measuring approximately 10,000 sq. m (107,500 sq. ft) selected to be sheltered from and not readily accessible to outsiders. The *qibla* orientation gives rise to a departure from the rigid street layout and allows for public passage through the

(Opposite) Project by Kamran Diba of DAZ Architects for a *jami* (1977), which explored a new formal language for the proposed mosque in the Shushtar New Town scheme (partially completed by 1978).

(Above) Plan and section for a neighbourhood mosque in Shushtar New Town. The section reveals Diba's use of 'light-catchers' and concrete structure.

(Below) Artist's impression of the Shushtar neighbourhood mosque in its urban setting; the building was intended to break the monotony of the grid through its orientation and the use of colour.

courtyard; the latter, decorated with colourful mosaics and ceramic tiles designed by a noted Iranian artist, Hossein Zenderoudi,[68] is thus linked to the pedestrian network, so enhancing the quality of the public spaces. The mosque is distinguished on the skyline by blue tiled surfaces rising above the *qibla* wall and courtyard. The roof forms are dome-like but on closer inspection are revealed as half-shells of brick with tiled surfaces which serve to catch both as wind and light. This practical solution, introduced earlier in the Jondishapur mosque, has here been elaborated with colour, but the essential quality remains – that of an alternative to the dome.

Khulafa Mosque, Baghdad, Iraq

When a historic minaret survives as a relic of a destroyed mosque, the architect must recognize this fact when commissioned to build a new mosque alongside it. In 1961, the Ministry of Awqaf commissioned the Iraqi architect Mohamed Makiya to design a mosque to be built on a site in the Sabbabigh al-All district of the old city formerly occupied by a ninth-century Abbasid structure, the Mosque of the Caliphs, and dominated by the then recently restored Suq el-Ghazl minaret originally built in the late thirteenth century. Makiya was called on to find a solution that would integrate the historic minaret into a new complex. He had therefore to reconcile the historic context of the site with the wish of the Ministry and Municipality to be 'modern' by projecting an image of a progressive Iraq while working

1 Main entrance on
  Khulafa Street
2 Old minaret
3 *Riwaq*
4 Courtyard
5 Prayer hall
6 *Mihrab*

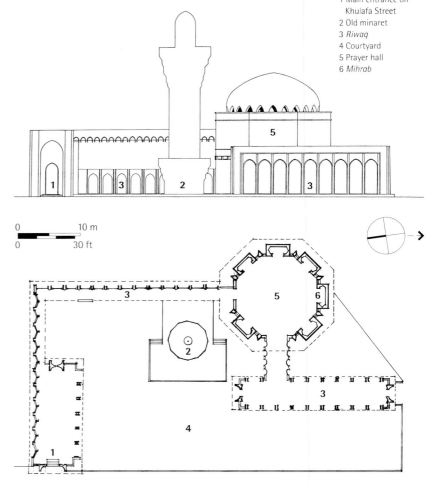

0   10 m

0   30 ft

within the constraints imposed by a very limited site.[69] By integrating the old and the new forms, he sought to create an illusion of greater space on what was clearly a rather awkward site, and to express 'traditional character in a new architectural ambience'.[70] Dealing with such a problem is not uncommon in the case of new buildings in historic cities of the Islamic world. The construction of the new mosque began in 1962 and was completed two years later.[71] As an advocate of a modernist style that respects and draws on building traditions, Makiya saw his professional responsibility as that of 'a trustee – like an archbishop. The architect is the representative of God on earth when he is designing because he is supposed to provide that extra dimension, those things which are called values – human values, ethical values, cultural values, time values.'[72]

Khulafa Mosque is located in a densely built-up district of Baghdad and is surrounded by commercial buildings. The historic minaret set the tone in design terms, determining the general disposition of the masses and the choice of building materials.[73] The built area occupies 1,800 sq. m (19,400 sq. ft) and consists of a domed octagonal prayer hall, with two entrance porticoes and arcades (*riwaqs*) lined with pointed arches which give access to the mosque and its courtyard from the adjacent streets on the western and southern boundaries. The passageways serve not only to connect the *riwaq* to the mosque, but also to link the various elements of the complex; they were designed to be extended at a later date into an adjacent market, but this has not been built. The use of an octagonal plan, traditionally associated with mausoleum architecture, is unusual for a mosque.[74] Here, the octagonal interior space is covered by a large dome supported by eight columns; between each pair of columns is a U-shaped freestanding brick niche, one of which is the *mihrab*.

Makiya explores the use of yellow brick as a decorative medium in the context of contemporary mosque design, ranging from simple bond patterns to complex geometric friezes and stylized calligraphy. The material was chosen chiefly as a means of harmonizing the new forms with the existing minaret. Local craftsmen were employed to execute the brickwork, thus preserving indigenous craft skills. Other materials used were local stone and wood, together with steel frames for the ceilings. An intricate steel-framed screen wall featuring calligraphic panels was used to form the boundary of the site along Khulafa Street on the west side, while the high east wall provides a backdrop for the complex. The use of suspended concrete arches as a structural and ornamental theme was a stylistic innovation. Like his colleague and contemporary Rifat Chadirji, Makiya employed this form during the 1960s in many of his designs. The motif of the pointed arch is used in a repetitive manner, providing a visual connection between the mosque and the minaret by echoing the *muqarnas* on the minaret.

In the Khulafa Mosque the architect has deliberately created an ensemble of varied elements, each with its own symbolism and character. The resulting mix of styles – from

(Opposite) General view of the Khulafa Mosque (1963), Baghdad, by Mohamed Makiya, built around a restored thirteenth-century minaret.

(Opposite below) The Khulafa Street elevation and site plan: the old minaret is framed by the new octagonal dome and the *riwaq* structures.

(Below) The detailing of the ornamental programme of yellow brickwork combined with carved plaster epigraphy was chosen to complement the existing historic monument.

(Bottom) View into the brick-covered dome of the mosque.

the oversized dome to the modernist concrete arches – is at once 'classical' and modern, creating an ambiguous and rich architecture. Makiya has characterized the architectural challenge presented to him by stating: 'I had to build a cathedral in an area suitable for a chapel.'[75]

Said Naum Mosque, Jakarta, Indonesia

In an area where the mosque had developed and retained its own regional form over centuries, but where the use of the dome (imported from the western regions of the Islamic world) is now making inroads, the Said Naum Mosque is an important building. In integrating new design features into the old and familiar architectural tradition, it also presents a challenge to the dome import.[76] Constructed within fifteen months and completed in 1977, the mosque was inserted into an existing dense urban fabric and was inspired by the traditional architectural language of Java. The new building also acts as a focal point for the local community. It formed part of a project resulting from a competition sponsored by the Jakarta Municipal Government (DKI) in 1975. Eight prominent Indonesian firms were invited to enter, and the competition brief stipulated that the design should reflect local character, make use of traditional and locally produced materials and be suited to the region's climate. In addition

Completed in 1977, the Said Naum Mosque in Jakarta designed by Adhi Moersid provides a refuge from the crowded urban environment with its landscaped grounds and verandahs providing shade. The design of the traditional Javanese roof is in this instance an unusual variation, the upper part being rotated through 45° (top). Arched openings lead from the verandahs to the prayer hall.

to the proposed mosque, the programme included an ablutions building, parking facilities and landscaped areas. Prior to the design stage, studies were undertaken by the municipality to establish the precise functional needs of the community which the project was to address.

The jury, headed by Ali Sadekin, Governor of Jakarta, included the heads of the Art Centre, the Social Directorate, and a number of other professionals. Their unanimous choice was the design submitted by Adhi Moersid of Atelier Enam, who had proposed a religious and social complex in a style which was developed from the Hindu-Javanese architectural tradition while retaining the spiritual concepts of Islamic philosophy.[77] His innovative reinterpretation of a regional form, that of the pyramidal *meru* roof, lends a distinctive Indonesian image to the building (for another example of this type of roof see the University of Indonesia Mosque, discussed in Chapter 4). Adhi Moersid, a well-known and prolific architect in Indonesia, was trained at the Institute of Technology in Bandung (ITB); he and five other ITB graduates banded together to create the firm Atelier Enam (or 'Six') after graduating in 1969.[78] By the 1980s, the firm had become one of the largest and most prominent practices in the country.

Moersid's competition entry included a design for a school (*madrasa*) which the municipality also planned to build on the site. This element was rejected, however, as the DKI was already provided with standardized school drawings which it implemented under the government's Division of School Construction.[79] In every other respect, the close collaboration during the design and construction processes between the architect, the client (represented by Ali Sadekin and Wastu Pragantha Chong, head of the government's Department of Construction and Restoration) and the contractor (P. T. Jaya) was particularly significant.

An unusual aspect of the project was the fact that part of the site had been used as a privately owned graveyard, and was donated for the purpose of building a mosque by Said Naum, an Egyptian residing in Jakarta. The rest of the site was owned by the municipal government which wanted to develop the entire area but considered the graveyard part unsuitable. Public objections to the building of a mosque on a former graveyard were raised, but after consultations had been held with religious leaders it was agreed that, subject to supervision by the religious and social authorities, a mosque could be built there.[80]

The architect conceived the mosque complex as an improvement in the urban environment and a potential stimulus for development in the community. Landscaping was an important aspect of the design, and the site was to provide a green and pleasant refuge for the community, acting as a buffer between the place of worship and the outside world.[81] From the parking area on the eastern boundary of the site worshippers proceed on foot through the main entrance to the ablutions building, after which they change direction to approach the mosque. (This shift in orientation helps to alert and prepare them mentally for

(Below) Section of the Said Naum Mosque showing the manipulation of elements of Javanese architecture in new ways, and site plan. The mosque is approached from the main road and car park through a courtyard that can also be used as overflow prayer space. The ablutions building is situated to the north of the courtyard.

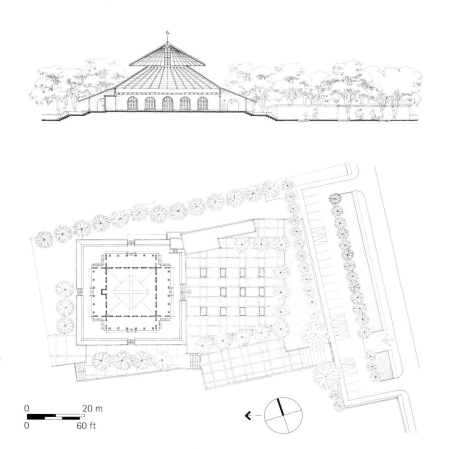

0   20 m
0   60 ft

the impending act of prayer.) A pathway leads first to the *madrasa* and finally up to the mosque, which stands on a raised two-tiered platform.

The mosque is symmetrical in plan, with deep verandahs on all four sides; the entrance and *mihrab* are laid out on the east-west axis with the west wall designated as the *qibla*.[82] The principal access to the prayer hall is through doorways on the east façade, but entrance is also possible from the verandahs. The plan is based on an open square with arched openings on all sides filled with protective wooden grills. The *mihrab* niche in the west wall is placed in the central opening and expressed externally.[83] The floor is finished in decorative tiles that delineate the praying rows, with space for up to 600 worshippers in the prayer hall measuring approximately 20 m (65 ft) square; the maximum capacity is 3,000 when the verandahs and the courtyard are also brought into use.

Concrete was employed for the columns, roof tiles and external paving. Cement mortar rendering and paint were used to cover the brick walls of the mosque, while ceramic tiles provide the finish on the verandahs and in the prayer hall; the latter is covered by a two-tiered tiled, pitched roof. The second tier is rotated through 45° and separated from the lower tier to form a lantern and provide ventilation.

(Below) The upper tier of the pitched roof, rotated as a stylistic feature and to provide ventilation and light.

(Centre) View from below into the lantern of the prayer hall revealing the lights arranged in a cross form, a Javanese symbol expressing the centrality and omnipresence of God.

(Bottom) The omission of the four traditionally sanctioned *saka-guru* timber supports allows for an unobstructed interior with a clear view of the *mihrab* and emphasizes the unity of the prayer space.

(Opposite) View into the roof lantern of the prayer hall.

The steel frame of the roof structure is concealed behind exposed timber rafters that run in pairs from the lantern to the edge of the roof over the verandahs. The roof lantern is executed in patterned painted glass along its ridges, allowing filtered light to enter the prayer hall from above.[84] The skylight takes the shape of an equilateral cross when viewed from the interior, an important Javanese symbol expressing the centre of the universe and the omnipresence of God.[85] The cross has sometimes been mistakenly read in Christian terms – a case of viewing the structure from another religious and cultural viewpoint.

The overall design integrates spatial concepts derived from Islamic building traditions and from regional Hindu-Javanese structures. The geometry of the plan, according to the architect, is inspired by the four *madhhabs*, or schools of Sunni law. Javanese house forms and the traditional Hindu-Javanese temple architecture of the region, featuring square plans, multi-tiered roofs, the sacred *cella*, and the four central pillars of the *saka guru* (the most spiritually invested area of the Hindu temple), are also important sources of inspiration.[86] The court, an integral element of Islamic sacred space, is also an important transitional space in Hindu-Javanese temples, where it is generally multiple, while the addition of verandahs is seemingly a later development in Javanese mosques.

As is the case in most traditional Indonesian mosques, there is no minaret.[87] In Said Naum Mosque, the daily call to prayer is delivered by means of a loudspeaker located in the roof lantern. In the past, a large drum was usually placed in a corner of a mosque and beaten in a particular rhythm to signal the hours of prayer. Here, the drum is placed in the verandah in deference to tradition, and is still used on festival days and special occasions.

Three important design innovations were made. The traditional Javanese form is retained in its outline, but is altered in its symbolic nature. Firstly, the rotation of the upper tier of the roof marks a departure from the traditional multi-layered *meru* roof. Secondly, the four central columns of the *saka guru* present in Javanese sacred architecture, and representing symbolic and architectonic vestiges of pre-Islamic architecture, are omitted.[88] This change has freed the interior and allowed an unobstructed view to the *mihrab*, while emphasizing the autonomy of the roof lantern. Thirdly, the mosque stands on a raised platform and, instead of the traditional timber roof structure, a light steel-frame structure was employed (engineered by Teddy Boen, based on the architect's sketches) to span the large interior space.[89] The last decision was, in part, a result of the client's wish to cover the roof with heavier, locally produced concrete tiles rather than the traditional shingles. Thanks to these supports, the mosque has acquired a new scale, and a more monumental approach, while still retaining a close relationship to human scale.

Symbolic content in the mosque is to be found less in the decorative scheme than in its structural and spatial composition. In fact, structure and symbol are inextricably

linked, while ornamentation plays only a minor role in the design.[90] The roof form, which emphasizes centrality and verticality of the space as well as unity, covers the whole area of the prayer hall and verandahs. Symbolic significance is also reflected in a functional solution which is uncommon in mosque design elsewhere in the Islamic world, though not perhaps in Indonesia. This concerns the absence of any built-in physical separation between men's and women's prayer space: instead, the architect, who considers human beings mainly in terms of their spiritual condition, has provided for a curtain to be hung inside the prayer hall, so symbolizing 'the fragile separation between male and female'.[91] An unusual detail of ornamentation which repeats this theme can be found in the abstract decorative motifs representing male and female figures on the skylight.

The project has been well publicized both in Indonesia and internationally.[92] It provides an indigenous model for new mosques in the region as opposed to the more modern or Indian-derived, pan-Islamic buildings in which domes and arches are employed.

Abu Bakar as-Siddiq Mosque, Kuala Lumpur, Malaysia

Located in Bangsar, a district of Kuala Lumpur, Abu Bakar as-Siddiq is a contemporary mosque with a modern, Indian-derived urban image. In its use of normative Islamic design elements, such as the dome, minaret and pointed arches, the design is representative of the pan-Islamic style that has become a feature of recent buildings in the Malay archipelago, where the popular desire to be seen as both Muslim and modern is clearly evident.

The idea of building a new neighbourhood mosque was put forward in 1978 by the Religious Affairs Department of Malaysia, which initially proposed to provide funds to match the contributions received from the Muslim community of Bangsar, a total of about 15,000 inhabitants. In response to the community's enthusiasm for the project, the Religious Affairs Department eventually offered to finance the greater part of the cost (about 70%), with some contributions from international sources. The client of record is the Malaysian Ministry of Federal Territory, which chose and acquired the site. In 1979, Haji Hajeedar bin Abdul Majid of the firm Hajeedar Dan Rakan Rakan (Hajeedar & Associates) undertook the design of the mosque. Construction began in July 1980 and was completed in April 1982.

Hajeedar's design is characterized by its use of various well-established Islamic design elements: the freestanding minaret crowned by an umbrella-like motif, reminiscent of the minaret of the Masjid Negara in Kuala Lumpur (see Chapter 2); the bulbous dome (made of aluminium and finished in gold leaf), a form that was introduced into the

Southeast Asian architectural vocabulary at the beginning of the twentieth century; and the use of stylized arches on concrete façades. The plan is based on the traditional Indian model in spite of its lack of a courtyard, perhaps omitted because of the awkward shape of the site.

The core of the structure is in the form of a cube which defines the main prayer hall for up to 1,000 worshippers. Additional prayer space extends behind and on both sides of the main prayer hall at first-floor level, as well as on the second floor which is connected to the main prayer hall by balconies. The extended prayer area accommodates 3,500 worshippers. The main prayer hall is an open square with a clear span of 72 ft (22 m); its dimensions, according to the architect, are meant to symbolize the greatness of Allah,[93] although it is unclear how this is to be interpreted. On the second floor, in addition to the extra prayer space, is with the women's prayer hall, secluded from the main prayer hall by plywood claustra work infilled with coloured glass. The ground floor accommodates the entrance area, the ablutions facilities, classrooms for religious education, office space and a library.

Apparently because of limited funds, the materials used were almost all of local origin: reinforced concrete for the structure; wood for the claustra work and the sliding screen doors which ventilate the mosque, as well as for carved Qur'anic inscriptions in the form of two large tablets on the *qibla* wall; terrazzo and mosaic tiles and carpeting. Four brass and glass chandeliers designed by the architect were fabricated locally as a cost-cutting measure. Both the architect and the community took pride in keeping the costs as low as possible, while maintaining a high standard of workmanship in the mosque.

Hajeedar, who by the mid-1990s had designed a dozen mosques, subsequently used the Masjid Abu Bakar As-Siddiq as a model for the design and the construction of the larger National Mosque (1984) in the Republic of the Maldives (see Chapter 2), whose government saw the building as both functional and suitable for its own climate and socio-cultural conditions.

Local authorities as branches of central government continue to play an important role in the funding and building of mosques in urban settlements. In spite of this control, the specific circumstances of each case have allowed for some degree of experimentation in design. Either the architect was able to push his own design agenda through the interstices of official bureaucracy, or the opportunity was provided by the key decision-makers within a bureaucracy, individuals whose own hopes and dreams were heard and incorporated into the newly reimagined spaces for worship.

(Opposite) Abu Bakar as-Siddiq Mosque (1982), Kuala Lumpur, does not follow the modernist lead of the Masjid Negara. Instead, a bulbous dome marks the centre of the prayer hall.

(Below) Section of the centrally placed square prayer hall surrounded by a women's prayer space and other facilities.

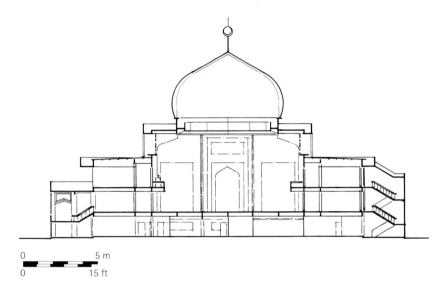

0   5 m
0   15 ft

(Above) Interior of the domed prayer hall looking towards the *mihrab*. An attempt has been made to soften the severity of concrete structures and surfaces by introducing wooden screens and doors.

Mosques for public and commercial institutions

As a frequent source of commissions for new mosque construction, social service institutions are significant patrons. Usually, such institutions derive their funding from central planning offices expressly created for that purpose by government authorities or ministries, often bypassing local government agencies, though a closer look at the decision-making bodies often reveals some overlapping memberships and responsibilities. Nevertheless, the choice of a designer usually falls to the governing body of a particular institution and its leader or leaders, who serve not only as the client of record but also as the effective decision-makers. Institutions dedicated to higher education and health care, as well as major providers of commercial and public transportation services, have in recent decades called for the inclusion of at least a prayer hall, if not a monumental mosque, in the facilities they aim to provide. In these contexts mosques are intended for the use of a select group, membership of which is based primarily on the nature and purpose of the institution, though their prestige and location may in the long run attract worshippers from a wider background. In surveys of public institutions, the most interesting and challenging examples are found in the context of university settings.

The incorporation of a mosque within a social service institution is clearly sanctioned by historical precedent, and the new examples may be taken as a continuation or recall of an already developed pattern of use and layout: one has only to call to mind great foundations such as the Ottoman educational complex and mosque known as the Süleymaniye in Istanbul or the mosque and hospital school of Bayezid II in Edirne, as well as the numerous Mamluk, Timurid and Mughal examples.[1] A closer look at newly created institutions and services and their immediate models and history, however, indicates that for them the inclusion of a mosque was a purposeful reinvention of (or return to) a tradition rather than a continuation of it. The new institutions, whether educational, medical or commercial, are of a size and complexity that have little direct design or functional relevance to the buildings and institutions of the past.

The recent history of universities and other institutions of higher learning in the Islamic world illustrates a complex evolution that is characterized more by divergence from pre-modern institutions of learning than by a sense of continuity.[2] The classic institution of higher learning, the *madrasa*, functioned mainly as a college for the Islamic sciences and religion: it did not expand physically to house other facilities, nor did it embrace other disciplines or subjects.[3] In the middle and early modern periods the *madrasa* remained as the locus for training men in the Islamic sciences as legal personnel, lawyers and judges.[4] In the context of the modernization efforts made in the nineteenth century in major centres of learning like Istanbul and Cairo, or Hyderabad and Aligarh in India, the leaders of the time did not see it as a viable locus for the training of specialists for the new nation-states, and established a series of technical and medical schools, as well as military institutions of higher learning. For instance, universities, higher technical schools and academies of fine arts were

(Above) The approach to the entrance of the mosque at Jondishapur University (1975) through an octagonal courtyard (see p. 156).

(Opposite) The mosque and its freestanding minaret at the King Khaled International Airport (1984), Riyadh, seen from its hexagonal plaza (see p. 176).

inaugurated in Turkey; their organization was based on German models.[5] The institutions were housed in new purpose-built structures on a massive scale and several storeys in height, also very much based on imported styles, as for example in the case of the Technical University in Istanbul.[6] Residential colleges, such as those established in the British colonies, in India in particular, or through the agency of American missionaries, can also be counted as implants from abroad, though ironically it was the medieval *madrasa* which had served as the model for the college concept in the first place.[7] In most cases, the programmes for the new institutions and their buildings had not included a mosque or a prayer hall, either because such educational bodies were conceived as special technical and secular institutions or because they were initially intended to cater for students drawn from non-Muslims living in the region. There were, however, a few exceptions that clearly indicated their religious affiliation, for example Aligarh University in northern India, the student intake of which was to be drawn solely from the Muslim population.[8] Another innovation – and one that provided a locus for anti-colonial sentiment, also being regarded as a counterpart to the secular state education system – was seen in Indonesia in the *pesantren* schools, where the teaching of Islamic sciences is combined with practical education.[9]

In the post-colonial era the number of new universities increased exponentially. They are generally programmed as extensive campuses – almost as separate neighbourhoods or villages. Whether it was because of the lack of inner urban sites sufficiently large for the scale of the institutions, or because it was deemed politically expedient to separate and isolate a large and often restive population of young people or because of the powerful impact of the campus planning model, the new universities are built well away from town centres. Their separation from the urban matrix, as well as their very layout, was in many cases directly influenced by the patterns of planning and building that had developed on American campuses of the 1950s and 1960s. Many close links exist between such new universities in the Islamic world and those in the United States: for example, the Middle East Technical University (METU) in Ankara and the Bangladesh University of Engineering and Technology (BUET) in Dhaka were established with close links to American universities through USAID funds.[10] Many of the early universities were not provided with mosques: both METU (1956) in Ankara and EPAU (Ecole polytechique d'architecture et d'urbanisme, 1970) in Algiers were created in states where the prevailing political ideology did not call for the inclusion of mosques. In more recent projects, particularly those located in less decidedly secularist settings, the mosque has made its appearance especially wherever these separate town-like settlements require a landmark as well as a locus for prayer. Within these new planned situations, especially since the mid-1970s, the mosque has played an increasingly more prominent role in terms of siting and physical presence.

Salman Mosque at ITB, Bandung, Indonesia

While the newest campuses have had a mosque planned into their overall programme, in the case of earlier, already established institutions of higher education mosques were generally built adjacent to the campus to serve the mainly male student community. One such early example in the post-colonial era is the mosque associated with Institut Teknologi Bandung (ITB) in West Java, Indonesia. ITB was founded by the Dutch colonial administration, and its buildings were designed by Henri MacLaine Pont between 1918 and 1920 in a style which consciously drew on the indigenous Minangkabau traditions for its outer forms, on Indian-derived Javanese ninth-century Hindu temples for their pillared structure and on *pondopos*, the open-sided pillared reception pavilions common in Java.[11] The mosque, which was initiated in 1959 but not completed until 1972, stands across the street from the main campus.[12] The building was conceived as a comment on and a criticism of the folkloric flavour of the original campus, as well as featuring thoroughly competent design in the modernist idiom. The well-known Indonesian architect Achmad Noe'man sought to create a spiritual space of great simplicity and beauty interpreted in concrete in the International Style. Inspired by a strict formal purism, his design is characterized by the absence of the architectural trappings of arch and dome, which he felt were nothing more than contingent, encumbering forms in mosque architecture. According to him, the true spirit in Islamic building did not lie in material existence or in techniques and theories, but rather in the extent to which the design and its implementation 'reflected submission to Allah's will and the laws of nature.'[13]

Noe'man, a lecturer in the department of architecture at ITB and a member of the mosque committee, personally took the initiative to develop a Master Plan for the 1.5-hectare (3³/₄-acre) site.[14] It is important to note here that the architect had the key voice on the mosque committee, and was influential with members drawn from the local community thanks to his reputation as a professional, a designer, and a pious Muslim. Because of his personal standing, he was able to persuade the committee to opt for a Modernist interpretation, despite the fact that the proposed design was not readily recognizable either as a local mosque type with pyramidal roofs or as an imported Middle Eastern type featuring a dome. In this instance, therefore, the role of the client was moderated by the influence of the architect himself.[15]

Because of a lack of funds (which had to be raised from a number of different sources), the project proved to be a piecemeal affair.[16] Temporary buildings were put up before the permanent concrete structures could be built. Financial difficulties, and the desire to keep the project a local one, led Noe'man to mobilize students, faculty members and staff, supplemented by help from a small number of skilled local craftsmen. Building materials were obtained locally whenever possible. As a result, the mosque was constructed

(Right) Site plan by Achmad Noe'man for the Salman Mosque and accompanying facilities.

(Below) The architect initiated an uncompromisingly modernist design for a new mosque and student centre across the street from the main campus of the Institut Teknologi Bandung (ITB) in 1959, but the complex was not completed until 1972.

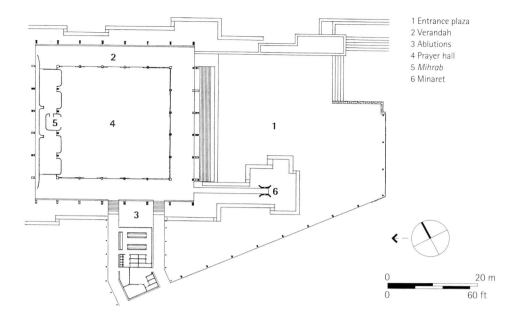

1 Entrance plaza
2 Verandah
3 Ablutions
4 Prayer hall
5 *Mihrab*
6 Minaret

0   20 m
0   60 ft

(Left) The main buildings of ITB dating from 1918–20 were designed by Henri Maclaine Pont in a style which drew on indigenous Mingankabu architecture for its external appearance, as well as on traditional Javanese reception pavilions.

(Above) The interior of the Salman Mosque and one side of the deep verandah which surrounds the prayer hall. The formal treatment of the *qibla* wall is limited to rounded concrete panels with a canopied *mihrab* niche at the centre, together with framing windows and teak shutters. The verandah normally serves as women's prayer space and can also be used to accommodate additional worshippers during religious festivals.

(Opposite) The mosque at Jondishapur University (1973–5) by DAZ Architects is a composition of brick volumes with rounded contours that distinguish it from surrounding buildings on the campus. The blue-tiled light tower at the entrance serves as a marker for the mosque, while the *mihrab* is expressed externally by a corresponding light tower built in brick.

for a relatively modest sum (equivalent to US$300,000), with the architect giving his services free of charge. The first permanent structure was the freestanding minaret (completed in 1966), marking the presence of the Muslim community in the ITB environment. The mosque itself drew praise from President Sukarno, which in turn gave the ITB leadership further impetus to see the entire project through to its completion in 1972.

The mosque complex was conceived primarily to serve the student population and members of their families residing on or near the campus. The programme for the mosque itself stipulated the location of the women's prayer space, on the verandah and mezzanine, or behind the men. Other features included a dispensary, offices, dormitories, a library with conference and lecture rooms, an auditorium, as well as publishing facilities and bookstore, a canteen, and a recreational centre offering a wide range of courses, from badminton to electronics to classical guitar. In all, the programme was more akin to that of a student union or community centre than a continuation of earlier traditions of religious educational complexes in Indonesia. In its architecture, the Salman Mosque makes no references to the past, nor does it evoke indigenous styles – unlike, for example, the Said Naum Mosque in Jakarta (see Chapter 3); instead, it employs a modern idiom that deliberately breaks with the past.[17]

Occupying a site at the northwest corner of the campus perimeter, the mosque complex is preceded by a stone plaza and a wide flight of steps leading to the prayer hall. The prayer hall, measuring 25 x 25 m (82 x 82 ft), and the surrounding verandahs can accommodate around 800 worshippers, and on festive occasions the use of the plaza triples the area available. The minaret – a tall tapering concrete shaft finished in glazed white mosaic tiles and latticework on two sides – stands on the plaza on an axis with the mosque. The ablutions facilities are in an annexe which was to connect the mosque to an auditorium and library wing (not realized).

A reinforced-concrete skeleton defines the interior of the prayer hall. The illusion of lightness conveyed by the 'floating' concrete roof supported by concrete columns epitomizes the architect's adherence to the International Style principle of revealing the structure. The interior, a single open space, is square in plan, with verandahs on three sides at ground-floor level and a mezzanine above providing extra space for prayer. The hall is enclosed on the same three sides by walls in teak alternating with reinforced-concrete columns and doorways (each having perforated concrete blocks above the lintel, thus admitting light to the interior). Between the wall partitions and the teak and masonite board ceiling runs a band of glass which also allows natural light to filter into the interior while emphasizing the dematerialized quality of the wall surfaces and revealing the difference between the structural and non-structural members. The formal treatment of the *qibla* wall is an intriguing aspect of the design: smooth, rounded concrete panels expressed as monolithic elements form a separate space with the concrete canopied *mihrab* niche in the centre; externally, the niche projects slightly beyond the structural envelope of the building. Decorative details were treated in a restrained way. Lighting fixtures in the prayer hall as well as on the verandahs take the form of clusters of cubes suspended from the ceiling; although they follow the International Style idiom, they may also be read as quotes from a *muqarnas*. The design statement of the Salman Mosque was in line with the progressive socialist, or quasi-socialist, aspirations that the Indonesian leadership of the time wanted to project. A similar tendency can also be detected in projects undertaken in other so-called 'progressive' states of the period.

Jondishapur University Mosque, Ahvaz, Iran

A progressive, modern image, albeit without the socialist bent, was pursued and embraced by the regime of Shah Reza Pahlavi in Iran, as well as by successive governments in Pakistan and Turkey. One hallmark of modernity in this definition was the introduction and construction of a number of new institutions, particularly those devoted to higher education. Almost the last to be built (the series was abruptly halted by the Iranian revolution of 1979), was Jondishapur University in Ahvaz, in the Khuzestan region of Iran, completed in 1975. Jondishapur was a name redolent of pre-Islamic Persian academic achievement.[18] Here, the existing educational facilities in the centre of the city were relocated to an expansive 375-hectare (925-acre) site on the periphery, developed from a scheme financed by the Iranian government. The new site, bordered by the Karun river with about 50 hectares (125 acres) of palm groves and gardens, was obtained for the purpose through Princess Ashraf Pahlavi, who at the time chaired the University Board of Trustees. The decision to relocate the university, then scattered in buildings throughout the city, was prompted by a desire to improve and expand the facilities. The fact that such a move was a convenient means of putting some

(Below and opposite below) First-floor plan, ground-level plan and section of the mosque. A pedestrian pathway passing through the courtyard provides a link to social and sports facilities on the university campus. The first-floor plan shows the extent of the women's gallery, while the section reveals the subtle manipulation of levels within the building to accommodate the particular function of each of the various spaces.

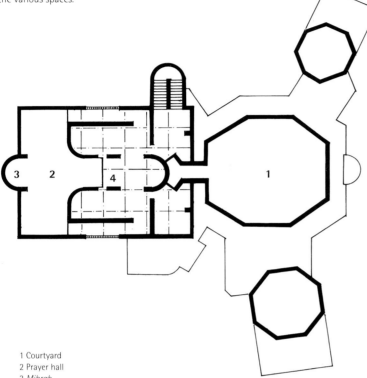

1 Courtyard
2 Prayer hall
3 *Mihrab*
4 Women's gallery

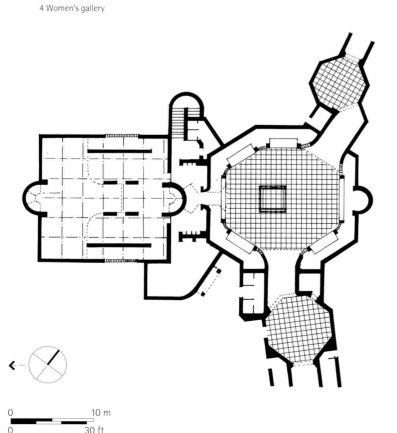

0   10 m
0   30 ft

distance between a potentially troublesome student body and the urban population cannot be ignored either.

In the early 1970s the Plan and Budget Organization of the Iranian government awarded DAZ Architects, Planners & Engineers the commission to prepare a Master Plan and architectural design for the university. Prior to this, in 1967, the same firm had been contracted to design the student cafeteria, and later, a sports complex and a mosque. Kamran Diba, principal architect in DAZ, was eventually also invited to design faculty housing and facilities for community services in another part of the campus, as well as a Graduate Centre for Religious Studies (which was seemingly never built). However, the University Vice-Chancellor, M. Ja'amei, who appears to have been the principal decision-maker on the client's side, subsequently rejected DAZ's Master Plan, and Kamran Diba was advised by Princess Ashraf's office to accept a joint venture with the American firm Perkins and Will.[19] The venture was ultimately dissolved as a result of difficulties in co-ordinating building programmes, though both consultants were retained and continued to work separately on their commissions. The Vice-Chancellor eventually brought in a third consultant, the Iranian firm MODAM, to undertake some of the academic buildings. Though he no longer held the commission for the entire Master Plan, Diba nevertheless managed to establish specific design principles for his part of the university and enjoyed the freedom to put them into practice without significant interference from the University authorities.

The site of the student union and cafeteria, mosque and sports complex consisted of 36 hectares (89 acres) of barren flat land on the northeast boundary of the campus and was traversed by an elevated irrigation canal. The only existing building was a student housing project located on the canal about halfway between the proposed mosque and sports complex.[20] Given the lack of a comprehensive and co-ordinated Master Plan for the university as a whole, Diba chose to develop an open-ended Master Plan for the limited site allotted to him. Having completed his first building, an extension to the gymnasium at the eastern end of the canal, he formulated the idea of a pedestrian axis connecting the gateway defined by the student cafeteria at one end of the site to the sports complex located at the opposite end, and in conjunction with it he projected the development of a larger building programme.[21] His intention was to create along the pedestrian axis 'a sequence of spaces modulated by variations in scale, texture, light and activity'.[22]

The siting of the mosque developed during the definition of the programme between 1967 and 1970. In response to the Chancellor's request for a cafeteria to be located on the edge of the campus along the main road, Diba suggested programming the building as a social centre, at which point the Chancellor asked him to include a prayer room. As Diba noted, 'I searched desperately for a way to connect it to the existing indoor gym, our first completed work on campus. The connection was through a pedestrian axis which I wanted to integrate with the existing irrigation canal.

We also had difficulty of design at the junction of two roads; therefore the solution was a structure which could articulate and resolve the change of direction [from] the cafeteria to the stadium. This is how the idea of the mosque was born. We simply took it outside of the cafeteria and gave it an independent identity and authority.'[23] Diba's solution gave the mosque the formal role of articulating and resolving the change of direction between the social centre and the gymnasium, achieved by positioning the courtyard over the intersection of the proposed pathway and the canal. In terms of urban design, this formulation was both ingenious and appropriate in that it integrated the mosque into the campus while also establishing the mosque's separate identity.

Designed in 1971–2 and built between 1973 and 1975, the university mosque is a sculptural brick composition of fragmented volumes featuring rounded edges to distinguish it from the other buildings nearby. From both directions access to the small courtyard is through a shaded, narrow passage leading to an octagonal *hashti*[24] which in turn creates a transitional space that makes possible the gradual discovery of the courtyard. Upon arriving in the courtyard – also octagonal – the worshipper may drink from the pool placed slightly off-centre, perform ablutions in a niche directly opposite the entrance to the prayer hall, or sit and rest in the shaded galleries. Small apertures in the courtyard walls offer glimpses of the surrounding landscape and act as visual connectors to the campus itself.

The entrance to the prayer hall is signalled by the blue-tiled rounded mass of a tower which stands in contrast to the otherwise monochromatic run of wheat-coloured brickwork used for the walls and the floors. It stands, half-cloaked by the walls of the courtyard, on the *mihrab* axis, diverting the worshippers around it before they enter the main prayer hall. The progression of space is subtly defined by changes in level between the courtyard, the entrance to the prayer hall and the prayer hall itself, which is somewhat lower than the entrance. To the right of the entrance are the ablutions facilities and a staircase leading to the women's mezzanine. In his review of the mosque, Samir Abdulac noted the 'movie theatre-like quality of the mezzanine' – a curious formal debt for a mosque.[25]

The interior space of the prayer hall is formed by two interpenetrating cubes; the larger of which, about 15 x 15 m (49 x 49 ft), is barrel-vaulted and accommodates the height and length of the women's gallery. The smaller cube, one

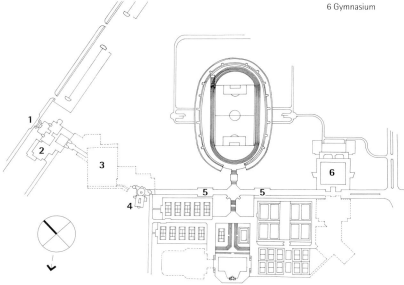

(Below) Site plan showing the mosque as a pivotal feature of the layout, including sports facilities and unbuilt elements (broken outlines).

1 Entrance to campus
2 Student Union
3 Religious studies centre (unbuilt)
4 Mosque
5 Pedestrian axis / line of old canal
6 Gymnasium

end of which forms the *qibla* wall, is covered by a flat roof with a plastered coffered ceiling. This complex interior space is provided with two sources of natural light, one in the tiled entrance tower, the other in the *mihrab* tower. Claustras in these towers also permit cross-ventilation, the air cooled by water in the canal.

The architect has stated unequivocally that he avoided the obvious elements of mosque architecture – arches, domes, ornamental work and calligraphy. Rather, he has chosen to celebrate the elements derived from southern Iranian architectural traditions and transmute them for his contemporary purposes. The use of patterned brick, the linear layout, the indirect entrance, and the shaping of courtyards and intermediate spaces are examples of such elements. Above all, he has taken the most dramatic aspects in Iranian domestic and monumental architecture, the roofscapes of desert towns with their vaults and wind-towers (*badgir*), and has reinterpreted them to produce the sculptural volumes of the mosque and its two towers.[26] Diba borrowed only the idea of the placement of the *badgir*, and used it to mark the *mihrab* on the exterior while introducing air and, particularly, light into the prayer hall. The treatment of the *mihrab* is a distant echo of the *mihrab* in the Mosque

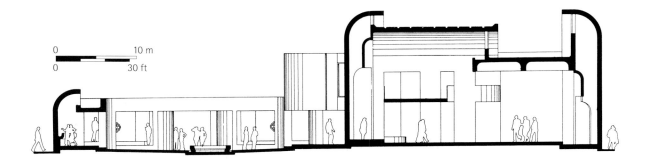

0 10 m
0 30 ft

of Amir Chaqmaq (1437) in Yazd, where a *badgir* was built over the *mihrab* to ventilate the dome chamber.[27] Devoid of any calligraphy or ornament, Diba's *mihrab* dominates the interior with its large, tri-lobed forms sculpted by the light effects and by the changes from brick revetment to plastered surfaces. This version of modernism has allowed him to evolve an architectural idiom appropriate to its location, while at the same time avoiding the easy solution of adopting traditional mosque forms. During the period of construction of Jondishapur University, the necessity of leaving room for expansion and change in the Master Plan led Diba to employ an idea that he would subsequently develop as a methodology which he was to call 'the Islamic approach to design'.[28] This idea consisted essentially of rejecting the monumental expression of the façade (he later regretted his early design for the monumental gateway to the student union) in favour of a less self-representative and more organically generated architecture, the essential qualities of which are apparent only from within. His project is a very sophisticated piece of urban design in terms of the progression of spaces, connectors, and the use of monolithic sculptural elements. Diba's design must rank as one of the major innovations and design solutions for the twentieth-century mosque. Despite being important and skilfully articulated in formal terms and in its effect on the visitor, this building has remained little known outside Iran.

Diba's design approach establishes a design vocabulary that is regionally specific yet modernist and minimalist in its expression and use of materials. It must be clearly differentiated from other buildings in the International Style which had appeared throughout the Islamic world as the hallmark of modernity in the 1960s and 1970s, well after that style had been extensively used in Europe and the USA; it thus belongs to a new regionalist sensibility.

Namaz Khaneh, Tehran, Iran

Kamran Diba's fine sense of urban design and architecture is illustrated in his Namaz Khaneh, a small open-air prayer space located in what was then called the Farah Park at the entrance to the Carpet Museum in Tehran. It was commissioned in 1977 and completed a year later within a larger project undertaken by the Farah Pahlavi Foundation and the Plan and Budget Organization for the enhancement of the entrance to the museum; this included the foundation office and a small plaza, and steps and a gate leading to the park. Diba, together with Parvin Pezeshski, was originally commissioned to design the landscape to the entrance area of the museum. The prayer room was an afterthought arising from the architect's observation that passers-by and local shop employees used the park, in which running water was available from the gardener's hose, to perform ablutions and to pray. In doing so, they created their own individual place

(Opposite and above) The Namaz Khaneh (1977–8) in Tehran by Kamran Diba. This small prayer space is open to the sky but protected by two enclosure walls from visual and aural distractions The rotation of the inner enclosing wall to conform with the *qibla* is clearly visible, while the outer wall is slit vertically along the sight line of a sculpture depicting the hand of Hazrat Abbas.

of prayer but also confused the *qibla* direction by mistakenly assuming that the street grid was oriented on a north-south axis.[29] Diba saw this informal practice as an opportunity to provide a correctly oriented prayer space which would, at the same time, be sheltered from the surrounding traffic noise and visual intrusion. The project, which is well composed and balanced, derives its existence from an accidental usage of a place: its lack of a formal programme, its limited size and its tiny budget were an opportunity for the architect to evolve a distinctive structural form out of the simplest requirements for prayer.

This prayer space, measuring approximately 9.20 m (30 ft) square, consists of a walled area open to the sky protected by a second outer wall. The outer enclosure is aligned parallel to the street, while the inner room is rotated within it to achieve the correct *qibla* orientation. The *qibla* direction is physically indicated by a narrow, vertical slit in the wall of the inner space which acts as a kind of *mihrab*; it is complemented by a slit in the outer wall which allows light to enter from outside. Given the stress on separation from the external world, the fact that this slit seems to be focused on a distant view of the sculpture representing the standard of the Hand of Hazrat Abbas in the park is fortuitous.[30] It not only re-emphasizes the orientation but binds the prayer area subtly to the surrounding park. The corridor walls around the rotated inner box are slanted and not parallel to each other, so creating a narrow corridor – a condensed and dynamic atmosphere of passage from the external world into the contained, controlled inner environment. The tightly defined interior surrounded by high walls meets the sky with a hard edge. The almost diagrammatic prayer space is an exercise in abstraction, inspired by the architect's own painterly past

(Below) The University of Petroleum and Minerals at Dhahran was designed to have its mosque as the focal point of the hilltop campus. The building, designed by Caudill, Rowlett, Scott and completed in 1974, rises out of an oasis pond; standing on a podium, it is covered with a canopy that is supported by slender columns. The interior is faced with marble, while the contrasting *mihrab* niche is accentuated by the use of gold and black mosaic decoration.

(Opposite top) Part of the coffered ceiling in the enclosed, air-conditioned prayer hall.

(Opposite below) Ground-floor plan of the mosque showing the area of the podium and roof canopy and the enclosed prayer hall.

and his admiration for the work of abstract artists such as Josef Albers. It was also very much in tune with the exercises in minimalist sculpture that were current at the time and present in his own works.[31] Applied to this particular instance, Diba utilized this abstraction to reduce the concept of the mosque to its essentials – the directional indication of Mecca, a clean space and a serene atmosphere.

University of Petroleum and Minerals Mosque, Dhahran, Saudi Arabia

In an interpretation of the International Style, the University of Petroleum and Minerals Mosque in Dhahran (1974) offers a case of a contemporary mosque in concrete and glass. The project to relocate the existing university was launched in December 1964, when the American firm Caudill, Rowlett, Scott (CRS) based in Houston, Texas, was invited to assist in selecting a site for the new campus. The University's initial request was extended the following month to include the development of spatial programmes, a Master Plan and the architectural design of the new buildings.[32] The Master Plan, which was phased in gradually from 1965 to the early 1980s, included faculty and student housing, academic buildings to house the four separate programmes offered by the university (a junior college, a technical institute, a school of engineering and a graduate programme in Saudi industry), as well as a water tower, shop facilities, a library, a conference centre, research facilities and community services, and a mosque.

Part of the site was occupied by an oasis, around which most of the community facilities, including the mosque, were located. The mosque, designed in 1969–70, constituted the second phase in the implementation of the Master Plan. Providing the focal point of the hill-top campus, the light, airy, multi-columnar structure has an area of approximately 27 x 45 m (88 x 148 ft) and, when seen at a distance, it appears to rise out of the water. Its presence is signalled to the university community by a contrasting, monolithic minaret, probably inspired by the typical stone examples found in many regions in Saudi Arabia.[33]

The key element of the mosque design is the podium which stands above the water and is shaded by an umbrella roof supported by slim arched colonnades. The prayer hall itself is an independent enclosure beneath this canopy and is closed off to permit mechanical air-conditioning. Square in plan, the hall is an open space without columns and is protected from the elements by walls consisting of marble panels. Light penetrates into the interior through vertical slits in the walls and through openings in the vaulted ceiling which is also lined with marble panels. The *mihrab* niche, recessed into the central panel, is decorated with black and gold inscriptions and vegetal motifs, and on its right is a freestanding marble *minbar*. The remainder of the podium is treated like a shaded courtyard. The perimeter colonnade with its slender proportions is meant to convey the memory of the palm-trees around an oasis, while the use of a band of inverted arches creates a mirror image,

University of Petroleum and Minerals Mosque, Dhahran, Saudi Arabia

thus successfully fulfilling the intended architectonic and emblematic function.

The concept of employing an umbrella structure to provide shade for other structures or functions beneath is not an entirely new idea. The device is common in hot climates, particularly in Southeast Asia and in India, for example in the sixteenth-century Padmanabhapuram Palace in Kerala. Yet, in Saudi Arabia, the recent Dhahran example was perhaps the first of its kind to be completed, followed closely by proposals put forward by Frei Otto in the preliminary design for the Mecca Conference Centre, in which he envisaged a massive tent sheltering the entire complex (see p. 172), and subsequently in the Diplomatic Club in Riyadh.[34]

In determining the essential character of the campus, the architects had to take into account two fundamental considerations: the desert environment and the desire expressed by the client that the architecture should reflect Saudi character. A response to the desert environment was the use of a local concrete mixture of sand, limestone aggregate and cement which was sandblasted to blend in with the natural colours of the surroundings, and the use of large canopies to provide shade. Their interpretation of the 'Saudi character' is thoroughly rooted and does not break

1 Courtyard
2 Minaret
3 Prayer hall
4 Mihrab

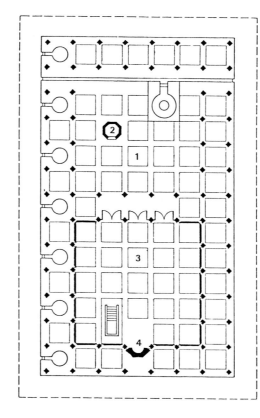

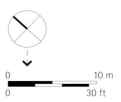

0   10 m
0   30 ft

out of the International Style and modernity, as seen by the client and architect.

The 1970s in Saudi Arabia witnessed many explorations of modernity in architecture. Institutions that had only recently been established saw themselves as progressive forces, even though they were usually controlled by members of the conservative élite. Various cultural and scientific foundations and service institutions provided commissions for a number of mosques in this mode.

King Faisal Foundation Mosque, Riyadh, Saudi Arabia

The concern with expressing local Saudi character was subsumed under the desire to be seen as 'modern' in the King Faisal Foundation Headquarters in Riyadh. This multi-purpose complex includes a noteworthy mosque. In 1976, the eminent Japanese architect Kenzo Tange (of Kenzo Tange & Urtec), who was already engaged in a number of projects in the country, was asked to design the project. Construction work on the complex, known as Al-Khairia, began a year later and was completed in September 1982.[35] It was built by a Korean firm, Hyundai Engineering and Construction Company.

The mosque stands at the east end of the site between two large rectangular blocks and a central plaza to its west, beyond which is an office tower. It consists of a square base pivoted towards Mecca away from the axis of the rest of the buildings; rising vertically out of the square is the cylindrical volume of the prayer hall. The top of the cylinder is sliced off at an angle so that when viewed from ground level it has the appearance of a crescent moon. A vertical slit inserted in the wall at its highest point marks the *mihrab*. This sculptural mosque is of reinforced-concrete cast *in situ*, using structural steel columns manufactured in

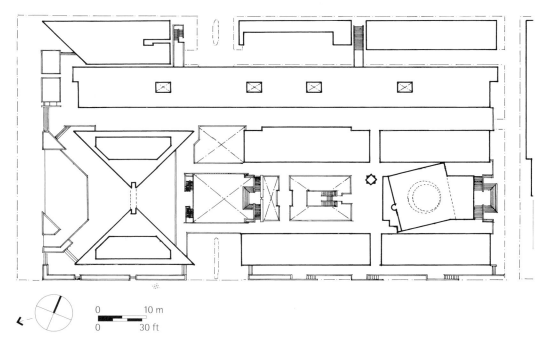

(Above) The mosque of the King Faisal Foundation (1981–2) in Riyadh, designed by Kenzo Tange, displays basic forms such as tower, cylinder, crescent and cube in an emblematic fashion. Deep-blue tiles were used to create a strong contrast between the vertical cylindrical form and the surrounding elements faced with white marble.

(Left) Site plan of the entire Al-Khairia complex, with the mosque turned within the grid to face Mecca.

(Opposite) Model for the dome of the projected mosque designed by Nader Ardalan in 1978 for the new Bu Ali Sina University in Hamadan.

Germany. Its off-white marble-clad exterior is monolithic and plain, while the interior is finished in rich lapis-lazuli and coloured tiles.

The architect's skill is evident in the handling of the site, in the massing of buildings, in the articulation of the spaces and their design expression. It is clear that the architectural styles of both this and the Dhahran building lie squarely within the modernist idiom and do not reflect specific local features such as those expressed in some of the other mosques discussed in this chapter, or in other later mosques in Saudi Arabia such as the Imam Turki bin Abdullah Jami by Badran and the Al-Kindi Plaza Jami by BEEAH (see Chapter 3).

Bu Ali Sina University Mosque, Hamadan, Iran (project)

A new institution devoted to higher education which was intentionally designed to convey a regional, even national, character, was the Bu Ali Sina University in Hamadan (the ancient city of Ecbatana) in northwestern Iran. With a proposed capacity for 6,500 students and begun in 1977,

the Master Plan was prepared by the Mandala Collaborative in Tehran and Georges Candilis in Paris; it comprised academic and research facilities to be built in phases, a teaching hospital with 600 beds, dormitory buildings for 3,000 students, faculty housing for 750 staff members, sports facilities, and a community centre incorporating a student mosque and social/recreational facilities. The complex, which was due to be completed in 1985, has only been executed in part.

The principal architect in charge of the Master Plan and of the design for the student mosque was Nader Ardalan of Mandala Collaborative. He was careful to preserve the existing orchards and farmland on the 172-hectare (425-acre) site, as well as an ancient pathway through the centre of the site connecting the city to the mountain passes of the nearby Alvand range. Much in the same way as the existing irrigation canal was used at Jondishapur University, the pathway became the spine of the university, serving as a link between academic, housing and recreational activities. Here,

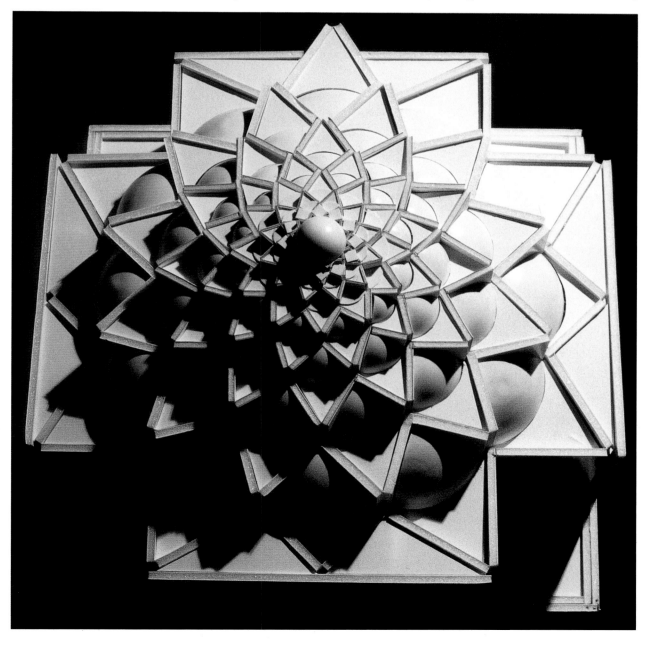

however, a community centre was designed in the linear bazaar form which Ardalan adapted from his studies of the city of Isfahan and the progression of spaces within its layout. Three principles set out in an essay entitled 'On Mosque Architecture' guided the design of the Bu Ali Sina University Mosque.[36] They are: the customary orientation towards Mecca; that of introversion as reflected in the gateway and portico, which the architect regarded as an important part of a design approach to 'positive space'; and the prominence given to the dome form, which highlights the qualities of centrality and symmetry in the mosque.

Designed in 1978 but not built, the mosque was to be identified by the presence of a fluted minaret located to the left of its gateway, while on the other (north) side offices and classrooms would be housed in a small block. A small hexagonal courtyard with a fountain in the centre would provide transitional space between the outside world and the mosque sanctuary. Using the *hashti* idea on a scale different from that used by Kamran Diba at Jondishapur, Ardalan chose this polygonal form as a means of resolving the change of direction between that of the path and the *qibla* and of dispersing access to the prayer hall and to other facilities.

The design proposed a synthesis of planar geometry and mystical ideas. The prayer hall, intended for 250 worshippers, was developed in plan as a square with a geometric design around it: elevated in section from its centre point, it forms a perfect cube. The latticed roof structure which was to be supported by a reinforced cast stone-concrete vaulting system, was infilled with quarter-domes in translucent fibreglass. Interpreted in new materials and geometry, the effect would be that of a *muqarnas* dome.[37] A translucent quarter-dome above the externally expressed *mihrab* would allow this feature to be illuminated in the interior. Developing logically out of the geometry of the design, the four corner rooms in the prayer hall, intended for individual prayer and meditation, were the architect's reference both to the *chahar taq* (places of worship of the sacred fire in pre-Islamic Iran) and to the dome pavilion of Seljuq mosques, as well as a way of anchoring the structure of his dome.[38] They appear to accentuate the centralized unity of the space, at the same time reducing the visible length of the *qibla* wall. The internal walls of the prayer hall were to be decorated with a band of Qur'anic calligraphy in glazed tiles at the spring point of the vaulting. Golden oak was to be used for the claustras, doors and the *minbar*, and a radiant heating system installed under the polished stone floor partially covered with locally woven carpets would help to counteract the effects of the severe winter conditions experienced in Hamadan.

The design proposed a synthesis of mysticism and planar geometry. In both plan and elevation, the mosque makes reference to esoteric Sufi traditions and the *mandala*, and the dome is presented as a mandalic form. Mandala was also the name chosen by Ardalan for his own firm; to him

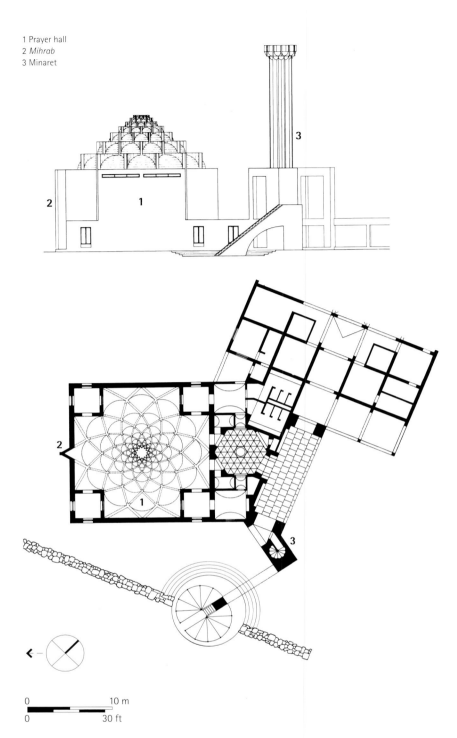

1 Prayer hall
2 *Mihrab*
3 Minaret

0   10 m
0   30 ft

(Above) South elevation and plan of the Bu Ali Sina University mosque. The lattice roof structure was to be supported by a cast reinforced stone-concrete system infilled with a series of quarter domes of translucent fibreglass: the effect would have been to produce a new interpretation of a *muqarnas* dome. The mosque is rotated out of the surrounding complex through a connecting pathway and a transitional hexagonal entrance courtyard.

it represented an important concept of symbolic unity, as is evident from his writings.[39] The dome is also seen as a absolute requirement in the semiotics of the mosque. Ardalan has faced squarely the issue of the legibility of mosque design from the standpoint of users, accepting the dome as a commonly felt requirement. He has also tackled the complex problem of designing a successful domed space in a modern context, taking into account the potential of new structural materials and the resulting need to reinterpret or reinvent techniques of dome-building.

Islamic Centre for Technical and Vocational Training and Research, Dhaka, Bangladesh

While the Hamadan mosque design by Ardalan was based on the harmonies of geometric pattern, championed the use of the dome, and evoked the linear layout of the bazaar in its relationship to the other elements of the master plan, the mosque complex for the Islamic Centre for Technical and Vocational Training and Research (ICTVTR), completed in 1987 on the outskirts of Dhaka, represents an intentional reinvention of a historical layout. Here, the Ottoman educational complex, the *külliye*, provided the inspiration for the design by Doruk Pamir and Ercüment Gümrük of the Turkish firm Studio 14.[40]

ICTVTR was initiated at the Ninth Islamic Conference of Foreign Ministers held in December 1978 in Dakar, Senegal, when the member countries agreed to finance the Dhaka Training Centre as a subsidiary institution of the Islamic Conference.[41] A Board of Trustees (comprising national representatives of Bangladesh, Gambia, Indonesia, Iran, Iraq,

(Above) The ceremonial entrance portal, set at one corner of the site and consisting of five freestanding arches, gives access to the Islamic Centre for Technical and Vocational Training and Research (1978–87), Dhaka. The design for the entire complex by the Turkish firm Studio 14 was guided by the principles of the historic Ottoman *külliye* layout. The freestanding minaret marks the centre of the complex and also serves as a rotational pivot for pedestrian circulation around the mosque.

Libya, Saudi Arabia, Senegal and Turkey) was appointed for the purpose, while each member country proposed a candidate designer from among its own nationals. The scheme submitted by Doruk Pamir of Studio 14 was selected by the Board in December 1979, and the design process was completed by mid-1983. The project manager was Gültekin Aktuna of Studio 14, and the client was represented by Dr Rafiquddin Ahmad, the Director of ICTVTR (1979–87).[42]

Located some 30 km (20 miles) north of Dhaka, outside the Jongi Industrial zone and in the vicinity of the Islamic University, ICTVTR is organized around a central courtyard. The core of the layout was programmed as a social-cum-administrative area including an auditorium for up to 500 persons, a cafeteria with a capacity of 1,000, a library and research centre, an administrative building with an arcade for exhibitions, shops and a mosque to accommodate 500 worshippers. The rest of the facilities, such as dormitories, academic buildings and workshops to the north, faculty and staff housing and a guest house to the west, and a student centre and sports facilities to the east, constituted an outer ring around the core.

The plan of the central courtyard and the surrounding buildings is governed by a rigid orthogonal grid. The need to rotate the mosque in the centre to achieve the orientation

(Below) Section and ground plan of the ICTVTR complex. The layout of the central court and surrounding buildings is governed by an orthogonal grid, within which the change of the mosque's orientation to the *qibla* creates a dynamic tension. The buildings are surrounded by water on three sides.

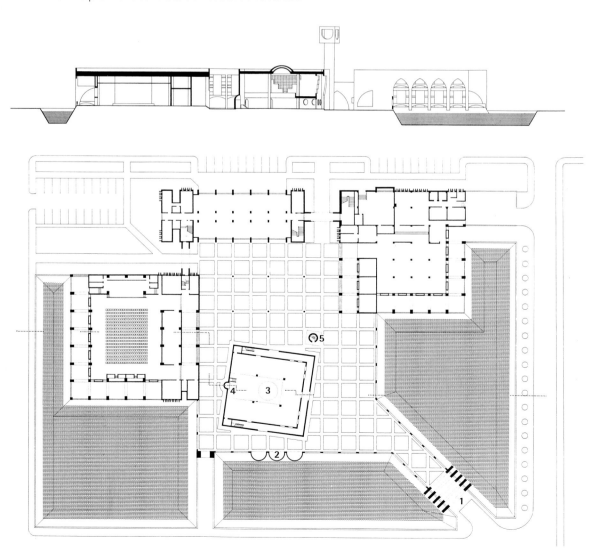

1 Ceremonial gateway
2 Ablutions fountains
3 Prayer hall
4 *Mihrab*
5 Minaret

0   20 m
0   60 ft

towards Mecca simultaneously creates a dynamic tension within the grid and represents a departure from the basic *külliye* layout. Three gates – the Gate of Knowledge, the Gate of Instruction and the Gate of Learning – allow pedestrian access to the court from the different zones of activity on the surrounding campus, while a fourth gate – a monumental entrance composed of five freestanding arches (representing the five pillars of the Islamic faith) – provides ceremonial access.

For climatic reasons, the courtyard was enclosed by buildings on three sides only, leaving the fourth open to the prevailing southerly breezes. The need to leave the south side open posed a design problem, for in the chosen *külliye* prototype the courtyard is enclosed on all four sides. The architects resolved this difficulty by locating the ceremonial gateway in the southeast corner, thereby giving the layout a new definition without departing from the organizing principles completely. With the exception of the minaret, 21 m (69 ft) in height, the buildings retain a uniformly low profile. Surrounding the core on three sides is a moat which combines the basic functions of two elements of Bengali architectural tradition, that of the tank which is commonly used for water storage and cooling, and that of the storm drain. In three places the moat widens to form reflecting pools, a ubiquitous feature in the architecture of the Indian subcontinent.

The labour force and constructional technology readily available in Bangladesh dictated the choice of construction materials, loadbearing brick and reinforced concrete, used throughout the complex.[43] Financial constraints obliged the architects to develop an uncomplicated design vocabulary derived from the architectonics of brick masonry and based on modular units which would allow construction to be carried out in stages. In order to vary the surfaces, different types of arch – pointed, segmental, shallow and inverted – were employed throughout the complex, though in the mosque itself only inverted, semicircular arches were used.

The mosque with its detached minaret – a simple cylindrical shaft with a single balcony pavilion echoing the cubical form of the mosque – occupies a prominent position near the middle of the central court. A freestanding entity in keeping with the *külliye* tradition, the mosque can be entered from three sides, all of which give access to a perimeter corridor with staircases on the north and south sides leading to the mezzanine level. The lateral entrances to the mosque are staggered in relation to the actual doorways of the prayer hall, while the entrance on the side facing the *mihrab* is direct. Square in plan, the prayer hall constitutes a single space with a shallow central dome (partially visible when viewed from the exterior) supported on four columns. The hemispherical *mihrab* niche is expressed externally.

In the architects' opinion, the most salient aspect of the ICTVTR complex is its combination of features from two distinctive cultures: an Ottoman prototype serving as an organizational scheme combined with local building technology; and the Bengali tradition of the relationship

(Top) The main entrance to the mosque. Cut-out forms in brick set up a dialogue with other examples of contemporary architecture in Dhaka engendered by Louis Kahn's design for the Capitol Complex.

(Above) A view along the exterior of the *qibla* wall demonstrates the dynamic intrusion of the bulk of the mosque and its projecting *mihrab* into the straight line of an access path for pedestrian circulation.

of water to buildings.[44] In addition, the complex owes much to Louis Kahn's design for the Sher-e-Bangla Nagar Capitol Complex in Dhaka in terms of its extensive use of brick masonry and particularly the centralized grouping of the primary functions, the connection with water, the tension in plan created by the orientation of the mosque, the double envelope of the façades, and the use of a circular layout and forms that have become associated with Islam in the subcontinent.[45] In the sense that the design is concerned with meaning expressed in the abstract through the use of pure geometry, as opposed to the reproduction of meaning through symbols limited to a local cultural context, the mosque epitomizes a 'style' that can be said to be universal. Taken as a whole, it is a dynamic descendant of Kahn's Capitol Complex idiom and makes a strong contribution to the contemporary architectural language of Bangladesh.

University of Kerman Mosque, Iran

If Pamir's mosque at ICTVTR can be considered a generic new type whose general outlines and solutions will find themselves being reflected in the myriad new mosques now in progress throughout the world, the example of the University of Kerman in southeastern Iran seems to represent a specifically local and unusual experiment.

This university began life as a private foundation in 1972, but after the Iranian Revolution it was taken over by the Ministry of Culture and Higher Education when construction started on its second phase, which included the mosque, in 1985. The university mosque, intended to accommodate around 150 worshippers, was completed in 1989 by the architectural firm Piraz based in Tehran, though the working drawings for it are those prepared by the originator of the plans, Bonyan Consultants.[46] The building is given visual prominence through being sited on the edge of the campus by the main vehicular entrance. (This choice of location differs somewhat from schemes for other campuses in which the mosque is more centrally sited.) An unusual aspect of the design in the history of mosque architecture anywhere in the Islamic world is that the cube of the Ka'ba in Mecca appears to have served as the model (as it did in the case of Bait ul-Mukarram in Dhaka; see Chapter 5). The architects have employed brick revetment and the type of

(Opposite) The Kerman University Mosque, completed in 1989, is given visual prominence by being raised on a mound. The prayer hall in the form of a cube is intended to accommodate 150 worshippers.

(Below) Entrance to the mosque is through a ground-level courtyard and ablutions area. In the interior the play of light brings out the horizontal band of calligraphic inscription on the brick walls and casts a yellow glow through the translucent marble of the *mihrab*.

(Bottom) Section and plan of the mosque and its courtyard.

1 Entrances
2 Courtyard
3 Ablutions
4 Prayer hall
5 *Mihrab*

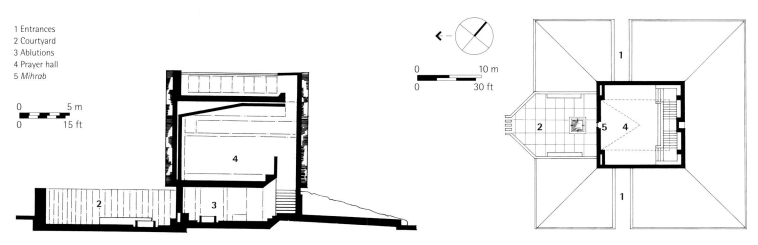

large-scale brick epigraphy that have apparently become fashionable in mosque architecture in Iran since 1980, as seen for example on the Al-Ghadir Mosque (see Chapter 5).

The isolated cube, raised on a grassy mound, has the aspect more of a monument or a mausoleum than that of a mosque. The mound is traversed by two entrance ways leading to a covered ablutions area and by a ground-level courtyard enclosed by a granite wall. The ablutions area receives light from the courtyard. The cubic prayer hall, with a floor area measuring 14 x 14 m (46 x 46 ft), is reached by two symmetrically placed flights of stairs from the ablutions area. The hall is skilfully and dramatically lit by sunlight streaming in from the top of the structure. The hanging vaulted ceiling serves to diffuse light along three of the walls. At night the same effect is produced by means of artificial lighting. The walls are ornamented on the exterior with a band of calligraphic inscription in brick relief executed in square Kufic script. The *qibla* wall features a narrow vertical slit filled with a panel of translucent Yazdi marble; the resulting continuous illuminated band, on which the word 'Allah' is inscribed, constitutes an innovative and dramatic contemporary expression of the *mihrab*.

University of Indonesia Mosque, Depok, Jakarta, Indonesia

An opportunity for innovation seems to have been missed in this university mosque, completed in 1990, perhaps because of the limitations placed on the design through the stated intention of the programme that the morphology of the entire university scheme should be based on indigenous architectural traditions. The University of Indonesia at Depok, on the outskirts of Jakarta in a new 100-hectare (250-acre) campus, forms part of a green-belt site with

(Below) The mosque of the University of Indonesia at Depok, completed in 1990, was designed by Triatno Yudo Hardjoko. It is sited close to the edge of one of a series of reservoirs which dot the campus. The morphology of the entire university was programmed to make use of indigenous architectural traditions.

(Opposite left) Axonometric partial site plan of the university showing the mosque, together with faculty and administration buildings.

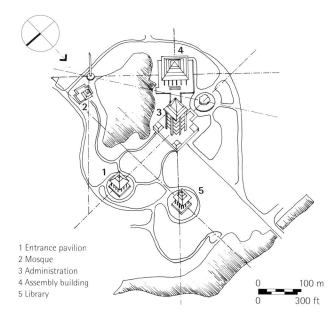

1 Entrance pavilion
2 Mosque
3 Administration
4 Assembly building
5 Library

0   100 m
0   300 ft

an area of 250 hectares (625 acres), partially occupied by several reservoirs providing water for the city. The nature of this location restricts the built-up area to 40% of the campus, with a height limit of eight storeys. The programme called for the creation of three teaching areas – medical, humanities, and environmental – served by seven faculty buildings designed by different architects. According to a set of vague design instructions for the guidance of architects, all buildings were to feature the typological characteristics of local architecture, though more precise guidelines were lacking – even to the extent of any reference to the context of Java. Construction on site was kept as straightforward as possible through the use of locally available materials and labour. The planning and building layout were undertaken by a team from the Limbaga Teknologi – FTUI.

Within these constraints, Triatno Yudo Hardjoko (who worked on the master plan and was also the architect of the Faculty of Engineering) designed the mosque; intended to serve the whole campus, it is sited close to the water's edge. The building features a *saka-guru* structure and a three-tiered pyramidal *meru* roof,[47] while the exterior – expressed visually in strong Central Javanese idiom – is somewhat incongruously combined with a lavish, marble-clad interior. The four columns of the *saka-guru* structure have here been joined by concrete arches (probably regarded as being more 'Islamic'), so introducing a discordant note by contradicting the traditional angular forms. A traditional interior using timber throughout would have been in keeping with the exterior, but the warm inviting ambience created by wood and wood-carving has now been replaced by fashionably modern polished marble surfaces. The *mihrab* niche, a series of diminishing rectangles, is seen through one of the interior arches, which the architect has chosen to call 'the arch of silence, contemplation and light' – evoking a mixed Islamic-Javanese symbol from the past.[48]

Given the successful resolution of the building's massing, appearance and general scale for a mosque intended to accommodate around 800 worshippers, it is unfortunate

(Top) The interior of the prayer hall, showing the diminishing rectangles of the *mihrab* niche and the entrance on the right; (above) a view of the women's gallery. In this building the use of internal arches and marble cladding brought the Indonesian mosque into line with pan-Islamic modern style.

that the appearance of the interior is marred by a choice of overweening imported ideas concerning the type of décor appropriate to a mosque.

Hotel and Conference Centre Mosque, Mecca, Saudi Arabia

While universities provide the largest sample among recent buildings that offer challenging solutions to the problem of contemporary mosque design, a number of those associated with other institutions also deserve mention. One of these, designed for a specialized commercial client, is the Inter-Continental Hotel and Conference Centre in Mecca, by the German team of Rolf Gutbrod and Frei Otto. Their project was the winning design in an invitational competition sponsored in 1966 by the Saudi Arabian Ministry of Finance and National Economy. It was an innovative proposal for a mast 60 m (200 ft) high, from which a large fabric structure (based on the idea of the Bedouin tent) would be suspended, while the buildings beneath it were to be organized around an artificial oasis. After the competition the architects were asked to develop their scheme for use on a different site, which they did in 1968.[49] The new site was located some 6.5 km (4 miles) west of Mecca along a dry river bed, with the Sirat Hills as a backdrop. Retaining the basic idea of the tent structure, the architects adapted their original design to incorporate a cluster of separate focal points, each with its own shading device.

Completed in August 1974, the Hotel and Conference Centre was intended to provide conference facilities and lodging for pilgrims making the *Hajj* and *umra*. As Mecca is inaccessible to non-Muslims, it proved difficult for the architects to supervise construction on site. This radical

(Top) The courtyard of the Conference Centre Mosque by Rolf Gutbrod and Frei Otto (1974), shaded by wooden lattice screens.

(Left and centre right) The *qibla* wall of the mosque from the exterior with its rectangular projections of the *mihrab*, *minbar* and the corner staircase minaret. The general view shows the mosque in the foreground in relation to the Conference Centre.

(Above) Detail of the Masjid-i Bilal, Mecca, the design of which provided a stylistic precedent for the staircase minaret of the Conference Centre Mosque.

handicap was overcome to some extent by installing TV monitors to help control the work in its early stages. A predominantly domestic labour force was employed and the architects made a point of employing local artists to make the population feel that the project belonged to them.[50]

In an effort to produce a scheme with recognizably Saudi Arabian design features, the architects combined three basic themes – the tent, a type of wooden lattice screen called the *kafess*, and the oasis – reinterpreting them through the medium of contemporary materials and technology. The scheme was divided into two parts, the hotel with 170 rooms and five large private suites, and the conference centre comprising: a main auditorium with seating for 1,400; three seminar rooms, each with a capacity of 200; a royal suite; six small meeting rooms; and offices. These were in turn articulated around two central cores within the oasis-like site.[51]

From the complex, a landscaped pathway leads to the mosque, which consists of three basic elements: a central courtyard, a shallow rectangular prayer hall, and a U-shaped office block raised on columns. The raised block serves as the entrance to the mosque, with an ablutions area at ground-floor level, above which are a reception area and office space on the first floor. Like the conference centre, this entrance block is built of concrete with exposed steel beams. The central courtyard is shaded by wooden lattice screens suspended from steel columns. Across the court from the raised block of offices rise the enveloping stone walls of the prayer hall and its pitched roof covered by ribbed aluminium sheeting. The juxtaposition of different materials, such as aluminium over the stone walls, and the arrangement of steel columns from which the wooden lattice screens are suspended provides a subtle and elegant comment on the continuity (and discontinuity) between the manufactured materials of the present and the natural materials used in the architecture of the past. The most memorable aspect of the mosque is its stone *qibla* wall. Incorporated into its exterior articulation are the rectangular projection of the *mihrab*, a smaller rectangle related to the upper part of the *minbar*, and most dramatically, into the corner, the staircase minaret. Even though the minaret is topped by a canopy of

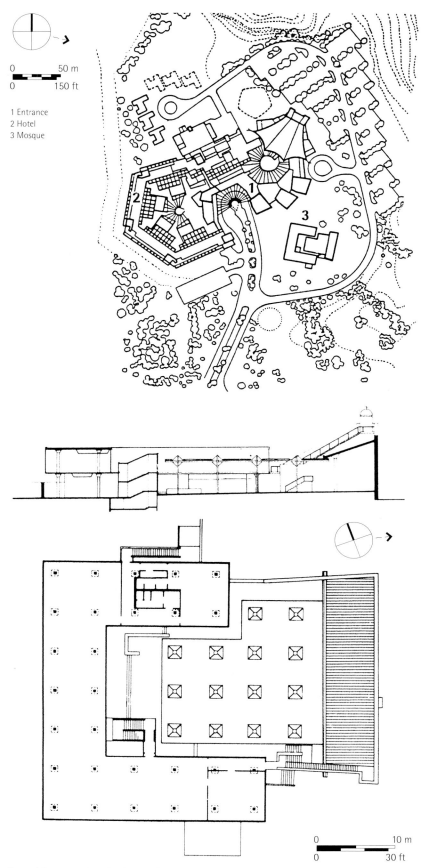

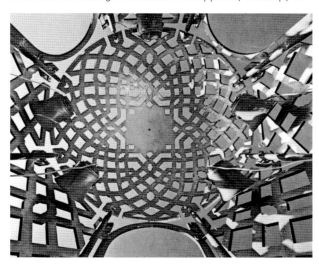

1 Entrance
2 Hotel
3 Mosque

(Above) Site plan of the Conference Centre complex and mosque; section and plan of the mosque showing the shaded courtyard and the appended administrative buildings.

(Left) A view into the aluminium lattice-work canopy above the staircase minaret.

Hotel and Conference Centre Mosque, Mecca, Saudi Arabia

173

aluminium latticework, its basic shape – adopted from that of the Masjid-i Bilal in Mecca – stems from a very old tradition in Arabia.[52]

King Khaled International Airport Mosque, Riyadh, Saudi Arabia

Comparable to the smaller state mosques in terms of size and scale, if not in its symbolic dimension, the King Khaled International Airport Mosque (1983) in Riyadh is suitably monumental, given its central and prominent location in what is physically one of the largest airports in the world. Situated some 32 km (20 miles) north of the city, the new airport was intended to solve the problem of air-traffic congestion and the absence of possibilities for expansion around the existing airport, which was already practically engulfed by urban growth, while providing an impressive gateway to the capital of Saudi Arabia. Gyo Obata, senior partner of Hellmuth, Obata & Kassabaum (HOK),[53] designed a magnificent airport layout in the setting of an artificial desert oasis with lush planted areas and fountains.[54]

The project was initiated in 1974 by the Ministry of Defence and Aviation (MODA) and International Airports Projects, a directorate within MODA. Among the prime movers of this project were Kamel Sindi, then head of the national airline Saudia, followed by Abdullah Mahdi and Nasser Al-Assaf, and General Said Yousef Amin in his capacity of head of International Airports Projects. Arabian Bechtel Co. (an independently incorporated subsidiary of Bechtel of San Francisco) was contracted to manage the design and construction. According to the architectural critic Mildred Schmertz, 'the Saudis' mandate to Bechtel was to give them the most beautiful and technologically advanced airport in the world by 1984'.[55] Bechtel in turn chose HOK to develop a Master Plan and design the airport. In the development of the airport site, the overall area of which was 149,000 hectares (94 sq. miles) there were few constraints and a budget of, reportedly, US$570 million – a sum that was exceeded by a factor of 5.6.[56] Bechtel's choice was no doubt based on HOK's wide experience in airport design (e.g. the extension to Dulles International Airport in Washington, DC, new airports in Atlanta, Georgia, Dallas/Fort Worth, Texas, and in Dubai), and the firm's

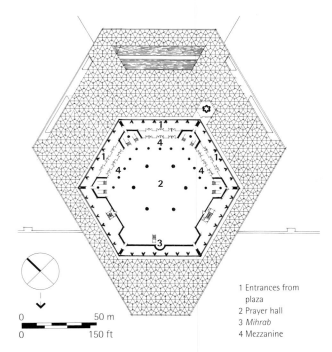

1 Entrances from plaza
2 Prayer hall
3 *Mihrab*
4 Mezzanine

0   50 m
0   150 ft

concurrent experience in Saudi Arabia with the King Saud University (1975–84) in Riyadh was also undoubtedly a particularly important factor.[57]

The programme for the airport buildings consisted of four passenger terminals, a royal terminal, a mosque with a capacity for 5,000 worshippers and an additional 4,000 outside, a ceremonial promenade, plus separate housing and support facilities for the airport personnel to the west. The layout also had to take into account projections for future traffic, suggesting that by the turn of the century 15 million passengers per annum would be passing through the airport; this was done by allowing for four new terminals, effectively doubling the original capacity.

Gyo Obata was assisted by a team of designers[58] who, during the design phase (1974–8), conducted an extensive study of Islamic architecture worldwide, and particularly in Egypt, Arabia, Morocco, Spain and Iran.[59] As a source of potential inspiration, Obata also examined traditional local Najdi architecture, the style of which he had earlier incorporated into the contemporary design of the King Saud University campus. Geometry played a vital role in the airport scheme: 'What I found in Islamic architecture is a tremendous use of geometry, and that's how the whole development of the airport grew – out of the triangle and using the triangle to keep building up the forms.'[60] Practical considerations led him to adopt the equilateral triangle as the primary design module, since it was an efficient unit, minimized distances and was infinitely repeatable in case of future expansion.

The mosque itself, which is hexagonal in plan, is a hybrid of design elements and space-age technology, though historically its obvious antecedent is the octagonal Dome of the Rock in Jerusalem. Sited on the central axis defined by a ceremonial promenade 12.50 m (41 ft) wide and 335 m (366 yds) long, the mosque functions as a pivot, connecting the four passenger terminals to the royal terminal. The theme

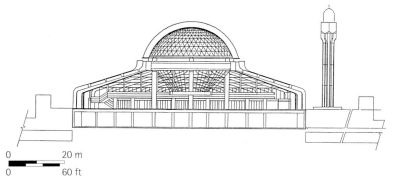

0   20 m
0   60 ft

(Above and top right) Transverse section through the dome of the airport mosque (1983), and plan showing the hexagonal forms of the building and its plaza.

(Opposite) Interior views showing the dome and the giant piers which support the compression ring decorated overall with tile-mosaic inscription.

of the triangular terminal buildings is developed here into a hexagonal motif reflected in the mosque's plan, structure and ornament.

Thus, the domed hexagon of the mosque is at the *qibla* end of a hexagonal plaza, the latter being enclosed by a colonnade with perforated screened wall. The mosque and its plaza are reached via a wide ceremonial stairway, also on the *qibla* axis, though no doubt the escalators which provide access to the prayer hall from the lower-level parking area and the adjacent terminals are used by just as many, if not more, people.[61] Doorways on three sides of the mosque lead directly to the main prayer hall, while internal staircases on two sides serve the women's gallery on the mezzanine level. The mosque also encloses a Qur'anic library occupying 1,700 sq. ft (158 sq. m), situated off the main prayer hall, as well as offices and lavatories along the walls. The minaret, standing at the northeast corner of the plaza, rises to a height of 128 ft (39 m), competing in the skyline with the taller control tower located between the mosque and the royal terminal.

The main floor of the mosque is approximately 16,500 sq. ft (1,500 sq. m) in area and the mezzanine 2,500 sq. ft (230 sq. m). The building is covered by a huge geodesic dome constructed in steel and concrete with a span of 110 ft (33.50 m) and rising to a height of 130 ft (40 m). The dome is formed from pitched-roof sections in lightweight concrete covered with glazed white ceramic tiles, and is supported by hexagonally shaped steel trusses that rest on six massive steel columns faced in concrete. The hexagonal dome is configured into the circular cap, the transition being marked by a clerestory, 7 ft (2.15 m) high, of coloured and clear glass and an ambulatory-like continuation of the canopy. The interior of the dome cap, but not the ambulatory, is finished

(Below) The airport mosque is situated between two of the terminal buildings and was conceived on the same scale. The hexagonal mosque surrounded by its own plaza and then in turn by an 'oasis' of plantings has become a magnet for the people of Riyadh, who come in large numbers to attend Friday prayers and for recreation.

with a total of 1,008 triangular bronze panels arranged in concentric registers. A continuous band of blue-and-white tile mosaic displaying passages from the Qur'an decorates the compression ring of the dome; covering an area of 2,600 sq. ft (240 sq. m), it is said to be the largest of its kind ever produced.[62] Tile-mosaic patterns, mainly in stylized vegetal motifs, fill the five panels of the deep, illuminated *mihrab* niche. Despite its bold ornamentation and illumination, the visual impact of the *mihrab* is reduced because its height is restricted to that of the top of the surrounding wall, above which a continuous glazed band below the ambulatory admits natural light, and because it is dwarfed by the vastness of the interior. The ornament both for the mosque and for the rest of the complex was commissioned by a special arts committee:[63] while the decoration of the terminal complex was included in HOK's contract, the decoration of the mosque was not. Instead, it was given to Vesti Corporation – an unfortunate move, according to Mildred Schmertz.[64] The interior of the mosque is elaborate and features the use of a wide variety of materials; the result of the approach and articulation adopted contrasts markedly with the ornamentation in the rest of the airport complex, which had been left in the architect's hands.

While the ornamentation is of a very high quality, its eclecticism and profusion is overwhelming; this decorative programme is probably one of the largest and richest in the contemporary world.[65] The exterior surfaces combine sand-blasted pre-cast concrete with marble facing decorated with floral designs carved in Italy. For the interiors, Vesti commissioned Brian Clarke to design the stained glass, and Edman Aivazian to undertake the mosaic decorations, carved stone, carved wood (for the 38 pairs of doors in the mosque) and ceramics. The stained glass, all hand-blown and fully leaded, was fabricated using new glass-cutting techniques that were dictated by the glass designs. Representing some 7,000 sq. ft (650 sq. m), the area covered by stained glass was the first to incorporate gold-plated brass and onyx.[66] Interior walls are faced with panels of Italian travertine marble, having a total area of 3.640 sq. ft (338 sq. m), etched with Arabic script in Bournemouth, England; the floors are of granite and travertine; and the prayer hall has a royal blue carpet with beige geometric designs woven in Hong Kong. The great circle of the Turkish chandelier, hung from points around the circumference of the dome, appears to float in space. It is clear that the client of record played a crucial role in formulating the final appearance and the visual impact of the mosque interior, contradicting the intentions of the architect.

The richness and the vast space of the interior, as well as the massive presence of the building within the airport complex and its oasis garden setting, have made the mosque a magnet not only for passengers in transit, but especially for the citizens of Riyadh who come in large numbers for Friday prayers and for recreation. Here, the monumental nature of the architecture, as well as the green surroundings have extended the attraction of the mosque beyond its

Details of the ornamentation programme of the airport mosque: wood carving of the many doors (top) and of the *minbar* (bottom) features geometric patterns. Vegetal patterns in tile mosaic are the main motif of the illuminated *mihrab* niche (centre).

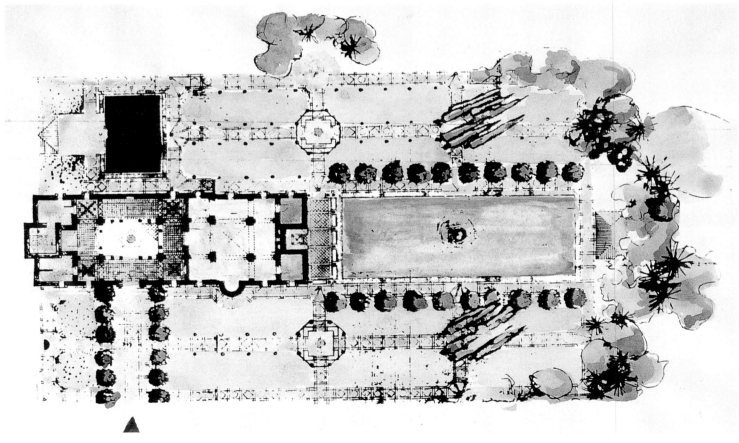

designated population of airport users to that of the capital city at large. The vast size and the ambitious nature of the programme for the airport mosque led the architect to seek inspiration from the most monumental concepts and design ideas in the history of Islamic architecture, and the client to demand embellishment of epic proportions.

Avicenne Military Hospital Mosque, Marrakech, Morocco

In contrast to the ambitious scale and intentions of the airport mosque in Riyadh, the Avicenne Military Hospital in Marrakech, Morocco, the commission for which was awarded to the prominent local architect Charles Boccara,[67] included a hospital with 300 beds and a small mosque adjacent to it for the use of patients, visiting families and staff. Boccara drew his inspiration for both elements from the local building traditions in which the materials used include fired and mud brick, *pisé, tadelakt* (a hard plaster) and eucalyptus wood, as well as ornamental materials like tile *zellij* mosaic revetment. Rejecting the modern precedent of high-rise hospital blocks, he chose rather to take as his model the low-built, horizontal architecture typical of the region. He also chose to adapt the design so as to conform with the existing foundations which had been laid for the hospital in the late 1930s. The mosque was built in 1982. By organizing the hospital buildings around planted courtyards (*riad*) with latticed pavilions, he created a pleasant, restful environment for patients and hospital workers alike. In his review of the project, Brian Taylor noted that 'Much effort was devoted to humanising the institutional environment through tasteful decoration using local materials . . .'.[68]

The mosque, 420 sq. m (4,500 sq. ft) in area, is located outside the main hospital complex to the west, and is approached through a paved courtyard with a central fountain. On the south side lies an ablutions area, an *iwan* or court, and access to the site of the projected but unbuilt minaret. To the north is the nine-bay prayer hall, the central bay of which is covered by a small lantern dome, protected by a pyramidal green-tiled roof. The dome is built of brick and finished internally with *tadelakt* coating. The deep, semicircular *mihrab* niche fills half of the middle bay and is easily identifiable as a projecting feature on the exterior. The prayer hall extends to the north as a porch open to a garden with large reflecting pool; an ideal place for meditation, convalescence and relaxation. The architect also designed extensive gardens to be laid out beyond the court of the mosque, but these were never executed due to lack of funds. In Boccara's words, 'wishing to demarcate spatially the sacred from the profane, we included a garden to provide the necessary transition'.[69]

An architect who operates in accordance with his own sense of place rather than within a theoretical framework, Boccara derived his inspiration in this case from traditional Moroccan mosque idioms. In order to humanize the institutional context, he sought to create an architecture that would evoke comfort and reassurance where they are

(Opposite top) Exterior view of the mosque, designed by Charles Boccara, built in 1982 in the grounds of the Avicenne Military Hospital, Marrakech, and site plan showing the mosque set in a formal garden landscape.

(Above) The central entrance to the mosque and a view into the enclosed garden (*riad*), which provides a peaceful and secluded area for meditation.

(Above) A view of the Dar Lamane Mosque,
designed by Abderrahim Charai and Abdelaziz
Lazrak, seen from the minaret showing the
inner courtyard, its exterior extension, and the
surrounding low-rise housing built in the 1980s
for a new community.

(Right) Site plan of the Dar Lamane housing
scheme, completed in 1983, which provides
housing for 25,000 people; the mosque is the
central feature of services provided for this
community.

(Opposite) The Dar Lamane Mosque, built in the
officially sanctioned Moroccan style, features a
square minaret, green-tiled roof and white
plastered walls.

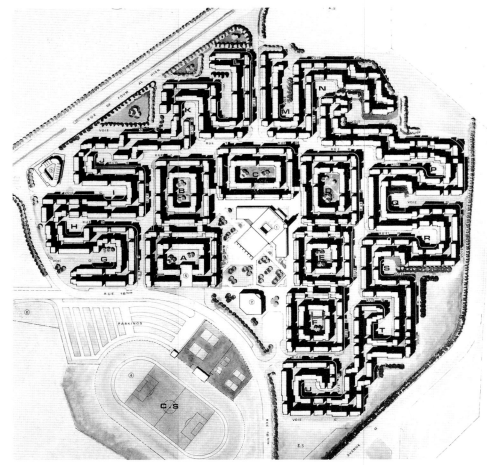

most needed. The spatial patterns, forms and ornament of the mosque, easily recognizable to its users, are carefully managed so as to establish a harmonious and balanced visual and physical environment.

Dar Lamane Mosque, near Casablanca, Morocco

Another example of the use of Moroccan idioms, but on a larger scale than that of the Avicenne Military Hospital, is the mosque at Dar Lamane near Casablanca. It was designed in the early 1980s to provide a focal point at the main entry to what was at the time the largest single lower- and middle-income housing scheme in the country. A private developer, Compagnie Générale Immobilière, developed a 37-hectare (91-acre) site comprising 4,022 units intended to provide housing for some 25,000 people. The client acquired the site in 1980 and charged the architects, Abderrahim Charai and Abdelaziz Lazrak, with the task of designing a new community scheme to relate to the 'surroundings and the general cultural milieu of Morocco'.[70] The overall scheme is interesting in itself, being arranged on three sides around a central public space that has the mosque as its focus, with a festival hall on one side and arcaded shops around the perimeter. Access for vehicles is via an approach road on the open side. The project, finished in mid-1983, was realized in the space of 30 months and under budget.

The Dar Lamane mosque, together with its external spaces, is substantial, covering an area of c. 7,000 sq. m (73,300 sq. ft). It serves as a local landmark and, while not special in terms of design, is well planned and executed using the traditional layout of a hypostyle prayer hall with courtyard, in a simplified architectural vocabulary that recognizably follows the officially sanctioned mosque style. The square minaret, green-tiled roofs and white plastered walls lend the unadorned exterior a pleasing aspect, while the interior is more embellished. One notable feature is the external open court on the west side, defined by a simple arcade, that serves as a forecourt to the mosque. The arcade encloses a transitional outdoor area which can be used as overflow space to accommodate additional worshippers and which can be shaded by temporary awnings. It is a simple and effective device that is both functional and tectonic.

The role of the private developer as a service organization providing amenities for a newly developed urban area is an old one, with a history dating back to the nineteenth century. The commercial property developer has now increasingly come to be recognized as an agent of change in the urban environment in both Asia and the Middle East. Despite the fact that the importance of this type of corporate (capitalist) institutional client continues to grow, instances of projects in which such a client provides facilities of architectural interest remain infrequent.

Chapter 5

Local community projects worldwide

Historically, a typical neighbourhood mosque community consisted of a small number of people known to each other personally (*jama ma'lum*), hence it was a locus of close association, but was not subject to state authority.[1] To a greater extent than in the great dynastic mosques, the type of atmosphere that characterizes older neighbourhood mosques is one for which a feeling of nostalgia clearly exists today, and one which communities organizing and building new mosques seek to replicate. This is as true in new areas of urban expansion as it is in spaces designated as mosques by migrant and immigrant communities. Rapid urbanization in conjunction with the migration of populations from rural areas has led to the formation of community groups (usually poor) in inner-city areas or in outlying developments. In other instances, these new communities are designed first on paper, as at Dar Lamane near Casablanca.

Such mosques were often constructed by builders and other skilled artisans from within a particular community. Although this practice still continues, many of the more recent buildings were designed by professional engineers and architects from elsewhere. Typically, these communities are more traditional in their outlook, for they are made up of groups of people having a common background in a particular sub-region of the country (e.g. the *mohajirs*, Muslim immigrants from India, or ethnic groups such as the Bengalis in Karachi). In some cases, there are new groups of converts to Islam, for example, African-Americans in the United States and the indigenous Chinese in Indonesia. In recent years, too, Muslims have moved into even more diverse societies, within which they make up only a small percentage of the population, as in Italy or Canada. Like many immigrant groups, they tend to live in close proximity to each other and to establish new communities. These differ significantly from each other because their members come from different geographical backgrounds and thus establish mutual ties through their need for observance of religious rituals rather than through any pre-existing ethnic, tribal or national affiliations that they might share.

The process of migration and movement of Muslims on a worldwide scale, especially since the 1960s (the so-called second wave of emigration), has also led to a redefinition of migrant communities in terms of 'otherness' in many societies. Notions of a community with roots no longer apply and traditional ties that defined communities have changed, resulting in a pluralistic mix. In these situations the prayer hall of the mosque forms part of a community centre which caters for most of the social and family needs of members of a newly assembled community – as the place of worship for Friday prayers, providing classroom space for lessons on Islam, as a venue for women's group meetings, and for weddings. Such a multi-functional complex provides an anchor in a new land, offering individual members of the community a protective and familiar environment.

It is worth noting that the concept of 'community' as client often refers not only to particular self-interest groups, for example Bangladeshis or African-Americans, Bohras or Ismailis or Shiites, but more narrowly to a committee set up by a particular community to act on its behalf. This is very evident both in larger cities of the Islamic world and in the United States, where the majority of community clients are Muslim associations, a notable example being the Islamic Society of North America (ISNA). Although such associations may be legal entities, they are in reality the embodiment of their communities and have therefore been included.

While community action has been accepted as an ideal and praised as such, under Islamic law no corporate body is empowered to act on such matters. Therefore, associations of individuals – be it a guild, brotherhood or community – cannot act as a legal entity in the buying and selling of property or enter into real estate transactions. Records relating to mosques seldom refer to the community as client, but in practice local communities have funded the building of mosques through *zakat* (alms-giving), using donations from individuals or groups. Community decision-taking at grass-roots level is, perhaps, one of the principal factors which have helped shape the urban fabric, notably in

(Opposite) Interior of the prayer hall in the
ISNA Islamic Center, Plainfield, IN, showing the
distinctive circular windows (see p. 219).

residential quarters. The ties between prominent individuals and their respective communities must be recognized,[2] because it is precisely in that nexus between individual and community that the decision to build a mosque as an act of piety and for the use of the community lies.

There is a difference between individual patronage, which is clearly located at the very summit of a specific political or social order, and the patronage of a group of individuals who take it upon themselves to initiate the building of a mosque – initiatives which are later appropriated by local neighbourhood groups. The will of the community is thus represented in a particular project and decisions to develop a funding base or to choose the architect and the design for the mosque invokes a sense of communal responsibility and commitment towards the local environment because the people are actively involved in forming as well as in maintaining it. Granted there is some overlap, but clearly the initiative and the bulk of the financial support for the construction of a community mosque do not come from government sources, but are contributed out of private funds. The nature of the design is dependent on the ability of the designer or architect to accede to the wishes of the local community and its memory of the 'mosque' concept while introducing his own ideas of mosque design.

In rural or village settlements, where traditional religious beliefs and practices continue more or less intact, or have been less disrupted than in an urban context, the function and place of the mosque in relation to the community have remained much as they always were. Each group would build its own mosque using whatever resources it had, in accordance with local traditions passed down through generations.[3] Such was the situation in the case of the Great Mosque (1973) in Niono, Mali, and of the Yaama Mosque (1982) in Niger, for example, where no architect in the modern sense of the word was necessary, and the actual construction was undertaken by a local builder/mason aided by members of the community.[4] Since the mosque was in similar circumstances intended to cater essentially to the basic religious needs of a particular group, it was usually a functional structure in the local vernacular style. In smaller neighbourhood mosques there were seldom any external signs distinguishing the building as a mosque because all the local people knew where it was and what it represented.

Usually the site on which a new community mosque is to be built is donated by a single individual, a family or a group. Another method of obtaining land for this purpose, particularly in areas where there is little scope for site selection, is by clandestinely building a mosque, or a shrine, on a vacant private or public plot. In this way, the site is appropriated by the community and, once the mosque has become established, it is almost impossible for the original landowner to recover this property.[5]

In the second half of the twentieth century, the building of neighbourhood mosques has become a considerably more complicated process because decision-making has been vested in centralized government authorities, both on the local and on the national level. In many Islamic countries, the authorities provide mosques not only as part of their obligation to cater for the religious needs of the population, but also significantly as a means of exerting a degree of control. Unfortunately, this also results in the removal of the community from the decision-making process and changes its relationship to the built environment. The consequences of this shift of power are particularly evident in the modern-day urban setting. In the past, the community mosque was almost without exception an integrated element in the urban fabric, central both physically and symbolically to the local population. This remains true of older urban settings where the close relationship was already established, and of new, informal urban settlements where traditional models are sometimes repeated. However, the problem of rapid growth in many cities has led governments to reach site decisions based exclusively on zoning considerations, that is, to create a number of 'strategically located' congregational (jami) mosques or other smaller mosques intended to be a feature of newly planned residential areas, but which are not usually integrated into the communities they serve.

Another development which has been expressed in a shift from particularism or regionalism in the built environment is the appearance of a pan-Islamic style incorporating easily recognizable 'universal' features (see Introduction). In new urban and rural situations, particularly in countries where Muslims are in a minority, the mosque is a very important collective symbol of a community's presence. A case in point, where the outward forms ensure immediate recognition by Muslim and non-Muslim alike, is the Muslim Village Mosque (1979) on the outskirts of Manila, Philippine Islands. Here, it was decided not to attempt a regional expression, but to opt for the new universal Islamic style, in which an Indian model featuring a rectangular plan with courtyard and dome was combined with a hypostyle prayer hall.[6]

Although the role of the Muslim community in making decisions about its own environment has been somewhat diminished by changing socio-political factors, and by the intervention of government and local authorities, there still exist many situations in which communities retain control over their environment through collective decisions. The process of building community mosques is in the main characterized by two tendencies: they are usually built in stages, and are expanded over a number of years. Quite often, in South and Southeast Asia and at times in Africa, the community mosque compound will also accommodate income-generating activities such as shops that help to pay for its upkeep – this continues the traditional link between mosque and bazaar, and blurs the boundary between ritual and secular spaces.

Great Mosque, Niono, Mali
This congregational mosque in West Africa is an example of a local mud-brick architectural tradition using local labour and building techniques, and was realized by deploying the community's own resources. The Great Mosque of Niono[7]

The imposing three-towered *qibla* façade of the
Great Mosque of Niono in the Upper Niger delta,
Mali, continues the regional vernacular style
established by the earlier Djenné Great Mosque.

is unusual in one respect, compared to the other mosques
presented here, for it was designed and built without the
aid of architectural drawings; although this is also true of
a number of traditional mosques all over the world, the
circumstances are unusual in the case of a mosque of this
size and importance.

Although it appears that a rural agglomeration pre-
existed it, the village of Niono was essentially constructed by
the French colonial administration c. 1937. The streets are
laid out in a grid pattern and, with the exception of a few
colonial-style buildings, the village consists of low, mud-
brick structures, occasionally with an upper storey. While
modern materials and technology are increasingly more
evident, the more economical local materials and techniques
are still very much in use. Prior to the construction of the
new congregational mosque, the only available place of
worship was a small wooden mosque situated on the
western edge of the village.

The initiative to build a larger new mosque to serve the
needs of the 5,000 inhabitants of Niono came from Dr
Diawara, a physician from Timbuktu who was working in the
village.[8] An organizing committee was created, presided over
by the *imam* of the existing mosque, in order to establish
the functional and aesthetic requirements for the new
structure, and to choose an architect-mason. The intended
site had been allocated for the purpose by the French
colonial administration, but the committee considered the
space to be insufficient for its needs.[9] As a consequence, Dr
Diawara acquired an adjacent parcel of land so as to permit
an extension of the designated area and thus accommodate
the dimensions of the proposed structure.

Construction began in 1948 under the supervision of
some local masons. For reasons which are now unclear, the
masons were relieved of the commission the same year and
Lassiné Minta became the new architect-mason in charge
of the project. He was responsible for all the subsequent
modifications, in which he was assisted by his eldest son and
another local mason. Minta, a member of this community,
originally moved from Djenné, where he had learned his
trade. After completing his apprenticeship with the small
group of masons there, and working for the French colonial
authorities during the 1930s on various projects, including
the Markala Dam in the Département of Niger, he settled in
Niono c. 1940.

Located in the centre of the village near the marketplace,
the site of the mosque – measuring 33 x 60 m (108 x 197 ft)
– is surrounded by an enclosure wall and is bordered on
three sides by streets, and on the fourth side by houses. It is
set in an L-shaped courtyard (on the west and south sides)
which was needed to accommodate the occasional overflow
of worshippers. Because of the successive extensions, the
reduced courtyard space now seems small in comparison to

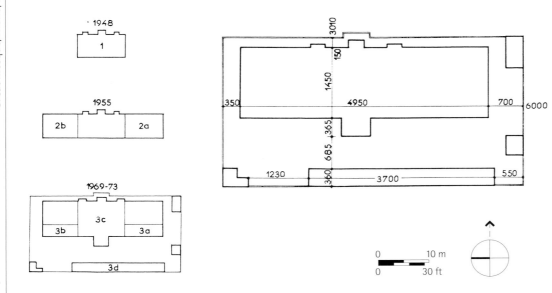

1948
1

1955
2b   2a

1969-73
3c
3b   3a
3d

3010
150
1450
350   4950   700   6000
365
685
1230   360   3700   550

0   10 m
0   30 ft

(Left) Schematic ground plans showing the phases of development of the Niono Mosque, as recorded by Raoul Snelder in 1983. It started as a small building in 1948 and was enlarged in several stages. After 1969 the central part was completely reconstructed; the final dimensions are shown in the larger sketch.

(Below) Detail of the exterior of the *qibla* façade of the Great Mosque, Djenné, the building which served as the model for the Niono mosque. Rows of projecting palmwood beams form part of the structure of the three main towers; their ends – akin to permanent scaffolding – facilitate the periodic resurfacing of the exterior.

(Opposite) The entrance to the Niono Mosque is flanked by traditional ancestral pillars, the shape and symbolism of which date back to a pre-Islamic period.

the monumental proportions of the mosque. There are several points of entry in the outer wall, but the main entrance is located on the south side, facing onto one of the main thoroughfares of Niono. A separate entrance for women is located near the southeast corner of the site.

In its present form the mosque is the result of three different phases of construction undertaken between 1948 and 1973.[10] The original mosque, a simple rectangular hypostyle prayer hall for the use of men only, had an area of 216 sq. m (2,260 sq. ft) and was composed of 24 bays, three from east to west, and eight from north to south, the *mihrab* being positioned on the east side on the axis of the fourth bay from the north end. In 1955, the committee decided to enlarge the building by adding six bays on the south side and four bays on the north side respectively, more than doubling the size of the interior. Between 1969 and 1973, the central part was entirely reconstructed and enlarged, with the *mihrab* being moved to the centre of the enlarged building and two bays being added to the west façade to accommodate women worshippers. As a result of these later extensions, the area of the prayer hall grew to 726 sq. m (7,800 sq. ft). Also at that time, a rudimentary ablutions building was added in the southwest corner, and a storeroom and guardian's house were built, flanking the main entrance on the south side. Subsequently, in 1983, the guardian's house was transformed into a tomb for the first *imam* of the mosque.

The form of the Niono mosque is based on the model of Djenné of the Dyula style associated with the Islamized inhabitants of the region[11]. The three-towered *qibla* wall of the Great Mosque of Djenné was the prototype for this feature in the Niono mosque. The treatment of the east façade is conventional insofar as it does not really diverge from the Djenné model – a central four-tiered tower over the *mihrab* flanked by two three-tiered towers. However,

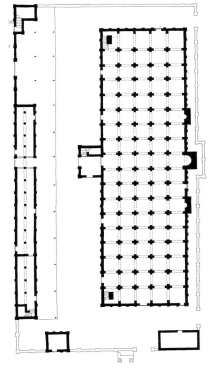

0   10 m

0   30 ft

(Above) Site plan of the mosque, drawn in the 1980s, showing how the main structure has grown to fill the greater part of the plot; the ablutions building lies to the west.

(Below) Interior of the hypostyle prayer hall with its forest of supporting columns.

Minta added a fourth tower at the entrance on the west façade on the *mihrab* axis. The boldness of this move can be appreciated fully only in the context of typological strictures applied in West African mosque architecture, rules which are particularly rigid in Mali. Not only is the west tower a typological rarity, but its alignment with the *mihrab* (thus emphasizing the east-west axis) has the practical effect of undermining the traditional predominance of the *qibla* axis. Architecturally, the west tower is unique in the local context. Some scholars have suggested the influence of colonial church architecture, examples of which Minta would certainly have had an opportunity to observe while working for the Département of Niger in the 1930s.

In the large courtyard secondary buildings run along the outer west sanctuary wall which encloses the entire mosque structure. The solid buttresses seen in the Djenné and Dyula models are here replaced by finer low-relief pilasters which, instead of rising to the full height of the wall, are connected by arches, echoing those within the prayer hall. Each pilaster is capped at the top of the façade with a pinnacle, a feature which continues somewhat eccentrically even over the main doors, where the rhythm no longer corresponds to the pilasters. The façades are punctuated by projecting palmwood (*toron*) beams, a decorative regional technique which serves a practical purpose, that of providing built-in scaffolding, facilitating both the initial construction and the subsequent maintenance of the exterior; it is also imbued with symbolic meaning.[12]

In the Niono mosque one can detect the assimilation of ancient pre-Islamic symbols – phallic, and those related to ancestor worship – in certain decorative features, such as the capitals of the pillars in the otherwise austere prayer hall, as well as the motif found in the niche just above the entrance on the west façade.[13] Pagan ancestral pillars are also thought to be an inspiration for the earthen buttresses in Dyula architecture. The distinctive verticality of the Dyula mosque type and the emphasis given to external surface decoration in contrast to the rather stark interior space are, according to Labelle Prussin, the result of the mosque's role in the past as a landmark, a 'logical response to the need for visual identification and the maintenance of stylistic cohesion and consistency'.[14] This tradition of mosque-building is born out of the overland trade routes that were opened up and developed as a result of the Islamic diaspora, and the pillars long associated with ancestor worship were translated into architectural forms which serve to define a prescribed space and which can be observed from afar in their entirety.

The Niono mosque's structure consists of loadbearing walls and pillars made of sun-dried clay bricks, from which spring arches along the longitudinal and transversal lines of the bays. Above the arches, closely packed wooden joists are laid diagonally across the corners, thereby ingeniously reducing the span to fit the roofing materials available. Other traditional materials include: clay mortar, with or without decayed rice bran; local wood for the roofing;

imported wood and wrought iron for the joinery; pre-cast concrete for the window frames; steel sections for the doors; quicklime for whitewashing; and tubular steel posts supporting the verandah on the west side of the enclosure.

The role of the builder-mason in the shaping of the representative aspects of the mosque was paramount, yet the major structural and symbolic elements of the building were held within the recognizable local architectural vernacular and the innovations were easily accepted by the villagers because they amounted to extensions of that language rather than a total break with it.[15]

Yaama Mosque, Tahoua, Niger

The Yaama Mosque, in the Tahoua region of Niger, is another notable West African mud-brick building, entirely financed by and built for the members of the community of Yaama using modest local resources. At the request of the village elders, the builder-mason Falké Barmou, a local farmer and a member of the community, designed and built this Friday Mosque as his personal contribution to the collective endeavour.[16] Aided by three other local masons and the villagers, he creatively used the local architectural vocabulary and the traditional mud-brick and rammed-earth construction techniques of the region to achieve a result that lies within the idiom of a particular West African building tradition, while displaying some original ideas. The new mosque was first brought to the attention of a wider public in 1986, when it received an Aga Khan Award for Architecture as an exceptional example of traditional popular architecture. In this context the Master Jury's citation noted that 'the living tradition of that culture is revitalized . . . [and] . . . the community participates in a ceremonial where every contribution becomes a sacrificial act to the Glory of God . . . There is an elemental beauty and integration in the whole complex. In this architecture, the issue of whether it is new or old becomes quite insignificant . . . in an era when traditional architecture is losing ground, this is a remarkable feat.'[17]

When the decision to build a Friday mosque was taken in 1962, the village elders initially proposed transforming one of the neighbourhood mosques in the village; however, opposition from the district head of government (*Chef de Canton*), who had not been informed of the decision, forced them to abandon the idea. The elders finally decided, with the acquiescence of the latter, to build a new Friday mosque. Having defined the functional characteristics of the mosque, they left decisions concerning the design and technical aspects to the master-builder. They envisaged a simple, functional rectangular hypostyle prayer hall, large enough to accommodate the village community, the only secondary feature being the externally expressed *mihrab*. No separate accommodation was planned for women worshippers,[18] nor was it felt that a Qur'anic school was necessary, and only very rudimentary facilities were provided for ablutions, located in a small building in a corner of the site where a jar of water is kept for the purpose. Construction was dictated

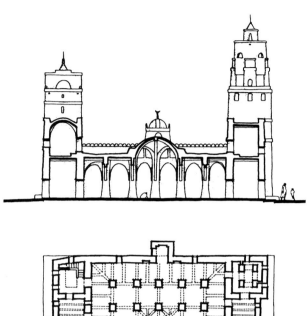

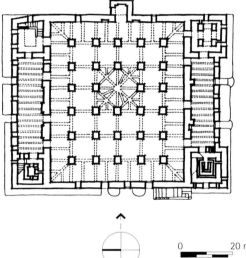

(Below) North-south section and ground-floor plan of the Yaama Mosque. The minarets and gallery on the north side were completed in 1980 and those on the south side in 1982.

0   20 m
0   60 ft

by the local weather conditions – it had to be erected and covered between rainy seasons.[19] At the time of construction, the mosque was situated on the edge of the village, at the end of the narrow main street which roughly bisected Yaama along its east-west axis. As a result of subsequent expansion, the mosque has become more centrally located.

The courtyard of the mosque is rather small relative to the building's overall size (as in the case of the Niono mosque, this is a result of gradual extensions). Surrounded by a low perimeter wall, it is used as an overflow prayer area. On two sides the compound is bordered by streets, while on the south side it opens into a large, open public space. On the east side, a smaller space separates the mosque compound from the buildings facing it. Access to the compound is via four gates in the enclosure wall: on the north side, the main entrance is located within an expanded portal, two gates are placed close together in the west wall, and another in the south wall leads to the open public space. The prayer hall itself has a door on three sides, and

The expressive forms of the Yaama Mosque (below) are based on traditional Hausa architecture, but were adapted to the local master builder's own aesthetic. Thus the covering of the prayer hall was changed into a series of shallow vaults using bundled reed arches as supports (opposite above).

(Far right) Diagrams by Raoul Snelder recording the growth of the mosque over three decades.

the *qibla* (east) wall has a direct private entry to the *mihrab* for the use of the *imam*.

The mosque is rectangular in plan, the east-west axis being slightly longer. The original structure had an area of c. 300 sq. m (3,230 sq. ft), with five rows of columns running east-west; there were six bays along the east-west axis and seven from north to south with a total of 30 columns. The *mihrab* was placed slightly off centre in the east wall to avoid it being entirely obscured by the central row of columns when viewed from the entrance on the west side. Barmou had considered using an arch-supported roof structure using bundled-stick arches (a technique he had learned from a Nigerian mason), but because the structure had to be covered quickly, he was obliged to opt for a less elaborate post-and-lintel system.[20] The structure is one commonly used for the large, sober mosques of the region: closely spaced thick columns (the column spacing/span ratio being roughly 1:3 or 1:3.5)[21] and thick loadbearing mud walls provided the support for the roof, which was formed from closely spaced beams made of bundles of sticks laid flat, criss-crossed diagonally and covered with mud. The internal walls curve at the top to meet the roof, and are pierced on three sides by several irregularly spaced and, for the most part, unornamented openings. The *qibla* wall itself is a blank façade, apart from two small windows flanking the *mihrab*.

In 1975, the prayer hall underwent major modification to repair its leaking and structurally unsound roof. Barmou took this opportunity to replace the old post-and-lintel structure with an arch-supported roof, using a method of binding sticks with a mud and straw mortar to form the voussoirs. This restructuring fundamentally altered the interior and meant that the original columns had to be extended to accommodate the new height. Also at that time, a dome supported on reed arches was inserted in the space formerly occupied by the four central bays by removing the third column in the middle row. The effect thus achieved has been described as 'a dimly-lit forest at the centre of which the central domed area forms a clearing'.[22] The hypostyle plan has become elaborated by much the same processes as those documented in the histories of traditional mosques and their development.[23]

A few years later, during the dry seasons of 1978–82, more ambitious improvements were proposed by the local builder-mason and carried out with the aim of embellishing the appearance of the mosque. On this occasion the mosque underwent major extensions, among which were four new corner towers, two-storey galleries in the north and south walls of the prayer hall, and an entrance building. In 1986, the *mihrab* superstructure was also embellished with a new crown-like top.

The additions of 1978 almost doubled the floor area of the mosque to c. 500 sq. m (5,380 sq. ft). Significantly, this major expansion did not for the most part constitute additional functional space; the towers and the second-floor galleries do not fulfil any specific need.[24] The four corner towers are all different in their formal treatment, and were included in an ornamental programme absent from the lower part of the façades. The towers are all multi-storeyed, slightly tapering and monolithic up to two-thirds of their height, at which point the elevations are pierced with numerous openings of varying shapes and sizes. The elevations are decorated with discontinuous frieze-like bands at different levels which are, however, not necessarily indications of changes in floor level. The culmination of each tower ends in a different finial. The two towers on the south side are taller and more imposing, probably because they form part of the façade overlooking a large open public space. On this side, too, the galleries have been recessed, so allowing the towers' contours to be more fully accentuated.

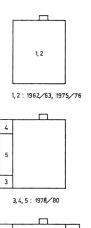

1, 2 : 1962/63, 1975/76

3, 4, 5 : 1978/80

6, 7, 8 : 1980/82

(Below) The only known representational drawing made by the builder of the Yaama Mosque.

The general layout of the mosque and the construction techniques fall squarely within the Hausa building tradition, with the possible exception of the arch technology which has been described as 'rendered wood' and is an unusual feature of a mosque in this region.[25] The materials employed are also specific to the region – the overall structure is of sun-dried mud brick reinforced with straw so as to prevent cracking, and mud mortar with cement addition.

Despite the fact that the mosque underwent a succession of transformations over the years between 1962 and 1982, its appearance remains harmonious, even though the basic functional austerity that characterized the original structure has gradually given way to a more explicit monumentality. The major innovations which the builder-mason brought to the design were of an aesthetic nature, accentuating the representational aspect of the mosque. From the post-and-lintel system of the prayer hall the structure evolves vertically through the use of tower and arch forms. Looking at the remarkable sculptural quality of the towers and the 'balanced interplay of masses and voids' of the whole composition, as it has been described by Raoul Snelder, one is struck by the experimental spirit of the design and an evident search for variety of formal and technical expression, at least in the upper part of the structure. This can be observed not only in the formal treatment of the towers, but on all four elevations, which vary in height and decoration and consist of crenellations above the parapets and, for the most part, plain bands in relief. The vaulted arches in part of the north gallery, which is otherwise flat-roofed like the south gallery, also tend to illustrate this experimental tendency, though it is not certain why Barmou did not extend the treatment to the rest of the galleries.

The gradual nature of the construction work allowed for an evolution of the mosque from a building of purely functional considerations to one where monumentality and, therefore, aspects of representation and aesthetics came to play an increasing role. In this process, the local people also supported Barmou's initiative completely by their participation in the project. The villagers contributed in cash or, more often, in kind by making mud bricks in their spare time, foraging for wood, carrying materials, or providing food. Individuals contributed in proportion to their means and ability. The labour might be regarded in the strict sense as unskilled, but the inhabitants of the region build their own houses and are thus already familiar with most of the techniques that were used. Notably, as a measure of its success in the region, the Yaama mosque has come to be regarded as a model for other communities wishing to build a more representational congregational mosque, not only because of its external monumentality but also because such a building is economically feasible.[26]

Because of the perishable nature of the materials, the structure is repaired and maintained each year during the dry season. Out of this constant process of renewal, communal participation in the act of building takes on a more profound meaning, though, at the same time, one

must beware of over-romanticizing a matter of necessity. One might even regard the collective nature of the building process as, in some sense, even more meaningful than the finished product, if one may speak of a finished product in this region. Concerning architecture as a process and a collective art, Abdel Wahed El-Wakil has stated apropos the building of mosques: 'Work is a prayer . . . an act of devotion.'[27] This attitude is not uncommon in tribal and rural societies where the rhythm of construction and collective participation in building are often regarded as a spiritual experience. While it is true that the ritual of renewal is rooted in the necessity to carry out constant maintenance, the regular re-enactment of this process over the years can also be seen as symbolizing the revitalization of the local culture and its regional building traditions.

Masjid-i Tooba, Karachi, Pakistan

As an example of a break with traditional style, the Masjid-i Tooba of the Defence Officers' Housing Society in Karachi presents an uncompromisingly modern image. The Society was formed as a co-operative in the manner of many Indian and Pakistani developments, where the central government

The concrete-shell structure of the Masjid-i Tooba (1969) in Karachi, designed by Babar Hameed, makes an uncompromisingly modernist statement. The circular mosque is approached by a formal walkway with a central pool and fountains.

made land available to specialist groups to be developed privately for their members, a process that was controlled by an elected committee made up of members of the co-operative.[28] The Defence Officers' Housing Society counts perhaps as the most affluent of such organizations. The Society's members wanted a Juma Masjid to serve the whole area, to be built on a plot occupying some 45,000 sq. ft (4,100 sq. m) adjacent to a main highway linking the port and the industrial area with Karachi's city centre, as a local landmark. In keeping with the progressive image of the state at the time and the military governments of the 1960s (the majority of the committee were retired officers), the desire for a modern design was not at all surprising.

What was unusual, however, was the choice of Babar Hameed as architect.[29] He had earlier left to study sculpture in Italy, and finally ended up in Rome training to become an architect. Upon his return to Pakistan in 1964, he obtained an internship with J. A. Ritchie working in Islamabad. At the time of receiving the mosque commission not long after his return from Italy, Hameed was better known for his sculpture than for his buildings (and subsequently he has not produced any other buildings of note). His connections with leading Italian designers and engineers did, however, stand him in good stead. He quickly produced the design for the mosque, and construction began in September 1966; the building was completed in November 1969.

The design of the mosque is based on a concrete-domed shell structure with a diameter of 212 ft (65 m), rising to a height of 51 ft 6 in. (16 m). The air-conditioned prayer hall accommodates up to 5,000 worshippers; a terrace provides additional space for an overflow of 8,000 and the gardens for a further 30,000. The shell is sited towards the centre of the site and is approached through walkways set in formal and somewhat uninspired landscaping. The engineers and contractors were MacDonald, Layton and Costain, Pakistan, who helped Hameed realize his design for what was at the time the largest shell structure on the Indian subcontinent. It is reported by the architect that when the noted Italian engineer Pier Luigi Nervi saw the design, he exclaimed, 'You have stabbed me in the back.'[30]

The mosque is well attended for Friday prayers and at Eid, even though its circular form seems to lack the essential directional quality so clearly evident in earlier monumental mosques. The single minaret, which rises to a height of 120 ft (36.50 m), is a separate freestanding structure that complements the shell; like so many other contemporary minarets, its design replicates an Ottoman model. The interior provides a single, shaded serene space. An outer covered walkway with *jali* block walls permits subdued natural light to enter, though the interior still needs to be mechanically cooled in the summer as it heats up quickly. The modern look of the building gained acceptance among other client groups in Pakistan and was copied in Lahore (on the Mall Road) and elsewhere. Even though the much smaller scale of these copies negates the essence of the structural achievement and the elegance of the Defence

(Opposite) A walkway around the periphery of the mosque is screened by a *jali* block wall; the perforations produce dramatic patterns of light on the interior.

(Below) Detail of the *jali* walls and the repeated arches of the roof as seen from the garden.

(Bottom) The circular prayer hall, a single domed space with a diameter of 212 ft (65 m), has to be artificially lit and mechanically cooled in the hot climate of Pakistan.

Officers Housing Society Mosque, this basic acceptance, as well as the initial choice of design, is a sure indication of the openness of these client groups and of their desire for outward representation in the modernist idiom.

Sherefuddin's White Mosque, Visoko, Bosnia

A break with local building traditions has on occasion been initiated by the architect himself, either with the approval of or at least with no overt objection from the community, precisely because the design offered to them appealed to their self-identification as sophisticated town-dwellers. Such a break took on a new and dramatic form in the case of Sherefuddin's White Mosque in Visoko, Bosnia (at the time an integral part of Yugoslavia). The design presented a modern projection of a longstanding Muslim community's presence in a non-Muslim socialist country. To judge by the reaction of the Muslim community itself, the design of the new mosque was initially regarded as representing a rupture with tradition, though its members eventually came to accept the building with pride as an important landmark in the town.[31]

Zlatko Ugljen, a nationally known architect and teacher, sought to translate the basic functional organization of the Bosnian mosque, and what he regarded as the spiritual and symbolic meaning in Islamic religious architecture, into an entirely modern architectural idiom.[32] The accent on modernity and new forms is all the more significant in a region where mosque design had until then remained more or less unchanged in the Ottoman style since the sixteenth century.[33]

The town of Visoko lies in the valley of the Bosna River, to the north of Sarajevo. It was the seat of the Bosnian kings when Bosnia was still independent, and was an important commercial centre during late-medieval times thanks to its location on a main trade route. Under Ottoman rule (1463–1878) the built environment of the town developed its particular Bosnian Muslim character. In 1911, a major fire destroyed a large part of the houses and mosques of the town which were built of wood, the most commonly used construction material in the region. The houses built more recently are two-storey masonry structures with pitched red-tiled roofs.

In 1967, the Muslim community of Visoko decided to build a new mosque after the central mosque – the largest of seven neighbourhood mosques then serving the town – was demolished. The site for the new building, which was intended to cater for the majority of the town's 30,000 Muslims,[34] was that of the old Sherefuddin Mosque in the heart of the commercial centre known as the Carsija (or 'cross-roads'). The community had maintained an active religious life under the socialist regime and the political climate in Yugoslavia at the time also allowed for such an initiative.[35] The decision to build was taken independently by the community, which provided 94% of the total costs through voluntary donations and provided the local labour.[36] Other funding came from local public sources (4%) and a

(Above) The powerful forms of Sherefuddin's White Mosque (1980), Visoko, designed by Zlatko Ugljen, are best revealed when viewed from the adjacent Muslim cemetery.

(Below) Section through the prayer hall. The complex form of the roof over the hall is apparent, as are the two main levels of the complex: the sunken courtyard and prayer hall, and the office and an annexe at street level.

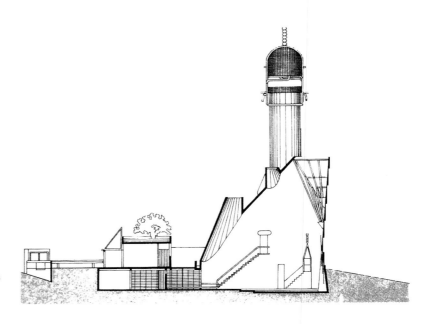

contribution from Saudi Arabia (2%). The architect, who is of Bosnian origin, gave his services free of charge.

The brief for the new mosque called for its integration into a development plan for the immediate surroundings – an existing market area and residences – in order to create a *külliye* complex which was to provide a new central focus for the town.[37] At the start, an annexe building in the front of the site was to house offices, a Qur'anic school and an assembly room, but later it was decided to use the space for a public library. Preliminary work by a state-run contracting firm began in early 1968, but the essential construction work was executed with long interruptions between 1970 and 1980 by a local private firm. The mosque was finally inaugurated in September 1980, in the presence of official delegations from a number of Islamic countries.

The site plan was shaped by two considerations: the existence of an old graveyard on the site and of the market area in front of the mosque. Graveyards for dignitaries and particularly pious individuals were a common feature of many Ottoman and, therefore, Bosnian mosques. Such memorial gardens were situated behind or to the side of the mosque, creating a green oasis in the middle of the built-up urban matrix. Here, too, the architect tried to recall the same relationship between the mosque and memorial garden or graveyard by juxtaposing the two, with no immediate visual access or connection between them. Hence the sides facing the graveyard are left blank.[38] As for the adjacent market area, the architect devised a solution that would exploit the topography of the sloping and slightly elevated site in relation to street level by locating the prayer hall in a hollow, below road level farther into the site, thus creating a more private and insulated space for prayer.[39] Moreover, the climatic conditions of the region, which experiences severe winters, made this an attractive option for thermal insulation. The prayer hall and the courtyard are on the same level, separated by a large glass panel that admits natural light and permits an uninterrupted view between the two spaces.

The total built area of the mosque itself is 435 sq. m (4,650 sq. ft), comprising five main functional elements: the entrance area and courtyard; the prayer hall; the annexe; the graveyard; and the minaret. Partially attached to the minaret, raised on stilts and reached by the staircase leading to the minaret from the interior of the prayer hall is a small cubic space intended for meditation. The annexe is treated as a simple block separate from the mosque and having its own entrance. The landmark minaret is in the form of a simple cylindrical shaft from which the *adhan* is broadcast by loudspeaker, and bears at its apex the name of Allah in green piping.[40]

From the street a sloping path winds via a low gate down to the small courtyard through which the mosque proper is reached. This is the main entrance, but the prayer hall also has a secondary entrance from the annexe block. In the courtyard is an ablutions fountain that is both functional and decorative. While the various elements combine to

(Above) A curved pathway leads down from the street to the courtyard of the mosque; to the left is the glassed-in entrance to the office at ground level.

(Below) Plan of the mosque and the annexe with its separate entrance.

1 Entrance path to mosque
2 Prayer hall
3 *Mihrab*
4 Minaret
5 Offices
6 Old cemetery

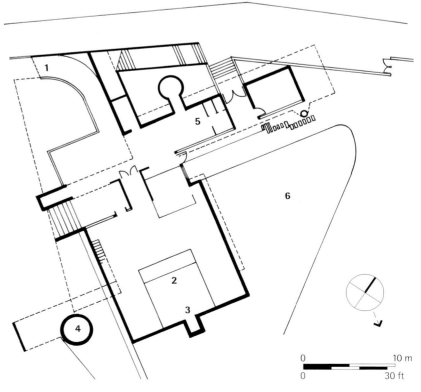

0   10 m
0   30 ft

197

create a multi-level composition with a complex circulation pattern, the general layout is inspired by existing Bosnian mosques based on the Ottoman single-unit domed type with courtyard.

The simplicity of the plan is at once complemented and challenged by the dynamic complexity of the elevation. 'Either covered by pitched roofs or cupolas, all Bosnian mosques respect a hierarchy of pyramidal organization; so are the mountains surrounding Visoko. The idea was to respect this principle.'[41] Here, the basic pyramid shape has been modified by the intrusion of several other crystalline forms. The meeting of the skylights and the stark white elevational planes of the building is manipulated in a self-consciously cubist manner so as to create a highly abstract dome form.[42] The composition taken as a whole culminates at the southeast corner of the façade in a symbolic gesture towards Mecca that would appear to represent the fusion of the vertical and horizontal axes.[43] The effect is somewhat softened by the adjacent cylindrical minaret.[44]

As a contrast to the hard edges of the external surfaces, the interior of the prayer hall is characterized by warped planes and curvilinear surfaces. Five strategically placed skylights (understood as symbolizing the 'five pillars' of Muslim belief) permit the creation of a play of light and shadow on the white walls and ceiling, while discreet and simply designed white lighting fixtures are placed at regular intervals along the walls. The *mihrab* recess, set in the east wall, is filled in with a composition of receding pinewood rectangles – a stylistic echo of a *muqarnas*. It is flanked by two calligraphic medallions in relief which recall the seventeenth-century examples in Aya Sofia in Istanbul and the Eski Cami (Old Mosque) in Edirne. To the right of the *mihrab* is the wooden *minbar*, made of pine painted white and topped with a pyramidal pavilion echoing the dome and the fountain. The floor of the prayer hall is covered in light-green carpet and at its centre there is a sunken area whose purpose is to permit a better view of the *mihrab*. This novel feature also has the effect of creating a raised walkway or arcaded area around it; however, within the prayer hall it results in worshippers being on two levels but without the separation of the prayer areas and walkways found in most mosques. Although this floor arrangement seems to have been accepted by the community, it does have the effect of causing one group of worshippers to be separated from another while at prayer.

All the standard architectural and functional elements generally found in mosques have been reinterpreted in a contemporary, modernist idiom. Structural elements are made of *in-situ* reinforced concrete, so allowing for a free arrangement of the various elements. The façades were rendered in white concrete, and local stone was used for the exterior paving. The decorative vegetal motifs on the *minbar* and the hangings in the prayer hall and on the ablutions fountain may well be derived from local folk designs.[45]

(Opposite above) The interior of the prayer hall is dramatically lit from above by the use of skylights.

(Opposite below) The ablutions fountain in the courtyard, separated from the prayer hall by a large glass partition.

(Above) The floor of the prayer hall is graduated towards the *qibla*. The *mihrab*, *minbar* and calligraphic medallion stand out against the plain white walls.

While clearly recognizing the overt and subconscious inspirations and background to both the form and the ornamentation of the mosque, the architect chose to move forward from European architecture of the 1950s which served as a springboard for this design. Possible inspiration derived from contemporary architects such as Le Corbusier – evident in the use of light and shade to create a dynamic spatial ensemble – leads to a comparison with the Chapel at Ronchamp in the respective architects' treatment of form and space. On the other hand, Brian Brace Taylor has suggested that the aesthetic of the new Visoko mosque is perhaps closer to Aalto's churches in Finland or to German architectural styles.[46] Yet to the local community, the design simply spoke of being sophisticated and modern. In the end the architect was able to convince the client that the shape of the mosque was not only acceptable, but also thoroughly representative of their desire to be seen as both Muslim and modern. In a similar vein, the later and larger Islamic Centre and Mosque in Zagreb projects an image of a modern Muslim community.

Islamic Centre and Mosque, Zagreb, Croatia

At the time of its construction in the 1980s when the Muslim population of Zagreb was *c.* 20,000, the complex was envisaged as the main Islamic centre for the city (and for Croatia). The new building was by no means the first modern mosque in the city: the Ustase leader Ante Pavelic had built one during World War II to please his Muslim subjects, and in the post-war years some 700 new mosques had been built under the socialist regime in the former Yugoslavia.

The Zagreb complex, with a built area of *c.*10,000 sq. m (104,300 sq. ft), was the first of its kind because it not only incorporated an auditorium, library, assembly rooms and classrooms, but also included a restaurant, a gymnasium and even a slaughterhouse so as to conform with Muslim dietary rules. This mix of functions makes it one of the largest twentieth-century complexes of its kind in Europe, comparable to other major Islamic Centres such as those in Rome and Lyon.

The idea for a centre was first proposed in 1960 by the *rais al-ulema* (religious leader of the community) during a visit to Zagreb, but no practical steps were taken until 1980. In the autumn of 1981, the foundation stone was laid and the mosque was due to be completed in 1984. That year, however, the shell dome was destroyed by fire, and subsequent administrative conflicts between the Muslim community and the city authorities delayed the completion and opening of the complex until 1987.

Designed by Mirze Goloze and Dzeme Celica (a former dean of the Sarajevo School of Civil Engineering), the Zagreb complex consists of two distinct parts: the mosque, inspired by the typical Ottoman layout featuring a central space and characteristic minarets, and community facilities housed in a two-storey structure designed in an International Style idiom of the 1960s. The construction was financed

(Opposite) Exterior view of the Islamic Centre and Mosque (1987), Zagreb, designed by Mirze Goloze and Dzeme Celica.

(Below) Entrance elevation and plan of the complex. The Islamic Centre to the left consists of an auditorium, gymnasium, library, slaughterhouse, classrooms and offices. To the right and set apart stands the sculptural mass of the mosque, with its freestanding minaret.

(Bottom) An interior view of the prayer hall showing the split plates of the dome.
(Overleaf) The white curving and sinuous forms of the interior are set off by the 700 carpets donated by Iran. The area of the gallery is proportionally one of the largest spaces provided for women worshippers in contemporary mosques.

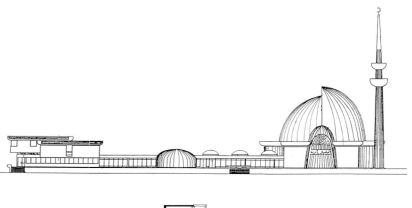

1 Entrance
2 Men's prayer area
3 Women's gallery
4 *Mihrab*
5 Minaret

0   20 m
0   60 ft

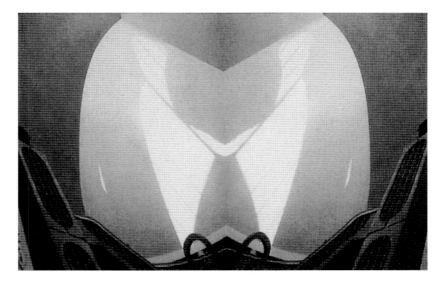

by donations from the Muslim population of Yugoslavia as a whole, and by several Muslim countries.

The mosque itself, which can accommodate up to 3,000 worshippers, consists of a hemispherical concrete shell split into two staggered sections, so permitting natural light to enter the prayer hall. As in Sherefuddin's White Mosque at Visoko, similar modernist and sculptural ideas are addressed here. The interior of the hall is further defined by the curving outline of the women's gallery which overhangs the main floor on three sides.[47] The plain plaster *mihrab* protrudes both internally and externally in a modern arch form flanked by two plaster roundels inscribed 'Allah' and 'Muhammad' respectively. The tall *minbar* surmounted by a dome and with screened sides that follow the outline of the balcony balustrade, is more traditional. The interior is simply lit by indirect light reflected from the off-white walls. The floor of the main men's hall is covered by some 700 Persian rugs woven in Kashan (all gifts from Iran), seventeen of which were personal donations from the Ayatollah Khomeini; the women's gallery is carpeted in green broadloom. In addition to prayer rugs, Iran also donated ceramic tiles, and several other Islamic countries provided building materials.

Although the style of the Zagreb Centre is recognizably Ottoman in inspiration, the building illustrates well the Modernist trend in mosque design in the late twentieth century – a mix sought by clients and architects alike.

Bait ul-Mukarram, Dhaka, Bangladesh

Having a predominantly Muslim population, Dhaka has been called the 'city of mosques' (estimated in 1984 to number almost two thousand, most built in the established Bengali-Indian idiom).[48] A few years after Independence in 1947 and as a result of changes to the political and religious climate that ensued in what was then East Pakistan, a decade-long wave of mosque building swept Dhaka. Situated in a busy commercial district of the city, Bait ul-Mukarram was one of this new generation of mosques. It was conceived to provide a centrally located mosque complex to serve the religious, social and cultural needs of the commercial district in particular. In addition to the mosque, the brief for the project called for a shopping complex, office space for the use of religious, political and cultural organizations, research facilities and exhibition space. Although the idea of a mosque with dependencies is a familiar one, in this case the chosen shape of the building as a mosque was without precedent.

The idea for a central mosque was first proposed in 1959 by Abdul Latif Bawany, a Pakistani industrialist and philanthropist. His idea was supported by other leading industrial and political figures, notably Major-General Umrao Khan, then Martial Law Administrator.[49] Funding for the mosque was provided entirely by the local community under the direction of the Islamic Foundation of Bangladesh

(Opposite) The axial approach from the south to the Bait ul-Mukarram (1986) in Dhaka is along a centrally located pool; this layout, conceived by Abdul Hossain Thariani, harks back to formal garden schemes of the Mughal Empire.

(Right and below) Ground-floor plan of the Bait ul-Mukarram, which is set in the central business district of the city, and site plan.

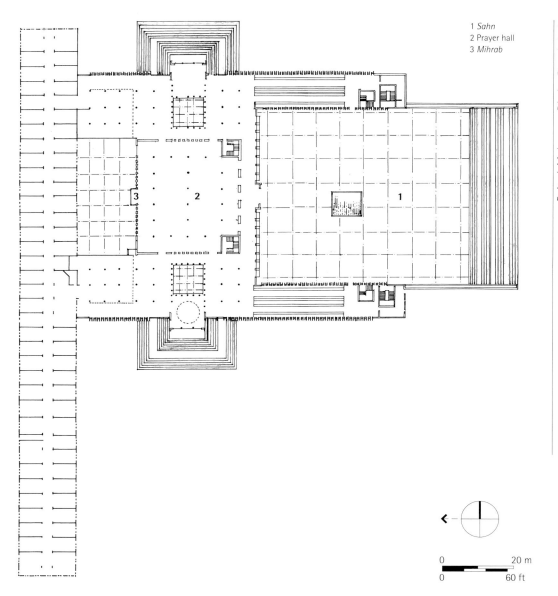

1 *Sahn*
2 Prayer hall
3 *Mihrab*

0   20 m
0   60 ft

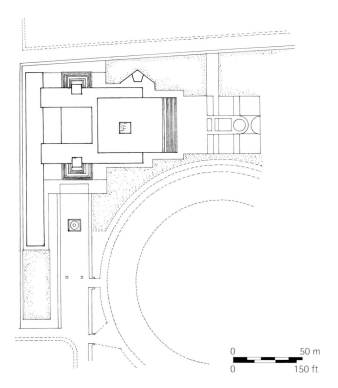

0   50 m
0   150 ft

and the Mosque Planning Committee, made up for the most part of industrialists and presided over by G.A. Madani, Commissioner of the Department of Works, Housing & Settlement of East Pakistan.

Construction began in 1960 and the mosque itself was completed and handed over to the community in 1963. The building of the other parts of the complex progressed gradually as funds and site became available, and work was completed in 1986. The project was overseen by the architect Abdul Hossain Thariani from Karachi until 1971, at which time the Directorate of Architecture of the newly formed state of Bangladesh took over the final construction phase. Trained in India, Thariani had one of the largest practices in the country with offices in West and East Pakistan.

The design was inspired by the form of the Ka'ba in Mecca, a choice apparently determined by a desire to give Muslims unable make the *Hajj* a tangible impression of the shrine.[50] In formal design terms, the eventuality of later high-rise development in the commercial district was taken into account, and the cubic form chosen for the structure

205

(Left) The mosque seen from the south gate.

(Below) The men's ablutions area, located at ground level.

(Bottom) Steps up to the south entrance, echoing the access on the north side.

(Opposite) The men's prayer hall is arranged on two levels connected by a mezzanine and a central well, and covered by an elongated dome.

(Below) In the main prayer hall of the Bait ul-Mukarram the *mihrab* is located on the mezzanine, which is supported by slim tapered columns.

was considered to provide an effective solution by which visual parity between the new mosque and its built-up surroundings could be achieved.

The site of the mosque is bounded on three sides by major avenues, and on the fourth by a large stadium. Approaching the mosque from the south, visitors pass under a structure of freestanding arches leading to a long processional pathway with a pool and fountains. The main entrance is on the east side, preceded by a 60,000 sq. ft (5,600 sq. m) *sahn*, above ground-floor level, which serves to accommodate any overflow of worshippers, as do the two other open spaces located at the north and south entrances. In addition to its planned use, the open space on the south side serves as an area for various activities ranging from political rallies to religious and socio-cultural events. The north and south verandahs give access to the prayer hall by way of a small colonnaded courtyard. The mosque as built has no minaret, despite the fact that the architectural plans show several possible locations for one.

The mosque itself, having a total floor area of 60,000 sq. ft (5,600 sq. m), rises five storeys above the rest of the complex.. On the first two floors are the men's prayer halls, connected by a mezzanine and a central balustraded well which allows a view of the dome at first-floor level, where the *mihrab* is located. The prayer halls are supported by slim, tapering mushroom columns, at the top of which artificial lighting fixtures have been installed. Natural light filters through the narrow elongated windows on the (west) *qibla* wall. The upper three floors are built around an interior central court open to the sky; these spaces are intended for undisturbed meditation and for use by religious groups. A women's prayer hall 4,500 sq. ft (430 sq. m) in area is located on the second floor on the north side, with separate entrance and ablutions facilities, as well as a women's centre. The men's ablutions facilities are located below.

The structure is a reinforced-concrete post-and-lintel system with brick infill. The distance between the columns was determined by the need to provide for a variety of functions at different floor-levels. The entire complex is painted white (as an expression of purity) with horizontal black bands (symbolizing tranquillity) as the sole exterior ornamentation of the mosque. The overall effect is one of functional simplicity in a modernist 1960s idiom, as is the structure and the detailing. Another symbolic element conceived by the architect was inherent in the height of the mosque, which measures 99 ft from the floor of the *mihrab*, corresponding to the ninety-nine Names of Allah.

In the Bait ul-Mukarram complex the bazaar (with 305 shops and 22 warehouses) is located on the ground floor; the income from this, combined with rents from office space, provides a largely sufficient revenue to provide for the maintenance of the mosque and its institutions. The activities which take place in the complex, as well as its location in a bustling commercial area, contribute to making Bait ul-Mukarram one of the most highly frequented of the city's mosques. In creating a multi-functional complex

around the mosque to encompass a multitude of everyday activities, embodying 'the all-embracing tenets of Islam' and highlighting the notion of 'unity' in the monolithic structure, the architect was inspired by traditional urban situations in which the mosque serves as the physical centre of all aspects of daily life. Yet, in the shaping of the mosque itself he departed radically from tradition. Direct formal reference to the most sacred shrine in Islam, the Ka'ba, had always been avoided in the past, whatever the location of a mosque. The unique quality of the Ka'ba as the *omphalos* of the Muslim world had precluded its use as a model for buildings elsewhere. The fact that Thariani chose to make such a direct reference, albeit on a totally different scale, indicates the existence of an almost complete rupture between the sense of the sacred in pre-modern Islam and its purposeful contemporary reinvention.

Al-Ghadir Mosque, Tehran, Iran

No less dramatically than Bait ul-Mukarram, this mosque in Tehran,[51] designed by Jahangir Mazlum, manifests another concerted attempt to reinterpret the sacred. In this case the architect has introduced polyhedral forms which had previously been associated solely with funerary buildings.[52] This crossing of symbolic boundaries seems not to have been noticed either by the community or by the architect. To the community this was a new design solution, albeit with an unfamiliar 'dome' form; from the architect's standpoint mausoleum architecture was simply a reservoir of forms, stripped of their original meanings.

Like Mohamed Makiya in his design for the Khulafa Mosque in Baghdad (see Chapter 3), Jahangir Mazlum had to deal with a site of restricted dimensions; the Al-Ghadir Mosque is also in polyhedral form and features patterned brickwork, though the result is very different. The mosque was commissioned in 1977 by a group of local benefactors who proposed to finance the construction of a religious complex for their neighbourhood community, with men's and women's prayer halls, a covered courtyard (atrium), library, amphitheatre, classrooms, office space and social facilities. The scheme met with some initial resistance from members of the local community who would have preferred a more traditional design for a mosque with minaret(s) and dome, but the architect's alternative concept was eventually realized in 1987.

Located on the busy Mirdamad Boulevard in an affluent neighbourhood of Tehran, the mosque is surrounded by modern residential and institutional buildings. The prayer hall is situated on the boulevard and connected to the social facilities and an atrium on the north side by an internal stairwell. The atrium, a space of transition between areas having different functions, was conceived and designed as a covered courtyard. A small building for social services is situated to one side of the main entrance to the prayer hall on the boulevard.

The twelve-sided prayer hall is raised above street level; the tallest part of the structure, it measures 15.20 m (50 ft)

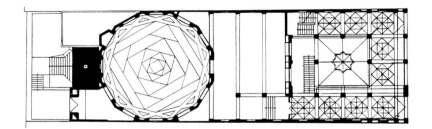

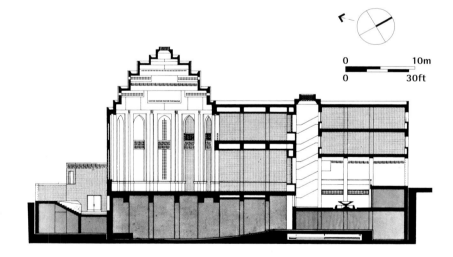

Al-Ghadir Mosque (1987), Tehran, by Jahangir Mazlum.

(Top) The entrance portal and the externally expressed *mihrab* at the corner of the site.

(Above) Plan and section of the 12-sided prayer hall and separate block for social facilities on the right. The section shows the stepped domical profile of the men's prayer hall, and the women's gallery; the social spaces on the left are arranged around a covered atrium, and an amphitheatre is located directly below the prayer hall.

(Top) The exterior view of the superstructure shows the projecting *mihrab* and decreasing, rotating squares serving as a substitute for a conventional domical vault. Calligraphic inscriptions in brick are a prominent decorative feature.

(Above) Calligraphy in square Kufic script continues the programme of ornament developed for the mosque into the amphitheatre below.

(Opposite) The tall narrow dome chamber of the Al-Ghadir Mosque is reminiscent of pre-modern memorial buildings found in the Tehran region.

across and fills the entire width of the site, accommodating about 80 worshippers. Additional space for prayer is provided in a triple-bayed annexe which includes a mezzanine for women worshippers. Externally, the prayer hall and entrance are visually related to the street, and the mosque is identified by the protruding *mihrab* in the *qibla* wall which is clearly visible to passers-by. On entering the mosque, worshippers are made gradually aware of the *qibla* wall on their left, through a visual progression of space. As with the exterior, the interior is rendered with brick revetment and highlighted with tile inserts bearing verses from the Qu'ran referring to the relationship of God and mankind.

The architectural form as a whole evolved from the inside out. This resulted from several considerations: the need on the part of the architect (and the community) to express the *qibla* and reconcile it with the difficult orientation and dimensions of the site; the desire to create an upward focus in the building; and the need to embody fundamental Shiite tenets such as the belief in the Twelve Imams, symbolically expressed through the dodecagonal form.[53] The polygonal form also resolves the problem of providing the means to orient at least one of the walls to face Mecca. In practice, however, this arrangement is awkward, as a direct view of the *mihrab* is not available to male worshippers in the bays or to women in the mezzanine.

The visual focus towards the heavens is accentuated by the roof form and the fragmentation of the interior surfaces of the prayer hall. The manner of interpreting the roof is a particularly original aspect of the design. The architect has adapted the basic dome form to produce a series of rotated superimposed and diminishing squares. The 'dome' is no longer treated as an arch rotating through 360°, but rather a geometric form that is abstracted from the squinches and multiplied in layers to form a dome-like covering. Thus, the corners are divested of their traditional structural purpose, and are treated simply as formal elements. The traditional Iranian dome has thus been reinterpreted in reinforced concrete and steel using contemporary technology.

'Another notable design feature in the al-Ghadir Mosque is the highly patterned brickwork through which the mosque distinguishes itself from its surroundings. It is derived from Iranian building ornamentation traditions, yet differs from them radically. The epigraphic program here has been rendered within the visual culture of its own time: posters, banners and massive revolutionary inscriptions. It covers the surfaces almost entirely, overwhelming the viewer with its insistent presence. Without being clear and legible, its scale, nevertheless, battles for attention successfully with the signs, movement and distractions of the modern street.'[54]

Objections can legitimately be raised concerning the architect's use of funerary forms in the mosque, and equally the extensive inscription programme has been criticized for overwhelming the structure, as if it were an object covered with textile. The repetitive nature of the surface decoration does not make it more easily legible.[55] Nevertheless, the high

(Above) View into the apex of the prayer hall;
the calligraphic and geometric ornament
executed in brick is illuminated by a central
brass chandelier.

(Right) The women's gallery, providing a partial
view of the *mihrab*.

quality of the brick revetment and its consistent use as a feature of the building, as well as the competent resolution of the persistent 'new' dome problem, make al-Ghadir one of the best and most interesting examples of contemporary mosque design appropriate to a confined urban setting.

Those wishing to build new mosques in towns and cities having a majority Muslim population may be faced with a variety of problems – such as financial, social or design considerations – before realizing their aims. Sometimes a proposed new building may be associated with a particular Muslim group, but in general it is not necessary for it to proclaim a Muslim presence. In other situations such as those in which a recently established Muslim community sets out to build a mosque, the group involved will be faced with a different set of problems. Here, the community has an additional and perhaps a different range of concerns, involving notions of self-presentation and representation, issues of acclimatization, integration or even absorption into the new setting. The community mosques in, for example, Europe and North America present an interesting series of experiments in both architectural and social terms. Thus, the buildings of immigrant groups often present architectural and social problems both for the newcomers and for the existing inhabitants.

East London and Brick Lane Mosques, London, UK

The expansion of the Muslim community in the London borough of Tower Hamlets is illustrated by the establishment of the East London Mosque in Whitechapel Road and the Brick Lane Mosque, Spitalfields, both of which serve mainly immigrants from Bangladesh. The Brick Lane Mosque was originally a Huguenot chapel built in 1742, later used as a synagogue by an orthodox Jewish society from 1895; in 1970 it was bought and converted into a mosque. Little was done to change its exterior (Georgian) character, but in 1985, encouraged by a visit by President Ershad of Bangladesh, the interior was substantially refurbished. New galleries were added, the pews were removed and the prayer areas were doubled in size to accommodate 1,200 worshippers. This change 'offended local [white] conservationists and highlighted the different approaches to the building. . . . No planning permission was required from the local authority but local conservationists protested at the way in which the refurbishment was undertaken. . . . Yet despite the growing power of the conservationist lobby the mosque's management committee was able legally to change the interior of the building to accommodate more worshippers.'[56]

In the case of the nearby East London Mosque, a strikingly different approach was adopted in order to represent the Muslim community's presence. It is a purpose-built structure designed by a London firm of architects and featuring easily recognizable elements such as a golden dome, an Iranian-style entrance portico, and minarets reminiscent of those overlooking the Ka'ba. The building had a £2 million (approx. US$3.25 million) budget, of which over half was funded by King Fahd of Saudi Arabia. The mosque committee (which included the Saudi Arabian Ambassador in London) was determined from the outset to remind local people of the building's religious function.[57] The regular broadcasting of the *adhan* from the minaret five times a day caused adverse reactions in the immediate neighbourhood and became the subject of much coverage in the local press. The controversy of how the building was used distracted most people from commenting on its basic architecture although, somewhat surprisingly, criticism did come from a few British Muslims, e.g. in the journal *MuslimWise*: '. . . when the consummation of the "Islamic" and the "regional vernacular styles" took place it gave birth to new and exciting art forms . . . Indigenous non-Muslims who look in horror at the dome-capped buildings we are erecting are as alien to them as they are to us. A good example of such a monstrosity is the East London Mosque in Whitechapel. It is a cold, characterless and impractical "word-processor" which is neither aesthetically nor spiritually attractive.'[58] Although this represents an extreme view, it is true that, despite the fact that the building is not a significant architectural statement, it is competently designed.

The emergence of mosques in London's 'East End' generated a wide debate amongst Muslims and non-Muslims alike – a phenomenon noticeable in many situations in the West where Muslims have formed communities relatively recently.[59]

The case of the establishment of Muslim communities in the United States serves well to illustrate these processes at work towards the end of the twentieth century. The first wave of Muslim immigrants in the late nineteenth and early twentieth century have been assimilated into the greater American society. Islamic organizations, such as those incorporated in 1914 in Michigan City, Indiana, consisting predominantly of Syrian and Lebanese immigrants,[60] were formed. For the most part new communities would rent halls for Friday prayers and other purposes, but the first purpose-built mosques, such as those in Michigan City (1924) and Cedar Rapids, Iowa (1929), date from this first influx, and were located mainly in the American industrial heartland. A Muslim presence only began to assert itself in North America on a larger scale, particularly in major urban centres, in the 1950s. Then, spurred on by representatives of Islamic countries, such complexes as the Islamic Center in Washington, DC (see Chapter 6), were constructed. Many of the mosque designs of that period reveal clear references to historical models in the Islamic world, and are neither innovative nor particularly significant architecturally. There are, however, a few contemporary mosque buildings that have broadened the architectural vocabulary and added to the symbolic discourse about place, identity and modernity among Muslims.

Dar al-Islam, Abiquiu, New Mexico, USA

The planned community of Dar al-Islam (House of Islam) was created as a centre for North American Muslims, many of them recent converts, to bring them into contact with each other and to educate them in the ritual and tenets of Islam. Its founders also intended it to serve as a model for future Muslim communities in North America. In a curious way the settlement, located in the countryside and isolated from other communities, is reminiscent of the communes which emerged in the United States in the late 1960s and 1970s. The settlement, designed by Hassan Fathy, is architecturally significant; the only building in North America to represent his philosophy of architecture, it reflects the spirit and values that were manifested in his project for New Gourna in Egypt (see Chapter 3), and has sometimes been regarded as a continuation of the same experiment.

The idea for the Dar al-Islam Foundation was conceived in 1978, when Nuridin Durkee, an American Muslim, met Sahl Kabbani, a Saudi Arabian engineer and industrialist who had studied in the United States. Durkee, who was studying in Mecca at the time, was concerned by the educational and socio-economic problems facing American Muslims who found themselves isolated from Islamic centres and denied the benefits of fundamental Islamic social structures. His concern was shared by Kabbani, and the two men decided to commit themselves to founding an Islamic Center in North America which could at the same time serve the purpose of introducing Islam in a tangible way to people of other faiths. The same year, Durkee's wife met the Princesses Moothie

and Johara, daughters of King Khaled of Saudi Arabia, who were likewise interested in the project and agreed to fund the search for a suitable site; they also brought the project to the attention of their father, who offered to donate money to buy the land.

Nuridin Durkee's own researches into the historical and contemporary architecture of minority Muslim communities led him to the conclusion that the traditional Muslim way of life tended to thrive particularly well in the context of rural villages where traditional crafts were also practised, and that Islam tended to take root readily in certain types of geographical environment. His findings were to be a crucial factor in the siting and conception of the new settlement. The search was restricted to the southwest of the United States, and a site in New Mexico was finally selected, located in the Chama Valley, close to the old Native American village of Abiquiu, near Santa Fe. Durkee has cited the principal reasons for this particular choice as being the topographical similarities of the site to various regions of the Muslim world present and past, such as Arabia, North Africa and Andalusia, and because of its proximity to areas with a strong tradition of Spanish-American and American Indian cultures, where he felt the local inhabitants were likely to be more receptive to a community such as Dar al-Islam than would be those with an Anglo-Saxon background.[60] Durkee had also opted for adobe as the main construction material, since it was already widely used in the region. He saw the use of adobe as being a tradition introduced by Spanish settlers, and one which ultimately had Andalusian roots.

The Dar al-Islam Foundation (1981), Abiquiu, NM, designed by Hassan Fathy. An aerial view of the settlement (above) shows the mosque set at an angle to the bulk of the complex. The mud-brick mosque, seen in its desert setting (opposite), was built by members of the Muslim community under the supervision of Nubian masons brought specially by the architect to New Mexico.

When the time came to choose an architect, Durkee and Kabbani approached Hassan Fathy about the project.[61] Even though Fathy had become famous by then, he had not been successful in promoting mud-brick construction and the use of vernacular idioms in his own homeland, Egypt, where both were too closely identified with poverty; hence adobe was regarded by the middleclass as a lowly material used only by peasants who could not afford anything better, and was also often rejected by the peasants themselves. The project thus provided Fathy with another opportunity of designing for a community, but this time in a more receptive environment. The client and user in this instance are one and the same – those involved were generally well travelled and educated, and in this respect were more akin to Fathy's private clients than to his institutional or governmental ones.

Fathy immediately took to the idea and agreed to draw up the master plan without fee.[62] It was further agreed that he would come to New Mexico in the summer of 1981, once the preliminary site work was completed, in order to teach the Dar al-Islam community how to build domes and vaults using traditional Nubian techniques. For this purpose, he brought with him two Nubian masons who worked for him regularly; they demonstrated the techniques in a workshop as the mosque was built.[63] With the help of participating community members who assisted by fetching and carrying the bricks, the masons completed the construction of the mosque, albeit on previously prepared foundations, in what must surely be a record time of two weeks.

The design of the mosque is simple and compact. It is based on the modular repetition of single domed cells and the use of other Nubian architectural forms such as the catenary vault, arch and cupola, all of which make up the basic vocabulary of Fathy's work. The domed cell is the basic spatial unit in Nubian mosques, tombs and domestic space – the dome being understood as the 'vault of heaven'. The construction of vaults originally had the purely practical function of supporting each dome, but Fathy developed them with openings decorated with claustras allowing light to filter into the interior. The clarity of the plan is evident from the façades. Hierarchy of space and function from west to east is expressed externally in elevation, and the south and west elevations are particularly coherent. The intersection of the *qibla* and *mihrab* axes is accorded dynamic symbolic emphasis in the dome over the *mihrab* niche and functional importance by the distribution of the prayer chambers, that for men being parallel to the *qibla* wall and the one for women being located on the *mihrab* axis.

Although Fathy had experimented with poured concrete and notably with the folded concrete slab while working in Greece with Doxiadis Associates (1957–62), he avoided the use of concrete technology in Dar al-Islam, except for the foundations. Otherwise, the entire construction was to be carried out in mud brick, a material that is well-suited to hot and arid climates, though it had some drawbacks in New Mexico, where snow and rainfall are frequent. Because of this, regular maintenance of the buildings would be more

(Below) Dar al-Islam: an interior view of the mosque showing the principal dome lit from above.

critical than in, say, Egypt. In the United States adobe construction is also more costly than poured concrete and, as a result, Fathy's 'reverse technology' applied in Abiquiu turned out to be rather an expensive venture. Materials and techniques which had evolved out of practical and economic necessities in one country had become a luxury in another. As Wael al-Masri has pointed out in his study of American Islamic Centres, '. . . the view of the essentialist nature of Islamic Architecture by both architect and the founders of the communities may be seen to reflect an . . . adoption of long established Western ideas of Islamic and Islamic Architecture as timeless and unchanging'.[64]

Fathy's master plan for Dar al-Islam underwent many revisions for reasons which remain unclear – at least one of these was attributable to El-Wakil and another to other Fathy protégés. In spite of this, the project undoubtedly represents a 'symbolic triumph', as James Steele has put it,[65] as a synthesis of the utopian ideals that led Fathy to become involved in the earlier and less successful projects at New Gourna and Bariz in Egypt. The intense media coverage that accompanied the building of the mosque earned him a far wider audience than any of his previous designs had ever done. This, and the recognition bestowed on Fathy through international awards,[66] made Dar al-Islam an important breakthrough both on the international architectural scene and in Egypt, where architects were finally having to take him and his 'reverse technology' seriously.[66] The essentially utopian experimental community of Dar al-Islam continued to grow and operate into the early 1990s, but gradually its members dispersed (including Durkee, who went to Cairo to pursue his Islamic studies at Al-Azhar University), leaving behind a shell of a community with a small number of 'caretakers' – a situation that Fathy did not live to see.

The Dar al-Islam community differs significantly from most other Muslim communities in that it is isolated and does not constitute an element within a larger neighbourhood. In many instances the Muslims tend to live in concentrated groups, one of the most significant examples of this recent social phenomenon in the United States being the African-American or Black Muslims in cities such as Philadelphia and New York. Their communities often take over a local shop and run it as a neighbourhood mosque and meeting place. These so-called 'shopfront' mosques can represent the first stage in a particular community's expression of establishment; on the other hand, they can also be viewed as evidence of the direct way in which religions interact within the community.[67] The Sunni Black American Muslims and the old Nation of Islam have undergone a political and social transition by reasserting their African identity. In major cities like Chicago, Philadelphia and Atlanta, African-American Muslims have established their own centres, to which other Muslims do not go to pray. Hence this ethnic division of Muslim groups continues to give rise to separate congregational spaces, each with its own identity.

However, as Sulayman Nyang has noted: 'The identity question is central to the Muslim presence in the United States. The American Muslim can maintain his identity only by holding steadfastly to the rope of *tawhid* (unity of Allah). . . . Though Muslims differ on some of the burning issues of American society, their sense of unity is evident in their common faith in *tawhid*, in their collective practice of Muslim rituals and in the expression of solidarity on matters affecting Muslims living in America.'[68]

The increasing manifestation of Muslim presence in North America can be seen in the building of mosques. Yvonne Haddad, who has studied many Muslim congregations in the USA, has found in them the desire for community expression. As she noted, in the context of second- and third-generation Muslims in Toledo, Ohio: 'There is a great deal of breaking away from tradition. Building a structure like the Toledo Mosque is a way for Moslems to celebrate themselves and not to hide anymore. It's a matter of pride.'[69]

Taric Islamic Centre, Toronto, Canada

In the case of the most significant mosques built in North America for community clients since the 1970s, each particular client has been represented by an association. Often an easily identifiable building with overt dome and minaret is requested, but sometimes the architect and client are able to agree on a design for a modern mosque, as in the case of the Taric Islamic Centre (1991). Here, the architect, Loghman Azar, an Iranian Canadian, produced a rectangular brick-clad building, forming the first phase of the project. This community hall was also used as a prayer hall pending the construction of the mosque itself. In order to lend the simple shed an 'Islamic character', he created a pointed arch on the surface with a *muqarnas* design articulated in coloured tiles. The interior is more elaborate. The second phase of the project – the mosque and ancillary services – went out to tender in 1996. Located in an urban situation overlooking a major road, the Taric Islamic Centre proclaims the presence of the Muslim community without resorting to the use of an alien form.

(Below) The Taric Islamic Centre, Toronto, by Loghman Azar. The first phase, completed in 1991, consists of a community hall which is also used for prayer. The exterior façade of the rectangular hall is patterned with arches and windows, and the *mihrab*-like protrusion is in fact a stage.

(Bottom) Site plan showing the existing community hall and the layout for the mosque and ancillary buildings to be completed in the second construction phase.

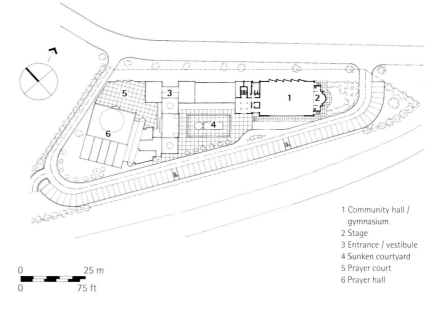

0   25 m
0   75 ft

1 Community hall / gymnasium
2 Stage
3 Entrance / vestibule
4 Sunken courtyard
5 Prayer court
6 Prayer hall

ISNA Islamic Center, Plainfield, Indiana, USA

Another kind of community is represented by the Islamic Students of North America (ISNA), founded in 1981, which incorporates older groups such as the Muslim Students Association and the Muslim Community Association.[70] ISNA provides a forum for Muslims to discuss all aspects of Islam and also publishes a number of periodicals.

The decision to build an Islamic community centre (often called the Islamic Center of North America, or ICNA) in Plainfield, Indiana, was taken in 1979 by the then Muslim Students Association. The project was designed by Gulzar Haider, a professor of architecture in Ontario, while the construction drawings were prepared by the associated architect (the architect of record), Mukhtar Khalil of Dana Architects & Planners of Chicago. The building was finally completed in 1983. Haider had by the 1990s established a reputation as perhaps the leading designer of mosques in North America – much in the way El-Wakil has come to be regarded in the Middle East. Haider, a Pakistani from Lahore, studied at the University of Illinois, where he obtained his M.Arch in 1969 before taking up a teaching post in Canada. He became involved in the Muslim Students Association and had designed a number of mosques as student projects, including a modernist entry for the Islamabad National Mosque competition.[71] His views on mosque design seem to have been modified later following a sabbatical (1977–8) in Saudi Arabia where he became aware of 'destructive and alienating forces of architecture' present in the modernist and imported designs.[72]

Haider was asked to design the ISNA Center to occupy an 84-acre (34-hectare) site and to incorporate in it a mosque

(Below and opposite) The mosque for the Islamic Society of North America (1983), designed by Gulzar Haider: detail of the protruding *mihrab*, and the main entrance. Shafts of sunlight stream into the prayer area through the circular window openings.

for up to 500 worshippers, a research library, offices for the headquarters of a school and dormitory accommodation for 500 short-term residents, staff housing for seven families, as well as recreational and outdoor facilities. This ambitious project was, however, not fully realized: only the mosque facilities (but not the proposed freestanding minaret) and the library have been built.[73]

The building is set in a landscaped area approached from a formal entrance plaza, and is divided into three sections: the mosque and offices (on one axis), and the library (on a perpendicular axis). No clear indications are provided on the solid brick-clad exterior to suggest the nature of the building's uses. The slit and circular windows provide glimpses of another world within, the idea being to express the concepts of *al-Batin* (Hidden) and *al-Zahir* (Manifest).[74] Haider has stated that: 'I chose to distinguish the exterior from the interior. I chose to veil this mosque. As a designer I invoked the need for meaningful and purposeful dissimulation.'[75]

The plan and three-dimensional spatial arrangement are derived from geometric principles associated with the square, octagon and circle. The octagon of the mosque is covered by a dome. Its abstract geometry and the use of light and shade achieved by high openings are reminiscent of the approach to modern design adopted by Louis Kahn.[76] The successful manipulation of interior space and the combining of mystical themes with Western design ideas to express a modern Muslim identity mark the building as one of the few examples of its kind in the USA – one that does not resort to any easy adaptation of historic or vernacular architectures from the Islamic world. (In this it has much in common with Kamran Diba's buildings in Iran.) 'ICNA is one of the significant examples of Islamic community centres in America because [it] is . . . justified by a narrative that essentializes [*sic*] architectural concepts, as well as by considerable understanding of the past from the perspective of the concrete circumstances of the present.'[77]

Looking back at the project in 1991, Haider made a telling remark: '[It] remains an enigma, especially to those Muslims who are used to seeing mosques and not praying in them.

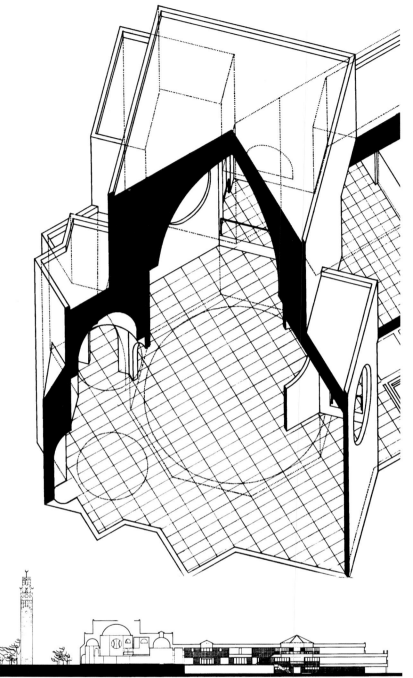

(Top) Axonometric projection of the prayer hall, revealing its geometric order and the insistent verticality in the treatment of interior space.

(Above and left) Section of the ISNA complex and an interpretive drawing by the architect, based on carpet and garden designs, to explore the overlapping geometric organization in relation to the progression of spaces in the ISNA layout as a whole.

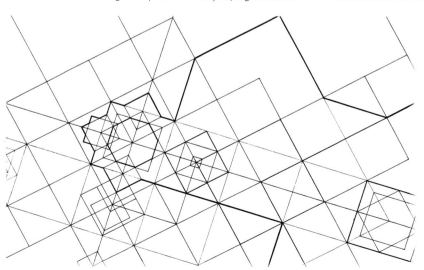

Those who have been inside are struck by the "mosqueness" of it all. It is fascinating [to note] that the clients who were very proud of their building a decade ago have now started to express what a Freudian [analyst] might diagnose as a "dome and minaret envy."'[78]

University of Arkansas Mosque, Jonesboro, Arkansas, USA

It may have been his experience with ISNA and the nature of his new client that caused Gulzar Haider to design a more 'normative' mosque for students of the University of Arkansas in Jonesboro. The mosque was commissioned in 1982 by the Saudi Arabian Department of Customs and the design was approved by its Deputy Minister. University representatives were also involved in the design approval process. The architects of record are Haider's associated firm for the project, Brackett Ktennerich and Associates based in Jonesboro. The project was completed in 1984.

In this building traditional Arabian red-and-white striped masonry, employed on the walls as well as on the entrance portal, is combined with a version of the Ottoman-style minaret. A bold brick frieze incorporating Qur'anic verses in Kufic epigraphy decorates the exterior. Nader Ardalan has pointed out that: 'The mosque design was very influenced by the cultural origins of the congregation, for it is of a Saudi Arabian style . . .'.[79]

Thus, the design transplants an alien architectural style into the region – something that Haider did not consider

The Islamic Center at Arkansas State University (1984), Jonesboro, by Gulzar Haider. The building features the use of red and white striped brickwork that is visually reminiscent of the treatment of stone architecture in Syria.

(Left) A view into the small entrance courtyard.

appropriate in his earlier work – and furthermore it did not correspond with his commitment to Islamic ideals that are not stylistic, nor indeed with his own interpretation of Islam. This building can therefore be regarded as marking the architect's entry into the realm of pan-Islamic designs in order to satisfy his client's wishes.

Bait ul-Islam, Maple, Toronto, Ontario, Canada

A third mosque designed by Gulzar Haider is that for the Canadian National Headquarters of the Ahmadiyya Movement in Islam,[80] an immigrant community which commissioned the Bait ul-Islam in 1987; construction started in 1989 and the building was opened in 1992. The project consists of the mosque, three offices and a small crèche. (The client owns other buildings in which social and administrative facilities are housed.) The men's prayer hall, measuring 80 x 60 ft (24.38 x 18.30 m) can accommodate up to 720 worshippers. A mezzanine is used by visitors and as an overflow space for prayer. An elegant feature, and the most successful part of the building, is the pattern of openings by which the interior of the prayer hall is filled with dappled light. A separate well-defined entrance leads to a women's prayer hall of equal size on the level below. This is one of the very rare instances in which the women's prayer hall is the same size as the men's. The architect opted for a historicist design in order to give the community a sense of established 'roots' and legitimacy through an eclectic mix of Mamluk dome, monumental Yemeni minaret, and internal spaces formed by columns and arches. Despite being an imposing edifice, this skilfully designed building is less convincing than the ISNA Islamic Center in terms of innovative or contemporary architectural design.

(Opposite) The interior of the prayer hall in the University of Arkansas Mosque, and a detail of the exterior brickwork and the slit windows.

(Below) The Bait ul-Islam (1992), Toronto, Ontario, by Gulzar Haider: general view; steps leading to the separate entrance of the women's prayer hall; and the interior of the men's prayer hall.

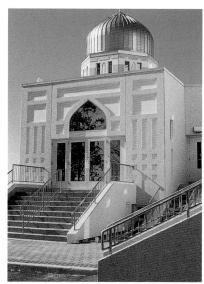

(Below) The Islamic Centre (1996), Kingston, Ontario, by Gulzar Haider. This building, rooted in the Canadian regional vernacular, features a three-stage tower that serves as a minaret signalling the presence of a Muslim community in the area.

(Bottom) Section and plan of the mosque and community hall (on the left) which can be used as overflow space for prayer. The main prayer hall has a protruding *mihrab*, and the women's prayer area is located in the centre (defined by a series of columns).

(Opposite) A view of the *mihrab* (above), in the form of a light tower, as seen from the women's prayer area. The steel structure of the main hall (below), featuring backward-sloping supports, is not only architecturally dramatic but also combines the original notion of a hypostyle hall with the local precedent of timber-framed barn construction.

Islamic Centre, Kingston, Ontario, Canada

The Kingston Islamic Centre is Haider's fourth mosque project in North America. The Centre, opened in 1996, stands on the site of a former slaughterhouse barn in a recently developed suburb to the north of the old city. The client, the building committee of the Islamic Society of Kingston (mainly composed of members of Queen's University), approached Haider as an architect already well known for his mosque designs. The results of the first design phase, begun in 1988, underwent numerous alterations. The architect of record, legally responsible for the work, was Mustafa Master of Domus Architects in Toronto. Problems arose as a result of disagreements between the architects and the building committee regarding both the construction design details and the costing of the project. As in the case of many such community mosques, there was a severe discrepancy between the funds available at the outset (around $50,000) and the demands of the design brief which suggested a building costing at least ten times as much, and the community eventually had to raise $900,000 to complete the work. Despite these difficulties, however, the mosque still reflects Haider's original concept; it was opened in February 1996, and was completed (with the addition of the minaret) some months later.

From the inception of the project the architects wanted 'to do a simple one level floor plan and express various activities within the space through light modulation and roof shape . . . [in] a building that will not only reflect its past but now serve the . . . spiritual and communal needs of a mostly immigrant community whose following generations will want to be at home in Canada'.[81] The design process entailed a dialogue between the architects, the contractor and the community's executive committee which, unusually, had active women members. The women managed to ensure that there would be a single entrance to the mosque, so avoiding the separation of men from women on arrival, and that women would pray on the same level as the men, rather than be allocated space in a mezzanine or in a basement area; as a compromise it was agreed, however, that the women would pray behind the men.[82] This solution is particularly relevant for Muslims in a more traditional Islamic setting where new forms and *mores* are developing. When it became clear that the community could not afford the building it wanted, the Government of Ontario was approached for financial assistance; but this could not be granted for a purely religious building. The scheme was then modified as a community social centre with an attached prayer space, and as a result it became eligible to receive government aid. At the time of its opening the building was used by about 100 worshippers for Friday prayers, but can accommodate up to 300 people.

Haider's scheme for a building on one level – a shed recalling the barns and indigenous architecture of the region – was well suited to the notion of a community hall. The mosque was designed over the existing slab of the old slaughterhouse, allowing for a change to conform with the

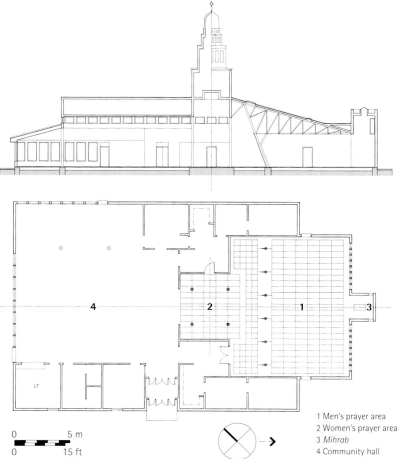

0   5 m
0   15 ft

1 Men's prayer area
2 Women's prayer area
3 *Mihrab*
4 Community hall

qibla orientation. The entrance area in the centre divides the building into two zones: the community facilities on one side and the prayer hall on the other. On festive occasions such as Eid the doors in the partition separating the two areas can be opened to unify the whole interior space. In section, the building can be read as a simple metal-covered shed, but the interior is more complex with a number of different kinds of spaces. The prayer hall itself contains five inclined columns, only 8 ft (2.44 m) apart, that develop into cantilever trusses reminiscent of tree trunks and serve as visual markers separating the women's prayer area from the men's. The backward slope of the columns is not only a dramatic aesthetic move, but also recalls the form of timber structures of the region. Above the women's prayer area in the centre of the building is a square minaret-tower supported by four columns. The tower is topped by a small fibreglass dome; the one clear use of an easily recognizable Islamic architectural feature. The *mihrab* takes the form of a simple light tower (8 x 8 x 16 ft / 2.44 x 2.44 x 4.58 m) with a single oculus to the sky, and in the *qibla* wall there are two slit windows that permit the *mihrab* niche to be bathed with natural light.

Of Haider's four mosque designs for clients in North America, this building is, in both cultural and constructional terms, closest to the characteristic features of its regional surroundings, introducing an innovative new direction for mosque architecture in Canada. An ambivalence remains, however, between his modernist building for ISNA and his historicist designs, reflecting the varied nature of Muslim community clients in America.

The representations of Islam described above reinforce cultural stereotypes through their respective architectural styles, both to Muslims themselves and to the people with whom the communities share their physical surroundings. For example, the modern low-cost and innovative Islamic Center in Albuquerque, New Mexico (1986–92), designed by the architect Bart Prince, was heavily criticized by Muslims in the area for 'having no sense of identity, no minarets, no dome'.[83] Soon after its completion, the local Muslim community planned an addition to the building which would provide 'traditional' elements, including a towering minaret. Zeynep Çelik has noted that Islamic cultures in the West 'continue to display themselves according to images drawn through the eyes of others, with references that rely heavily on nineteenth-century legacies and that broadcast simultaneously old and new value systems. This complex and multilayered dialectic – within each culture and between cultures – may play the most important role in the rapidly changing cultural definitions of the twentieth century.'[84] And although there are numerous examples of modern buildings to be found both in the West and in the Islamic world, at the end of the twentieth century one is conscious of the 'historicist lobby' gaining greater credence in the design of new mosques.

Chapter 6

Representative Islamic Centres in the West

Mosques built as symbolic statements of Muslim presence in the West, as distinct from those built by communities for normal everyday use, are usually found in capitals or other cosmopolitan cities. Such major projects are funded and commissioned by the diplomatic or other leading overseas representatives of Muslim states, and the buildings serve as important manifestations of common identity for a diverse group with different origins and backgrounds living within a foreign and non-Islamic cultural context. In this sense major Islamic centres fulfil the role of ambassadors of Muslim countries even more than do their official representative buildings, the embassies.

Projects for mosques expressing a Muslim presence in non-Muslim countries started to take shape in the 1950s, coinciding with the establishment of independent states in the Islamic world. With the rise of nationalism came a growing sense of an 'Islamic identity' which began to be expressed in the 1960s in a large number of state mosques and other major mosques built by governments as symbols of Islamic nationhood, such as the King Faisal Masjid in Islamabad, the Masjid Negara in Kuala Lumpur, and the Istiqlal Mosque in Jakarta (see Chapter 2).

The former longstanding colonial associations, however, that had existed between countries like England and India, France and Algeria and Morocco, or Italy and Libya, were retained. Early mosques in the west include England's first purpose-built example in Woking, Surrey, founded in 1889 by Shah Jehan Begum, wife of the Nawab of Bhopal, and inspired by the Taj Mahal; this building, in a typically Mughal-style, displays its Indian connections just as the design of the Paris Mosque built in the 1920s was inspired by Andalusian architecture.

During the 1950s and 1960s a 'second wave' of Muslim immigrants arrived in England, France and other parts of Europe, as well as in North America. By the 1960s, the burgeoning immigrant communities began to express their presence by building new mosques. Various projects that had been initiated in the 1950s, such as the Islamic Centre in Hamburg, built between 1960 and 1973 and funded jointly by the Iranian community resident in Germany and

by religious institutions in Iran, were finally seeing the light of day. Very often, the prime movers in such situations are accredited members of Muslim diplomatic missions who use their position and influence to raise the necessary funds from their own and other Muslim governments. Like their counterparts, the State Mosques in Islamic countries, large-scale mosques built in the West as statements of Muslim identity are usually financed either entirely or in part by Muslim governments, particularly by that of Saudi Arabia – the nation which has been responsible for financing more

(Above) The mosque at Woking, Surrey, inspired by the Taj Mahal and dating from 1889, is one of the earliest purpose-built examples in Europe.

(Opposite) The prayer hall of the Islamic Centre in Rome (1975–94), featuring a superstructure of intersecting ribs supporting domed bays (see p. 243).

227

mosques outside its own boundaries than any other Muslim country.

Mosques built in foreign cultural settings are usually characterized by three tendencies:

(1) The design is tempered by the specific context, modified in response to pressures from the local non-Muslim community or by local regulations and laws.

(2) Especially in the earlier examples, the design makes references back to regional Islamic traditions, the external architectural form being influenced in most instances by a single dominant style from a particular country or region, depending on who is financing, leading or designing the project; in this sense, the design may reflect the self-identity and aspirations of the group that takes the initiative in the project. The internal layout or plan generally follows that of the external architecture. However, internal ornamentation is quite frequently eclectic and inspired by a potpourri of styles that often has no direct connection with the external form. While the outside must be made to fit into a non-Muslim cultural context, the inside may be exuberantly decorated with characteristic Islamic ornament in order to emphasize the fact that that space belongs to Muslims (in this sense these buildings are similar to community mosques built in the West).

(3) Since the 1980s, there has been a conscious search for a contemporary architectural expression that attempts to

(Opposite) Architect's renderings of the Mosque and Muslim Institute in Paris (1922–6): general view and principal courtyard. The first purpose-built mosque in France, it was designed in the typical Andalusian-Maghrebi style with the full complement of ornamentation, which not only communicated a Muslim identity in the urban surroundings of the French capital, but also continued a representation already familiar to Parisians from the international exhibitions of the recent past.

(Below and bottom left) Longitudinal section of the mosque complex showing the domed prayer hall and the *hammam* on the right; and interior perspective of the prayer hall, with decoration featuring elaborate carved woodwork and plasterwork.

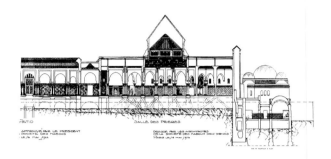

achieve some kind of synthesis of traditional principles and modern forms. A significant number of such mosques and Islamic centres were built in Europe and North America – many of the earliest examples were directly based on a historical Islamic model, a few were modernist in nature, and the later ones attempted to achieve some kind of synthesis between the two.

Mosque and Muslim Institute, Paris, France

This project, realized in the 1920s, is the earliest of the mosques presented here. While it lies outside the time-frame of this book, and was the result of different intention and participation, the Paris Mosque has been included because it illustrates the historicist tendency in mosque building. Sometimes called the Great Mosque of Paris, it is a fine example of Moorish architectural and decorative design, and the first mosque to be built in France. As a collaborative effort sponsored by the French government of President Alexandre Millerand and commissioned by the Association of *Habous* of Holy Places,[1] it was intended to emphasize the close ties that existed between France and its colonies in North Africa, namely Morocco, Tunisia and Algeria.

The idea for such a mosque in Paris was projected as early as 1895, when the Commission on French Africa, with the patronage of Prince Ahrenberg and the French diplomat Jules Cambon, first suggested the possibility, though it was never realized due to the lack of funds. However, in the years following World War I the idea was again put forward to the French government, this time by Si Kaddour ben Ghabrit, a Moroccan statesman and the president of the Association of *Habous* of Holy Places. Anxious to find some way of recognizing the Muslims of North Africa who had fought alongside the French forces during the war in the defence of Paris against the German invasion, the French government requested 500,000 francs[2] from parliament, and this sum was made available to the Association to be used as

it saw fit. At the same time, an administrative commission was set up, presided over by Edouard Herriot with several other French dignitaries,[3] and the Paris Municipal Council donated a large and prominent site of 7,500 sq. m (78,000 sq. ft) in the 5th *arrondissement* of the city, just behind the Jardin des Plantes and the Museum of Natural History, where the old Hôpital de la Pitié built by Marie de Médicis once stood. Contributions were also received from French overseas territories, from the governments of Algeria, French West Africa, Cameroon and Indo-China, from the protectorates of Tunisia and Morocco, as well as from individuals in North Africa. The project cost amounted to approximately 5 million francs.[4] Egypt donated the *minbar*, as well as copies of the Qur'an prepared in Cairo, and continues to provide an annual allocation of funds from the Ministry of Awqaf. The Bey of Tunis donated the mosaic tiles in the *hammam*.

Work began in 1922 and was completed in July 1926. Several architects were involved in the project, all of them French and all having had extensive experience in North Africa, particularly in Morocco. The original plans were prepared by Tranchant de Lunel, Inspector-General of the Ecole des Beaux-Arts in Morocco, and Maurice Mantout, an architect working in the same department. The definitive plans, however, were eventually drawn up by M. Eustache (a recipient of the coveted Prix de Rome), Robert Fournez and Maurice Mantout.[5]

Although not a product of Muslim governments in the West, the mosque complex illustrates how those who designed the earliest buildings of this kind sought to reflect historical models of the past, and it thus seems to have set a precedent. A similar design approach was adopted later and in very different contexts in the United Kingdom and the USA, signalling the emergence of mosques abroad commissioned by representatives of Muslim states.

London Central (Regent's Park) Mosque, London, UK

The London Central Mosque, perhaps better known as the Regent's Park Mosque, was built to provide a focus and inspiration for the half million Muslims in Great Britain. Completed in 1977, it was by no means the first mosque to be built in Great Britain, where there were already over four hundred public places of prayer, thirty-five of them having been purpose-built as mosques. Proposals to build a mosque in London were first put forward in 1920, but no decisive action was taken until 1940. Prompted by Hassan Nashat Pasha, the Egyptian Ambassador to the Court of St James, an initial approach was made by Lord Lloyd, Chairman of the British Council, to the Prime Minister of the day, Neville Chamberlain. Lord Lloyd proposed that the British Government purchase a site for the mosque as a reciprocal gesture to the Egyptian Government, which had donated land in Cairo for the building of an Anglican cathedral some years before.

The Prime Minister accepted the proposal and the present site (occupying 0.93 hectares/2.3 acres) at Hanover Gate in Regent's Park was purchased. The Muslim community's choice of such a centrally located site for a major mosque spoke clearly of its desire to be recognized as an important minority group in England where, in the past, mosques had been built only on the outskirts of cities. The site was formally handed over in November 1944 by the Crown Land Commissioners to the Mosque Committee, which at that time consisted of twelve ambassadors from Muslim countries. An Islamic Cultural Centre was established in the existing house known as Regent's Lodge until funds could be raised to build the mosque.

A design for the mosque, submitted to the Committee by the Egyptian architect General Ramzy Omar, was accepted in the late 1940s, but the project was delayed until 1959 when it appeared that all was finally ready for construction to begin. However, the London County Council and the Fine Arts Commission intervened, objecting that Omar's design was unsuitable in the context of the neighbouring buildings facing Regent's Park. As a result, the Committee was obliged to reject the design and no further steps were taken until 1969, when interest in the project was revived, largely thanks to the efforts of the then Ambassadors of Saudi Arabia, Pakistan, Lebanon and Kuwait. It was decided that the best way of finding an acceptable design would be to organize an international competition, with prizes on offer for the first four designs selected.

Fifty-two entries were received from architects in seventeen countries. The entries were assessed by a jury composed of Sir Robert Matthew, President of the Royal Institute of British Architects, A. Ahed from Pakistan and L. Blanco Soler from Spain. The winning design was that of the British architect Sir Frederick Gibberd.[6] After certain modifications, the design was finally approved in 1973 by the Trustees and construction began early in 1974, using the funds that had been donated by the Mosque Trust made up of a number of Muslim governments.[7]

The brief required that the design be developed in three separate parts: the mosque, an Islamic cultural centre (to include a library, conference rooms and a cafeteria), and living accommodation for the staff. Gibberd decided to combine these three functions as a single composition 'to underline that Islam is not just a religious observance but a way of life'.[8] Another requirement of the competition was that overflow space be provided for festivals such as Eid. To this end, the architect opted to extend the rectangular prayer hall laterally by installing folding doors which open onto terraces covered by marquees. Thus, the capacity of the main prayer hall (965 worshippers, a figure which was considered large at the time) could be increased – by using the entrance hall, court and the marquees – to nearly 4,500 (small in comparison to the capacity of state mosques in Muslim countries).

The triangular site is almost entirely fulled by the Mosque and Cultural Centre. To facilitate pedestrian circulation, particularly during festivals such as Eid, the building can be entered from different points on the site. An underground

(Above) The London Central Mosque (1969–77) by Sir Frederick Gibberd features the use of modern building techniques to express a pan-Islamic form. The mosque is seen against the background of Regent's Park; the courtyard is covered, so providing additional prayer space for major festivals.

(Below) Section through the mosque complex; the dome profile is modelled on major Iranian examples, particularly those of Safavid Isfahan.

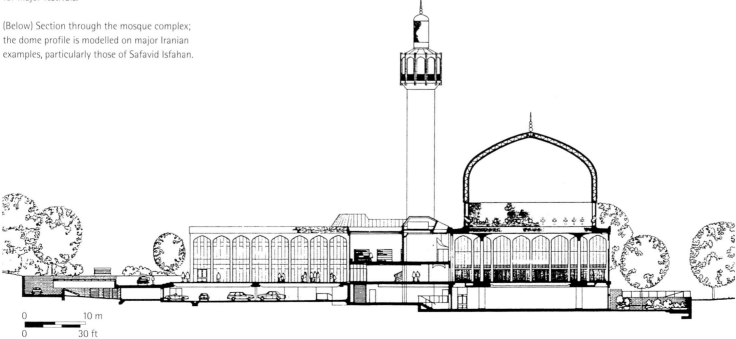

0   10 m
0   30 ft

(Below) Plans of the mosque at upper-floor, ground-floor and basement levels showing the square prayer hall and the L-shaped section occupied by the library, administrative offices and utility spaces. Parking facilities are located beneath the courtyard.

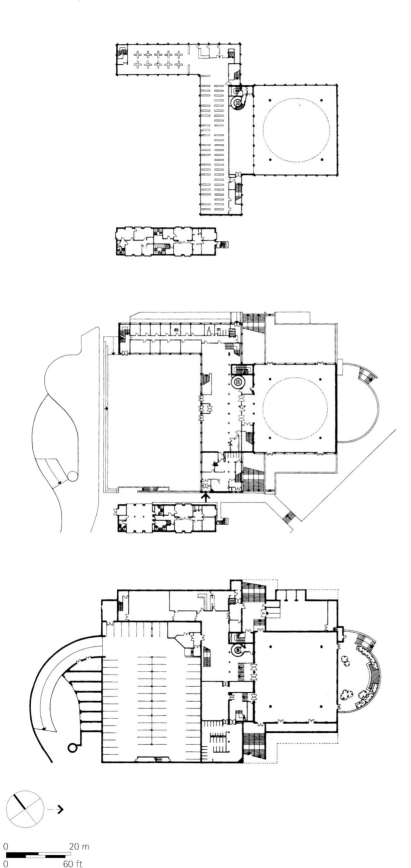

0   20 m

0   60 ft

car park, accessible from the front of the site, is located below the courtyard so as to minimize traffic on site and preserve an atmosphere of tranquillity. The *qibla* wall, the feature considered by the architect and client alike to be the most important element of the mosque, is pushed to the edge of the site overlooking Regent's Park and facing Mecca, so that all the other functions occur behind it.[9]

The dome and minaret (the latter incorporated into the main building) are respectively 25 m (82 ft) and 43 m (141 ft) in height and are the most prominent features of the building. The rest of the structure is relatively low (9.50 m/31 ft high) so as not to dominate the surrounding park and Nash's Hanover Terrace (*c.* 1825) just across the road. Furthermore, a Derbyshire spar aggregate was judiciously chosen for the external finish of the building to harmonize with the adjacent buildings.

The volumetric disposition of the building is governed by a module of 3.15 m (10 ft 4 in.), a rationalized unit (based on standardized norms adopted in the building industry at the time) which testifies to the architect's concern with the use of modern technology. The layout is linear in terms of the transition from the courtyard to the entrance foyer, and from there to the prayer hall. The main entrance serves as a filtering space providing access to all other areas. Separate ablutions facilities for men and women are located in such a way as to permit direct access from these areas to the prayer hall. The main entrance foyer is L-shaped, and above it on the first floor are the library, expressed on the exterior by its vaulted ceiling,[10] and the administrative offices. Beneath the prayer hall, a multi-purpose hall of identical size is provided with separate entrances on the lower level, one of which is from a sunken garden located at the *qibla* end of the site.

The rectangular plan of the prayer hall was chosen in a pragmatic spirit (since all prayer mats are rectangular, as Gibberd pointed out, the most logical solution is to make a prayer hall that reflects this shape).[11] The women's gallery is recessed into the west wall facing the *mihrab* and its area represents about one-fifth of the floor space of the main prayer hall.

The prayer hall is covered with a steel-framed dome, comprising eight tubular ribs connected by circumferential ring beams and having an internal diameter of 20 m (65 ft 6 in.). It rests on a cylindrical drum which is supported by four mushroom columns, and is clad in diagonal timber boarding and finished in gold-painted copper sheeting. The form of the dome is derived from that of the Iranian four-centred arch, employed as a repeated formal element in the mosque. Its design is clearly inspired by the Isfahan tradition, characterized in part by shiny domes with a four-point profile. The dome is surmounted by a finial with a symbolic crescent.

All the façades are composed of identical pre-cast concrete elements consisting of two columns joined at the top by the Iranian four-centred arch. These units are placed side by side around the entire structure but not fixed together. They are infilled with either glass or blank panels finished in white mosaic. In the opinion of the architects, the repetition of units like these throughout the building symbolizes unity, as does the plan of the L-shaped wing which houses the library and the administrative offices. (However, this rationalization could have been interpreted and expressed in different ways and can be read as part of an Islamist rhetoric.) Above the wall units is a continuous upstand pre-cast structural beam finished in mosaic which serves as a parapet to create a horizontal line around the building, thereby counteracting the verticality of the arched wall units.

The London Central Mosque was designed to present an expression of Islam in which the use of modern technologies was combined with pan-Islamic design elements that are considered recognizably Islamic in the eyes of all Muslims, without being representative of any one culture. The design, and more specifically the treatment of the arches, was very strongly influenced by the modern technological concerns of the time, and is indebted to the technological language developed by the architects Rifat Chadirji and Mohamed Makiya in the 1960s – an international language that was concerned with the formal expression of contemporary building materials.[12]

The use of modern materials such as concrete and steel allowed for the inclusion of a powerfully expressed dome. However, this new technology expressed formally by the repeated arches is somewhat inconsistent in relation to the treatment of the older and more traditional elements – the minaret and the dome. This creates a problem of clarity insofar as the structural imagery of the mosque as a whole is concerned, and gives the impression that in terms of its design the priority was simply to feature some kind of dome constructed with modern materials.

Islamic Center, Washington, DC, USA

In the United States, over 600 mosques serving some three million Muslims were in active use by the mid-1980s.[13] The earliest representational mosque was the Islamic Center in Washington, DC, established by a group of ambassadors from Muslim countries and completed in 1957. In addition to providing a mosque to serve the religious needs of the Muslim community in the capital, the client conceived it to promote a better understanding of Islam in a country where the Muslim religion was not well known and as a vehicle by which to improve relations between the United States and the Muslim world.[14]

The project is notable for the breadth of its functions and for the perseverance of the client in the face of financial constraints to realize the building, the completion of which took almost fifteen years. The scope of the initial project included a wide range of services, including a museum to exhibit works of art from different Islamic countries, an institute of higher learning for history, art and *Shari'a* (Islamic law), Arabic and religious studies for children, an academic magazine and various publications dealing with Islamic issues, lectures and library facilities. While some of

(Below) The Islamic Center (1945–57), Washington, DC, designed by Mario Rossi: general view of the street façade, the style of which follows formal aspects of Mamluk architecture; and the main entrance decorated with a monumental Qur'anic inscription executed in light-blue and white marble chips.

the client's objectives were never fulfilled due to lack of funds, personnel and space (the museum, Islamic institute and publication of the magazine were never realized, and the lecture hall has since been subdivided to provide a number of small classrooms), the Center as built has been used intensively since its completion.[15]

Aside from funding difficulties, the Board was also confronted with the task of building a major mosque in a non-Muslim country where such an idea was still quite novel. Projected as early as 1944, it is one of the early purpose-built mosques in the United States. It is also interesting to note that the inception of the idea for the

Washington project was roughly contemporaneous with that of the London Central Mosque (initiated four years earlier by Hassan Nashat Pasha, Egyptian Ambassador to the Court of St James; see above). Moreover, it is not improbable that the undertaking in England may have influenced events in Washington, as Muhammad Abdul-Rauf, the mosque's *imam*, has suggested.[16]

The idea to build a mosque grew out of a conversation which took place in Washington in November 1944 between the Ambassador of Egypt, Mahmoud Hassan Pasha, and A.J. Howar, an American-Palestinian building contractor who had entered the United States as an immigrant in the first decade of the twentieth century. Both regretted that there was no mosque in the Washington area in which to hold a prayer service for their deceased friend, the Ambassador of Turkey, or even regular prayers for the Muslim community.[17] Plans solidified in February 1945, when the Washington Mosque Foundation was officially established with the Ambassador of Egypt as its president and Mr Howar as Secretary-Treasurer, along with two other members whose names have not been recorded.[18]

The project was marked by solidarity, not only among Muslims but also between Muslims and non-Muslims. The cost of building the mosque was met entirely by donations received from Muslim and Arab Christian communities and individuals in other parts of North America, and from other communities and governments all over the Islamic world.[19] The eventual realization of the building was largely due to the involvement of a number of Muslim diplomats[20] who sponsored the original idea and convinced their respective governments to lend financial support to the project; they included Ambassador Hassan Pasha who contributed his time to fundraising for the Center as President of the Board of Governors until his mission came to an end in 1948, and Ambassador Abdul-Rahim who succeeded him in these functions until 1953, though he was to continue his efforts even after his mission had ended.[21] Among the prominent private contributors were Mr and Mrs Howar, the Nizam of Hyderabad, King Farouk of Egypt, and King Saud Ibn Abdul Aziz of Saudi Arabia, and many others who donated money as well as furnishings for the Center.[22] The broad extent of the sources of donations attests to the concern of Muslim governments, organizations and individuals to express their presence and to be recognized by other communities as co-habitants of the capital city.

The Board's search for a suitable site began in 1945. Early on, it was offered a large site as a gift, but this was turned down because the location was too far from the centre of the city.[23] It finally selected a prominent plot, 30,000 sq. ft (2,800 sq. m) in area, in the heart of the embassy quarter, purchased for $95,000 in 1946, using the donations received from King Farouk of Egypt and the Egyptian government, as

(Above left) Detail of the minaret; minarets constituted an important feature of all new mosques built by Mario Rossi in Egypt in the 1930s and 1940s.

(Above right) A view through one of the side archways that give access to the garden; the courtyard beyond functions as a public transitional space leading to the prayer hall.

(Opposite) Examples of ornamental details derived from Mamluk architecture used throughout the complex and reinterpreted as a new series of vegetal designs.

well as those obtained through the Board's national fund-raising campaign. The prestigious site on Massachusetts Avenue slopes down slightly towards the park. It is bordered by 200 ft (61 m) of public frontage on Massachusetts Avenue and 150 ft (45.75 m) on the western and eastern sides.

By 1950, sufficient funds, boosted by large donations from Pakistan ($296,000) and Egypt ($331,806), had been accumulated to permit construction to begin. However, the amount of construction undertaken each year depended on the sporadic nature of the funding by large donations, with the result that it was difficult to orchestrate the work; in fact, activity ceased for several months during 1953 due to lack of funds, and the building was eventually completed in March 1957.

It was Ambassador Mahmoud Hassan Pasha who used his official position and authority to convince the Egyptian Ministry of Awqaf to design the Washington Islamic Center and to prepare construction drawings. In Cairo, the Ministry assigned an Italian architect, Mario Rossi (1897–1961), who was resident in Egypt and employed by the Ministry of Works there, to design the new Islamic Center.[24] Rossi was influential as an architect in Egypt at that time and was a specialist in mosque architecture and decoration. Among his better-known designs are the Mosques of Zamalik and Omar Mukarram in Cairo, and the Mahatat al-Raml, Muhammad Karim, and Abi al-Abbas al-Mursi Mosques in Alexandria. Writing of the architect's work in general, Ihsan Fethi has noted that 'Rossi's mosque designs show a basic adherence to tradition, especially in his repeated use of the Ottoman centralised dome type. His experiments were mostly stylistic, in the decoration of the mosque and in the shape of the minaret, dome, etc. . . . In most of his designs he did away with the open courtyard altogether, and raised the mosque well above street level, thereby treating it as a totally enclosed monument. The mosque was reached by ascending a flight of steps that led to a colonnaded portico instead of the customary *iwan* gateway. The omission of the open courtyard, in particular, became popular, because it was difficult to find large enough plots in town centres. Rossi's notable stylistic innovations include new forms of arabesque (*tawriq*) decoration, especially for the filigree masonry screens, which he used extensively and which became very popular in Egyptian mosques; carved stone domes in the corners of mosques in addition to the main central dome; and his treatment of the minaret, whose form and height he sometimes exaggerated, at the Mahatat al-Raml Mosque (1948–51), which soars to 73 meters [240 ft] above ground level.'[25]

Rossi's design for the Washington Mosque essentially reflects this description. It is a highly symmetrical building, obviously based on Cairene models, and is constructed in concrete and steel, faced with smooth limestone panels. From Massachusetts Avenue the building is reached by a flight of steps leading to the main colonnaded portico entrance, decorated with a tall band of stylized Arabic calligraphy in light-blue and white marble chips. The text of the Qur'anic inscription reads: 'In houses which Allah has permitted to be raised to honour, for celebration, in them His name: in them He is glorified.' (XXIV: 36)[26] The entrance is flanked by identical two-storey wings with flat arched windows on the first floor and pointed arched windows above. Each wing culminates in a bay composed of perpendicular arches supported on a single column at the corner and covered by a pitched green-tiled roof, reminiscent of Andalusian and North African architecture. In the wings a Qur'anic library and a gift shop are located at ground-floor level, with administrative offices on the upper floor of the east wing; the upper floor of the west wing has no specific function. A lecture hall for up to 300 people is located in the basement of the Center, as are the ablutions and sanitary facilities.[27]

Beyond the main entrance is a colonnaded courtyard in which stands an ornamental pink marble fountain; this leads in turn to the vestibule of the prayer hall. The colonnades are composed of slender granite columns in the composite order that support highly stylized and slightly pointed tucked arches decorated with calligraphic inscriptions intertwined with vegetal motifs. These are executed in rough-textured light-blue and white marble chips that contrast well with the smooth limestone finish of the overall structure. Lateral entrance gates give access to the courtyard from the small car park situated on the eastern side which continues around the back of the prayer

Exterior view of the *qibla* façade, with emergency escape stairs leading down to street level.

hall (the parking area was not a feature of Rossi's original plan), and from the western side where there is a large open space which contains a marquee (probably used for religious classes), a temporary structure furnished with Persian carpets, and a kitchen. The whole structure is crowned by stylized crenellations and by the minaret, 160 ft (48.75 m) in height, the design of which was inspired by a number of Mamluk examples in Cairo, Palestine and Syria. The minaret consists of a tall square base with a cylindrical shaft and a bulbous 'teardrop' finial, and is decorated with *muqarnas*, crenellations, and geometric and interlacing designs, as well as Qur'anic inscriptions.

As a result of local planning requirements the drawings had to be modified by a Washington firm, Irving S. Porter & Sons, which was contracted at the end of 1949 to finalize the design. This process involved, among other things, the question of the orientation of the façade. Since zoning regulations required that the façade be parallel to the street like all other buildings on Massachusetts Avenue, it was necessary to reconcile this requirement with the imperative of the *qibla* orientation. Thus, the directional transition is accommodated within the courtyard in order to effect the change between the axis of the main façade and that of the prayer hall facing towards Mecca.

Another important development in the implementation of Rossi's design lay in certain changes to the original plan of the building which occurred at an unspecified point in the design process. In Rossi's original plan the vestibule was integrated into the main entrance on the principal façade, while the courtyard led directly to the prayer hall. In turn, the prayer hall was surrounded by a number of small rooms, some opening onto the prayer hall and having separate lateral entrances from the porticoes in the courtyard, and a large rectangular volume housing the *mihrab* and *minbar*. The minaret was integrated into the main façade next to a vestibular space, and the western and eastern boundaries of the site were enclosed by porticoed arcades with pedestrian entrances from the street. In the definitive version of the plan the courtyard and the vestibule are inverted so that the vestibule becomes the immediate entrance to the prayer hall. The courtyard is therefore divested of its more sacred dimension in the earlier plan, and thus becomes a rather more public transitional space. The actual position of the minaret is rather unusual and worth noting. In relation to its earlier proposed position it was moved back and placed right in the centre of the vestibule, where it marks the main entrance to the prayer hall, flanked by two smaller doorways. In all likelihood the minaret was set back further into the site because it was probably thought that it would be too prominent. While this reshuffling of spatial and formal elements may appear somewhat gratuitous at first glance, it may be noted that Mamluk architecture, which is based on modular and repeated elements, lends itself well to this treatment, and in its heyday experiments were often made with the rearrangement of building components, as Grabar has pointed out.[28]

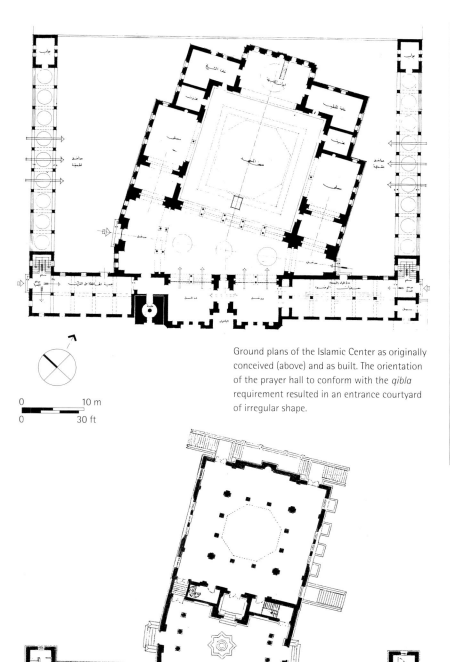

Ground plans of the Islamic Center as originally conceived (above) and as built. The orientation of the prayer hall to conform with the *qibla* requirement resulted in an entrance courtyard of irregular shape.

The prayer hall itself is almost square in plan and covered by a dome. On the lower part the outer walls are ornately decorated with a running band (approximately 6 ft/2m high) of Turkish tiles based on Iznik designs,[29] donated by the Turkish government and installed by a team of specialist craftsmen sent from Turkey and supervised by Hakky Izzat, an architect and professor at the Ghazi Institute of Ankara. The middle section of the outer walls is in white plaster with plaster screens in the lateral walls to admit natural light. Higher up are perforated screens and decorative tile panels. Set in the *qibla* wall, the *mihrab* is an arched niche covered with Turkish tiles and inscriptions. The *minbar*, donated by the Egyptian government, is particularly remarkable, for it consists of over 10,000 pieces of hand-carved wood segments inlaid with bone and ivory, all fitted together by an Egyptian craftsman without using a single nail.

The dome (60 ft/18.25 m in height) is supported on an octagonal drum with arched windows and rests on a square base that is decorated with plaster mouldings of floral motifs with painted calligraphic inscriptions. This in turn is supported by four stone pillars, one at each corner, and between each pair there are two stone columns faced in Vermont marble; these form narrow, pointed triple arches decorated with painted calligraphy and vegetal motifs. The dome is placed over the centre of the prayer hall, not above the *mihrab*. Egyptian craftsmen were brought specially from Cairo to execute the plasterwork and the calligraphy which features verses from the Qur'an and the names of God, the Prophet and the four Orthodox Caliphs in Kufic script.[30] At the time of construction the question of whether or not to admit women to the mosque remained unresolved. Today, a small curtained space is provided for female worshippers in the southeast corner of the prayer hall.

Between 1980 and 1983, the Islamic Center suffered extensive damage as a result of a fire, roof leakage, frozen water pipes and general neglect due to insufficient funds for maintenance. Also, an intra-Muslim community conflict, in which opposing Iranian factions occupied the building and disrupted everyday activities for over a year, resulted in further damage. In early 1983, Mokhless Al-Hariri of the Georgetown Design Group was commissioned by the Center's Board of Governors to undertake the design and construction management work required to restore and refurbish the building. The original concrete structure remains unchanged. The limestone and pre-cast panel facing was cleaned and restored, but the majority of the work seems to have been focused on the restoration of the damaged ornamentation on the walls and ceiling, and a security perimeter fence was also built. The restoration effort was funded mainly by Saudi Arabian donations.

There is an interesting postscript to the project that has changed its nature. It was originally set up as a non-profit organization run by the Director-*imam*, Muhammad Abdul-Rauf from Egypt, whose services were paid for by Al-Azhar University in Cairo. (This is also true of the Manhattan Mosque discussed below.) However, disputes between Shiite and Sunni users of the mosque and the resulting occupation led to a number of appointments of shorter-term *imams*, and the job was divided so that by the mid-1980s there was a Director and an *imam*, as well as visiting *imams*. The majority of the funding for the running of the mosque came from Saudi Arabia and was overseen by that country's Ambassador to the United States. By the 1990s these funds have been supplemented by the community of mosque users. A second change, and one that is more important to the fabric of the building, is the way in which the Center is being used. When it was first established little attention was paid to women's needs; as women began to take a more active role in congregational activities, their needs, including

the provision of a permanent prayer area, had to be met. With changes in the balance of the mosque, it was gradually appropriated for the benefit of the city's Muslim community and has now become as much a local socio-religious centre as a representational and symbolic building.[31]

Islamic Cultural Foundation Mosque, Petit Saconnex (Geneva), Switzerland

The Islamic Cultural Foundation Mosque (1978) located in Petit Saconnex, Geneva, was conceived as a means of providing for the religious needs of the Muslim community living in and around Geneva, members of which (working for the most part in the diplomatic corps and for international governmental organizations) had had to use rented space for daily prayers. The desire to achieve a more permanent solution led Dr Sheil El Ard, the Saudi Arabian Ambassador to the United Nations, to initiate a programme in 1974 to create religious facilities for the estimated 6,000 Muslims in the area.

El Ard solicited financial support from the late King Faisal of Saudi Arabia, who agreed to finance the entire project.[32] In addition to providing the financing, the government of Saudi Arabia had the foresight to set up a foundation and to donate other real estate in Geneva, the rental income from which is used to cover the continuing maintenance costs of the Centre. The Geneva-based firm of Osman Gurdogan and Jean-Pierre Limongelli was chosen to design a mosque complex which, due to local building regulations and site constraints, was initially to include only underground parking facilities.

At the instigation of the architects, the scope of the project was expanded in response to the site conditions in the vicinity of the United Nations headquarters. The site selected, 4,200 sq. m (45,000 sq. ft) in area, set in a residential zone of high-rise apartment blocks, was that of a former estate with an existing manor house and farm building. First, permission had to be obtained from the authorities concerned for the construction of a cultural centre in a residential area, and a condition was imposed in the sale of the land which obliged the architects to integrate all the existing structures into their proposed design. As a result, a larger range of facilities – including a conference room, library and language laboratories in the manor house, a Qur'anic school in the farm building, and a cafeteria and morgue – were incorporated into the programme which was developed during the winter of 1974/75. The design stage was completed towards the end of 1975 and construction began in January 1976.

The Centre is divided into two distinct parts, and has separate entrances to the public and the religious areas. The public functions are centred around the courtyard, while the prayer hall is expressed as a distinct entity through its octagonal form and its prominent position on the site. The choice of an octagonal plan appears to have been a logical response to the problem of orientation towards Mecca and the position of the entrance, given that the

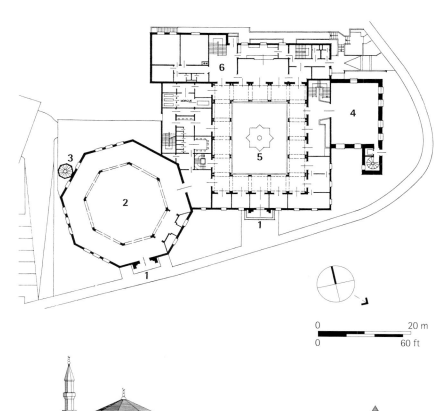

1 Entrances
2 Prayer hall
3 Minaret
4 Old manor house
5 Public area/courtyard
6 Old farm building

(Left) Plan and street elevation of the Islamic Cultural Foundation Mosque complex (1974–8), near Geneva, by Gurdogan and Limongelli. The mosque and cultural centre are linked to the older buildings on the site by means of a central courtyard. The external appearance is restrained, so allowing the new complex to fit into the village atmosphere of Grand Saconnex.

(Bottom) The simple exterior of the prayer hall and minaret reveal the stylistic inspiration of Ottoman sobriety in the use of stone facings.

0   20 m
0   60 ft

qibla axis faces the street. However, the drawback to this arrangement is that worshippers arriving late for prayers tend to join the rows on the sides instead of those at the rear of the hall, so creating minor disturbances. The existing manor house to the east of the site and the farm building to the north are incorporated into the overall design by means of the central courtyard.

The mosque itself is a sober edifice, inspired in elevation by Ottoman architecture and distinguished by its octagonal shape, with dome and minaret. The colonnaded courtyard with a fountain was considered a necessary and integral design element serving to identify the complex as Islamic.[33] However, the overall plan of the complex is not particularly Ottoman in layout, but rather inspired by a generic tradition of courtyard-type mosques. Separate ablutions facilities for men and women are located within the public part of the complex, and a mezzanine prayer area is provided for the use of women.

The external surfaces of the whole complex are treated very simply, using materials and design elements that harmonize with the existing buildings. Thus, the mosque, constructed in reinforced concrete, is faced with Savonnière stone and the existing buildings have been restored using local stone (*crépi*), while the formal treatment of apertures such as windows and entrances is in keeping with the style of the manor house.

Despite the architects' heavy reliance on Ottoman precedent,[34] Sheil El Ard expressed a preference for the use of Moorish ornamentation in the interior spaces of the complex. The contrast between the simplicity of the façade and the ornateness of the interior is not unusual, and such a combination is in keeping with ideas of space in Muslim society where interiors, especially of mosques, are often lavishly decorated while the façades are left blank. However, in this context external simplicity was primarily a response to another concern, that of Muslims in a predominantly

The *mihrab* niche and detail of the octagonal prayer hall showing the transitional area below the dome. The ornamentation executed by craftsmen sent by King Hassan II of Morocco reveals characteristic North African features.

Christian country who prefer 'to remain reserved on the outside, wishing only to be present'.[35]

Aside from the ceilings in the library, conference room and courtyard, all of which are decorated with gold-painted glass and turquoise in the Byzantine/Umayyad vein, the ornamentation is distinctly North African.[36] In the prayer hall, Moroccan influence can be seen in the pointed arches and the eight coloured wood panels made in Casablanca by Moroccan craftsmen (incidentally the only part of the construction to have been executed off-site). King Hassan II of Morocco offered the services of numerous Moroccan craftsmen from Fez, Marrakech and Casablanca, and sent them to Geneva to execute both the ornate *zellij* work[37] using imported Venetian mosaics and the plasterwork which adorns the surfaces of the complex.

The building's architectural articulation and scale give it the general aspect of a neighbourhood mosque. Perhaps this tempered modesty can be partially explained by the nature of the society within which it is located. The Geneva Mosque illustrates well the translation of a historical model into a twentieth-century idiom.

Islamic Centre and Mosque, Rome, Italy

In contrast to the preceding examples, the Islamic Centre and Mosque of Rome and the New York Islamic Cultural Center Mosque (discussed below) offer an architectural expression in a more contemporary vein. The buildings of the Rome project were first opened for occasional use in mid-1992, and were officially completed in 1994. Here, a contrasting solution to the problem of establishing a link with the past has been devised. Eschewing modernist attitudes, which tend in the main to prefer open interior spaces with large roof spans, the architects Paolo Portoghesi and Vittorio Gigliotti chose rather to evoke the historical model of the Great Mosque of Cordoba (8th–10th century) in terms of horizontality and the organic image of the 'forest of columns', which they felt captured an atmosphere of spirituality. In addition to the Moorish influence, Turkish and Persian imagery was combined with Italian (and specifically Roman) imagery to reflect both the varied background of the client as a group and the *genius loci* of Rome. Careful attention was paid to the nature of the site and its surrounding landscape.

Before the construction of the mosque, the Muslim community had had to use rented apartments in the city for religious and cultural gatherings. However, the Rome Islamic Centre, in existence since 1959, had served as much as a point of assistance for Muslim refugees as a place of prayer. Recognizing the imperative need to provide a mosque for the benefit of some 20,000 Muslims (1990 estimate) residing in Rome, a Vatican decree issued in 1963 had declared that it would not oppose the construction of a mosque in Rome on condition that the new building be located out of sight of St Peter's Basilica and that its minaret be no taller than the dome of St Peter's.[38] This declaration led to the founding in 1966 of the Islamic Cultural Centre of Italy. A visit to Italy

(Below) An aerial view, plan and section of the Islamic Centre and Mosque (1975–94) in Rome, designed by Portoghesi, Gigliotti and Moussawi. The layout of the entrance plaza, the gardens and the auxiliary services is conceived within the monumental building traditions of Roman, Baroque and Islamic architecture. Access to the main prayer hall is via a staircase leading to the podium on which it stands.

1 Prayer hall
2 Minaret
3 Subsidiary prayer hall
   for everyday use
4 Islamic Cultural Centre
5 Reception hall
6 Library
7 Conference hall
8 Meeting rooms and
   museum

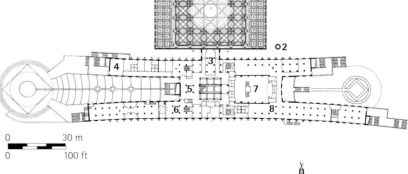

0   30 m
0   100 ft

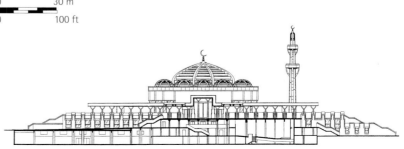

by King Faisal of Saudi Arabia in the early 1970s seems to have been the event which triggered action on the part of Rome's Muslim community in taking definitive steps to build the new mosque.[39]

The eventual design was the outcome of a competition held in 1975; out of forty-seven entries there were four first prize winners. Two of these projects, one by the Iraqi architect Sami Moussawi and the other by the Italians Paolo Portoghesi and Vittorio Gigliotti, were ultimately selected by a jury composed of professors from Islamic universities, Italian historians, and a number of ambassadors (notably those from Oman and Egypt). The architects were asked to collaborate in a joint effort on the final design. A committee of thirteen ambassadors (chaired by Pakistan) sponsored the project and twenty-four Muslim countries participated in financing it, while the 2.5-hectare site (6 acres) in the district known as Monte Antenne was donated in 1974 by the Rome city council. Once the definitive project had been approved by the Mayoralty in January 1979, work began immediately, only to be interrupted soon afterwards (seemingly because of insufficient funding) until 1984,[40] when it resumed concurrently with the receipt of a Saudi Arabian donation of $10 million. The foundation stone was laid in December 1984, nine years after the original competition had been held. The project was, as the Italian critic Marcello Palumbo's metaphor describes it, a 'theatre of constructions'.[41]

Surprisingly, the client specifically requested a building with a strong anti-seismic design, even though Rome is not officially listed as being in an active earthquake zone. Aesthetic and functional durability were also required. The architects and engineers studied and tested materials to meet the client's stipulation, and their painstaking work won several European awards for the study and treatment of concrete, as well as for the structural design which resulted from it.

(Above) The *mihrab*, which is covered in blue, green and ochre ceramic tiles, offsets the varying tonalities of the white interior, while on the exterior its position on the *qibla* wall is indicated by a recessed niche on either side of which part of the horizontal glazed band can be seen.

(Right) Historic Andalusian-Maghrebi mosques with ribbed domes, such as this example over one of the bays adjacent to the *mihrab* in the Great Mosque in Cordoba, provided the inspiration for the superstructure of the Rome prayer hall.

(Opposite) Views of the interior showing the superstructure of the prayer hall and the ribbed dome; supported by eight columns, the dome's appearance is dematerialized by seven rings of glazed openings.

Islamic Centre and Mosque, Rome, Italy

(Above) Interior detail of one of the flanking colonnades which unify the entire complex.

(Right and opposite) Exterior details showing the library with its floating slab roof supported by externally expressed columns, and the freestanding minaret, 40 m (130 ft) in height, with two-tiered galleries.

The sloping triangular site is divided into two distinct parts – the prayer hall area at the centre, and the library and cultural centre on the north-south axis – separated by a colonnaded court. Flanking the court on both sides, gently curving colonnades frame the prayer hall which is situated towards the higher (road) side and set against the mass of Monte Antenne. The library and cultural centre are kept relatively low so as to maintain a harmonious relationship between the architecture and the natural surroundings. The landscaped grounds featuring the use of local flora, together with the strong geometric layout, bring to mind both Persian and Italian formal garden layouts. The low horizontality of the brick colonnades is characteristic of many of Portoghesi's earlier designs, while their curves relate well to the hilly site, creating continuously changing perspectives in a manner reminiscent of Michelangelo's Campidoglio on the Capitoline Hill in Rome. In this context Christian Norberg-Schulz remarked perceptively in his book on Portoghesi and Gigliotti that the colonnades 'echo the enclosing walls of Islamic architecture, at the same time as their curved outline make us remember the inflected surfaces of Borromini and the contours of the *forre* [of ancient Etruria].'[42] The progression of space, read as a series of interconnected functions, was conceived to give the complex the feeling of an urban experience.

The circular geometry seen in this particular project is a recurring theme in the work of Portoghesi and Gigliotti, observed for example in their project for the Royal Court in Amman, Jordan, even more rigorously formalistic in its expression of structure than the Rome project, and in the urban planning and beautification of Khartoum.[43]

The dynamic quality of the layout of the complex and the visual progression of space is in contrast with the static quality of the prayer hall in which 'the effects of lightness, dematerialization and static paradox found in classical Islamic architecture [serve] to create an atmosphere of sacredness and solemnity'.[44] The main prayer hall is the most successful element within the Rome complex. Designed to accommodate up to 2,000 worshippers, it is sited on an axis perpendicular to that of the colonnades, and can be reached either directly from the elevated court or through the main entrance located beneath it.[45] The prayer hall which has an area of 2,500 sq. m (26,775 sq. ft) and a central domed space matches the reputed size of the original house/mosque of the Prophet in Medina (41 x 41 m/132 x 132 ft);[46] rising almost to the height of a cube, the hall is flanked by two-storey arcades. Its design combines the modular and circular systems of the classical Arab hypostyle prayer hall and the domed Ottoman style. An intriguing design element of the Mosque of Rome is the roof structure of the prayer hall, inspired by historic precedents such as the domes in the Great Mosques of Cordoba in Andalusia and the twelfth-century Tlemcen in Algeria. The roof consists of the central ribbed dome with 16 subsidiary domes, all supported by a complex system of interwoven arches and columns. The columns, each composed of four double-curved pillars and

a central mast held together by a compression ring, are concerned essentially with design, not structure, and are used to conceal heating and lighting fixtures. The seven-stepped central dome, almost 22.80 m (75 ft) in diameter, is supported on eight columns. Its mixed historical references find their inspiration in a cosmological image symbolizing the Seven Heavens in the Prophet Muhammad's *mi'raj nama*, or Ascent to Heaven,[47] and include an apparent allusion to Borromini's design for the cupola in the church of S. Ivo alla Sapienza (mid-seventeenth century) in Rome.[48] The central space is enclosed by non-structural suspended walls supported by the rigid system of subsidiary domes and capitals. The richness of the tall *mihrab* niche, which is covered with decorative ceramic tiles and a band of *nastaliq* calligraphy in blue, green and ochre tile, is offset by the different tonalities of white in the interior.

The prayer hall is lit by glazed apertures in the domes and the *qibla* wall, and by a continuous running band of glass that also plays a formal role in that it helps to break up the volumes. An important process in the elaboration of the design was the determination of the different qualities of light in the prayer hall by day and by night; studies were undertaken to calculate the varying degrees of light and shade. Four huge hanging chandeliers, based on old Turkish designs, are suspended beneath the dome.

Separate women's sections, raised as galleries covering some 10% of the total prayer area, run along two sides of the prayer hall, from which they are screened by carved latticework and richly decorated in *zellij*. The tiles and the screens are executed with delicacy and their rich traditional patterning and colours contrast in a striking manner with the monochrome structure, as do the carpets.

The form of the thirty-two pillars in the prayer hall is also used as a design motif on a larger scale in other parts of the complex. For example, the architects regard the minaret – 40 m (130 ft) in height – as a structural projection of these columns on an urban scale. The minaret is thus seen as being not only an expression of the mosque (the two-tiered form being one that is found throughout the Islamic world), but also as integrating well into the urban context.

Using modern technology and materials, the architects intended to create an atmosphere combining sacredness and solemnity by incorporating – according to Portoghesi – 'the effects of lightness, dematerialization and static paradox found in classical Islamic architecture to evoke the atmosphere of ancient mosques.' In this, the prayer hall is successful. Even if the complex as a whole raises questions as to its significance as a major work of architecture, it is none the less an important landmark building. Instead of displaying overt references to precise regional traditions or styles, the Mosque of Rome is a neutral expression of pan-Islamism, in that it represents an attempt to employ an architectural style that will be accessible to all Muslims, regardless of their geographical origins.

The Islamic Cultural Center of New York, USA

Like the Rome Mosque, the Islamic Cultural Center of New York features easily recognizable elements traditionally associated with mosque architecture to produce a building in a modern idiom. Sponsored by the Islamic countries represented at the United Nations headquarters, the Center is located at East 96th Street and Third Avenue on New York's Upper East Side. In Greater New York, where no more than a dozen mosques existed in the 1970s, the number had risen to around 250 by 1995.[49] The Muslims of New York form a wide ethnic and cultural mix – those with Lebanese, Pakistani, Yemeni and Turkish origins being predominant groups – and are the most highly educated in the Muslim *umma*.[50] It appears that a new 'American Islam' may be emerging, distinguished by a general desire on the part of Muslims living there to be seen as 'modern', whether they are religiously liberal or conservative. This also holds true for the Muslim states represented at the UN. It is not surprising, therefore, that the mosque was conceived as both a place of prayer and a venue for social contact, and viewed as a pan-Islamic symbol reflecting diversity.

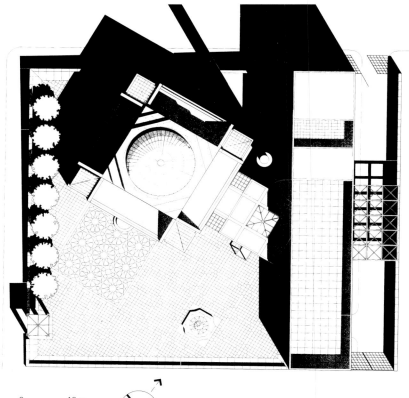

0   10 m
0   30 ft

The site was acquired in 1966 by the governments of Kuwait, Saudi Arabia and Libya, and a Board of Trustees for a non-profit entity was set up to develop and administer the project. Initially, several ambitious proposals were under consideration, including one for the construction of a 40-storey building on part of the site to provide an income to pay for continuing costs of maintaining and operating the Mosque and Cultural Center – in effect, instituting a modern *waqf* building. A joint venture with a New York developer led to the design for a 'skyscraper mosque', and other schemes were also considered. Such ideas proved to be too ambitious, however, and the whole project was scaled down and put on hold. When the scheme was relaunched in 1981, the problem faced by the Board of Trustees (consisting of ambassadors from Muslim nations to the United Nations, led by the representative of Kuwait)[51] was the same as had arisen in the context of projects in London, Washington, DC, and Rome – namely, how should the external appearance of the building be treated?

The project was first given to the Iranian architect Ali Dadras, but his design did not satisfy the Board and was deemed unbuildable. The Board then decided that it wanted a building that would reflect its New York location and be designed to engage the sophisticated design sense of New Yorkers. In 1987, it commissioned the New York office of Skidmore, Owings & Merrill (SOM) to undertake the design under the leadership of Michael McCarthy (who was known to the client for his work in Kuwait and for the Chancery of Kuwait in Washington, DC). The minaret was commissioned separately – for reasons that are unclear – from Swanke Haden Connel Associates, and was designed by its Turkish architect Altun Gürsel.[52] The architects were advised by two committees of experts selected by the client to assist with project definition. The two committees had conflicting viewpoints: one urged the architect to follow historic motifs literally, while the other, consisting of art and architectural historians and critics, encouraged a more contemporary style of expression with due respect for Muslim beliefs and architectural traditions, but which would relate more closely to the urban context of New York.[53] The architects were influenced by the latter and the client insisted that the Center must include a dome and a minaret.

In addition to the mosque itself, the project included a separate building for a school, a library, a small museum, an apartment for the *imam* and some shops. The first stage of the project (the mosque) was built according to this plan. The rest is being built separately. The mosque includes a main prayer area, below which is a large multi-purpose hall, ablutions facilities for men and women, offices for the administration and storage and service areas.

The site of the mosque at a busy urban intersection prompted the architects to design a self-contained building set back from the street to provide overflow space, as well as to exclude distractions created by noise and movement from the prayer area, which is angled to the rectangular city grid. However, this approach also has the effect of accentuating

The Islamic Cultural Center of New York (1987–91), by Skidmore, Owings & Merrill.

(Opposite) General view of the entrance façade, and site plan of the mosque showing the building angled away from the street grid to conform with the *qibla* requirements.

(Overleaf) Interior of the prayer hall, and a detail showing the *mihrab* niche. The low-level lights hung in a chandelier-like circle help to retain a feeling of human scale, while the subtly lit glazed interior of the *mihrab* represents a new rendition of the traditional *muqarnas*.

Exterior corner detail and section through the prayer hall. The single dome of the mosque sits on a transitional zone of stepped reinforced-concrete beams infilled with etched-glass panels. The use of uniform square panels of either granite or glass on all four walls gives the interior a sense of order.

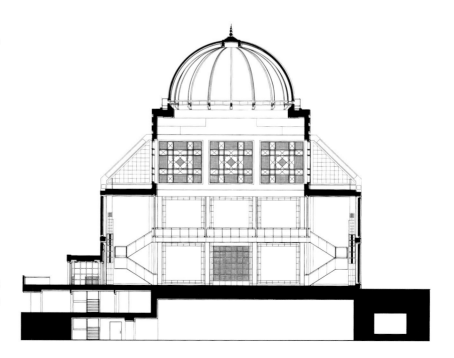

249

(Below) Plans of the mosque at mezzanine and
ground-floor levels.

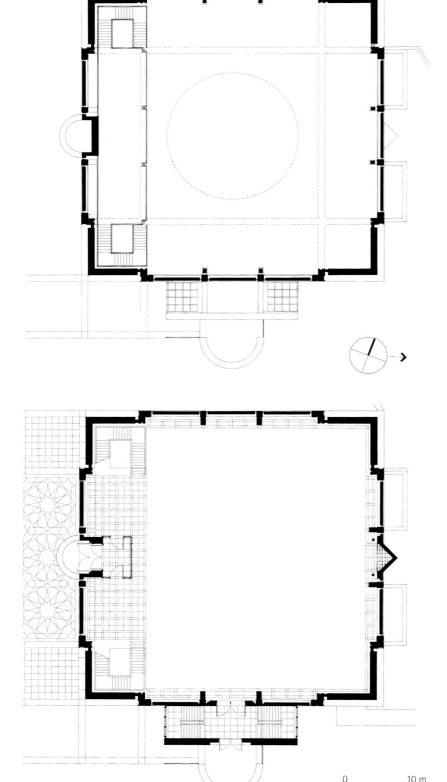

the new mosque in its otherwise anonymous urban setting,
presenting it as an object on a raised platform. Its resulting
isolation was the price that had to be paid for establishing a
strong presence in the neighbourhood. Granted that the site
presented difficult and conflicting conditions, the resolution
of this scheme is nevertheless less satisfactory than in other
similar situations, such as the Al-Ghadir Mosque in Tehran
(see Chapter 5) or the Ismaili Centre in London and the
Shafiq Amash Mosque in Beirut (see Chapter 1), which take
account architecturally of the adjacent streets.

Of the various Islamic countries which helped finance
the project, Kuwait donated over 50% of the funds and
effectively also controlled the construction through its
representative, Ziad Monayir. The foundation stone was
laid in September 1988 by the Emir of Kuwait, Sheikh Jaber
Al-Ahmad Al-Sabah, and the first stage of the Center was
completed and opened in 1991.

Set at an angle to the street grid because of the usual
orientation requirements, the building is based on a square
grid and is itself essentially a vertically extended cube
covered by a central dome. The design was modelled on the
single-domed Ottoman mosque type, as proposed by the
project architects who included Mustafa Abadan, himself
a Turk. The original concept was retained, but was revised
and substantially reworked over time. The central space has
a clear span 90 ft (27 m) in height, made up of four trusses
that support the concrete dome clad in steel and copper and
from which the women's mezzanine below and at the rear
of the hall is suspended. The trusses below the dome contain
decorative square openings which are a source of natural
light in addition to the skylights at each of the four corners
of the cube which serve to illuminate the prayer area. 'The
stepping pendentive-like beams at the corners, in addition
to their structural role in supporting the dome, help to
visually connect the trusses to the dome, thus allowing a
smooth transition between the square and the dome . . .
Moreover, the steel-ribbed structure of the dome expresses
its modernity, and the tectonic expression of the supports
of these ribs, with their minimum proportions, reinforced by
the light penetration, creates a distinctively modern floating
effect . . . It is effectively expressed in a contemporary
language.'[54] The mosque accommodates approximately 900
male worshippers, while the mezzanine for women has an
area about 20% of that allotted to the main prayer hall. The
women's area above is kept behind the men's prayer area
so that it should not be directly above it.[55] In architectural
terms this arrangement helps to reinforce the *mihrab* axis,
but functionally the route between the ablutions facilities
and the women's area means that female worshippers have
to cross the prayer hall and thus cannot avoid mingling with
the men – a notion that can be viewed either as progressive
or as problematic, depending on one's attitude.

The interior decoration, which does not rely on the use
of ornamentation in the traditional manner, seeks rather
to achieve a new style within the technical contraints of
the structure. The whole space is carefully articulated and

0   10 m
0   30 ft

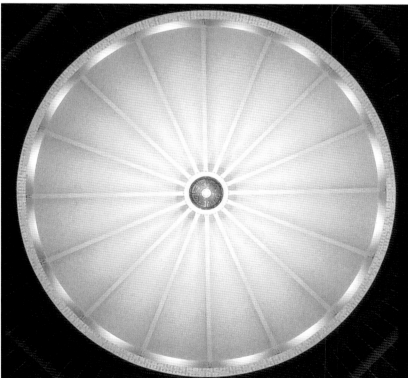

(Top) The main entrance to the prayer hall, which, like the *mihrab*, features a modern version of the *muqarnas*.

(Above) The interior of the dome showing the use of steel ribs and a ring of windows around the base to admit natural light.

designed in such a way as to create a contrast between the simplicity of monochromatic materials, including panels of blue tiles and greenish opaque glass[56] in the upper areas of the hall, and the *mihrab* in the form of a striking pale-blue *muqarnas* in glass bordered by a frieze consisting of Qur'anic verses in Kufic script. The main entrance portal also features the same device of the glass *muqarnas*. Artificial lighting is provided by a circle of lamps suspended from steel wires – an echo of the suspended circles of oil lamps found in medieval mosques. The corners and the top of the main structure are chamfered to emphasize the dome, surmounted by a gilded crescent finial, while the interior is decorated with nine of the Names of Allah.[57]

The minaret is a freestanding element 130 ft (40 m) in height, having a square shaft and an internal staircase that leads to a balcony from which the *muezzin*'s call to prayer is made, as is the case with most new mosques, using an amplified recording. The client attached great symbolic importance to the provision of a minaret, and the Emir of Kuwait personally paid $1.5 million for it following his visit in 1988. His decision to do so, rather than apply funds to provide more community facilities, once again confirms the representational aspect of the building. It also reflects what Oleg Grabar has called 'the official image of Islam'.[58] The simplified elemental design and the elegant contemporary finishes – granite, marble, glass, and wood – have made this building a Manhattan landmark.

By commissioning major buildings in Western cities, Muslim clients present a permanent public statement in non-Muslim surroundings. The direct involvement of officials such as ambassadors from Islamic nations has ensured an overtly representative aspect in such buildings. Stylistic concessions have been made in deference to local contexts, though only to a limited degree. The ambivalent attitude to the presence of women in the mosque persists, the separate prayer areas assigned to them being restricted to less than 20% of the available space, regardless of their numbers as a proportion of the mosque-going population.

Retaining a recognizable Muslim image has remained the primary concern. The buildings of the earlier twentieth century were, in the main, more literal in their historicist expressions, often couched in almost Orientalist terms. The more recent buildings of the 1980s and the 1990s reveal a desire to achieve a more 'modern' expression. The concept of a Muslim 'modernity' was manifested later abroad than in the homelands, ironically just as the modernist experiment in the West began to lose ground in favour of reiterations of models from the past, now again regarded as manifestations of political and religious authority and legitimacy.[59]

As multi-ethnic and multi-cultural Muslim communities continue to present themselves worldwide through the presence of a mosque, they will be challenged to do so in a manner which, while establishing their identity, also attests to their involvement in a chosen nation and locality.

Notes on the text

Introduction

1 Renata Holod and Ahmet Evin (eds.), *Modern Turkish Architecture*. Also see Sibel Bozdoğan *et al.*, *Sedad Hakki Eldem*. Also by Bozdoğan, 'Modernity in the Margins: Architecture and Ideology in the Early Republic', *Proceedings of the XVIII International Congress of the History of Art*.
2 See Sami A. Hanna and G. Gardner, *Arab Socialism: A Documentary Survey*.
3 On the International Style and socialist state architecture see, for example, Jean-Louis Cohen, *Le Corbusier and the Mystique of the USSR: Theories and Projects for Moscow, 1928–1936*. The histories of building in individual countries mentioned have not yet been assembled. On Iraq a partial view, focused more on the role of individual architects, is presented in the works by Rifat Chadirji, particularly *Concepts and Influences: Towards a Regionalized International Architecture,* and in the monograph on Mohamed Makiya by Kanan Makiya, *Post-Islamic Classicism*.
4 See Kamil Khan Mumtaz, *Architecture in Pakistan,* and the Capital Development Authority publication, *Islamabad, the City of Peace*. Also see Doxiadis Associates, 'Islamabad, the New Capital of Pakistan', *Ekistics* 18, pp. 331–6.
5 On regionalism see William Curtis, *Modern Architecture since 1900*, pp. 356–66. Hassan Fathy's work embodies the quest for regionalist expression, as does that of Sedad Hakki Eldem.
6 A history of the building programmes of the Pahlavi regime has yet to be written. Little attention seems to have been paid to mosques, even though some very interesting ones were designed; see, however, Nader Ardalan, 'Architecture: Pahlavi, After World War II', *Encyclopaedia Iranica,* vol. II, pp. 326–55. After the overthrow of the Shah, the new regime took over a wide variety of public places for large-scale prayer rallies; mosque building as a programme did not emerge. Although some private initiatives have been evident, little has been published on this topic.
7 On the building boom in Saudi Arabia in the context of the development of the country, see Fouad Al-Farsi, *Modernity and Tradition*.

8 The concept of 'creolisation' is one coined by U. Hannerz, 'The World in Creolisation', *Africa* 57, pp. 546–9, and in 'Cosmopolitans and Locals in World Culture', M. Featherstone (ed.), *Global Culture: Nationalism, Globalization and Modernity*.
9 For a discussion of the formula, see Oleg Grabar, 'The Mosque in Islamic Society Today', in Martin Frishman and Hasan-Uddin Khan (eds.), *The Mosque*, pp. 242–6.
10 On the discussion of the nature of the Muslim diaspora, see Akbar Ahmed and Hastings Donnan (eds.), *Islam, Globalization and Postmodernity*, particularly pp. 1–20.
11 For example K.A.C. Creswell, *Early Muslim Architecture* and *Muslim Architecture of Egypt*; Prisse d'Avennes, *Arab Art as Seen Through the Monuments of Cairo from the 7th Century to the 18th*; Owen Jones, *The Grammar of Ornament*; A.U. Pope and P. Ackerman (eds.), *A Survey of Persian Art*. These are all publications which have been designated – often pejoratively – Orientalist, but which nevertheless played an essential role in forming the visual culture of the contemporary Muslim client. More recent publications such as Derek Hill's *Islamic Architecture and its Decoration* (with introduction by Oleg Grabar); Nader Ardalan and Laleh Bakhtiar, *The Sense of Unity: The Sufi Tradition in Persian Architecture*, and Issam el-Said and Ayse Parman, *Geometric Concepts in Islamic Art*, have enriched the visual vocabulary of the architects, and partially also of the clients. Ironically, even non-architectural studies of Islamic societies have been utilized to support particular arrangements in mosques; see for example the study published some 150 years ago, Edward Lane, *An Account of the Manners and Customs of the Modern Egyptians*.
12 On the nature of building trades in Egypt and the importation of skilled labour in the earlier part of the twentieth century, see Roger Owen, 'The Cairo Building Industry and the Building Boom of 1897 to 1907', *Colloque International sur l'Histoire du Caire*, pp. 337–50. The history of the development of new technically skilled cadres still needs to be written on a region-by-region and country-by-country basis. The subject is

mentioned in passing in respect of Turkey in Holod and Evin, op. cit., pp. 1–10. In general, though, much of the recent building boom has relied on the use of an international skilled labour force for the most technically sophisticated buildings.
13 For post-Islamic formulation, see Kanan Makiya, *Post-Islamic Classicism: A Visual Essay on the Architecture of Mohamed Makiya*.
14 Ironically, such a trend is occurring at the same time as works have been published showing the extensive particularism and separate developments of regionally and chronologically distinct schools that are present within the history of Islamic art and architecture. See, among some of the most recent publications: Catherine E.B. Asher, *Architecture of Mughal India*; Sheila Blair and Jonathan Bloom, *The Art and Architecture of Islam 1250–1800*; Robert Hillenbrand, *Islamic Architecture: Form, Function, and Meaning*; Michael Meinecke, *Die Mamlukische Architektur in Ägypten und Syrien*; Gülru Necipoğlu, *Architecture, Ceremonial, and Power: The Topkapi Palace in the Fifteenth and Sixteenth Centuries*; Lisa Golombek and Donald Wilber, *Timurid Architecture of Iran and Turan*; and Bernard O'Kane, *Timurid Architecture in Khurasan*.
15 For Indonesian examples see Josef Prijotomo, *Ideas and Forms of Javanese Architecture*; also Yuswadi Saliya, Hariadi and Gunawan Tjahjono, 'The Indonesian Experience', in *Expressions of Islam in Buildings*; and Hugh O'Neill, 'South-East Asia', in M. Frishman and H.U. Khan (eds.), *The Mosque*, pp. 225–41.
16 For a definition of the groups which can be designated as such see Hisham Sharabi, *Neopatriarchy: a Theory of Distorted Changes in Arab Society*.
17 On new calligraphers and artists, see among others, Wijdan Ali (ed.), *Contemporary Art from the Islamic World*.
18 For a critique of the competition for the projected Iraq State Mosque in Baghdad, see Mildred Schmertz, 'Mosque as Monument', *Architectural Record*, June 1984, pp. 142–9, and Oleg Grabar, 'From the past into the future: On two designs for State Mosques', op. cit., pp. 150–1.

19 The prolongation of the construction periods of mosques due to a lack of funds is evident in major public and private efforts and in the smaller community mosques, regardless of whether they are built in the Islamic world or in the West. This is borne out by our study of such mosques – both those included here and others not featured in this book.

20 Baber Johansen's unpublished paper, 'The Mosques: places of religious integration or political agitation?' (pp. 13–17), includes a discussion of *jami* or congregational mosques. We thank the author for making it available to us. See also 'Masjid', *Encyclopaedia of Islam* (2nd ed.), for a historic introduction to the mosque before the twentieth century.

21 On the role of the *waqf* in the twentieth century see also G. Busson de Janssens, 'Les Wakfs dans l'Islam contemporain', *Revue des Etudes Islamiques*, vol. XI, pp. 43–76. For a more recent review, see Faruk Bilici, *Le Waqf dans le monde musulman contemporain XIXe–XXe S. Fonction sociale, économique et politique*, Institut Français d'Études Anatoliennes, Istanbul, 1994.

22 Johansen, op. cit., pp. 2–5 and 19–22.

23 *Dahir portant loi no. 1-84-159 1984 relative aux édifices affectés au culte musulman, B.O. no. 3753* (Johansen, p. 4).

24 Décret no. 88-50 du mars 1988 relatif à la construction, à l'organisation et au fonctionnement des mosquées, *Le Journal Officiel de la République Algérienne*, no. 11, 6 mars 1988, pp. 317–18. The decree defines the mosque as the house of God in which prayers are held and the Qur'an is read and where 'the believers listen to what is useful to them in their religion and their life'. It follows the classical Islamic tradition in defining the types of mosques. There are three: the historical mosques, which in Algeria are classified jointly by the Ministry of Pious Affairs and the Ministry of Historical Monuments; the big mosque; and a third group of buildings which do not belong to either. The province maintains the historical mosques, while the municipalities take charge of the others of the first two categories. The authorities control the style of the mosque, making sure that it has a 'national character'. It is the Ministry of Pious Affairs which decides whether and when to open the doors of the mosque to the public. The mosque association may also equip the mosque and give money to support it, and these funds are constituted as a *waqf*. The subsequent maintenance of the building is taken over by the municipal and provincial administration. The personnel of the mosque are appointed by the Ministry of Pious Affairs. The *imam* is responsible for order and security in his mosque and is in charge of all the mosque's property and of all donations received. He is responsible for raising funds, but must apply to government authorities for permission to do so (after Johansen, op. cit., pp. 21–2).

25 Mohammed Arkoun, 'The Metamorphosis of the Sacred', in M. Frishman and H.U. Khan (eds.), *The Mosque*, pp. 268–73. Judging by the events of the 1990s in Algeria, these measures seem not to have even slowed the use of the mosque as a rallying centre for the Islamist cause – a 'lair and springboard'.

26 Loi no. 88-34 du mai 1988 relative aux mosquées, *Journal Officiel de la République Tunisienne, 6 mai 1988,* which emphasizes that the authorities are unwilling to tolerate any political agitation in the mosque: these spaces are not to be used for public speeches, assembly or the dissemination of written material by persons who are not part of the board of the mosques, which body is also directly under the control of the Prime Minister's office (after Johansen, op. cit., pp. 23–4).

27 Ottoman legal opinion considered it sufficient that a mosque's administrator or founder received the Sultan's permission to perform prayer. This legal opinion shows the degree to which ties between the political and military authorities on the one hand, and Friday mosques on the other, had loosened. This was accepted among nineteenth-century Hanafi judges (Johansen, op. cit., pp. 16–17).

28 The building of mosques in Europe was on the whole a much more charged issue – see Chapter 6. For example, the design of the Mosque and Islamic Centre in Rome had to conform with certain conditions laid down by the Vatican. (However, the height restrictions placed on the proposed design are equally applicable to all new buildings in Rome.) One may wonder whether a reciprocal initiative would be entertained in the same way in the Islamic world.

29 There is a growing volume of literature describing the circumstances of women in various Muslim societies, discussing a variety of issues pertaining to this theme. See for instance Valentine Moghaddam (ed.), *Gender and National Identity: Women and Politics in Muslim Societies*; Leila Ahmed, *Women and Gender in Islam*; and Nikki Keddie and Beth Baron (eds.), *Women in Middle Eastern History: Shifting Boundaries in Sex and Gender.* Fatima Mernissi's numerous works are very important in this context, for example, 'Women, Saints and Sanctuaries', *Signs* 3, pp. 100–11; *Doing Daily Battle: Interviews with Moroccan Women*; and *Femme et Pouvoir: Collection,* as well as *The Veil and the Male Elite: A Feminist Interpretation of Women's Rights in Islam.* Barbara Stowasser's *Women in the Qur'an: Traditions and Interpretation* sheds new light on these issues.

30 See a special issue of *Arts of Asia*, 1990, on the subject of women as patrons of architecture. See also the pioneering study of Ülkü Bates on the building activities of women in Seljuq and Ottoman society, 'Women as Patrons of Architecture in Turkey', in Nikki Keddie and Lois Beck (eds.), *Women in the Muslim World*, pp. 245–60. Also see Lucienne Thys-Senocak on Ottoman *valides* as patrons, *The Yeni Valide Mosque Complex in Eminonu, Istanbul*; Bernard O'Kane, op. cit. (n. 14), pp. 79–100, on Timurid women's building activities, particularly that of Gawhar Shad; see Yasser Tabbaa, *Circles of Power . . .* (in preparation), on Ayyubid women as patrons in Aleppo; Noha Sadek on the Rasulid women of Yemen; Renata Holod, 'Patronage and the Place of Women in the Monumental Architecture of Pre-modern and Early Modern Iran', in Guity Nashat (ed.), *Women in Iran* (in preparation), and D.F. Ruggles (ed.)., *Women, Patronage and Self-Representation in Islamic Studies* (in preparation). The present royal ruling élites such as those of Morocco, Saudi Arabia, Kuwait or Jordan do not appear to provide such an outlet for piety, power and recognition for their women, or none has been architecturally notable.

31 On women's religious life, see for example Laal Jamzadeh and Margaret Mills, 'Iranian Sofreh: From Collective to Female Ritual', in Caroline Walker Bynum, Stevan Harrell and Paula Richman (eds.), *Gender and Religion: On the Complexity of Symbols,* pp. 23–65; Anne H. Betteridge, *Ziarat: Pilgrimage to the Shrines of Shiraz*; Nancy Tapper, 'Gender and Religion in a Turkish Town: A Comparison of Two Types of Formal Women's Gatherings', in P. Holden (ed.), *Women's Religious Experience*.

32 On uses of shrines, see Fatima Mernissi, *Signs*, op. cit.; Roya Marefat, 'Beyond the Architecture of Death: the Shrine of the Shah-i-Zinda in Samarkand'; Hayat Salam, op. cit., pp. 97–101. No detailed study yet exists.

33 For example, women are shown in a thirteenth-century copy of the Maqamat as part of an audience for the sermon. Equally, in a seventeenth-century Persian miniature they appear in the galleries at a sermon; see Renata Holod 'Patronage and the Place of Women . . .', op. cit. (in preparation). Shrines seem to have been generally much more accessible for women and very much part of their religious life.

34 See articles: 'Hidjab', 'Pardah', 'Wudu' and 'Ghusl' in the *Encyclopaedia of Islam* and in the *Encyclopaedia Iranica*.

35 See the totally specious arguments concerning the location of the gallery of the Regent's Park Mosque in London, citing objections to women praying above men; the source given for this opinion was the mosque committee with reference to Edward Lane in his work of 1842. See Ronald Lewcock, 'London Central Mosque', *Architects' Journal*, August 1977, p. 266.

36 Fatma Sabbah, *Women in the Muslim Unconscious*; Abdelwahab Bouhdibaa, *Sexuality in Islam*; Basim Musallam, *Sex and Society in Islam*.

37 Zamakhshari al-Mahmud ibn 'Umar, *al-Kashaf'an haqa'iq ghawamid al-tanzil, (Matba'at al-istiqama)*, vol. 1, p. 277; Jalal ad-din Muhammad bin Ahmad al-Mahalli and Jalal ad-Din Abd al-Rahman al-Suyuti, *Tafsir al-Quran al-Azim, (Matba'at al-Istiqamat)*, p. 52; al-Razi, *al-Tafsir al-Kabir, (al-Matba'a al-bahiyya al-misriyya)*, vol. 8, p. 47, after Stowasser, p. 163.

38 The separation of the sexes in ritual contexts is a persistent pre-modern phenomenon. In the Eastern Church, for example, the interior space (facing the altar) was clearly divided with women on the left and men on the right. In pre-modern, and Orthodox, Jewish settings, women, if allowed into the synagogue at all, had to enter via a separate door leading to a gallery. In Italian medieval settings, temporary screens were set up to separate women and men in order to promote the attention of the congregation during sermons given by the great preachers. See Richard C. Trexler, *The Christian at Prayer: An Illustrated Prayer Manual Attributed to Peter the Chanter, Church and Community 1200–1600: Studies in the History of Florence and New Spain*, and *Public Life in Renaissance Florence*; also, as editor, *Gender Rhetorics: Postures of Dominance and Submission in History* (our thanks to Paul Watson for these

citations). On the role of women and the segregation of the sexes, see Yvonne Haddad and Ellison Banks Findly, *Women, Religion, and Social Change*; also Haddad and Adair Lumis, *Islamic Values in the United States*. See also Elaine Combs-Schilling, *Sacred Performances*, esp. pp. 135–255.

39 This seems to be increasingly the case in Diaspora mosques, as noted by Gulzar Haider and Muhammad Mukhtar in an unpublished paper, 'Islamic Architecture in Non-Islamic Environments', p. 30.

40 For example, recall the incident in Ayodhya in Northern India, where the Baberi Masjid, located in an area populated by Hindus, was destroyed by right-wing extremists in December 1992. In a subsequent act of reconciliation, an architectural ideas competition was held with the notion of building a new mosque and a Hindu temple on the same site; see the booklet by Aron Puri, *Yeh Bhumi!*, in which he discusses the ideas submitted by a number of Indian architects.

Chapter 1

1 According to the *Hadith* of the Prophet (and applied to men only): 'Man's deeds come to an end with his death, and only three things do not pass away from the world with him: charity which endures forever, knowledge which benefits others, and a virtuous son who prays for him.' (after al-Tirmidhi in Ibn Qudamah, *Al-Mughni*, v. 5, pp. 640–2; as noted by Jamal Akbar, *Crisis in the Built Environment: the Case of the Muslim City*, p. 203).

2 Although historically women have been important patrons of mosques, there are almost no examples of this type of patronage within the time span covered by this book.

3 AKAA Archives, Client's and Architect's record, 1985.

4 See Osamah El-Gohary, *Mosque Design in Light of Psycho-Religious Experience* (in preparation), on the necessity for visual and physical separation during prayer.

5 The information on the project is based on a personal site visit and on an exchange of correspondence (1990–1) between the architect and H.U. Khan.

6 It is unclear as to how extensively the Bhong Mosque is used by the villagers. An unconfirmed verbal report in 1995 suggested that the building was closed to the villagers,

who use the community mosque nearby. Another report asserts that they use the new building only on major religious occasions.

7 See for example Catherine Asher, *Architecture of Mughal India*, and Raymond Head, *The Indian Style*.

8 The mosque was a controversial winner of the Aga Khan Award for Architecture in 1989; the citation described it as a 'monumental achievement . . . It enshrines and epitomises the "popular" taste in Pakistan with all its vigor, pride, tension and sentiment. Its use – and misuse – of signs and symbols express appropriate growing pains of an architecture in transition . . .'. See I. Serageldin, *Space for Freedom: the Search for Architectural Excellence in Muslim Societies*, p. 150.

9 The colourful and exuberant *ars vulgaris* paintings and decorations on trucks in Pakistan have been explored in an essay by Hasan-Uddin Khan, 'Mobile Shelter in Pakistan', in *Shelter, Sign and Symbol*, pp. 183–96. See also article by Kamil Khan Mumtaz, 'Mistree Haji Ghulam Hussain', *Mimar* 10, pp. 8–13.

10 For Mamluk buildings see K.A.C. Creswell, *Muslim Architecture of Egypt*, and Michael Meinecke, *Die Mamlukische Architektur in Ägypten und Syrien*. The work of Egyptian architects has had a wide impact throughout the Arab world, particularly in Libya, Saudi Arabia and the Gulf States in the 1960s and 1970s; for example, they were responsible for the design of the reconstruction of the Mosque of the Prophet in Medina and for the Ka'ba enclosure and surrounding area in Mecca.

11 The Othman Mosque (also known as the Kuwaiti Mosque), donated to the city by Abdullah Abdullatif Al-Othman (a Kuwaiti), was designed by Mohammed Farra, a Damascus-based architect. Construction work was delayed due to the patron's death.

12 On the first Mamluk revival and Cairene architecture of the period, see Mercedes Volait, *L'Architecture moderne en Egypte et la revue al-'imara (1939–59)*, and Mohammad Al-Asad, *The Modern State Mosque in the Eastern Arab World, 1828–1985*; also on the al-Rifai Mosque in *Proceedings of the XVIII International Congress of the History of Art*, 1993.

13 The total cost of the project (excluding land) was 80 million pesetas. The client's representative was Eyad Kayali; the client

was a member of the Saudi royal family, and his exact role in the project development is unclear.

14 The brochure *La Mezquita del Sheykh Ibrahim bin Abdulaziz al-Ibrahim en Caracas*, published in 1993 (in Spanish and English) by the foundation, documents and illustrates the project.

15 Two other individuals who played a role on behalf of the Foundation were its Vice-President, Sheikh Khaled al-Ibrahim, and its Secretary-General, Fahad al-Yahya.

16 The project team was advised by the Saudi firm Zuhair Fayez and Associates and by Maria Luisa Fernandez, who had received her doctorate from Harvard University with Oleg Grabar, who was then the Aga Khan Professor there. The construction management company was Arquiobra, CA. All the artists and specialists involved in the works were Venezuelan.

17 Brochure, op. cit., p. 7.

18 Henry Vicente, 'A Formal Episode within a Millenary Typology' (brochure), op. cit., p. 36.

19 El-Wakil eventually closed his offices in England when commissions in the Middle East dried up; he moved to the USA, where he set up a practice in Florida in the 1990s.

20 For example, the Juffali Mosque sponsored by Ali al-Juffali; the Aziziyya Mosque sponsored by Regab Abdel Aziz and Silsila Abdullah, and the municipality of Jeddah. The whole programme of mosque building was supported by the Deputy Minister of Hajj and Awqaf, Sheikh Husam Khashoggi, and by the Mayor of Jeddah, Mohammad Said Al-Farsi. One could say that El-Wakil had an integrated vision of what mosques should be, at least, from the late 1970s onward, a vision that was accepted by his clients.

21 The eleven mosques by El-Wakil are: (in Jeddah) the small Corniche, Ruwais, Binladen and Island Mosques, and the community mosques of Sulaiman, Harithy, Aziziyya, Juffali and King Saud; and (in Medina) the Qiblatayn and Quba Mosques. With the exception of the Sulaiman Mosque, built in 1980, and the Ruwais Mosque, which remains unfinished, all the others were completed between 1986 and 1989.

22 The architect had just been commissioned by the sheikh to build him a palace. See 'El-Wakil's Buildings', *Mimar* 1 (1981), pp. 48–55.

23 The King Saud Mosque (funded by King Fahd of Saudi Arabia and given to the people of Jeddah), designed by Abdel Wahed El-Wakil

in Jeddah, is an interesting example in this context. 'The main dome of brick rises to a height of 42 m (136 ft) and spans 20 m (65 ft). Reliance on reinforced concrete is minimized and usually limited to foundations and platforms. Every one of El-Wakil's designs includes direct and often literal quotations from monuments belonging to the enormous corpus of Islamic architecture. For example, the composition of the portal and courtyard of the King Saud Mosque show the influence of those parts of the fourteenth-century Cairene mosque of Sultan Hasan. Its plan arrangement and the interior articulation of its main dome are based on those of the Great Mosque of Isfahan (eighth–seventeenth centuries) . . . . In contrast to his mentor Hassan Fathy, who drew exclusively from the vernacular architecture of the Egyptian countryside, El-Wakil relies on a wide variety of traditions including those of Mamluk Egypt, Saljuq Iran, Ottoman Turkey, and Rasulid Yemen.' Mohammad Al-Asad, 'The Mosques of Abdel Wahed El-Wakil', *Mimar* 42 (1992), p. 34.

24 Quote from El-Wakil, in an interview with Osamah El-Gohary, *Al-Benaa* 34, p. 17.

25 Al-Asad, op. cit. pp. 34–9.

26 Mayet has the same philosophy as El-Wakil. He has written: 'A mosque has to be "original". This does not mean it has to be different. It means it should relate to the "origin": the archetype through which all prototypes evolve.' See 'The City Room' in *Architecture SA* (South Africa), July–August 1994, p. 26.

27 As reported by Catherine Slessor in an article on the mosque, 'Sacred Room', *Architectural Review*, March 1995, pp. 68–9.

28 A short history of the building and a record of its architecture from the client's perspective can be found in the booklet *The Ismaili Centre*.

29 The main consultants for the interiors were Karl Schlamminger and Thomas Weil. Surat and Gulgee also contributed to the geometric and artistic references. There were also a great many specialist sub-contractors and suppliers, all co-ordinated by the project managers, Montagu Evans & Son.

30 Booklet, *The Ismaili Jamatkhana and Centre, Burnaby.*

31 The landscape design concept was developed also by Garr Campbell, who had worked for Sasaki Associates in the USA before he became the Aga Khan's landscape

planner and designer in France. Campbell worked on many of the Aga Khan's institutional buildings and centres, and his approach to geometry and planting is evident both in the London Centre and at Burnaby. This also set the pattern on which others later developed the landscape designs. The landscape architects of record for Burnaby are Vagelatos Associates of Vancouver.

32 Quoted from the first page of the booklet on Burnaby.

33 As quoted in 'Counterpoint' of the exhibition catalogue *Contemporary Houses, Traditional Values* by Brian Brace Taylor, pp. 10–11.

34 The king sponsored a major study devoted to Moroccan architecture and crafts: André Paccard, *Le Maroc et l'artisanat traditionnel Islamique dans l'architecture.*

35 Its first director, Abdou Filali-Ansary, a Moroccan, answers to a Board whose members comprise Saudis, Moroccans and other North African representatives.

36 The size and ambitious intent of the project are similar to the *Grands Projets* of Paris of the 1980s. Another parallel in the Francophone world is found in the Ivory Coast, where President Houphouet-Boigny inaugurated the largest Christian basilica in the world in 1989, modelled after St Peter's in Rome.

37 Mohammed Arkoun, 'The Metamorphosis of the Sacred', in Martin Frishman and Hasan-Uddin Khan (eds.), *The Mosque*, p. 272.

38 It is interesting that the king selected a foreign architect, but that he was French came as no surprise because of the long-established cultural connections between Morocco and France. In earlier major commissions foreign architects were also selected: the Vietnamese Vo Toan for the Mausoleum of Mohammed V and the Frenchman André Paccard for many royal palaces and other projects. Each worked under the close supervision of the king.

39 These figures (and more) are given in the 'official' book *La mosquée Hassan II*, with text by Mohammed-Allat Sinaceur.

40 These figures are given in: Tim McGirk, 'Strong-arm Tactics are used to Finance Hassan's Mosque', *The Independent* (London), 11 April 1989; Giles Milton, 'Hassan's Dream', *Telegraph Magazine* (London), 29 May 1993, p. 32; and 'Hassan Inaugure sa Mecque à Casablanca', *La Libération* (Paris), 30 August 1993, p. 14 – to name but three features in European newspapers.

41 A front-page banner which appeared above the title block of the Moroccan newspaper *Le Matin* in January 1995 proclaimed: 'Citoyens, citoyennes, répondez à l'appel de S.M. Hassan II, Amir Al-Mouminine, le Réunificateur, le Sauveur et le Rassembleur – Et si vous ne l'avez encore fait, souscrivez pour la maintenance, l'entretien et la gestion de la Mosquée Hassan II.'

42 The lotus blossom, more often associated with Hinduism, in Islam represents *sidrah* or highest wisdom. Such blossoms were found on the seventh (highest) heaven by the Prophet in his journey to the heavens – the *Miraj Nameh*. (We thank the religious scholar Nurcholish Madjid for pointing this out during a visit to the mosque in 1995.)

43 See M. Elaine Combs-Schilling, *Sacred Performances: Islam, Sexuality, and Sacrifice*, especially Chapter 8, pp. 157–74, concerning Al-Mansur's celebration of the Prophet's birthday. We are indebted to her also for her unpublished paper, 'Performing Monarchy, Staging Nation' (April 1994), in which she notes that 'by the early 1400s, a blood descendant of the Prophet re-emerged in Morocco using lineage to legitimize governance. The staging of the Prophet's birthday became a time of recalling this legitimacy. But it was not until the reign of al-Mansur ("the Victorious") in the 16th century that this performance became embedded into popular consciousness. Al-Mansur built the magnificent Baadi Palace in Marrakech after defeating the Portuguese in 1578 on Moroccan soil and re-establishing his sovereignty. The opening of the palace in 1593 was made to coincide with the Prophet's birthday and was attended by diplomats from all over the Mediterranean – the Hapsburgs, Castilians and Ottomans amongst them. In the celebrations [which occur in much the same way all over the Islamic world – author's note] a sequence of acts was realized. First, on the eve of the birthday a candle-lit procession led to the palace and poetry was read that evoked the place of both men and women in society. The next day the king, as symbolic head or "light" of the State, led the prayers in a unifying act of submission to the will of God. (The Prophet is often referred to as "God's light".) Later, surrounded by light, the king, his subjects and visitors, heard poetry chanted in praise of the Prophet and his descendant on the throne. "The Mantle of the Prophet", which was usually recited on these occasions, drew together the individuals all dressed in white robes into a cohesive unity. In anthropological terms, the king in this staging of central power becomes an emblematic figure that stands in for God, religion and state. Al-Mansur's staging of the birthday was an important act that consolidated nationhood within the population. The combining of ritual and place became a powerful icon that traversed time and reconfirmed the relationship between ruler and the ruled both as members of humanity under one God. The Sa'di dynasty ended soon after the death of al-Mansur in 1603, but the celebration of the birthday continued and was replicated elsewhere.' See also her 'Casablanca 1993: Negotiating Gender and Nation in Performative Space', *Journal of Ritual Studies* 10 (Summer 1996), pp. 3–35.

Chapter 2

1 AKAA 1988, Architect's Record for Istiqlal Mosque, p. 4.

2 Another indication of the concern to express a nationalist image can be found in the dome over the prayer hall, which has a diameter of 45 m. It apparently refers symbolically to the year in which Indonesia achieved independence. Op. cit., p. 9.

3 The second prize was awarded to R. Utojo and the third prize to Hans Groenewegen. Of the 27 designs submitted, 22 were seen by the committee in charge of the competition as being acceptable on the basis of the stated requirements of the programme. The entries were submitted under code names: Silaban's code name was 'Ketuhan' (Believer in God); Utojo's was 'Istiqfar' (Seer); and Groenewegen's was 'Salaam' (Peace). Op. cit., p. 4.

4 As Rex Mortimer in his essay 'The Place of Communism' and others in the book *Indonesia: Australian Perspectives* have noted, President Sukarno used both nationalist and liberation ideologies to consolidate his own power, '. . . the origin of the Marxist movement in Indonesia or Asia is the same as the origin of his own [Nationalist] movement' (p. 617). The period started with the revolution (1945–9), followed by phases of parliamentary democracy (1950–7), 'Guided Democracy' (1957–65), at a point when Sukarno felt slighted by the USA and turned to the Soviet Union for help, and the New Order (from 1966 onwards), when he controversially decided to clamp down on the activities of the powerful PKI (Parti Komunis Indonesia).

5 *Sukarno. An Autobiography*, p. 298, as told to Cindy Adams.

6 Trevor Boddy, 'Political Uses of Urban Design: The Jakarta Example', in *The Southeast Asian Environment*, pp. 31–41. His comments on the mosque as one of several new symbolic projects are interesting: 'Among the most lavish of these projects was the Istiqlal Mosque, built out of a sense of architectural competition to the national mosque of Malaysia in Kuala Lumpur . . . Forsaking the grace and refinement of the Malaysian example for simple, hulking grandeur . . . this construction required the elimination of Jakarta's most important historic sites' (p. 37).

7 As reported by Soedarmadji Damais in a conversation with H.U. Khan, 1989.

8 See Ismudiyanto and Parmono Atmadi, *Demak, Kudus & Jepara Mosques: A Study of Architectural Syncretism*, Jakarta, 1987. In Indonesia the corrected orientation of the mosque towards Mecca was a twentieth-century development. Early mosques had always been oriented on a simple east-west axis, in accordance with the established Hindu-Javanese tradition.

9 For Indonesian traditions of architecture, see Barry Dawson and John Gillow, *The Traditional Architecture of Indonesia*.

10 Indonesia's national philosophy, *pancasila*, is embodied in the preamble to the 1945 Constitution. Its points are: 'Belief in the One Supreme God; Just and Civilized Humanity; Unity of Indonesia; the People's Sovereignty guided by the wisdom of unanimity in deliberation among representatives; and Social Justice for all the people of Indonesia.' Although Indonesia has the world's largest Muslim population, it does not style itself an 'Islamic Republic'. See E. Darmaputera, *Pancasila and the Search for Identity and Modernity in Indonesian Society*, pp. 146ff.

11 See Roger Caratini, *Le génie de l'Islamisme*, p. 694. Caratini's estimates are based on the latest available population figures from various national censuses taken between 1986 and 1990. In the 1950s, Malaysia's Muslim population was estimated at around 48% of the total; more recent estimates suggest that the proportion is about 50%.

12 Clifford Geertz, *Interpretation of Cultures*, New York, 1973, p. 245.

13 *Masjid Negara*, a 53-page booklet issued on the occasion of the inauguration of the mosque on 25 August 1965, is a particularly important and informative document. In it are outlined the ideological intentions of its inception as expressed by the Prime Minister of Malaysia, Tunku Abdul Rahman Putra. He wrote: '. . . I conceived the idea of building this Masjid Negara when I first assumed leadership of our people and nation. In addition to being able to serve the nation, I was desirous of serving the cause of Islam, the official religion of the country. The Masjid Negara, impressive and centrally situated in the nation's capital . . . '. The booklet also contains a detailed description of the completed complex, a detailed chronology of its financing, design and construction, as well as lists of individuals who sat on the major organizing and programming committee. It also features a brief but useful history both of the spread of Islam and of mosque architecture in Malaysia.

14 Apparently it was the Prime Minister who ultimately selected the site near the railway station. When he made his decision public, some critics argued that the site was too far away from Muslim residential areas and that it was bisected by a ravine. The ravine was subsequently filled in with the earth excavated from the site of the nearby Negara Stadium.

15 *Masjid Negara*, op. cit.

16 Once the federal government had agreed to contribute $4.5 million, the working party began an official nationwide fundraising campaign, the first to be launched in the country. In each state a committee headed by a Chief Minister was set up to collect contributions from the public. Among the many individuals and groups whose cash contributions fell in the category of public donations were the first gift from Brunei of $25,000 and $26,000 from the Shaw Foundation. The South Indian community contributed $18,716 and Senator J.S. Crawford gave $250 per month from the time the campaign was launched.

17 *Masjid Negara*, op. cit..

18 See Ken Yeang, *The Architecture of Malaysia*, p. 239.

19 *Masjid Negara*, op.cit.

20 The client considered this a revolutionary design: 'The mihrab, where the Imam leads the prayer, is revolutionary in design. Rectangular in shape instead of the usual arch, it looks like a door.' From a colour brochure available at the National Mosque, p. 26.

21 The second and third prizes were awarded to C.H.R. Bailey of Edwards & Partners, and Fong Ying Hong respectively.

22 The Malaysian Architects Co-Partnership (MAC), formed in 1960 by three British-trained architects, Chen Voon Fee, Lim Chong Keat and William Lim, was the first local architectural firm to coin a group name instead of using the partners' names. The partnership was dissolved in 1967 when Lim Chong Keat, Lim Chin See and Baharuddin Abu Kassim combined to form Jurubena Bertiga (Team 3), Chen Voon Fee formed Akitek Berakan, and William Lim started his own practice in Singapore.

23 An existing off-site car park near the State Assembly Hall provided sufficient space for users.

24 'Negeri Sembilan State Mosque Architectural Competition', *PETA*, vol. 4, nos. 3 & 4, pp. 42–50.

25 In the early 1980s, the government actually tried to define by law what Islamic architecture should be. They ran into problems, because architects would define it one way and bureaucrats another. The bureaucrats adopted early Malay houses as their model, and this produced a great deal of resentment among many architects and planners in Malaysia, the majority of whom are ethnic Chinese. Attempts to create a national architecture that satisfies three or four groups continue to be made. At a seminar held in Kuala Lumpur, the question of identity in architecture was raised again, but those discussing the issue carefully skirted the concealed antagonism that exists between the Chinese who run the building industry and the Bumiputera Malays (meaning literally 'sons of the soil') who control the country. The topic was discussed in veiled terms because no one wanted to see a repetition of the communal violence that erupted in 1960s, but the underlying tension was nonetheless present. See Hasan-Uddin Khan, 'Some Recent Large-Scale Projects in Asia', in *Continuity and Change: Design Strategies for Large-Scale Urban Development*, pp. 14–15. It should be noted that by the early 1990s the situation seems to have improved, thanks to equal opportunities being available to the Chinese, Indian and Malay members of the population.

26 The minarets were recorded in the 1988 *Guinness Book of Records* as the world's tallest.

27 Construction of the mosque, named after the Sultan, began in 1977 and was to have been completed in time for his Silver Jubilee in 1985. The building was inaugurated in March 1988, on the Sultan's birthday, at a ceremony attended by leaders from all over the Islamic world, including the Sultan of Brunei. The building cost $162 million and was paid for by the State, the richest in the Federation of Malaysia.

28 Described by Ken Yeang in *The Architecture of Malaysia*, p. 332. Moussawi was one of the prize-winning architects in the earlier Rome Mosque competition; although the Sarawak State Mosque owes much to that building in terms of its rectangular exterior design and the interior of the prayer hall, the result is not as elegant a solution and is more historicist in its realization.

29 The Commission was set up in 1959 by the head of the martial law administration, Gen. Ayub Khan. It had the following terms of reference: (1) to consider the suitability of Karachi as the capital, and (2) to recommend an alternative site if Karachi was deemed unsuitable. The decision was reached in June 1959, and the plan rather rapidly realized in 1960. The Capital Development Authority (CDA) was established in 1960. See *Islamabad: The City of Peace*.

30 The competition entries were judged by Samir Abu Bakr Ghaffar (Saudi Arabia), Aptullah Kuran (Turkey), Philip Khouri (Lebanon), Mazharul Islam (East Pakistan; now Bangladesh), and the Chairman of the Capital Development Authority, Lt-Gen. K.M. Sheikh.

31 The jury members chose Dalokay's design by a 4 to 1 majority. In an article entitled 'The Shah Faisal Mosque' in *Habitat Pakistan*, vol. 2, no. 2 (pp. 22–3), Sikandar A. Khan records the jury's comment on the winning scheme: 'The classical approach of formal mosque architecture is blended in this project with modern forms and technology. The simplicity of the general layout . . . is appreciated.' However, some revisions were recommended so that it would '. . . more strictly conform to a modernist paradigm . . . and all "traditional" references be eliminated.' The second prize was awarded to Ozer, Eren and Tokcan, and the third prize was awarded to N. Bindal; interestingly, both projects proposed radically

259

modern roof forms and tall Ottoman-style minarets. Makiya & Associates also took part in the competition.

32 The initial project cost in 1966 was estimated at US$10 million; the final cost amounted to US$40 million, due in part to the increase in the size of the programme, but also as the result of cost over-runs and fluctuations in currency conversion rates for imported items.

33 See 'The Shah Faisal Mosque' (op. cit.), p. 21.

34 Also see Imran Ahmed, 'Expression of Nationhood'.

35 AKAA 1985, Architect's Record for the Great Mosque of Kuwait. In the programme the mosque was to be referred to as the 'Great State Mosque'. The authorities later dropped the word 'state', and the mosque is now known as the 'Great Mosque'. See Mohammad Al-Asad, *The Modern State Mosque in the Eastern Arab World, 1828–1985*. Our discussion of this mosque is indebted to Dr Al-Asad's work.

36 See Kuwait, Ministry of Public Works, *Masjid al-Dawlah al-Kabir, Mutatallabat* (Great State Mosque, Requirements).

37 Ibid. For a characterization of the brief, see also the comments by Kanan Makiya in Lawrence Weschler, 'Architects Amid the Ruins', *The New Yorker*, 6 January 1992, p. 49, where the brief for the mosque is referred to as 'The Kuwait State Mosque and Multi-Storey Car Park'.

38 M. Al-Asad, op. cit., p. 97.

39 M. Al-Asad notes: 'As a result of its massive size and the existence of a number of entrances located in different parts of the complex, this arrangement initially may be difficult to visualize by the approaching visitor. The predominance of right angles is contrasted by the curving surfaces of the large dome and the octagonal section of the minaret. Also, it is interesting to note that even though the monument is surrounded by open areas consisting of landscaped terraces and wide boulevards, the massive size of the structure does not allow for full views of its longer facades.' Op. cit., p. 98.

40 AKAA 1985, Architect's Record for the Great Mosque of Kuwait.

41 Ibid., p. 7.

42 Ibid., p. 6.

43 Makiya's suggestions were made in a letter dated 4 April 1988 sent by him to the Kuwaiti Minister of Public Works (M. Al-Asad, op. cit., p. 100). See, however, Kanan Makiya's

comments on the imposed over-decoration of the original scheme (op. cit., p. 50).

44 Ibid., p. 107. M. Al-Asad identifies part of the problem as being related to the mosque's proximity to the Emir's palace/administrative headquarters.

45 Al-Asad, op. cit. The Kuwait Water Towers won an Aga Khan Award in 1980. See R. Holod with D. Rastofer (eds.), *Architecture and Community: Building in the Islamic World Today*.

46 The project was never realized due to the continuing Iraq-Iran conflict and, later, to the events associated with the Gulf War of 1991 and its consequences for Iraq.

47 Statement by the Competition Organizers in 'Regenerative Approaches to Mosque Design', *Mimar* 11, p. 45.

48 If built, this mosque would have an area second only to that of the Great Mosque of al-Mutawwakhil at Samarra (847–861), also located in present-day Iraq, which measured 376 x 444 m (i.e. an area of 166,944 sq. m). At the time of the programming of the mosque competition these were the dimensions to be exceeded. Now, one can regard the recently reconstructed Mosque of the Prophet in Medina and the Mosque of Hassan II in Casablanca as the largest in the world.

49 John Simpson, writing in *The Times* in August 1995, stated that President Saddam Hussein had 'laid the foundation stone of the largest mosque in the world' in 1994. Whether this means that the winning state mosque competition entry will eventually be built or whether some other scheme will be erected on the site remains unclear.

50 For a fuller description of the climate within which the building campaign came about, see Lawrence Weschler, op. cit., p. 50.

51 For additional information on the organization of the competition, see *Competition Programme, International Design Competition for the State Mosque, Baghdad, Iraq.*

52 Chadirji's involvement in Baghdad's projects of the time has a rather curious history. He had been imprisoned in 1978 on charge of allegedly misappropriating funds. He was released in 1981 and required to head the building programme, having been granted plenipotentiary powers to bypass the regular course of government bureaucracy. The story of the conditions of his release was narrated to the authors by himself, as well as by Mohamed Makiya.

53 See Competition Programme, op. cit.

54 This choice of architects was based on Chadirji's desire to involve a diverse group of participants, including some with international reputations. This consideration was equally true for other projects undertaken in the context of the entire campaign for the beautification of Baghdad. Each participant in the mosque competition was paid an honorarium of approximately 20,000 Iraqi dinars (over US$60,000) for expenses. Information from a personal communication with R. Holod; see also M. Al-Asad, op. cit., pp. 132ff.

55 Makiya in a conversation with R. Holod and H.U. Khan in 1982.

56 Among them were The Architects' Collaborative, Josep Lluis Sert, Harrison & Abramovitz, Jørn Utzon and Henning Larsen. See M. Al-Asad, op. cit., p. 134.

57 These statements are reproduced in 'Regenerative Approaches', op. cit., pp. 50–63.

58 Al-Asad, op. cit. p. 138.

59 In addition to the problems arising from the rejection of the jury's decision, the impetus for proceeding in an orderly fashion to construction of the mosque was in any case dissipated due to preoccupations with the war with Iran; also by the beginning of the following year the main force behind the competition, Rifat Chadirji, had left Iraq.

60 See 'Regenerative Approaches . . .', op. cit., pp. 56–7. Badran's expert advisor on Islamic architecture was Oleg Grabar.

61 Ibid., p. 56.

62 Ibid., pp. 60–1.

63 See for instance M. Al-Asad, p.139.

64 See 'Regenerative Approaches . . .', op. cit., p. 62.

65 Ibid., p. 50.

66 Venturi was given advice on Islamic architecture by Renata Holod and on Islamic history and the inscription programme by Muhsin Mahdi. His calligrapher was Mohammed Zakariya.

67 For another opinion, see Al-Asad, op. cit.

68 Quotations from typed instructions to the architects dated 17 March 1980 issued by the Government of Libya.

69 The building is permanently closed to non-Muslims.

70 The architect is reputed to be an Italian, but in spite of several attempts to ascertain his name, the authors were unsuccessful.

71 Cited in Alexandra Tyng, *Beginnings: Louis Kahn's Philosophy of Architecture*, p. 91.

72 The process of design and change is well documented in Chapter 9 of Lawrence Vale's book *Architecture, Power and National Identity*, 'The Acropolis of Bangladesh', pp. 236–71. See also David B. Brownlee and David G. De Long, *Louis I. Kahn: In the Realm of Architecture* (catalogue to accompany a travelling exhibition [1992–4] organized by the Museum of Contemporary Art, Los Angeles), pp. 374–83.

73 Richard Saul Wurman, *What Will Be Has Always Been: The Words of Louis I. Kahn*, 1986, p. 216.

74 Cited in Heinz Ronner, Sharad Javeri and Alessandro Vasella (eds.), *Louis I. Kahn: Complete Works 1935–1974*, p. 230.

75 Although Pakistan called itself an Islamic Republic in its formative years, state and religious acts were usually kept separate. Part of the worry was that religious and ethnic differences could be disruptive – as was demonstrated by the events that led to the separation of East Pakistan in 1971. Islam became the official religion of Bangladesh in 1988 under President Ershad.

76 At one time several Bangladeshi architects felt the *qibla* orientation to be incorrect. However, as Lawrence Vale has pointed out: 'This perception may even withstand a cursory glance at the plans. Upon examination, however, it seems clear that it looks this way only because the orthogonal South Plaza outside the mosque entrance is itself not cardinally oriented . . . in his orientation of the mosque at least, Kahn stayed in line with prevailing local sentiment. That some in Dhaka have raised misorientation as an issue, however, may be symptomatic of other concerns about the building and about its imported designer's interpretation of the role of Islam.' (op. cit., p. 263).

77 Ibid.

78 Kahn's address delivered to the Boston Society of Architects, April 1966, published in *Boston Society of Architects' Journal* 1 (1967), pp. 5–20.

79 The story of Dalokay's mosque design is quite complex. Apparently the shape of the proposed concrete shell caused an uproar. It was compared to a garage in Chicago and the minarets were called rockets. In fact, the project was aborted after the foundation had already been poured.

80 For a discussion of the creation of the new capital and its main government buildings in the late 1920s and 1930s, see Renata Holod and Ahmet Evin (eds.), *Modern Turkish Architecture*.

81 Aydan Balamir and Jale Erzen, 'Contemporary Turkish Mosque Architecture'.

82 See Balamir and Erzen, op. cit., and AKAA 1992, Architect's Record. Also involved were Orhan Berk (Associate Architect) and Arican Kurtay (Civil Engineer).

83 The architects state: '. . . the purpose of the design is the creation of a "transitional space" within which an intimate one-to-one relation with God is to occur. . . . the main space respects and encourages the knowledge and belief that in Islamic worship the eyes are not raised skywards – reconfirming the motto of "modesty rather than glorification" . . . prototypical elements (*riwak,* courtyard, minaret, etc. are abstracted to serve as familiar signs.' AKAA 1992, Architects' Record, p. 2.

84 The actual costs (without land) were 2,800 million Turkish lira or US$1,670,000 – totally funded by the government. Source: AKAA 1992, Architects' Record.

85 Rough construction was executed by Molin Construction Firm; finishes were carried out by the construction department of the Department of Pious Foundations (Vakılfar). It is interesting to note that the use of reinforced-concrete techniques has developed into an advanced skill among Turkish construction workers, probably due to their association with industry as 'guest workers' in Germany and Holland.

86 See Balamir and Erzen, op. cit.

87 AKAA 1992, Architects' Record, p. 5.

88 The mosque received an Aga Khan Award in 1992. See 'Mosque of the Grand National Assembly', in Cynthia C. Davidson (ed.), *Architecture beyond Architecture*, London, 1995, pp. 124–31.

Chapter 3

1 Turkey has been an important model for 'modern' government in many newly independent Islamic countries. On the state mechanisms within Turkey see, *inter alia*, the work of Ilhan Tekeli and S. Yerasimos.

2 Since the mid-1980s the situation has changed somewhat in some countries. For example, in Turkey municipalities have floated bonds both nationally and internationally to raise funds for projects. Similarly, they are also empowered to levy local taxes. However, these new fiscal arrangements have not yet affected the funding of mosques anywhere.

3 In *Gourna: A Tale of Two Villages*, Fathy speaks of four tribes and five hamlets which defined the social groupings of the local population. The fifth group may well have been Coptic Christians; if so, it would explain why a church was also built and why there were only four *iwans* in the mosque (where the Muslim tribes gathered). It does not, however, explain why Fathy speaks of only four different sectors in the village. This aspect is not made sufficiently clear in his account.

4 Fathy explains his reasons for this in *Architecture for the Poor*, p. 75: 'I thought it proper to begin with this building as the spiritual centre of the village and thus most fitting for a ceremonial foundation stone laying, and also because the orientation of the mosque is predetermined – in this case, I have been careful to ascertain, it was 121 degrees 10' from N.'

5 Cf. *Architecture for the Poor*, pp. 74–5.

6 Fathy said: 'To make a building that should have that sober and calm air that leads to quiet meditation and prayer, I had to consider how the light would fall upon its walls and be distributed in its rooms.' (*Architecture for the Poor*, p. 74).

7 On the topic of the environment necessary for concentration during prayer, see Osamah El-Gohary, *Mosque Design in Light of Psycho-Religious Experience* (in preparation).

8 One can cite numerous projects as examples of this wider impact, e.g. the Agricultural Training Centre (1977) in Nianing, Senegal; the Halawa House (1975) in Agamy, Egypt; and the village of Abiquiu (1984) in New Mexico, USA. See R. Holod with D. Rastofer (eds.), *Architecture and Community*, pp. 236–46, as well as the subsequent monograph, *Hassan Fathy*, by James Steele. The task of tracing all the influences still remains to be undertaken.

9 A number of young architects and students attached themselves to Fathy for short periods in the 1970s. Prominent amongst them were the Egyptians Umar Farouk and Abdel Wahed el-Wakil (examples of whose work are covered in this book); also students from the Architectural Association School of Architecture in London and from other European schools, including the members of the Development Workshop who worked with him in Oman and later independently in Iran and West Africa. A little later, others, such as the group CRATERE from Grenoble in France,

ADAUA in Switzerland and West Africa, and individuals such as Rami Dahan of Egypt and Elie Mouyal of Morocco, modelled their philosophies and work on Fathy's example. It can be argued that Fathy is perhaps the most influential twentieth-century architect of the Islamic world.

10 For coverage of this project see Sawsan Noweir, 'The El Miniawy Architects', *Mimar* 8, April–June 1983, pp. 7–17, and *Techniques et Architectures* 329, March 1980.

11 Mohammed Arkoun spoke about the Algerian Agrarian Revolution programme (launched by President Boumedienne in 1971) at an Aga Khan Award seminar held in Beijing; his views were published as 'The Socialist Villages Experiment in Algeria' in *The Changing Rural Habitat*, vol. 1, pp. 45–50.

12 Mohammed Arkoun has noted that in the 1980s the mosque was used for political purposes, as a refuge for fugitives and as 'a lair and springboard' from which to launch their activities. For his analysis of the function of the mosque see 'The Metamorphosis of the Sacred', in M. Frishman and H.U. Khan (eds.), *The Mosque*, pp. 268–77. Also see B. Johansen on the role of the mosque, cited above in the Introduction.

13 Judith Nagata, 'How to be Islamic without being an Islamic State: Contested Models of Development,' in Akbar Ahmed and Hastings Donnan (eds.), *Islam, Globalization and Postmodernity*, pp. 63–90.

14 Reported by Abbad Al Radi in the AKAA 1992, Technical Review Summary of Timber Modular Mosques, p. 1.

15 He states: 'In the context of rural mosques, much can be learnt from the climatically sensitive Malay traditional buildings. The essential features consist of elements such as the covered verandahs, open terraces, raised floors, extended overhangs, central air-well, and courtyards. These traditional architectural elements are often the result of an instinctive ("unselfconscious") design response to local climate and life style. Designs must respond to nature so that the buildings harmonize with the environment. They must also respond to the Malaysian climate. Roof and spatial design should provide shade to keep out the sun and rain whilst encouraging cross-ventilation. Local architecture should respond to local technology and materials and many designs incorporate timber of which Malaysia has an abundant supply. The relatively lower level of sophistication in

workmanship can be exploited in the sense that characteristics such as roughness and imperfections can be accentuated.' As related by Abbad Al Radi, (op. cit., p. 4).

16 Roof types originate in different house forms, for example: *bambung lima*, with its hipped roof; *bambung perak*, with a gambrel roof influenced by the Dutch style; and *bambung limas*, the pyramidal shape used for mosques but seldom in houses. Tile and wood shingles are traditional. *Merbau* or *meru* (a medium hardwood) is the timber utilized most commonly in the region. The Kampung Laut Masjid was probably modelled on the Demak Mosque (c. 1478) in Java, Indonesia.

17 For details of mosque types, design and locations, see the AKAA Technical Review Summary, op. cit.

18 Ibid., p. 7.

19 The Public Works Department (PWD) cost estimate for a typical masonry mosque with capacity for 250 persons was around 1.4 million Malaysian ringitts (US$425,000), whereas the equivalent ASPA 'B'-type mosque cost 260,000 ringitts (US$104,000). The larger 'C'-type cost MR 350,000 (US$144,000). Cf. Technical Review, op. cit., p. 9.

20 The Housing and Development Board was founded in 1960 as the statutory authority for public housing in Singapore – its responsibilities cover the construction of housing as well as the preparation of new town-planning schemes, the provision of public facilities in these towns, and the management and maintenance of all these properties. By the mid-1980s over 80% of the population was accommodated in over 500,000 units built and managed by HDB. For a review of projects see *Designed for Living: Public Housing Architecture in Singapore*, produced by the HDB.

21 AKAA 1989, Technical Review Summary, p. 5, quoting an HDB report.

22 See *New-Generation Mosques in Singapore and their Activities*.

23 Op. cit., p. 4.

24 In the AKAA 1989 Technical Review Summary for the Darul Aman Mosque, Romi Khosla suggests that 'the enormous roof over the central space precludes any illusions of being within a courtyard which the plan certainly hints at . . . [the building] indicates the courtyard concept of many traditional mosques, and yet at a perceptual level, it is close to the indigenous architecture of this region', p. 4.

25 'For Muslim Singaporeans living in a modern and highly urbanized Singapore their participation and involvement in these dynamic new-generation mosques provide the material and spiritual needs of their daily lives.' (ibid., pp. 11–12).

26 The false ceiling is of gypsum board, and the exterior façades are of brick plastered over with a grit finish. The woodwork for the *mihrab* and the *imam*'s chair were executed by Ikram Arts Pvt. Ltd and the contractors were M/s Guan Hong Construction Company. The actual cost of the project was S$2,310,037 (S$922 per square metre) in 1986, and the architect claims that his costs were below prevailing construction costs for public buildings at the time of completion. Ibid., p. 7.

27 For a formal exploration of the Malay roof, see also the unbuilt project in Penang by Fawziah Kamal published in *Mimar* 1 (1981); see also Chapter 6, 'The Indonesian Experience', in Hayat Salam (ed.), *Expressions of Islam in Buildings*, pp. 190–3.

28 For an introduction to modernist city building see, among others, Norma Evenson, *Chandigarh*, and Lawrence Vale, *Architecture, Power, and National Identity*.

29 The term 'Ekistics' was formulated by Constantinos A. Doxiadis (1913–75) in the mid-1940s to designate a new field of knowledge dealing with the science of human settlements; it embraced various disciplines such as economics, social sciences, history, anthropology, and city and regional planning in combination with new technology, and sought to apply this knowledge using systematic, mathematical and scientific techniques. See C. A. Doxiadis, *Ekistics: An Introduction to the Science of Human Settlements*; see also Gerald Dix (ed.), *Ecology and Ekistics*.

30 See Kamil Khan Mumtaz, *Architecture in Pakistan*, pp. 184–8; the CDA booklet, *Islamabad*; and Chapter 5 entitled 'Designed Capitals since 1960' in Lawrence Vale, *Architecture, Power, and National Identity*, pp. 128–34.

31 Anwar Saeed remained Chief Architect of CDA for some thirty years; his architectural output includes a number of significant mosques, the designs for which are in a similar vein to that of his 'C-type' Ahle Hadith Mosque.

32 See for example the works of Edward D. Stone and Arne Jacobsen.

33 It is unclear what role they played in the oversight or control of the project. It appears that, because of the President's initial interest, the design team was given a fairly free hand.
34 The design advisors were Mohamed Mahmoud Hamdi, Seif Eddin al-Sadiq, and Seddiq Abdelwahab. The senior engineers were Hashim Khalifa and Khalid Fadou al-Saeed. The British Aluminium Company was responsible for the design and manufacture of the cladding system, the elements of which were fabricated in Britain and assembled on site.
35 The project was budgeted at US$3.3 million in 1976. The doubling of the cost was mainly due to the very high rate of inflation which adversely affected the cost of imported materials.
36 The architect felt that the relationship of his building to the forces of nature was a crucial factor in the design: the same principle was also used to justify the shape of the building (personal communication with H.U. Khan in 1987).
37 See article 'Bid'a' in Encyclopaedia of Islam (2nd ed.). Islamic jurisprudence has always differentiated between two different kinds of bid'a, the good (hasan) or praiseworthy (mahmuda), and the bad (sayyi'a) or blameworthy (madhmuma); only the latter is referred to here.
38 AKAA 1985, Client's Record Form. Concerns with the design were voiced by a number of people, while others (including the President) supported it. It is unclear what the specific 'religious and symbolic' issues at the time were.
39 Oleg Grabar, 'From the Past into the Future: On Two Designs for State Mosques', Architectural Record, June 1984, pp. 150–1.
40 See Yasser Tabbaa, 'The Muqarnas Dome: Its Origin and Meaning', Muqarnas 3 (1985), pp. 61–74, and Oleg Grabar, The Alhambra.
41 On the destruction of the domes of mausolea, see, for instance, Abdulla Bokhari, Jeddah (Ph.D. dissertation, University of Pennsylvania), 1978, pp. 191ff..
42 For a series of typical examples see Kaizer Talib, Shelter in Saudi Arabia.
43 The contractors for the project were Korean. The total cost (just under budget) was 123.6 million Saudi rials (equivalent to approximately US$39 million); the cost per square metre, SR2,278/$715, was below the general average in the country at that time. This is borne out by comparison with the construction costs of other mosques built

in Saudi Arabia. For more on Al-Kindi Plaza, see James Steele (ed.), Architecture for Islamic Societies Today, p. 99.
44 By 1990, Rasem Badran, principal of SBA (formerly Shubeilat, Badran and Keilany) had become one of the most prominent practitioners in the Islamic world. He was educated in Germany and worked there until his return to Amman in 1973. His firm (started in 1976) has undertaken major projects all over the Middle East, in Spain and in Malaysia. He has won many architectural competitions and his prolific output includes houses, housing schemes and universities, as well as large institutional and commercial complexes.
45 For an illustration of the design evolution, see Badran's presentation in Margaret Ševčenko (ed.), Theories and Principles of Design in the Architecture of Islamic Societies, pp. 149–60.
46 The project was overseen by the Riyadh Development Authority (RDA), formerly known as the High Commission for the Development of Riyadh, under Mohammad bin Abdulaziz Al-Shaikh, Minister of Municipal and Rural Affairs. The guiding commission for the second phase included its leaders, Al-Shaikh as Director-General, Planning and Programmes (and later President of RDA), Ahmed bin Mohammed Assalloom as Director-General, Construction, Operations and Maintenance, and Ibrahim bin Mohammed Assultan in his capacity as Director of Construction.
47 For an exploration of this relationship in early Arab Muslim cities, see Nezar Alsayyad, Cities and Caliphs: On the Genesis of Arab Muslim Urbanism, and Hisham Djait, Al-Kufa, Naissance de la ville islamique.
48 Rasem Badran in the unpublished text of a lecture given in April 1993 entitled 'The Justice Palace (Qasr Al Hokm) and the Jami Mosque', p. 4.
49 As reported in 1993 by Stefano Bianca, one of the competition organizers, in a personal communication to H.U. Khan.
50 On the history and geography of Jeddah, see Bokhari, op. cit., and Angelo Pesce, Jeddah, Portrait of an Arabian City.
51 See 'An Island Mosque in Jeddah', Mimar 19 (1986), pp. 12–17; also Mohammad Al-Asad's 'The Mosques of Abdel Wahed El-Wakil', Mimar 42 (1992), pp. 34–9.
52 Similar developments include those in Beirut in the 1970s and the waterfront area

of Kuwait City, as well as Jakarta's 'Ancol' recreation area.
53 The mosques designed by El-Wakil for Jeddah and Medina were reviewed by Mohammad Al-Asad in 1989 for the Aga Khan Award for Architecture; see his Technical Review Summary 'Saudi Mosques'. Al-Asad studied seven mosques as possible recipients of the Award and was positive about El-Wakil's group 'that provides us with an important contribution to the Islamic world'. The Award Jury appeared to have considered the three small mosques – Island, Corniche and Binladen – most seriously as candidates for a joint award, and eventually selected the Corniche Mosque as a representative award-winning project.
54 This led to subsequent commissions from the Ministry of Hajj and Awqaf to realize several other mosques in Jeddah and Medina, as well as other buildings elsewhere in Saudi Arabia. A curious detail concerning the history of the small mosques is related by El-Wakil, who recalls that the mayor, Mohammad Said Al-Farsi, originally approached him with a suggestion for a series of sculptures to be sited around the city. When the architect proposed a series of small mosques, the mayor immediately took to the idea and set about making arrangements for the project. For an account of the project history see 'An Island Mosque in Jeddah', op. cit.
55 It is surmised that Farsi chose not to ask El-Wakil to design his mosque as to have done so might have been interpreted as evidence of favouritism (based on a conversation between the mayor and H.U. Khan in Jeddah in January 1985).
56 Unlike the other projects, there was no general contractor for the Corniche Mosque.
57 The Island Mosque cost SR5.5 million at SR13,750 (equivalent to US$3,700) per sq. m, whereas the Corniche Mosque cost SR1.5 million (or US$2,050 per sq. m). Like El-Wakil's other mosques, these buildings are relatively expensive mainly because of their decorative finishes and the use of structural brick, an uncommon building material in this region.
58 See J. Steele (ed.), Architecture for Islamic Societies Today, pp. 110–15.
59 Chris Abel, 'Model and Metaphor in the Design of New Building Types in Saudi Arabia', in M. Ševčenko (ed.), Theories and Principles of Design in the Architecture of Islamic Societies, p. 173.

60 Ibid.

61 Ibid.

62 Abdel Wahed El-Wakil in *Mimar* 17 (1985), p. 13.

63 See 'Results of Mimar Competition III' in *Mimar* 17 (1985), pp. 9–29. Sixteen of the projects were published in this issue.

64 'As a jury we were very aware of the impact our choices could have on younger designers and the search for a combination of beauty, spirituality, place and function became much more serious in our minds as we discussed the projects. (I suspect we were more serious than earlier juries because of two factors: the works were being judged in the heartland of Islam, Saudi Arabia, and that religious buildings resonated strongly with our own beliefs and the faith itself.) The judgment process became much more than just judging "good design" and took on the broader debate on architectural symbolism and regionalism, culture and the message conveyed by our choices to architects and clients, especially those in the Islamic world. Perhaps this is why the jury as a whole was "conservative." Hasan-Uddin Khan, ibid., p. 11. For statements made by the other members of the jury, see pp. 11–13.

65 Diba, the principal architect, was assisted by Parvin Pezeshki, Mamnoon, C.P. Saberwal and S.K. Manchandra. It is unclear what the roles of individual members of the team were.

66 Diba in *Kamran Diba: Buildings & Projects*, p. 11.

67 Diba's Shushtar project was 'Highly Commended' in the 1986 Aga Khan Award for Architecture. See Ismail Serageldin, *Space for Freedom*.

68 Zenderoudi (born 1937) has been labelled a 'neo-traditionalist' (*saqqah-khaneh*); he works with calligraphic and geometric imagery that makes references to Shiite religious motifs and talismanic writings. For a short discussion of *saqqah-khaneh* artists and of Zenderoudi, see the chapter on Iran by Kamran Diba in W. Ali (ed.), *Contemporary Art from the Islamic World*, pp. 152–4.

69 Lawrence Weschler, 'Architect Amid the Ruins', *The New Yorker*, 6 January 1992, p. 46.

70 AKAA 1985, Project Record Form, Khulafa Mosque.

71 The cost of construction, at 55 Iraqi dinars per square metre (a figure considered fairly high at the time), amounted to 100,000 dinars (then equivalent to US$341,000). Some uncertainty exists as to the year of completion – 1964 or 1965 – but the mosque was certainly open to the public in 1965.

72 *The Middle East Times*, 4–11 February 1984.

73 The form of the minaret is of interest since it is the only extant example built on a dodecagonal base, although polyhedral bases are not unknown in Iraq. In fact, it is one of a series of brick minarets built in Anatolia, Iran and Iraq during the twelfth and thirteenth centuries. The base is decorated with four rows of *muqarnas* which in turn support a twelve-sided gallery decorated with a geometric frieze. The shaft is decorated with a pattern of brick plugs carved with leaf motifs. The upper part features more *muqarnas*, with a band of Kufic inscriptions below, and the whole is surmounted by a dome. The structure is made exclusively of brick and is decorated with geometric patterns of ornamental brickwork.

74 On mausolea and their forms, see Robert Hillenbrand, *Islamic Architecture: Form, Function and Meaning.*

75 Quoted in Kanan Makiya, *Post-Islamic Classicism*, p. 43; here the design is discussed in detail as representing Mohamed Makiya's first major and formative work.

76 Ready-made metal domes are available for sale in Indonesia at roadside stands: these bulbous lightweight forms are often mounted on older mosques or used for new ones.

77 AKAA 1986, Technical Review of Said Naum Mosque.

78 Each partner runs his own projects independently, but all six confer with each other and use the 'central services' of their offices. Among their completed projects are numerous office buildings, hotels and academic complexes.

79 In the event, the actual layout of the *madrasa* as well as the footpath linking the mosque to the *madrasa* did not differ substantially from Moersid's proposal. In fact, certain aspects of the design of the *madrasa* attempted to reflect the form of the retaining walls and arches of the mosque.

80 The AKAA 1986 Project Record Form indicates that the human remains were exhumed and reinterred elsewhere; also in personal communication of Soedarmadji Damais with Renata Holod, 1989.

81 The architect wanted to distinguish the complex as being separate from the parking area and the street by landscaping the entrance. He intended to use palm trees, but those planted were fast-growing, economic and bushy Angansa trees commonly used by the government. The trees bordering the main entrance were later felled on the order of the *yayasin* (foundation) to allow a clear view of the mosque from the street and to provide more space for worshippers on special occasions.

82 All older mosques in Java follow this orientation, which was derived seemingly from Hindu-Javanese architectural principles. Yuswadi Saliya, Hariadi and Gunawan Tjahjono observe that 'in the first phase of Islamisation [. . .] the Muslims made new interpretations by designating new functions and meanings to old structures or buildings. Thus, the *West* was then named *qiblat* (direction to Kaaba) [. . .]. The preservation of the cardinal directions (north-south; east-west) for a mosque, is an example of how at its early stage of Islamisation, a compromise by the new religion was made. This may signify the role of the dominant *political power* in enforcing the siting of a mosque in front of *alun-alun* (public square). In the later phase of its spread, however, the *qiblat* prevailed. It may characterise the building among other masses which usually follow the east-west direction to minimise the exposure to the sun.' From 'The Indonesian Experience' in H. Salam (ed.), *Expressions of Islam in Buildings*, pp. 194–5.

83 Because of their geographical location the direction in which Javanese Muslims must turn in order to face Mecca directly is northwest. However, in Javanese mosques the *mihrab* is most commonly placed on the west side, as is done in the case of Said Naum.

84 The artificial lighting, provided mainly by neon tubes, remains a weak point of the design.

85 According to Darab Diba. See AKAA 1986, Technical Review, Annex II, p. 26.

86 The court, often an integral element of Muslim religious buildings, is also an important transitional space in Hindu-Javanese temples, where it is generally multiple; the presence of verandahs is seemingly a later development in Javanese mosques. According to Josef Prijotomo, it became common to add one or more verandahs to the main structure at later dates. This was apparently the case in the Demak Mosque, one of the earliest surviving mosques in Indonesia. '[The] verandah, furthermore, also functions as a place where other religious events like marriage, Islamic

court, etc. [take] place. Prior to this additional structure, such events were held in the mosque.' AKAA 1986, Technical Review, p. 50.

87 '[An] element that is characteristic of Islamic architecture is the minaret. This tower traditionally functioned as a place from which to call Muslims to pray. However, this element surprisingly did not become an integral element of the Javanese mosques . . .', in Josef Prijotomo, *Ideas and Forms of Javanese Architecture*, p. 50.

88 'In pre-Islamic Java, the cross and five points symbolised God's omnipresence ("He is North, South, East, West, as well as with us"). In religious buildings the *saka guru* structure of four pillars converging at a [vertical] point reflected this symbol of God's omnipresence. The symbol was translated into the "Five Pillars of Islam" and also represented the unity (*tawhid*) when *saka guru* buildings became *masjids*.' See Darab Diba, AKAA 1986, Technical Review Summary, p. 21.

89 Design innovations also led to a saving of about 20% in relation to usual local costs. The building cost the equivalent of around US$650,000 in 1977.

90 'Traditional architecture tried basically to reconstruct a series of components with symbolic content'; Adhi Moersid in an article on Indonesian architects by Udo Kultermann in *Mimar* 21 (1986), p. 46.

91 AKAA 1986, Technical Review of Said Naum Mosque.

92 The project received an honourable mention in the 1986 cycle of the Aga Khan Award for Architecture. The Jury's citation noted: 'The approach is innovative yet faithful to the region's indigenous architecture. What failings there may be in concept or execution are far outweighed by the courage of the architect and client in re-interpreting the traditional idiom and contributing to the production of an authentic yet modern regional architecture.' I. Serageldin (ed.), *Space for Freedom*, p. 187.

93 AKAA 1982, Architect's Record Form, p. 5.

Chapter 4

1 On the layout and organization of the great Ottoman educational complexes, see Aptullah Kuran, *Sinan: The Grand Old Master of Ottoman Architecture*. On the hospital-mosque complex of Bayezid II in Edirne, see Godfrey Goodwin, *A History of Ottoman Architecture*. On the Timurid complexes, see

Lisa Golombek and Donald Wilber, *The Timurid Architecture of Iran and Turan*; on Mamluk complexes see Michael Meinecke, *Die Mamlukische Architektur in Ägypten und Syrien*; on Mughal examples see Catherine E.B. Asher, *Architecture of Mughal India*; and on *madrasa* plans see Robert Hillenbrand, *Islamic Architecture*.

2 On one case study of the history of universities in the Islamic world, see Donald M. Reid, *Cairo University and the Making of Modern Egypt*. See also Jean-Jacques Waaredenburg, *Les Universités dans le monde arabe actuel*, Paris, 1964.

3 For the history of the formation of the *madrasa* as an institution, see George Makdisi, *The Rise of Colleges: Institutions of Learning in Islam and the West*; and a recent work dealing with the history and structure of *madrasa* education is Jonathan Berkey, *The Transmission of Knowledge in Medieval Cairo*.

4 Roy Mottahedeh, *The Mantle of the Prophet: Religion and Politics in Iran*, on the current *madrasa* curriculum.

5 See Renata Holod and Ahmet Evin (eds.), *Modern Turkish Architecture,* Chapters I and II.

6 In Egypt the modernization campaign of Muhammad Ali and his successors led to the establishment of technical schools. In particular, Ali Mubarak Pasha, the Minister of Public Works for Khedive Ismail, was instrumental in initiating educational reforms. In the Ottoman Empire, the military and medical schools were the first introductions.

7 Christian missionary activity, both Catholic and otherwise, was responsible for the introduction of these types of institutions. For example, the American University in Beirut (1866) was a foundation of the Presbyterians, while the Université Saint Joseph (1881) was a Jesuit institution. Their student bodies originally consisted exclusively or mainly of local Christians and were expanded only later to admit others.

8 Aligarh University, founded by Sir Sayeed Ahmed Khan, was built as a residential college. The funds were collected from the Muslim community in British India, initially to finance the building of a mosque as part of an institution of higher learning.

9 The *pesantren* schools are traditional training colleges for the study of Islamic sciences and all are privately owned by the individual *kyai* (guide / religious leader / teacher); the emphasis is on ethical behaviour, and a life of sincerity, purity

and learning is an obligation and dedication to God. Such schools were probably first established in the reign of Prabu Kertawijaya of the Majapahet Kingdom in the seventeenth century. On the history of the *pesantren* schools, see Zamalkhsyari Dhofar, 'Islamic Education and Traditional Ideology on Java,' J.J. Fox, R.G. Garnault, P.T. McCawley, J.A.C. Mackie (eds.), *Indonesia: Australian Perspectives*, vol. I, pp. 263–71.

10 For example, Holmes Perkins, then Dean of the School of Fine Arts at the University of Pennsylvania, was instrumental in the planning of the Middle East Technical University in Ankara. In the 1970s and 1980s, Skidmore, Owings & Merrill was engaged in university building projects in the Arab World, including, in 1977–8 in Saudi Arabia, King Abdul Aziz (now Umm al-Qura) University, Mecca (by Richard Dober and Fazul Rahman Khan), and, in Benghazi, Libya, in 1966–74, Garyounis University (by James Cubitt).

11 The Royal Institute for Higher Technical Education in the Netherlands Indies commissioned MacLaine Pont to establish the first university-level institute for the training of Indonesians: its syllabus and structure was modelled on the Technische Hochschule in Delft.' Pont felt it important to express indigenous cultural values in the Bandung design. Through this choice of style . . . he affirmed his faith in the ability of Indonesian architecture to provide a basis for future development.' See Helen Jessup, 'Dutch Architectural Visions of the Indonesian Tradition', *Muqarnas* 3 (1985), p. 141.

12 Construction commenced in 1964, with the first element, the *mihrab*, completed in 1966.

13 Ahmad Sadali in AKAA 1979, Project Record; also see *Expressions of Islam in Buildings*, p. 33.

14 Udo Kultermann, 'The Architects of Indonesia', *Mimar* 21 (1986), p. 46. Incidentally, the first Department of Architecture established in an Indonesian university was created in 1954 at ITB, where Noe'man himself was trained.

15 The client of record was the Yayasan Pembilna Masjid Salman (Foundation for the Development of the Salman Mosque).

16 The funds were eventually raised in widely varying proportions from: municipal government (25%); national government (10%); international sources (2.5%); and ITB (65.5%). See AKAA 1979, Project Record.

265

17 It is interesting to note that, soon after construction was completed, 'although the mosque had a minaret/tower, at a glance people did not recognise that the building was a mosque. This was because previously there were no such mosque idioms either in the traditional buildings of the region or imported from the Middle East. The only recognisable element was the direction of the qibla.' M.P. Effendi, *The Development of the Mosque in Indonesia*, p. 16.

18 Jondishapur had been the location of a famous medical school in the Sasanian period; see *Cambridge History of Iran*, vol. 4: *The Parthians and Sasanians*. Glorification of the pre-Islamic periods from the Achaemenid to the Sasanian era (c. seventh century BC–sixth century AD) had been a major element in the political and cultural campaign waged by the Pahlavi dynasty in the early 1970s.

19 The Aga Khan Award for Architecture Project Summary, June 1980, p. 3. Samir Abdulac, the project's Technical Reviewer, claimed that one of the difficulties in designing and locating the buildings was the lack of a Master Plan at the time, combined with the preference on the part of the Chancellor for 'piecemeal planning' and physical separation of the different faculties on the campus. Diba's relationship to the University authorities is summed up by his own statement, '. . . we were sometimes obliged to deal with unreasonable bureaucrats who tried to impose their personal taste on public projects. We always accommodated such whims, keeping our original plans in the drawer, while waiting for the particular technocrat's term of office to expire. But sometimes we simply showed them what they wanted and built our own design.' *Kamran Diba, Buildings and Projects*, p. 54.

20 Two of the partners of MODAM, Reza Moghtader and Andreev (who were the French architect Michel Ecochard's partners in Iran), were responsible for designing the first Master Plan and the very first building on the campus, a student housing project with outdoor sports facilities, in the late 1950s. Their scheme incorporated the canal as part of a pedestrian axis in the composition.

21 For example, Diba secretly projected student dormitories to the north and south of the walkway, though he was aware of the fact that the Chancellor was opposed to the idea of allowing student dormitories

on campus, as he was to the inclusion of any spaces with potential for student congregation and the fomentation of unrest. The pedestrian walkway later came to be used as a track for bicycles and motorcycles.

22 AKAA 1980, Project Summary, p. 1.

23 Diba in a handwritten annotation to one of his drawings sent to Hasan-Uddin Khan in Paris, 1989.

24 In Iranian architecture the *hashti* is usually the octagonal foyer or entrance hall which was most often covered with a dome. This feature occurs in public as well as domestic architecture and is best known from examples of Safavid architecture of the sixteenth-seventeenth centuries and from buildings of later periods; see, for example, Maxime Siroux, *Caravansérails d'Iran et petites constructions routières*, also in R. Holod (ed.), *Studies on Isfahan*, his 'Anciennes voies et monuments routiers de la région d'Ispahan suivis de plusieurs autres édifices de cette province'.

25 See AKAA 1980, Project Summary, p. 8.

26 On *badgirs* see Elizabeth Beazeley, *Living with the Desert: Working Buildings of the Iranian Plateau*. Also Susan Roaf, 'Badgir', in *Encyclopaedia Iranica*, vol. III, pp. 368–70. Diba has also utilized the idea of a 'light tower' (based on a wind tower) in his Tehran Museum of Contemporary Art, though on a different scale and employing different materials. See *Kamran Diba, Buildings and Projects*, pp. 30–47.

27 On Amir Chaqmaq Mosque, see Golombek and Wilber, *Timurid Architecture of Iran and Turan*, pp. 421–3.

28 Describing the design process of the proposed Graduate Centre for Religious Studies, Diba wrote, '. . . it gave me pleasure to execute the idea of destroying or blocking the exterior elevation by another structure – a practice common in indigenous vernacular architecture . . .', *Kamran Diba, Buildings and Projects*, p. 3. He went on to state that 'The mystery of many examples of Islamic urban architecture is that facades are internal and are not destroyed or affected by attached buildings. The occasion used to put into practice an expansion of our open-ended scheme, making facades and external character of buildings disappear and give way to new buildings while the interior stays orderly and intact. This was a new discovery on my part which I tried to formulate into a methodology called "Islamic approach to design" which was adopted in the design of

future schemes. In summary, by creating a physical setting, which maintains inherent physical and social characteristics of a given Islamic culture, and caters to a Moslem population, I believe that I am, with a key in hand, at the doorstep of contemporary Islamic architecture.' AKAA 1980, Project Record Form, p. 5.

29 In Tehran the *qibla* customarily faces west.

30 The exact location of the sculpture was consciously sited in relation to the Namaz Khaneh. The Shiite standard represents the severed hand of Hazrat Abbas, half-brother and standard bearer of Husayn. It also symbolizes the five 'pure ones' in Shiite Islam – Muhammad, Fatima, Ali, Hasan and Husayn. See also Jean Calmard and James Allen, 'Alam va 'Alamat', *Encyclopaedia Iranica*, vol. I, pp. 785–91.

31 For example the minimalist sculpture of Dan Flavin.

32 The client of record was the University under the aegis of the Ministry of Petroleum and Minerals. The contract covering the first building phase was awarded to Taisei Construction Company of Tokyo and all the subsequent phases, including the mosque, were carried out by Consolidated Construction Company of Beirut.

33 The design principal for the project was Charles Lawrence; the partner-in-charge was Joe Thomas and the project manager was Conrad Neal. According to the architects, 'the UPM mosque fosters the Islamic spirit without resorting to literal copies of historic examples. . . . The mosque epitomises engineering precision and quality of reinforced concrete.' AKAA 1979, Architect's Record Form (signed by William Caudill), p. 4. On historic minarets see Geoffrey R.D. King, *The Historical Mosques of Saudi Arabia*.

34 The Inter-Continental Hotel and Conference Centre (1966–74) in Mecca has an auditorium with a hanging roof structure using the principles of modern tent design developed by the German engineer Frei Otto – the first hi-tech construction of its kind in Saudi Arabia. See R. Holod (ed.), *Architecture and Community*, pp. 151–61. Later projects such as the Hajj Terminal (1982) at the international airport in Jeddah, the world's largest tent structure, by Skidmore, Owings & Merrill, and the Diplomatic Club (1985) in Riyadh by Omrania (with Otto as engineer), developed both the technology and the covering membrane in glass fibre coated

with Teflon. See William Curtis, 'Diplomatic Club, Riyadh', in *Mimar* 21 (1986). This type of tent structure and its imagery have been extensively used in the country in buildings ranging from palaces to stadiums.

35 AKAA 1985, Project Summary and Client's Record Forms.

36 See *Architecture and Community*, pp. 56–7. Although published only later, the principles had in fact been articulated by the architect at the time of designing the mosque, and mentioned to the authors in conversations held in late 1978.

37 For examples of *muqarnas* domes, see Sheila Blair, *The Ilkhanid Shrine at Natanz*, and, with Jonathan Bloom, *The Art and Architecture of Islam, 1250–1800*, concerning ideas of post-Timurid dome vaults in Isfahan and Kerman.

38 According to him, mosques in Iran, Central Asia and Afghanistan rely heavily upon the place-making concept implicit in the *chahar taq*. See 'On Mosque Architecture' in R. Holod (ed.), *Architecture and Community*, pp. 56–7.

39 See especially Nader Ardalan and Laleh Bakhtiar, *The Sense of Unity*, p. 31, apropos the use of this language for architectural expression.

40 The layouts of *külliye* in, for example, the Süleymaniye complex in Istanbul and the Bayezid II complex in Edirne. See Aptullah Kuran, *Sinan*, and Godfrey Goodwin, *A History of Ottoman Architecture*.

41 The Islamic Conference is a pan-Islamic political organization, established by the late King Faisal of Saudi Arabia, which holds summits and the annual meetings of the Foreign Ministers of Muslim states. It derived its impetus from the first Islamic summit in Rabat in 1969; the first conference was held in 1970 in Jeddah, where the organization now has its headquarters.

42 AKAA 1985, Architect's Form, p. 5. The engineering design was prepared in Turkey by HES Ltd in Ankara (preliminary design), co-ordinated by Suner Tuncer, and in Bangladesh by Sheikh Shaheedullah of Shaheedullah Associates of Dhaka (construction drawings). Specifications were drawn up by A.K.M. Rafiquddin of Development Design Consultants.

43 Jahangirnagar Islamic University, designed by Mazharul Islam in 1971, is a mainly brick-clad structure. The availability of brick and the influence of Louis Kahn's Capitol Complex seems to have influenced Pamir in his choice of building material. Pamir counts himself among the disciples of Louis Kahn, having attended his master classes at the University of Pennsylvania.

44 AKAA 1988, Architect's Record, pp. 4–5. William Curtis also discusses this matter in his definition of 'Authentic Regionalism', noting that 'the realm of what we might call archetypes within architectural thought, of basic forms in Bangladesh has to do with the fusion of two centralised traditions, one from Islam and one ultimately from Buddhism and the relationship to water in the wet humid cultures of Southeast Asia.' See essay 'On Regionalism' in R. Powell (ed.), *Regionalism in Architecture*, pp. 73–7.

45 See Abu H. Imamuddin, 'Islamic Centre for Technical and Vocational Training and Research', *Mimar* 37 (1990), pp. 34–8. He also notes that 'the formal nature of the campus is viewed . . . as a physical manifestation of the discipline in Islamic lifestyle and living . . .' (ibid., p. 38).

46 Darab Diba, 'Iran: The University of Kerman', *Mimar* 42 (1992), pp. 62–4. AKAA 1988, Architects' Record Form (signed by Y. Shariatzadeh). The architects of the university were Piraz, Tehran, Y. Shariatzadeh, M. Mirheydar, Y. Razzaghi and B. Farahvashi. Bonyan Consultants drew up the preliminary plans in 1972. From 1984 on Piraz carried out the design and supervision of the construction of the auditorium and other academic buildings. Working drawings for the prayer hall are by Bonyan.

47 The architect, according to Saliya, Hariadi and Tjahjono, was guided by the following principle: 'In the Javanese context, heaven and wholeness have to be represented by the one-point pyramidal roof, which suggests a strong central power commanding its four quarters. Both pyramid and four quarters with a centre are related to spatial archetypes, the archaic image in the human unconscious.' From H. Salam (ed.), *Expressions of Islam in Buildings*, p. 192. For another example of the use of the traditional *meru* roof form, see the Said Naum Mosque, Jakarta, discussed in Chapter 3.

48 See Budi A. Sukada, 'The University of Indonesia, Depok', *Mimar* 42 (1992), p. 69. So powerful is the arch as an identifying feature of a mosque that even an avowed modernist such as Noe'man has moved away from the style of his earlier Salman Mosque and incorporated a heavy screen of arches, so masking what would otherwise have been a mosque design in full harmony with the pitched-roof style of the Islamic University at Bandung.

49 The design team leader for the project was Hermann Kendel, working with E. Baur, A. Charif, A. Claar, H.J. Collmar, H. Dannenberg, I. Grimm, H. Kiess, V. Keckstein, D. Mailander, P. Netzer and S. Schulze. Munir was the Islamic motif designer. Ove Arup and Partners of London were the engineers.

50 AKAA 1979, Project Record Form III, p. 3 (signed by H. Kendel). The client of record was the Saudi Ministry of Finance and Natural Economy. However, it appears that the operators, the Inter-Continental Hotel Group under its Regional Vice-President, Raymond G. Khalife, had a major say in the design. See AKAA 1979, Client's Record Form, p. 2.

51 In 1980, this complex won an Aga Khan Award for Architecture. The Master Jury cited it in the 'Search for Innovation' category as an example which '. . . combine[s] modern technology and functional forms in the context of Islamic culture . . . and represents a step in the search for an appropriate architectural language'. *Awards 1980*, brochure, unpaginated.

52 On staircase minarets, see Jonathan Bloom, *Minaret, Symbol of Islam*. See also Geoffrey R.D. King, *The Historical Mosques of Saudi Arabia*, p. 190.

53 Obata was a former student of Eero Saarinen at the Cranbrook Academy. The influence of Saarinen's TWA Terminal (1956–62) at J.F. Kennedy International Airport, New York, can be felt in Obata's airport projects.

54 AKAA 1983, Architect's Record, p. 5. Since there was no natural vegetation on the site, it was necessary to import all the plants. An 18.8-hectare (47-acre) greenhouse complex established by Bechtel supports the quarter-million plants and shrubs in the airport.

55 Mildred Schmertz, 'Affording the Best', *Architectural Record*, March 1984, p. 114.

56 Although the total initial budget for HOK-designed facilities was US$570 million, the actual cost of building the airport was about US$3,200,000,000. The cost of the mosque alone was estimated at SR150 million. According to Walter McQuade in *Architecture in the Real World . . .*, p. 216, '. . . the airport job, managed by Bechtel Company of San Francisco, with HOK designing all the terminal buildings, is within budget and on schedule.'

267

Bechtel arranged 66 contracts, half of which were required only during the construction period, such as that for temporary housing for the labour force (which peaked at 15,000 in 1982). The ten largest contracts (averaging $100 million) were mostly with Korean, Japanese and other foreign companies. However, the project illustrates increasing participation by locally based firms, which benefited from a decree requiring that works representing at least 30% of the cost of every contract be executed by companies in Saudi ownership. See *Engineering News Record*, 27 October 1983.

57 The King Saud University was HOK's largest university campus project, built at a cost of US$3,500,000,000. Cf. *Mimar* 42 (1992).

58 The design team consisted of William E. Valentine, Robert E. Stauder, Roslyn Brandt, Floyd W. Zimmerman, Janis Purgalis, Richard E. Quinn, Charles M. Oraftik, Carl W. Martin, Ronald H. Thompson, Bradley James Hill, Rolf E. Muenter and Sara Liss Katz. Oleg Grabar acted as consultant on Islamic architecture.

59 In 'A Special Report on the Saudi Arabian Capital', *The International Herald Tribune*, Paris, 11 November 1983.

60 'KKIA: Riyadh's "Royal Airport"', *Airport Forum* 2, 1984.

61 The fact that the direction of the ceremonial promenade coincided with the southwesterly *qibla* axis was fortuitous. The architect relates that the direction of the runways dictated the planning and organization of the layout and only afterwards did he relate the terminals and mosque to the runways orthogonally, so producing an alignment which happened to be precisely that of the direction towards Mecca (op. cit.).

62 See *Mimar* 12 (1984), p. 8.

63 The committee members were Maj.-Gen. Amin, the architect Ronald H. Thompson and, as consultants, Talai Kurdi of Jeddah, Stellio Skamanga of Geneva and Wayne Anderson of the Vesti Corporation based in Boston, Massachusetts.

64 'The decoration of the mosque interior, unfortunately, was not in HOK's contract. The masterful relationship of ornament to architecture found in HOK's interiors and especially in the royal terminal, is sadly missing in the mosque. Put together by Vesti Corporation under separate contract to Bechtel, the individual works, many created by superb craftsmen, are lovely. The

ornament, however, is not painstakingly related to structure, proportion and space as it is in the terminals. The architects who embellished the HOK interiors really knew and understood their buildings. Vesti, it would appear, came a bit late to the mosque', *Architectural Record*, March 1984, ibid.

65 It is cited as being 'the largest integral art project in the modern world'. *Mimar* 12 (1984), p. 8.

66 Owing to the size and scope of the project the stained-glass production was divided among five West German studios in order to meet the construction deadlines imposed. Other specialists who participated in the project include: woodworking companies in Switzerland, Syria and Jeddah, which executed geometric designs on the teak, mahogany and oak doors; craftsmen from Munich who set the vast calligraphic mosaic band; a well-known Querceta stone-carving studio (headed by the sculptor Henry Moore's chief artisan) using traditional techniques in Carrara, Italy, which crafted the travertine arches of the *mihrab*; and an associate of Picasso in southern France who glazed the ceramic tiles decorating the *mihrab*.

67 Charles Boccara was trained at the Ecole des Beaux-Arts in Paris; he returned to Morocco in the early 1960s and worked for the well-known architect E. Azagury in Casablanca before setting up his own practice in Marrakech.

68 Brian B. Taylor, 'Hospital, Marrakesh', *Mimar* 14 (1984), p. 45.

69 Quoted in 'Hospital Mosque, Marrakesh', *Mimar* 15 (1985), p. 48.

70 See 'Dar Lamane Housing Community', in Ismail Serageldin (ed.), *Space for Freedom*, pp. 90–101. The scheme won an Aga Khan Award for Architecture in 1986.

Chapter 5

1 For example, nineteenth-century Hanafi judges understood the people of the quarter (*ahl al-mahal*) to be an autonomous mosque community. See Baber Johansen, 'The mosques: places of religious integration or political agitation?', pp. 16–17.

2 This type of patron should not be confused with the individual who donates a mosque to a particular community (see Chapter 1 for a discussion of individual patronage). In most cases a patron such as a sultan or a wealthy landowner would finance the building of a

mosque, but the decision-making process remained collective, thus allowing the community to participate in shaping its own environment.

3 That romantic picture can be modified to read in the opposite direction: that the landowner was clearly the patron and the design decision-maker for the local mosque as often as not. For instance, most of the monumental examples in the historic record, such as the Iranian Yazdi suburban mosques, were funded by individual patrons (see Golombek and Wilber, *Timurid Architecture*). On the other hand, the mosque at Ghardaia in Algeria seems to have been a collective venture.

4 Although there was no architect in the modern sense of the word, specialists in different trades, such as carpenters, masons and calligraphers, were active participants.

5 In a paper published in 1985 and entitled 'Community Mosque – A Symbol of Society', A.H. Imamuddin, S.A. Hassan and D. Sarkar explain that communities will 'construct a rudimentary makeshift structure for prayer on an abandoned or unused government or disputed plot and subsequently on repeated appeals and persistent efforts of the people, the concerned authority allocates the land for future construction of [a] permanent mosque – since there is an unwritten law that once a mosque is built on a site it cannot be removed from that space.' (*Regionalism in Architecture*, p. 61). In order to recover such land the government must act quickly, for once a new mosque is a recognized and established entity, the authorities can no longer lay claim to the site. In instances where the land is privately owned, the owner is almost always unsuccessful in any claim to regain possession.

6 Note also the mosque in Zagreb discussed in this chapter.

7 The term Great Mosque is from the French *Grande Mosquée*, the term employed by the builder.

8 See AKAA 1983, Technical Review of the Great Mosque of Niono by Raoul Snelder, p. 7.

9 Niono was planned in the 1930s by the French Colonial Administration to house the indigenous labour force under colonial rule. The layout of the village and the design of the buildings at that time were influenced by Western urban models. See also Brian B. Taylor, 'Rethinking Colonial Architecture',

Mimar 13 (1984), pp. 16–25, and Gwendolyn Wright, *The Politics of Design in French Colonial Urbanism.*

10 Unfortunately, no documents from this period are available to establish the precise requirements that were set out. Information concerning the mosque comes from the collective memory of the villagers through interviews conducted by Raoul Snelder with the village dignitaries and with the son of the mosque's first *imam*. Some uncertainty exists as to what each phase comprises. In his review of the mosque for the AKAA, Raoul Snelder noted that 'Il est évident que sur ce point ne peuvent être avancées que des tentatives d'interprétations: le recul, l'absence de documents, les problèmes de communication et les particularités de procédures vernaculaires doivent conduire à une certaine réserve.' (AKAA 1983, Technical Review Summary, p. 8). Our description of the construction process is based on Snelder's account and by reference to his drawings, which are to some extent contradictory.

11 The known history of the successive reconstructions of the Great Mosque at Djenné is summarized by Raoul Snelder in *Mimar* 12 (1984), pp. 66–74, and by Labelle Prussin in *Hatumere: Islamic Design in West Africa*, pp. 182–9. Inspired by the indigenous heritage of the Manding people in the region now occupied by the republics of Mali and Niger, the Islamized population, the Dyula, rebuilt the mosque in Djenné in the sixteenth century, giving rise to the West African mosque type. The monumental Djenné mosque was subsequently rebuilt on several occasions. The present Great Mosque dates from 1907 and appears to be a colonial reconstruction of a building dating from 1830. It is the 1907 version that is considered as representative of the 'Djenné style' which is characterized by sculptural verticality (repetitive pinnacled buttresses) and by the three-towered *qibla* wall (a *mihrab* tower flanked by two smaller towers). It is not known for certain whether the three-towered east façade of 1907 was a new addition or whether it had figured in the initial versions of the mosque. Labelle Prussin suggests that the 'Djenné style' is inspired by the 'attached pillar and projecting pinnacle' which are the distinguishing features of Dyula architecture: 'Extension of these pillars as corner quoins and pinnacles above earthen parapets, incorporation into portal entrances and

extended architraves and lintels, integration into an intricate register of balustrades, and arrangement into a cohesive cluster bounding space are elaborations on this central theme.' (op. cit., p. 162).

12 See Labelle Prussin, *Hatumere*, p. 168. This motif concerns a type that she labelled as 'anthropomorphic representation' during the Aga Khan Award Seminar held in Dakar, Senegal, in November 1982. Its origin, function and meaning are not as yet agreed upon.

13 In many ethnic groups of the region, similar motifs are found in ancestor worship.

14 L. Prussin, op. cit., p. 170.

15 For a further account of the mosque (which received an AKAA in 1983), see S. Cantacuzino (ed.), *Architecture in Continuity: Building in the Islamic World Today.*

16 The question of design in this case consisted of marking out the actual dimensions of the building layout on the ground. No drawings were prepared.

17 Master Jury's Statement on the Yaama Mosque in I. Serageldin (ed.), *Space for Freedom: The Search for Architectural Excellence in Muslim Societies*, pp. 133–6.

18 On the place of women in mosques see Introduction.

19 Raoul Snelder, AKAA 1986, Technical Review Summary, pp. 8–10.

20 Before embarking on the construction of the Yaama Mosque, Falké Barmou apparently learned this technique from a Nigerian mason who had been hired by the Chef de Canton to build a house for his son. Interestingly, Falké Barmou used the same technique in building his own house (Snelder, ibid., pp. 17–18). Snelder implies that the technique differs somewhat from those generally used in domestic structures in Yaama, where the most important rooms are covered either by a slightly sloping system of wooden rafters supported by a central post and covered with sticks and branches that, in turn, support a mud roof; or by a shallow dome-like roof covered with branches and mud mortar which is supported on sets of right-angle arches in the corners made from bundles of sticks covered with a thick layer of mud.

21 Raoul Snelder, ibid., p. 15. The ratio was determined by the materials used and by spatial requirements for prayer, allowing sufficient space for one person in between the columns and some additional space for circulation.

22 Snelder, ibid., p. 23. Note the parallel in Iranian mosques on the insertion of a dome into a hypostyle mosque. Hypostyle mosques lend themselves to this type of elaboration.

23 The best investigated is the archaeology and history of the development of the congregational mosque of Isfahan: for an introduction to these issues, see Oleg Grabar, *The Great Mosque of Isfahan*, where he presents an analysis of the archaeological and restoration work done by Eugenio Galdieri.

24 Snelder, p. 10. While the ground-floor galleries could conceivably be used to provide overflow prayer space, the upper galleries do not lend themselves to this function because they are entirely separate from the main prayer hall, and reached by staircases in the towers.

25 'Technology and architecture are purely local, or rather, regional, as some elements may have originated in Northern Nigeria, others elsewhere in the Sahelian region.' Snelder, ibid., p. 23. He also suggests that the outside staircase is 'a sculpture all by itself reminiscent of the Dyula architecture of central West Africa.' Ibid., p. 14.

26 'The fact that [the mosque] is appreciated even outside Yaama is underlined by the fact that other villages seek to follow its example and solicit the services of the same architect-mason. In an era where traditional architecture is losing ground this is a remarkable feat.' Ibid., p. 24.

27 Abdel Wahed El-Wakil, in an interview with the editors, *Mimar* 1 (1981), p. 46.

28 The development consists of a number of sectors, each with its own social and commercial facilities, in addition to the housing; see M. Ahmed Ali, *Town Planning in Pakistan & India*, on the housing societies in Pakistan.

29 It is unclear how the architect was selected, but it appears that he was personally known to a number of influential members of the Society Committee.

30 Personal communication with H.U. Khan in 1989.

31 Atilla Yücel mentions that during the talks at first the community was 'sceptical'. Its members were persuaded 'when they saw the result and also when foreign visitors came and appreciated' their new mosque. Now, he reports that they describe their mosque variously as 'beautiful', 'interesting', 'quiet', 'impressive' and 'perfect'. Likewise, the *imam* praises the mosque because 'its

architecture will also be meaningful for the coming generations'. AKAA 1988, Technical Review Report, pp. 10–11.

32 Sherefuddin's White Mosque received an Aga Khan Award for Architecture in 1983, at which time the Master Jury commended it for its 'boldness, creativity, and brilliance. . . . While acknowledging the tradition of the Bosnian mosque, the design extends the architectural vocabulary of the mosque into the twentieth century and therefore contributes to the changing architectural heritage . . . The combining of technological and vernacular building is extremely convincing. The lighting and ambience of the interior, though modern, exactly maintain the traditional atmosphere of the mosque, and the choice and conjunction of materials, old and new, is refined and elegant.' In R. Holod (ed.), *Architecture in Continuity*, p. 105.

33 See Machiel Kiel on Ottoman mosques in the Balkans. Few significant monuments were built after the eighteenth century. Therefore, there is really no continuously evolving tradition of local mosque building as such. Also mentioned by Ibrahim Krzovic in an appendix to the AKAA 1988, Technical Review Summary by Atilla Yücel.

34 This figure cited in S. Cantacuzino (ed.), *Architecture in Continuity*, p. 106.

35 The decision might well have corresponded to a tendency of the time in Yugoslavian social politics, whereby a new emphasis was given to religion, especially for the benefit of Muslim communities concentrated in Macedonia and Bosnia-Herzegovina.

36 The architect has estimated the voluntary labour of community workers, skilled and unskilled, to account for one-third of the total cost of the project.

37 It remains uncertain as to whether this development plan has been completed to date, though some of the shop blocks shown in the plan, destined to be located on the edge of the mosque site, have been built. They were designed by another architect, Oruc Ibrahim, reflecting a pseudo-vernacular style.

38 In traditional Bosnian mosques the graveyard encircled the mosque, creating a protective outer layer. The buffer function does not appear to operate here as the graveyard is isolated, in the 'backyard' of the mosque, to shield it from the residences behind the site.

39 Most often the prayer hall in a mosque is situated at ground level or above it, though underground winter prayer halls exist in areas subject to severe cold, such as Iran and Central Asia. It is also very rare to find changes of level within the prayer hall itself, with the exception of a platform for the *imam* or a *minbar*.

40 Although the piping is said to read 'Allah', no one, to our knowledge, has been able to decipher it correctly.

41 Zlatko Ugljen's words as recorded by Atilla Yücel in the AKAA 1988, Technical Review Summary, p. 5.

42 'At the seminar during the Istanbul Award presentations, the architect described his study and research into Arab geometric patterns, and his efforts to distil these into a pure "Cubist" geometry compatible with modern sensitivities.' (Brian Brace Taylor in *Mimar* 10, 1983, p. 20).

43 'Another connotation the architect recognises in the asymmetrical form of the cupola has some anthropomorphic reference to the praying man: the cupola on the south-eastern facade "bends forward to Ka'aba", following the direction of prayer.' (Yücel, ibid., p. 5).

44 'The steel grating can also be related to similar solutions of the domes of the old *türbehs* in Travnik and Mostar, where the domes of the *baldachins* are marked by iron bars.' (Krzovic, ibid., annex, p. 4).

45 Yücel thinks that they were conceived 'as simple, spontaneous objects similar to those encountered in the streets. They reflect a spirit very close to folk design, and [their] forms were reduced to an elementary level'. (ibid., p. 6).

46 B. B. Taylor, 'Directions in Diversity', *Mimar* 10, p. 21.

47 In this mosque the women's gallery is unusually large – its area is about 40% of that of the men's prayer space. Its curious shape, like that in the Jondishapur mosque by Diba (Chapter 4), is reminiscent of the curvilinear cinema mezzanines of the 1950s and 1960s.

48 Cf. Perween Hasan, writing on 'The Indian Subcontinent', in M. Frishman and H.U. Khan (eds.), *The Mosque*, pp. 159–80.

49 East Pakistan was overseen from the centre (West Pakistan) under the military government of Ayub Khan, represented in the East by an Administrator who was *de facto* head of government.

50 The architect in a conversation with H.U. Khan in 1986.

51 The mosque, construction of which began in 1977, was opened for worship in 1980, and finally completed seven years later. Also see M. Falamaki, 'Al-Ghadir Mosque, Tehran', *Mimar* 29, pp. 24–9.

52 Cf. mausolea such as Varamin. On the subject of mausolea in Iran, see Robert Hillenbrand, 'The Development of Saljuq Mausolea in Iran', in O. Watson (ed.), *The Art of Iran and Anatolia from the 11th to the 13th century A.D.*, pp. 40–59; also the chapter on mausolea in his *Islamic Architecture*, 1994.

53 As expressed by the architect to the authors.

54 M. Falamaki, 'Al Ghadir Mosque' *Mimar* 29, p. 26.

55 We refer here to personal communications with Oleg Grabar.

56 John Eade, 'Islam, Religious Buildings and Space in London' (unpublished paper), 1991. Eade, who has studied London Muslim communities over many years, discusses both the Brick Lane and East London mosques. We are indebted to this study and to some of his other publications that shed light on Muslims and their buildings in the UK.

57 J. Eade, ibid., p. 8.

58 K. Manzoor (features editor) writing in *MuslimWise*, December 1980, as cited in J. Eade, op cit., p. 10.

59 In the USA a similar situation arose with the Islamic Society of Quincy when it applied to build a mosque in Milton, Massachusetts. Local building codes necessitated a reduction in the size of the dome and minaret. The community members took their case to court but were unsuccessful. Later, during the Gulf War of 1990, the centre was subjected to arson attacks.

60 E. A. Richardson, *East meets West*, pp. 150–1.

61 Apparently Durkee was introduced to Fathy by another convert to Islam, Abdullah Schleifer; see his essay 'Hassan Fathy's Abiquiu', *Ekistics* 304 (1984).

62 Fathy was assisted in the layout and design by Dr Hisham Sameh, Mahmoud Nessim and Hassan El Sayed, all of whose names appear on the 1981 drawings of the village.

63 The masons had worked for Fathy in New Gourna and also for Abdel Wahed El-Wakil in Saudi Arabia, as well as for other builders and architects whom they instructed in the art of adobe vault construction.

64 Wael al-Masri, *Architecture and the Question of Identity: Issues of Self-*

Representation in Islamic Community Centers in America (unpublished M.Sc. thesis, MIT, Cambridge, MA), p. 75.

65 James Steele, *Hassan Fathy*, p. 119.

66 Among the many awards which Fathy received were the Aga Khan Award for Architecture Chairman's Award in 1980 and the International Union of Architects' (UIA) Gold Medal in 1984.

67 On shopfront mosques see Susan Slymovitz, 'The Muslim World Day Parade and "Storefront" Mosques of New York City', in Barbara Daly Metcalf (ed.), *Making Muslim Space in North America and Europe*, Berkeley, CA, 1996. Another interesting example occurs in the very different context of Indonesia. Shop-houses in Jakarta and some other Javanese cities have been converted in predominantly Chinese neighbourhoods. These buildings often incorporate some form of dome and minaret clearly visible from the street to proclaim the adherence and identification with the country's predominantly Muslim population.

68 Sulayman Nyang in Yvonne Haddad (ed.), *The Muslims of America*, p. 40.

69 Yvonne Haddad in 'Moslems making their mark on Ohio', *New York Times*, 25 November 1984.

70 The pan-American nature of such associations, which include the Federation of Islamic Associations (FIA) established in 1952, coincides with the desire to build representational mosques in both the USA and Canada.

71 On Dalokay's winning project Haider remarked: 'And when we saw the winner we were amazed at how any contemporary Jury could select such a "traditional" scheme with four minarets!', quoted from 'Space and the Practising Architect' in H. Salam (ed.), *Expressions of Islam in Buildings*, p. 156.

72 Ibid., p. 158.

73 The office complex was commissioned later by a subsequent ISNA committee from another architect.

74 *Al-Batin* (Hidden) and *al-Zahir* (Manifest) are two of the Ninety-nine Names of God. Nader Ardalan has described them as: ' . . . God as Manifest *(Zahir)* is the reality of universal externalisation . . . in the second, complementary view of God as Hidden *(Batin)* there is an inward movement within the microcosm of man . . . moving towards his spiritual centre . . . the two schemes correspond to each other, at the same

time that one is the reverse of the other.' N. Ardalan and L. Bakhtiar, *The Sense of Unity*, p. 11.

75 See Haider in *Expressions of Islam in Buildings*, p. 159. Also see Gulzar Haider and Muhammad Mukhtar, "Islamic Architecture in Non-Islamic Environments" (unpublished paper on ICNA), 1980.

76 The 'cut-outs' in the prayer hall and its strong spatial character are akin to Kahn's mosque in the Dhaka Capitol complex – a project which Haider has studied carefully. However, Haider says that they are more the result of his interest in geometry – as expressed by him at a conference on the 'Mosques of North America', held at the Massachusetts Institute of Technology (MIT) in November 1995.

77 Wael al-Masri, op. cit., p. 126. We are indebted to al-Masri's research on ICNA where he discusses the symbolism of the mosque in detail, and we have used it in addition to personal ongoing dialogue with the architect himself.

78 Haider in H. Salam (ed.) *Expressions of Islam in Buildings*, p. 160.

79 Nader Ardalan, 'Architects in America Design for Islamic Cultures', *Arts & the Islamic World* 3 (Autumn 1985), p. 48.

80 The Ahmadiyyas, a small Muslim sect (estimated membership 800,000), originated in the Indian Punjab. After independence in 1947 they transferred their headquarters to Rabwa in Pakistan. They were declared 'out of Islamic bounds' in Pakistan and suffered doctrinal eviction. In the 1980s they established their base in the multi-cultural Canadian environment.

81 Personal communication with H.U. Khan, September 1996.

82 Apparently there was one woman, a respected convert to Islam, who was the prime mover for this arrangement. Haider recalls that 'The conservative men lost grudgingly. A questionnaire was circulated to about sixty Islamic authorities across North America and internationally to get their opinion on the location of women in the mosque. About thirty replied and the answers were varied. The community then had another general meeting, at which it was decided that women would be "at the same level but behind men". Now this was not an earth-shattering new idea, but what was new and encouraging was the process in which participatory democracy was used.'

(communication with Hasan-Uddin Khan, September 1996).

83 Quoted from an article by Steve Brewer, 'Peace of Worship. Where is the Mosque?', *Albuquerque Journal*, 26 July 1992.

84 Zeynep Çelik, *Displaying the Orient: The Architecture of Islam at the Nineteenth-Century World's Fairs*, p. 198.

Chapter 6

1 Created in 1917, the Association of *Habous* (or Awqaf) of Holy Places was a North African organization composed of dignitaries from Morocco, Tunisia and Algeria. Its function was to organize pilgrimages to Mecca and in this context it provided services such as hostels in Mecca and Medina to receive pilgrims from North Africa, as well as sanitary facilities, security, etc.

2 Figures are given in *anciens francs*; many years later, in 1958, as a consequence of devaluations and post-war inflation, the government of Charles de Gaulle introduced the *nouveau franc* (1 *nouveau franc* = 100 *anciens francs*). Thus, the sum made available by a decree dated 19 August 1920 bears no relationship to present-day values.

3 The names of the members appear in an undated booklet entitled *Institut Musulman de Paris*, probably produced in the 1920s.

4 In 1924, total contributions amounted to roughly 4,700,000 francs, of which 3,800,000 came from Moroccan Muslims. Figures from the booklet cited in note 3.

5 See *La Construction moderne*, 2 November 1924, pp. 50–5. Following the death of Eustache he was succeeded by Heubès, who also supervised the construction of the mosque. The French architect Valroff, who was in charge of the artistic work, had spent ten years in Morocco prior to working on the mosque in Paris; he spoke fluent Arabic and was thus able to communicate easily with the 450 Moroccan craftsmen working on the project.

6 The second prize was awarded to a Turkish architect and the third prize was won jointly by designs from Egypt and Morocco.

7 The construction costs amounted to £4.5 million (approximately $10 million at 1970 conversion rates).

8 AKAA 1979, Architect's Record.

9 Apparently, the precise orientation of the buildingtowards Mecca was calculated using a computer only after the competition; this

demonstrated that the line established
for the purpose of the competition was
inexact. The site boundaries were so tight
that the design for the building could not
in practice be made to conform with the
correct orientation; however, the Crown
Commissioners agreed to an adjustment of
the building line so that the Mosque could
be built as designed (AKAA 1979, Architect's
Record). At the design stage, which coincided
with the transition from the use of imperial
measurements to metric standards in the UK,
the original plans were drawn up in feet and
inches; the working drawings and engineering
specifications were, however, prepared using
metric measurements.

10 The architect considered the library to be
an important element in the scheme, serving
as a reminder that historically mosques were
also centres of learning.

11 Hasan-Uddin Khan's communication with
Gibberd's office in 1986. Apparently this was
formulated in conjunction with the client –
the Mosque Committee.

12 Illustrations of their ideas can be seen
in the Khulafa Mosque and the University of
Dhahran Mosque. It is interesting to note
that Rifat Chadirji also submitted a design to
the London Central Mosque competition.

13 'View from a Jersey City Mosque', *The New
Yorker*, 27 September 1993, p. 31.

14 In a fundraising letter sent in May 1951
to the Secretary-General of the Arab League
in New York City, Abdul-Rahman Azzam,
Ambassador Abdul-Rahim summarized the
goals of the Washington Islamic Center: it
was 'not set up merely to provide a place of
worship in this capital, to rebut falsehood and
attacks against Islam and its culture and to
provide guidance for Muslims in this land –
though these are all lofty aims – but it also
fundamentally aims at promoting the
interests of the Arab and Muslim world
politically and economically and to reveal to
the inhabitants of the New World the beauty
and purity of our great religion in its
authentic garb. I hardly need to emphasize
the importance of the USA and its influential
role in world policy. So, to bring the Muslim
world to the Americans is one of the basic
objectives of setting up this Foundation; and
success in this direction will no doubt be very
beneficial, God willing, from all aspects to all
Muslim countries.' (see *History of the Islamic
Center* by Dr Muhammad Abdul-Rauf, p. 33).

15 Ibid., pp. 41, 78–84 for more details.

16 Ibid., pp. 12–13. Dr Abdul-Rauf became the
seventh Director-*imam* of the Washington
Islamic Center in 1971.

17 Ibid., p. 12.

18 Ibid., p. 13.

19 The contributions can be broken down as
follows: Construction costs – $1,094,017
(Afghanistan, Egypt, Indonesia, Iraq, Jordan,
Kuwait Libya, Pakistan, Saudi Arabia, Syria,
Turkey and Yemen); Operating expenses –
$66,554 (Afghanistan, Iraq, Libya, Morocco,
Pakistan, Saudi Arabia and Syria). The
Egyptian government paid the craftsmen's
wages, and the cost of providing the *minbar*
and chandelier in the prayer hall. Other cash
contributions from private sources amounted
to $136,873. Iran donated ten large carpets,
Afghanistan donated a marble-topped table,
and Turkey donated tiles and the services of
craftsmen for their installation. For more
details on the contributors, see Muhammad
Abdul-Rauf, *History of the Islamic Center*,
p. 95.

20 The list is too long to include here.
However, all those involved are credited in
History of the Islamic Center.

21 Ambassador Abdul-Rahim was also
instrumental in initiating the search for the
Washington Islamic Center's first *imam*. Dr
Mahmoud Hobballah was nominated in 1951
after the Ambassador had contacted Al-Azhar
University in Cairo, requesting that one of its
professors be seconded as *imam*. He held this
office 1952–5.

22 Mr & Mrs Howar built and donated the
fountain in the courtyard. In his professional
capacity, Mr Howar also recommended the
local architectural firm of Irving S. Porter &
Sons to build the mosque. Following an
official visit to the mosque in February 1957,
King Saud Ibn Abdul Aziz promised to pay
for a Muslim cemetery which was to be
purchased, owned, and controlled by the
Islamic Center, as well as the cost of building
a fence around the building. See *History of
the Islamic Center*, p. 70.

23 Ibid., p. 16. Unfortunately, Dr Abdul-Rauf
does not specify the source of the offer.

24 Professor Rossi was inspired by the old
mosques of Cairo and became widely known
in Egypt for his own mosque designs. He 'was
influential in the development in Egypt of a
new, but still basically conservative, style of
mosque design. His mosques in Cairo and
Alexandria are an attempt to create a
synthesis of the Ottoman and Mamluk styles,

with some innovations of his own. Rossi came
to Egypt while in his twenties and was first
employed by the Ministry of Works, which
assigned him duties in the Royal Palaces.
Later, in 1928, he was commissioned to
design the Abi al-Abbas al-Mursi Mosque
in Alexandria, which took sixteen years to
complete. During this period Rossi was
converted to Islam and began his systematic
study of mosque architecture in Egypt. He
compiled an impressive atlas of Islamic
architecture and decoration, which remains
unpublished and is kept by the *awqaf.*' See
Ihsan Fethi, 'The Mosque Today', in Sherban
Cantacuzino (ed.), *Architecture in Continuity:
Building in the Islamic World Today*, pp. 58–9.

25 Ibid., p. 59.

26 The writing itself, which is without the
customary diacritical marks and even includes
a spelling error, is of relatively poor quality
when compared to calligraphic inscriptions,
on other historic buildings. See Richard
Ettinghausen, 'Arabic Epigraphy . . .'.

27 According to Abdul-Rauf, the basement
was not part of the original plan. It was a late
addition arising from the need to dig deeper
than had been anticipated to reach firm
ground for the foundations. See *History of
the Islamic Center*, pp. 87–8.

28 See Oleg Grabar (ed.), 'The Art of the
Mamluks', *Muqarnas* 2 (1984), p. 9.

29 Tiles were fabricated in Turkey at the
Sümerbank Yildi Porcelain Factory.

30 These were Abdelaal Hassan and his two
assistants, M. Mahdi and T. Ahmed, whose
names appear on a plaque in the prayer hall.

31 We are indebted to Mokhless Al-Hariri for
information concerning the latest phase of
the design and use of the mosque; this was
presented in part at the conference 'Mosques
and Islamic Centers in North America' held
in November 1995 at the Massachusetts
Institute of Technology.

32 King Faisal of Saudi Arabia was an active
architectural patron, just as King Abdul Aziz
al-Saud had been before him; he personally
financed a number of important international
projects, e.g. the State Mosque in Islamabad
and the Islamic Centre in Rome.

33 AKAA 1983, Nomination Form for the
Islamic Cultural Foundation in Geneva.

34 Ibid.

35 Ibid.

36 Ibid.

37 There exist two techniques for making
zellij, or mosaics, in North Africa. The first

technique consists of covering the surface with enamel onto which standard designs are formed by hand using a special hammer. The enamel side is laid face down on the ground and the repeatable patterns are then traced on the back using paper or earth. The second technique consists of scraping away the enamel surface so as to leave raised geometric or calligraphic patterns. The surface is cut into sections and eventually mounted on the chosen surface in the building.

38 As reported in the *Middle East Economic Digest*, 25–31 July 1987, p. 22. According to the architect, however, the only real factor affecting the height of the minaret was a restriction imposed by the municipal building code. The minaret is 40 m tall, about one quarter of the height of St Peter's, and was never intended to provide any 'competition'. A taller structure would have been out of scale with the Centre itself (Portoghesi, in a conversation with H.U. Khan in 1991). However, at least one of the competition entries did feature a minaret higher than the dome of St Peter's and reportedly this caused the Vatican concern; it is probable that indeed a discreet word was put out to indicate that this was unacceptable.

39 Among those present, Prince Amin Abul Gassem deserves recognition for his role as a prime mover of the project; he was present through all its phases.

40 The building permit lapsed and a new application had to be made; this was issued in 1987.

41 Marcello Palumbo, 'La Moschea de Monte Antenne', *Storia dell'Arte*.

42 Christian Norberg-Schulz, *Architetture di Paolo Portoghesi e Vittorio Gigliotti*, p. 102.

43 Ibid., p. 200.

44 Portoghesi in a personal communication on the mosque sent to H.U. Khan in 1992.

45 This is the official capacity tied to parking requirements; however, the prayer hall can accommodate around 2,500 worshippers.

46 The architects base this dimension on the reconstruction drawing by Jean Sauvaget, *La Mosquée omeyyade de Médine*, Paris, 1947.

47 According to Portoghesi, the iconography of the Prophet's journey to Heaven came to Europe in the fourteenth century, appearing, moreover, in Dante's *Divine Comedy*. This idea has been disputed, however.

48 Portoghesi has admired and studied Borromini's architecture over the years and is author of the monograph *Francesco Borromini* (1967 and 1984). Portoghesi also credits the exploration of the ribbed structural system in the fifteenth century to Leonardo da Vinci, 're-proposing it for the *tiburium* [dome over the crossing] of Milan's Duomo in a version that presented Gothic arches. It was Borromini, though, who discovered the iconological value of this syntagma as an allusion to Oriental Tradition.' Portoghesi, 'The Architecture of Harkening', in Demetra Spigolature (ed.), *The Mosque in Rome*, p. 16. (This book presents perhaps the most complete published analysis and discussion of the project.)

49 'View from a Jersey City Mosque', *The New Yorker*, 27 September 1993, p. 31.

50 For a study of Islam in the United States, see Yvonne Haddad and Adair Lumis, *Islamic Values in the United States*. The information included here is extracted from this study published in 1983, which still remains valid at the turn of the millennium.

51 The Kuwaiti ambassador, Muhammad Abulhassan, became the main mover behind the project.

52 One reason mentioned for changing architects was SOM's high fees, though this has not been verifiable. SHCA received the commission because the firm was known to the Kuwaitis: amongst other works, Gursel had designed the permanent mission of Kuwait to the UN in 1987.

53 It is reported by McCarthy that Oleg Grabar, a member of the second committee, threatened to resign from it if the building included a dome and minaret. The committee succeeded, nevertheless, in encouraging the architect to explore, and the client to accept, the ornamental qualities of new materials, including glass. Its members also included Marilyn Jenkins of the Metropolitan Museum of Art, New York, Maan Medina of Columbia University, New York, Mildred Schmertz of *Architectural Record* and Renata Holod.

54 Wael al-Masri, 'Architecture and the Question of Identity . . .', p. 94.

55 There is a continuing debate amongst the *ulema* both in Europe and North America and in the Islamic world as to whether having women praying above (or below) men is an acceptable practice. In both the Regent's Park and Manhattan mosques the client rejected the idea of placing the women's prayer area above the main prayer hall. Also see Ronald Lewcock, 'London Central Mosque', *Architects' Journal*, vol. 166, no. 32, 10 August 1977,

p. 266; Marcel Boisard, *Humanism in Islam*, p. 77; and Gulzar Haider and Muhammad Mukhtar's unpublished paper, 'Islamic Architecture in Non-Islamic Environments' (1980), p. 30.

56 The colour green, used widely in Islam, was stipulated by the client to symbolize hope and fertility.

57 The nine are: *Allah, Al-Rahman, Al-Rahim, Al-Malik, Al-Quddus, Al-Salaam, Al-Mumin, Al-Mukarjamin* and *Al-Aziz*.

58 As quoted in James Traub, 'The Road to Mecca', *New York Times*, 24 June 1991, p. 40.

59 The issue of legitimacy and authenticity in the architecture of the Islamic world is one that is currently the subject of debate and concerns scholars of Islam, modernity, and their cultural expressions. The historian Mohammed Arkoun has argued in several publications that contemporary Muslim governments, such as that of Morocco, resort to the use of historically accepted architectural styles in order to reinforce an image of longevity, permanence and legitimacy. Such architecture is viewed as having the weight of authenticity. For discussions on authenticity, see Hasan-Uddin Khan, 'Meaning in Tradition Today: An Approach to Architectural Criticism', and Michael Sorkin, 'Counterpoint', in Robert Powell (ed.), *Criticism in Architecture*, pp. 53–68. For a more detailed exploration of issues of legitimacy and Islam facing modernity, see Arkoun, *Ouvertures sur l'Islam*, as well as 'The Metamorphosis of the Sacred' in M. Frishman and H.U. Khan (eds.), *The Mosque*, pp. 268–77.

Key mosques and Islamic Centres

The following list includes a selection of built examples that are important for architectural and/or social reasons. The list may be used as a guide or for easy reference. The examples are arranged alphabetically by country, with brief details of: the location of the building; the dates of commission and completion of the project (when only one date is given, it is the latter); the name and city of the architect's practice (at the time of publication); the official client of the work, sometimes including the names of particular individuals who were important to its realization; and a short description of each project, with salient details concerning materials, siting, stylistic features etc.

Bangladesh

Project Bait ul-Mukarram,
67 Purana Paltan, Dhaka
Dates 1959–63
Architect Abdul Hossain Thariani,
Karachi, Pakistan
Client Islamic Foundation of Bangladesh &
Mosque Planning Committee
Providing religious, social and cultural facilities in the city's central commercial district, the mosque complex also includes a bazaar, and is inspired by traditional urban models in which the mosque is the physical focus of daily life. The formal inspiration of the five-storey cubic building is the Ka'ba – an early and rare use of the shrine in Mecca as a formal reference for a contemporary mosque. (See Chapter 5.)

Project Islamic Centre for Technical and Vocational Training and Research (ICTVTR), West of Dhaka
Dates 1979–87
Architect Studio 14 (Doruk Pamir & Ercüment Gümrük), Istanbul, Turkey
Client Board of Trustees, Islamic Conference of Foreign Ministers/Rafiquddin Ahmad
The general layout of ICTVTR relies on the organizing principles of the Turkish *külliye*, with some adjustments for climate and function, while the cubical mosque and the cylindrical minaret break the orthogonal grid of the complex to achieve the orientation towards Mecca. Contemporary expression, modular brick and reinforced-concrete construction, and the functional and symbolic presence of water are among the notable characteristics of the project. (See Chapter 4.)

Project Capitol Complex Mosque, Sher-e-Bangla Nagar, Dhaka
Dates 1962–83
Architects Louis Kahn (died 1974); David Wisdom & Associates, Philadelphia, Pennsylvania, USA
Client Public Works Department/Government of Bangladesh
Designed as part of a large modern complex to house the nascent Bangladeshi state government, the unadorned cubical prayer hall is remarkable for its powerful geometry. The spiritual quality of the interior is created by the modulation of light and the play of geometric forms, while the only sign of the religious function apparent from without is its angle relative to the main building, resulting from the change of orientation required to face Mecca. (See Chapter 2.)

Bosnia

Project Sherefuddin's White Mosque, Visoko
Dates 1967–80
Architect Zlatko Ugljen, Zagreb, Croatia
Client Muslim community of Visoko
Situated in the town centre, the mosque is a sculptural, modernist interpretation of the Ottoman single-unit domed type exemplified by many old Bosnian mosques. The forms and elements of the mosque, including an unusual minaret, are treated in an abstract manner and constitute a radical departure from familiar mosque forms. The building has become an important landmark for its town. (See Chapter 5.)

Canada

Project Ismaili Jamatkhana and Centre, Burnaby (Vancouver), British Columbia
Dates 1982–94
Architect Bruno Freschi, Vancouver, British Columbia
Client The Ismaili Community of Canada/ The Aga Khan
Located on a flat suburban site and serving the local Ismaili community, the modern, well-crafted building has a citadel-like appearance with a soaring portal entrance and three-dimensional window niches in geometrically patterned glass. Natural light is also diffused from the thirteen octagonal domes and skylight, and rich materials, such as the contrasting coral and marble panels in the *mihrab*, are used in the interior detailing. (See Chapter 1.)

Croatia

Project Islamic Centre and Mosque, Zagreb
Dates 1980–7
Architects Mirže Golože and Dzeme Čelića Zagreb, Croatia
Client Muslim community of Zagreb
Probably the largest Islamic Centre in Europe, the mosque projects both a recognizably Ottoman image, seen in the large dome covering the central space and in the typical minarets, and a contemporary expression for the community in a modernist idiom. The concrete shell is split into two staggered sections permitting natural light to enter the large prayer hall, the mosque's most dramatic design aspect. (See Chapter 5.)

Dubai (UAE)

Project Bin Madiya Mosque, Al Nasser Square, Deira
Dates 1982–90
Architect A.N. Tombazis & Associates/ Alexandros Tombazis, Athens, Greece
Client/Patron Majid Al Futtaim
A modern mosque donated for public use by a private patron, it is noteworthy for the manner in which the architect handled the difficult siting in a dense urban location, and for the stepped roof and clerestory windows which create a striking profile. The outer walls and minaret are clad in sand-coloured hand-made brick, while the prayer hall, lit from above, features a *qibla* wall decorated with blue and beige glass mosaic and calligraphy. (See Chapter 1.)

Egypt

Project New Gourna Village Mosque, New Gourna, near Luxor
Dates 1945–8
Architect Hassan Fathy (died 1989), Cairo
Client The Egyptian Department of Antiquities/Osman Rustum & Alexander Stopplaere

Though outside the time frame of this book, the village mosque in New Gourna partakes of its architect's lifelong philosophy of using local technology and responding to the prevailing conditions of climate and rural poverty in his native Egypt. In building the domes and vaults of the mosque Fathy used the vernacular of mud-brick construction techniques of Upper Egypt, thus establishing an important Arab model for later mosques in hot, dry climates. (See Chapter 3.)

France

Project Mosque & Muslim Institute, Place du Puits-l'Ermite, Paris 75005
Dates 1922–6
Architects M. Eustache, Robert Fournez and Maurice Mantout
Client The French Government and the Association of *Habous* of Holy Places and Si Kaddour Ben Ghabrit

Although strictly outside the time frame of this book, the complex illustrates an early historicist trend that is still prevalent in mosque design. The first mosque to be built in France, it is a fine example of Moorish architecture and decorative design, with intricate wood and plaster work executed by Moroccan craftsmen, and includes inviting courtyards and gardens. (See Chapter 6.)

Indonesia

Project Salman Mosque, Institut Teknologi Bandung (ITB), Jalan Ganesha 9, Bandung
Dates 1959–72
Architect Achmad Noe'man, Bandung
Client Mosque Committee

The progressive modernist idiom of the design marked a radical departure from accepted norms of mosque building in Indonesia. The frank expression of structure and materials in the concrete minaret and the floating concrete roof supported by reinforced-concrete columns, to the exclusion of more obvious and recognizable historical or regional references, was unprecedented. (See Chapter 4.)

Project University of Indonesia Mosque, Depok, Jakarta
Date 1990
Architect Triatno Y. Hardjoko, Jakarta
Client The University of Indonesia

The architect was asked to design the mosque in accordance with the typological characteristics associated with Central Javanese architecture. The design is a close interpretation of the three-tiered pyramidal *meru* roof and the *soko guru* structure commonly employed in local mosques and in Hindu Javanese temples. While the exterior follows typical local mosque design, the treatment of the interior is unusual, with surfaces finished in imported polished marble rather than locally available wood. (See Chapter 4.)

Project Istiqlal Mosque, Taman Wijaya Kusuma, Pintu Air, Jakarta Pusat
Dates 1955–84
Architect F. Silaban (died 1986), Jakarta
Client State Committee/President Sukarno

The design for this state mosque was influenced by aspects of the monumental secular architecture of the Soviet Union and Turkey, in addition to Ottoman imagery in the urban landmark minaret. The large building with two courtyards reveals local influences in terms of its orientation and layout, and is related visually to the nearby National Monument. (See Chapter 2.)

Project Said Naum Mosque, Kel. Kebon, Kacang, Tanah Abang, Jakarta
Dates 1976–7
Architect Atelier Enam (Adhi Moersid), Jakarta
Client Jakarta Municipal Government (DKI)/ Ali Sadekin & Wastu Pragantha Chong

Prominently sited in a dense urban location and built to provide a religious and social centre for the local community, the mosque follows the Hindu Javanese architectural tradition of the region while retaining spiritual concepts of Islamic philosophy. The rotated two-tiered roof forms a pyramid; it represents a novel reinterpretation of the regional *meru* roof type. (See Chapter 2.)

Iran

Project Al-Ghadir Mosque, Mirdamad Boulevard, Tehran
Dates 1977–87
Architect Jahangir Mazlum, Tehran
Client Neighbourhood community/Mosque Board of Trustees

Located on a restricted urban site in a residential neighbourhood, the mosque is noted for its dodecagonal plan – a form usually associated with funerary architecture – and for the use of decorative geometric patterns and calligraphy in both the exterior and interior brickwork. The abstracted dome form in reinforced concrete and steel clad in brick is created out of a series of rotated superimposed squares producing a contemporary and unusual external expression using a traditional material. (See Chapter 5.)

Project Jondishapur University Mosque, Ahvaz, Khuzestan
Dates 1971–5
Architect Kamran Diba (DAZ Architects), Paris, France
Client Plan and Budget Organization, Government of Iran

The sculptural brick building is located on a pedestrian axis connecting scattered buildings on the campus. The modern design features elements of southern Iranian architecture, patterned brickwork and blue-tiled *badgir*s, but deliberately avoids the more obvious elements usually associated with mosque design, such as dome and ornamentation. (See Chapter 4.)

Project University of Kerman Mosque, Kerman
Dates 1985–9
Architect Bonyan Consultants/Piraz, Tehran
Client Ministry of Culture & Higher Education

The university mosque refers to the cubic form of the Ka'ba in Mecca as its primary model. Brick revetment and the large-scale brick epigraphy used as a decorative device here were popular in Iran and appeared in many new mosques built in the 1980s. The design of the top-lit vaulted prayer hall is particularly remarkable for the innovative contemporary expression of the *mihrab*. The building, raised on a mound, is entered at ground level. (See Chapter 4.)

Project Shushtar Neighbourhood Mosque, Shushtar, Khuzestan
Dates 1974–8
Architect Kamran Diba (DAZ Architects), Paris, France
Client Iran Housing Company/Sazeman Khaneh Sazi/Karoun Agro-Industry
In the new town built to provide housing for the employees of the Karoun Agro-Industry, the neighbourhood mosque is fully integrated into the urban plan, passage through its outer parts being treated as part of the pedestrian network. Local brick, colourful mosaics and ceramic tiles were used and regional architectural elements like the dome-like wind-catchers have here been reinterpreted to signal the mosque's presence. (See Chapter 3.)

Iraq

Project Khulafa Mosque, Baghdad
Dates 1961–3
Architect Mohamed Makiya, London, United Kingdom
Client Ministry of Awqaf
Located in a densely built urban district on a restricted site, partially occupied by a thirteenth-century minaret, the mosque reflects a contemporary expression of traditional materials and forms, in which brick is used as a decorative and structural medium. The distinctive suspended 'Islamic' arches, geometric friezes, Kufic calligraphy, and the unusual octagonal plan of the prayer hall are notable features. (See Chapter 3.)

Italy

Project Islamic Centre and Mosque, Av. della Moschea, Monte Antenne, Rome
Dates 1979–94
Architects Sami Moussawi, Manchester; Paolo Portoghesi and Vittorio Gigliotti, Rome
Client Mosque Committee of Ambassadors
The mosque is the most successful element of the large complex, particularly the roof structure of the main prayer hall, the interior of which is modelled on the Great Mosque of Cordoba in Spain, with its forest of graceful columns and arches. The design combines the modular and circular systems of the classical Arab hypostyle prayer hall and the domed Ottoman type and attempts to express a neutral pan-Islamism capable of being understood by all. (See Chapter 6.)

Kuwait

Project Great Mosque of Kuwait, Kuwait City
Dates 1976–84
Architect Mohamed Makiya, London, United Kingdom
Client Major Works Department, Ministry of Public Works
The design reflects the point of meeting between the modernist sensibilities of the architect and the client's wish to see more emphasis on the ornamentation and crafts perceived as specifically Islamic. References to historic examples coexist with modernist treatments such as the development of a repeatable wall bay unit and the liberal use of exposed concrete. (See Chapter 2.)

Lebanon

Project Shafiq Amash Mosque, Mostafa Kamil, Ras-Beirut
Dates 1982–4
Architect Nabbil Tabbara, Beirut
Client/Patron Mohammad Al Amine Islamic Association/Saeb Salaam & Rabih Amache
The modern structure was a response to the contraints of a restricted urban site, and maintains an unusual open visual connection between the interior of the prayer hall and the street. The design is based on variations of the square and cube. (See Chapter 1.)

Malaysia

Project Abu Bakar as-Siddiq Mosque, Bangsar, Kuala Lumpur
Dates 1978–82
Architect Hajeedar & Associates (Hajeedar bin Abdul Majid), Kuala Lumpur
Client Religious Affairs Department/ Malaysian Ministry of Federal Territory
The mosque is a representative example of the pan-Islamic style popular in the Malay archipelago. It projects an Indian urban image, using well-established Islamic design elements such as the minaret, pointed arches, and onion-shaped dome, here executed in aluminium. (See Chapter 3.)

Project Masjid Negara, Jalan Sultan Hisamuddin, Kuala Lumpur
Dates 1957–65
Architect Baharuddin Abu Kassim/The Public Works Department, Kuala Lumpur

Client Central Organizing Committee
A folded concrete plate roof in the form of a parasol covers a large prayer hall, square in plan, in a contemporary interpretation of the dome form and the traditional Malay wooden roof. Ottoman imagery is introduced in the minaret and in the centrepiece of the dome. The state mosque is an integral feature of a complex of buildings housing a variety of facilities, and is used for important occasions. (See Chapter 2.)

Project Negeri Sembilan Mosque, Seremban
Dates 1962–7
Architects Malayan Architects Co-Partnership (Datuk Lim Chong Keat and Chen Voon Fee); later, Jurubena Bertiga International, Kuala Lumpur
Client State Committee
Influenced by the previous example, the design of this smaller state mosque borrows the imagery of the concrete parasol roof, under which all the facilities are gathered, but interprets more specifically the Chinese Malay roof type found in the region. (See Chapter 2.)

Mali

Project Great Mosque, Niono
Dates 1948–73
Architect/Mason Lassiné Minta, Niono
Client Community of Niono/Dr Diawara
Built without the aid of drawings by a local mason and the community it was to serve, the mosque is derived from the Great Mosque of Djenné in Mali, which has a large hypostyle prayer hall and a three-towered *qibla* wall, and from Dyula architecture with its strong emphasis on verticality. Using local sun-dried brick, the architect/mason extended a regional architectural language without breaking with it. (See Chapter 5.)

Morocco

Project Avicenne Military Hospital Mosque, Marrakech
Date 1982
Architect Charles Boccara, Marrakech
Client Avicenne Military Hospital
In a low-rise hospital setting, the mosque has its own courtyard and garden, which provides a peaceful and pleasant oasis; its style was inspired by local building traditions and idioms. (See Chapter 4.)

Project Great Mosque of Hassan II,
Corniche, Casablanca
Dates 1986–93
Architect Michel Pinseau,
Paris, France
Client King Hassan II of Morocco
Noted for its grandiose scale, the quality of
craftsmanship, and its location at the very
edge of the sea overlooking the Atlantic
Ocean, the mosque draws exclusively on
Moroccan historical precedents, particularly
those dating from the Almohad period. Its
minaret, 200 m (650 ft) in height, is a major
local landmark, and its extensive ancillary
facilities include a public library, a museum
and underground swimming pool. (See
Chapter 1.)

Niger

Project Yaama Mosque, Yaama, Tahoua
Dates 1962–86
Architect/Mason Falké Barmou, Yaama
Client Community of Yaama
Financed by the local community and built
under the leadership of a local mason, the
mosque features the use of the regional
techniques of mud-brick and rammed-
earth construction and of the vernacular
architectural language of the region. Rising
high above the village, the four-towered
structure has a courtyard and a rectangular
hypostyle prayer hall. Over the decades it
has undergone successive modifications
and improvements. (See Chapter 5.)

Pakistan

Project Bhong Mosque,
Bhong, near Rahimyar Khan, Punjab
Dates 1932–83
Architect/Patron/Client Rais Ghazi
Muhammad
The mosque follows the tradition of the
Mughal mosque type and has a profuse and
eclectic programme of ornamentation that
draws on Multani and Victorian colonial
traditions, in addition to the Mughal style.
It forms part of a private compound of
buildings and gardens in the village of
Bhong, and is notable for its exuberance.
(See Chapter 1.)

Project King Faisal Masjid,
Shahrah-e Islamabad, Islamabad
Dates 1960–86

Architect Vedat Dalokay (died 1981),
Ankara, Turkey
Client Capital Development Authority
A major landmark in the new capital, the
colossal tent-like structure epitomizes both
monumentality and modernity. The architect
used the latest in contemporary structural
techniques and materials, combined with
historical references to mosques of the
Ottoman Empire, in this centralized structure
and four pencil-thin minarets. Facilities
include an Islamic University and Research
Institute. (See Chapter 2.)

Project Jamat Ahle Hadith
('C'-type Mosque), Islamabad
Dates 1969–73
Architect Anwar Saeed (Capital
Development Authority)
Client Ministry of Awqaf
The architect, who was influenced by the
modern movement, designed an economical
and flexible mosque for the newly created
neighbourhoods of Islamabad that could be
adapted to communities of varying sizes.
Choosing easily identifiable motifs such as
arch and dome, he employed a basic grid
articulated by concrete vaults and columns.
(See Chapter 3.)

Project Al-Tooba Mosque (Masjid-i Tooba),
Phase 1, Defence Officers' Housing Society,
Karachi
Dates 1964–9
Architect Babar Hameed, Karachi
Client Defence Officers' Housing Society
At the time of its construction, the circular
domed structure was a technological feat
in the region. Featuring the largest shell
structure on the subcontinent, as well as
a towering, landmark minaret, the mosque
presented an uncompromisingly modern
image. (See Chapter 5.)

Saudi Arabia

Project University of Petroleum and
Minerals Mosque, Dhahran
Dates 1969–74
Architect Caudill, Rowlett, Scott (CRS),
Houston, Texas, USA
Client University of Petroleum and Minerals
Located in an oasis, the mosque is set on
a podium over the water. It is shaded by
an umbrella roof carried on slim arched
colonnades which covers both prayer hall

and courtyard. The design projects the
International Style for the mosque built in
concrete and glass. (See Chapter 4.)

Project Corniche Mosque,
Corniche, Jeddah
Date 1986
Architect Abdel Wahed El-Wakil,
Miami, Florida, USA
Client Ministry of Pilgrimage and
Endowments and the Municipality of
Jeddah/Mohammad Said Al-Farsi
This is a small, sculptural mosque set in a
popular recreation area by the sea. Regional
techniques for dome construction in local
brick were employed and the walls are
finished in white plaster; this is an eclectic
compact building with a dome and minaret.
(See Chapter 3.)

Project Al-Harithy Mosque, Jeddah
Date 1986
Architect Abdel Wahed El-Wakil,
Miami, Florida, USA
Client Muwaffak Al-Harithy
References to Ottoman architecture,
combined with the use of materials and
crafts drawn from Mediterranean cultures,
are integrated into the design of this
community mosque. The courtyard can
be covered by a retractable canopy roof.
(See Chapter 1.)

Project Island Mosque, Corniche, Jeddah
Dates 1983–6
Architect Abdel Wahed El-Wakil,
Miami, Florida, USA
Client Ministry of Pilgrimage and
Endowments and the Municipality of
Jeddah/Mohammad Said Al-Farsi
This is a small sculptural mosque sited in
a popular coastal recreation area near the
Corniche Mosque (see above). It was built
using the same technology and materials
as the Corniche Mosque, has a dome and
minaret, but makes different stylistic
references. (See Chapter 3.)

Project Sulaiman Mosque, Hamra, Jeddah
Date 1980
Architect Abdel Wahed El-Wakil,
Miami, Florida, USA
Client Sheikh Abdel Aziz al-Sulaiman &
brothers
The mosque draws from the historic Mamluk
and Ottoman architectures and integrates

modern construction techniques with those historically used in Upper Egypt. (See Chapter 1.)

Project Al-Kindi Plaza Jami, Hayy Assafarat, Riyadh
Dates 1983–6
Architect BEEAH (Ali Shuaibi), Riyadh
Client Riyadh Development Authority
Located in the Diplomatic Quarter of the capital, the large mosque features a hypostyle prayer hall and is organized around a courtyard with two tall minarets marking its gateways. Built in concrete and covered in sprayed earth-coloured stucco to resemble traditional mud plaster, it was designed in the idiom of Najdi architecture. (See Chapter 3.)

Project Imam Turki bin Abdullah Jami, al-Adl Square, Qasr al-Hokm, Riyadh
Dates 1988–92
Architect Rasem Badran, Amman, Jordan
Client Riyadh Development Authority
Comparable in scale to many state mosques, the building features a hypostyle prayer hall, and is located in the historic core of the city. It has two tall square minarets indicating the direction of Mecca in the cityscape, but avoids conventional arch and dome forms altogether. As in the previous example, the design employs the regional idiom of Najdi architecture. (See Chapter 3.)

Project King Khaled International Airport Mosque, Riyadh
Dates 1974–83
Architect HOK + 4 – a consortium/ Hellmuth, Obata & Kassabaum (Gyo Obata), St Louis, Missouri, USA
Client Ministry of Defence and Aviation and International Airports Projects
The large freestanding mosque with dome and minaret has a pivotal location in the airport. The design makes historical reference to the Dome of the Rock in Jerusalem and is executed using advanced technology. The lightweight concrete dome supported by steel trusses and columns is striking and the decorative programme lavish. (See Chapter 4.)

Singapore

Project Darul Aman Mosque, Changi Road and Jalan Eunos, Singapore
Date 1986

Architect Housing Development Board (Mohamed Asaduz Zaman), Singapore
Client The Muslim Religious Council of Singapore (MUIS)
The design is based on local Malay architectural forms, with the use of traditional pitched, two-tiered *meru* roofs and timber construction, here supplemented by structural reinforced concrete and steel. It avoids the use of stylistic features of mosque design derived from the Anglo-Indian vocabulary which have become popular in much of Southeast Asia. (See Chapter 3.)

South Africa

Project Jumma Masjid, Kerk Street, Johannesburg
Dates 1992–6
Architect Muhammad Mayet, Johannesburg
Located in the central business district of the city, the mosque makes reference to Egyptian Mamluk architecture and El-Wakil's mosque designs in the Middle East. Load-bearing brick construction is combined with a tall landmark minaret; with the design and the ornamentation are similar to those of El-Wakil's Al-Harithy Mosque in Jeddah, Saudi Arabia, listed above. (See Chapter 1.)

Sudan

Project Nilein Mosque, Omdurman, Khartoum
Dates 1974–84
Architect Gamar Eldowla Abdel Gadir, Khartoum
Client Government of Sudan
Sited near the confluence of the White Nile and the Blue Nile, the mosque comprises familiar forms of dome, minaret and arch, which are given contemporary expression. The dominant element, the dome, is in the form of an aluminium space-frame faceted with rhomboid forms. The interior decoration was executed by Moroccan craftsmen. (See Chapter 3.)

Switzerland

Project Islamic Cultural Foundation Mosque, 34 chemin Colladon, Petit Saconnex, Geneva
Dates 1974–8

Architect Osman Gurdogan and Jean-Pierre Limongelli, Geneva
Client Government of Saudi Arabia/Dr Sheil El Ard
The mosque was built on a site with existing buildings which had to be incorporated into the complex. Ottoman architecture is the dominant reference to the past in the domed prayer hall and minaret, while Moroccan ornamentation characterizes the interior surfaces. The marked contrast between the sober exterior and the ornate interior is noteworthy. (See Chapter 6.)

Turkey

Project Grand National Assembly Mosque, Ankara
Dates 1985–9
Architect Altug, Behruz and Can Çinici (Behruz Çinici), Ankara
Client The Turkish Parliament
The contemporary design is inspired by the Turkish *külliye* model, inserted into an existing complex of government buildings. Modern in the abstraction of the *mihrab* and minaret forms and in the reinforced-concrete construction, the building is a successful non-stylistic example of mosque design. (See Chapter 2.)

United Kingdom

Project Ismaili Centre, Cromwell Road and Exhibition Road, South Kensington, London
Dates 1979–84
Architect Casson Conder Partnership (Neville Conder and Kenneth Price), London
Client/Patron The Ismaili Community of the United Kingdom/The Aga Khan
The mosque is located on a very difficult site across the road from the Victoria and Albert Museum and attempts to reflect the 'mood' of Islamic architectural tradition in a modern building. The prayer hall on the third floor is a rectangular space, tiled and carpeted, and has a low ceiling, in contrast to the vertical emphasis so often associated with major places of prayer. (See Chapter 1.)

Project London Central Mosque, Regent's Park, London
Dates 1969–77
Architect Sir Frederick Gibberd (died 1984), London

Client Trustees of the Central London Mosque

The mosque was designed as an expression of Islam using modern technologies and pan-Islamic design elements considered as recognizably Islamic to all Muslims, such as the powerfully proportioned dome inspired by those in Isfahan. The architect was very strongly influenced by the contemporary technological concerns and the formal expression of contemporary building materials in the mosque using modular and pre-cast elements. (See Chapter 6.)

United States

Project University of Arkansas Mosque, Jonesboro, Arkansas
Dates 1982–4
Architect Gulzar Haider, Ottawa, Ontario, Canada; Brackett Ktennerich & Associates, Jonesboro, Arkansas
Client Department of Customs, Saudi Arabia
A small mosque in pan-Islamic style; the striped exterior draws on the regional architecture of Saudi Arabia, and the minaret reflects Ottoman design. For an alternative approach by the same architect, see the ISNA Mosque in Plainfield, Indiana (listed below). (See Chapter 5.)

Project Islamic Center, Massachusetts Avenue, Washington, DC
Dates 1949–57
Architect Mario Rossi (died 1961), Cairo, Egypt; later renovations by Georgetown Design Group (Mokhless Al-Hariri), Washington, DC
Client Board of Governors of the Islamic Center, Washington, DC
Modelled on Cairene Mamluk examples, the mosque is a symmetrical building with minaret and dome, constructed in concrete and steel and finished in limestone and blue marble chips. The interior ornamentation is a mix of Moroccan, Turkish and Egyptian traditions reflecting the identity of the countries contributing to the costs of building the mosque.(See Chapter 6.)

Project Islamic Students of North America (ISNA) Mosque, Plainfield, Indiana
Dates 1979–83
Architect Gulzar Haider, Ottawa, Ontario, Canada; Dana Architects & Planners (Mukhtar Khalil), Chicago, Illinois

Client Muslim Students Association (now part of ISNA)
The plan and three-dimensional spatial arrangement of this elegant contemporary mosque are derived from geometric principles of the square, octagon and circle. The abstract geometry and use of light and shade from high openings, and the combination of mystical themes with Western design ideas to express a modern Muslim identity are noteworthy aspects of the design concept. Some debt to Louis Kahn is perceptible. (See Chapter 5.)

Project Dar al-Islam Mosque, Abiquiu, New Mexico
Date 1981
Architect Hassan Fathy (died 1989), Cairo, Egypt
Client Dar al-Islam Foundation/Nuridin Durkee
The mosque was built by and for a new experimental community, whose members received instruction from Fathy and his team of Nubian masons (who came to the USA specially for the purpose) in the low-technology building techniques of vault and dome construction used in Upper Egypt. Constructed entirely with mud brick, the mosque has loadbearing walls that carry arches vaults and domes which cover the prayer hall, itself divided into single domed units. (See Chapter 5.)

Project Islamic Cultural Center, East 96th Street, New York, NY
Dates 1987–91
Architect Skidmore, Owings & Merrill (Michael McCarthy), New York
Client Government of Kuwait and other Islamic countries
Angled to the city street grid, the mosque is a vertically extended cube of glass and granite covered by a central dome. Lit by skylights, the prayer hall features a programme of ornamentation that is generated through the possibilities offered by contemporary technical means. A freestanding minaret was included for symbolic value. (See Chapter 6.)

Venezuela

Project Al-Ibrahim Jami, Santa Rosa Boulevard, Caracas
Dates 1990–3

Architect Oscar Bracho, Caracas
Client/Patron Al-Ibrahim Foundation/ Sheikh Ibrahim bin Abdulaziz al-Ibrahim & Sheikh Bakar Khomais
Located in a rapidly changing area of the city, this historicist mosque features the use of dome, minaret and portal to signal its presence in the urban landscape, and devices such as the octagonal hall rising up from a platform to a circular dome to achieve the transition between the street and the interior of the prayer hall. (See Chapter 1.)

Select bibliography

The sources and publications listed relate to the works cited in abbreviated form in the Notes on the Text; the latter also include various very specific citations in the context of the projects to which they refer.

Archival material, Aga Khan Award for Architecture (AKAA), Geneva

Bangladesh
Islamic Centre for Technical and Vocational Training, Dhaka: Architect's Record Form, 1988

Bosnia
Sherefuddin's White Mosque, Visoko: Project Summary Form; Technical Review Summary (Atilla Yücel), 1983

Indonesia
Istiqlal Mosque, Jakarta: Architect's Record Form, 1986
Said Naum Mosque, Jakarta: Project Record Form; Technical Review Summary (Darab Diba), 1986
Salman Mosque, Institut Teknologi Bandung: Client's Record Form and Project Record Form, 1979

Iran
Jondishapur University Mosque, Ahvaz: Architect's Record Form; Project Summary; Technical Review Summary (Samir Abdulac), 1980
University of Kerman Mosque: Architect's Record Form, 1988

Iraq
Khulafa Mosque, Baghdad: Project Record Form, 1985

Kuwait
Great Mosque, Kuwait City: Architect's Record Form, 1985

Lebanon
Shafiq Amash Mosque, Beirut: Client's Record Form and Architect's Record Form, 1985

Malaysia
Abu Bakar as-Siddiq Mosque, Kuala Lumpur: Architect's Record Form, 1982
Timber Modular Mosques, Pahang State:

Architect's Record Form; Technical Review Summary (Abbad al-Radi), 1992

Mali
Great Mosque, Niono: Project Summary (Raoul Snelder), 1983

Niger
Yaama Mosque, Tahou: Technical Review Summary (Raoul Snelder), 1986

Saudi Arabia
Corniche Mosque, Jeddah: Technical Review Summary (Mohammad Al-Asad), 1989
Hotel and Conference Centre Mosque, Mecca: Client's Record Form and Project Record Form, 1979
Al-Kindi Plaza, Riyadh: Project Record Form, 1989
King Faisal Foundation Mosque, Riyadh: Project Summary Form and Client's Record Form, 1985
King Khaled International Airport Mosque, Riyadh: Architect's Record Form, 1983
University of Petroleum and Minerals Mosque, Dhahran: Architect's Record Form, 1979

Singapore
Darul Aman Mosque: Technical Review Summary, 1989

Sudan
Nilein Mosque, Khartoum: Client's Record Form, 1985

Switzerland
Islamic Cultural Foundation, Geneva: Nomination Form, 1983

Turkey
Grand National Assembly Mosque, Ankara: Architect's Record Forms, 1992

United Kingdom
Regent's Park Mosque, London: Architect's Record Form, 1979

Lectures, personal communications and correspondence

Azzam, Abdul-Rahman: Letter of May 1951 to the Secretary-General of the Arab League in New York City, regarding fundraising for the Islamic Center, Washington, DC
Badran, Rasem: 'The Justice Palace (Qasr al-Hokm) and the Jama'a Mosque' (lecture, 1993), and discussions with the authors.

Bianca, Stefano: Conversation with H.U. Khan, 1993, on the Baghdad State Mosque Competition
Chadirji, Rifat: Conversations with R. Holod, 1982–3, about the Baghdad State Mosque Competition and Iraqi architecture in general
Damais, Soedarmadji: Conversations with R. Holod, 1979, and with H.U. Khan, 1989, on the Istiqlal Mosque, Jakarta
Diba, Kamran: Conversations and correspondence with H.U. Khan and R. Holod, 1988–9, on his architecture
Al-Farsi, Mohammad Said: Conversations with H.U. Khan, 1985, on the Jeddah Corniche mosques and site visits
Gadir, Gamal El-Dowla Abdel: Correspondence with H.U. Khan, 1987, on the Nilein Mosque
Gibberd, Sir Frederick: Correspondence with his office, 1986, on the Regent's Park Mosque, London
Grabar, Oleg: Discussions with H.U. Khan and R. Holod, 1989, particularly on the Al-Ghadir Mosque in Tehran and the project for the Osman ibn Affan Mosque in Qatar
Haider, Gulzar: Communications with H.U. Khan, 1996, concerning the Islamic Center, Kingston, Ontario
Hameed, Babar: Correspondence with H.U. Khan, 1989, on the Defence Officers' Housing Society Mosque, Karachi
Makiya, Mohamed: Conversations with R. Holod and H.U. Khan, 1982–3, on his design for the Kuwait Great Mosque and the Baghdad State Mosque competition
Portoghesi, Paolo: Conversation, site visit with the architects and exchange of correspondence with H.U. Khan, 1990–1
Saeed, Anwar: Conversations with H.U. Khan, 1987, about the mosques in Islamabad
Tombazis, A.N.: Correspondence with H.U. Khan, 1990–1, on the Bin Madiya Mosque, Dubai

Books and articles

'Abdel Wahed El-Wakil', *Mimar* 1 (1981), pp. 48–55
Abdul-Rauf, Muhammad, *History of the Islamic Center, [Washington]*, Washington, DC, 1978

Abel, Chris, 'Model and Metaphor in the Design of New Building Types in Saudi Arabia', in Margaret Ševčenko (ed.), *Theories and Principles of Design in the Architecture of Islamic Societies*, Cambridge, MA, 1988, pp. 169–83

Adams, Cindy, *Sukarno: An Autobiography*, Indianapolis, IN, 1965, and Hong Kong, 1966

Ahmed, Akbar, and Hastings Donnan (eds.), *Islam, Globalization and Postmodernity*, London and New York, 1994

Ahmed, Imran, *Expression of Nationhood* (M.S. thesis, Massachusetts Institute of Technology), Cambridge, MA, 1992

Ahmed, Leila, *Women and Gender in Islam: Historical Roots of a Modern Debate*, New Haven, CT, 1992

Akbar, Jamal, *Crisis in the Built Environment: the Case of the Muslim City*, Singapore, 1988

Ali, Ahmed, *Town Planning in Pakistan and India*, Karachi, 1971

Ali, Wijdan (ed.), *Contemporary Art from the Islamic World*, London, 1989

Alsayyad, Nezar, *Cities and Caliphs: On the Genesis of Arab Muslim Urbanism*, Westport, NY, 1991.

Ardalan, Nader, 'Architecture: Pahlavi, After World War II', *Encyclopaedia Iranica*, vol. II, pp. 326–55;

–, 'Architects in America Design for Islamic Cultures', *Arts & the Islamic World* 3 (1985), p. 48

Ardalan, Nader, and Laleh Bakhtiar, *The Sense of Unity: The Sufi Tradition in Persian Architecture*, Chicago, 1973

Arkoun, Mohammed, 'The Socialist Villages Experiment in Algeria', *The Changing Rural Habitat: Case Studies*, vol. 1, Singapore, 1982, pp. 45–50;

–, 'Islamic Cultures, Developing Societies, Modern Thought', in Salam Hayat (ed.), *Expressions of Islam in Buildings*, Geneva, 1990, pp. 49–68;

–, *Ouvertures sur l'Islam* (2nd ed.), Paris, 1992;

–, 'The Metamorphosis of the Sacred', in M. Frishman and H.U. Khan (eds.), *The Mosque*, London and New York, 1994, pp. 268–77

Al-Asad, Mohammad, 'The Modern State Mosque in the Eastern Arab World, 1828–1985' (Ph.D. dissertation, Harvard University), 1990;

–, 'The Mosques of Abdel Wahed El-Wakil', *Mimar* 42 (1992), pp. 34–9;

–, 'The Re-invention of Tradition: Neo-Islamic Architecture', *Proceedings of the XVIII International Congress of the History of Art*, Berlin, 1993;

–, 'Applications of Geometry', in M. Frishman and H.U. Khan (eds.), *The Mosque*, London and New York, 1994, pp. 55–70

Asher, Catherine E.B., *Architecture of Mughal India*, Cambridge and New York, 1992

Avennes, Prisse d', *Arab Art as Seen Through the Monuments of Cairo from the 7th Century to the 18th* (translated from the French *L'Art Arabe*, Paris, 1877, by J. I. Erythraspis), reprinted London, 1983

Badran, Rasem, 'Historical References and Contemporary Design', in Margaret B. Sevcenko (ed.), *Theories and Principles of Design in the Architecture of Islamic Societies*, Cambridge, MA, 1988, pp. 149–60

Baghdad, **Mayoralty of**, *Competition Programme, International Design Competition for the State Mosque, Baghdad, Iraq*, Baghdad, 1982

Balamir, Aydan, and Jale Erzen, 'Contemporary Turkish Mosque Architecture' (unpublished paper), 1990

Bates, Ülkü, 'Women as Patrons of Architecture in Turkey', in Nikki Keddie and Lois Beck (eds.), *Women in the Muslim World*, Cambridge, MA, 1978, pp. 245–60

Beazeley, Elizabeth, *Living with the Desert: Working Buildings of the Iranian Plateau*, Warminster, 1982

Berkey, Jonathan, *The Transmission of Knowledge in Medieval Cairo: A Social History of Islamic Education*, Princeton, NJ, 1992

Betteridge, Anne H., 'Ziarat: Pilgrimage to the Shrines of Shiraz' (Ph.D. dissertation, University of Chicago), 1987

Blair, Sheila, *The Ilkhanid Shrine Complex at Natanz, Iran*, Cambridge, MA, 1986

Blair, Sheila, and Jonathan Bloom, *The Art and Architecture of Islam, 1250–1800*, New Haven, CT, 1994

Bloom, Jonathan, *Minaret, Symbol of Islam*, (Oxford Studies of Islamic Art VII), Oxford, 1989

Boddy, Trevor, 'Political Uses of Urban Design: The Jakarta Example', in Douglas R. Webster (ed.), *The Southeast Asian Environment*, Ottawa, 1983, pp. 31–41

Boisard, Marcel A., *Humanism in Islam*, Indianapolis, 1988

Bokhari, Abdulla, 'Jeddah' (PhD dissertation, University of Pennsylvania), 1978

Bouhdibaa, Abdelwahab, *Sexuality in Islam* (translated by Alan Sheridan), London, 1985

Bousquat, G.H., 'Ghusl', *Encyclopaedia of Islam* (2nd ed.), vol. II, p. 1104

Bozdoğan, Sibel, 'Modernity in the Margins: Architecture and Ideology in the Early Republic', *Proceedings of the XVIII International Congress of the History of Art*, Berlin, 1993

Bozdoğan, Sibel, Suha Özkan and Engin Yenal, *Sedad Eldem: Architect in Turkey*, Singapore, 1987

Brownlee, David B., and David G. De Long, *Louis I. Kahn: In the Realm of Architecture*, New York, 1991

Busson de Janssens, G., 'Les Wakfs dans l'Islam contemporain', *Revue des Etudes Islamiques*, vol. XI, 1953, pp. 43–76

Calmard, Jean, and James Allen, 'Alam va'Alamat', *Encyclopaedia Iranica*, vol. I, pp. 785–91

Cantacuzino, Sherban (ed.), *Architecture in Continuity: Building in the Islamic World Today*, New York, 1985

Caratini, Roger, *Le génie de l'Islamisme*, Paris, 1992

Çelik, Zeynep, *Displaying the Orient: The Architecture of Islam at the Nineteenth-Century World's Fairs*, Berkeley, CA, 1992

Chadirji, Rifat, *Concepts and Influences: Towards a Regionalized International Architecture, 1952–1978*, London and New York, 1986

Chelhod, J., 'Hidjab', *Encyclopedia of Islam* (2nd ed.), vol. III, pp. 359–61

Cohen, Jean-Louis, *Le Corbusier and the Mystique of the USSR: Theories and Projects for Moscow, 1928–1936*, Princeton, N.J., 1992

Combs-Schilling, M. Elaine, *Sacred Performances: Islam, Sexuality, and Sacrifice*, New York, 1989;

–, 'Performing Monarchy, Staging Nation', paper delivered at the Middle East Center, Harvard University, 1994 (unpublished)

Creswell, K.A.C., *Early Muslim Architecture* (2nd ed.), Oxford and New York, 1969;

–, *Muslim Architecture of Egypt* (reprint), New York, 1978

Curtis, William, *Modern Architecture since 1900*, Oxford and Englewood Cliffs, NJ, 1983;

–, 'On Regionalism', in Robert Powell (ed.), *Regionalism in Architecture*, Singapore, 1985, pp. 73–7;

–, 'Diplomatic Club, Riyadh', *Mimar* 21 (1986), pp. 20–5

Darmaputera, E., *Pancasila and the Search for Identity and Modernity in Indonesian Society*, Leiden, 1988

Dawson, Barry, and John Gillow, *The Traditional Architecture of Indonesia*, London, 1994

'Décret no. 88-50 du mars 1988 relatif à la construction, à l'organisation et au fonctionnement des mosquées', *Le Journal Officiel de la République Algérienne*, no. 11, 6 March 1988

Designed for Living: Public Housing in Singapore, Housing and Development Board, Singapore, 1985

Dhofar, Zamalkhsyari, 'Islamic Education and Traditional Ideology on Java', in J.J. Fox, R.G. Garnault, P.T. McCawley, J.A.C. Mackie (eds.), *Indonesia: Australian Perspectives*, vol. I, Canberra, 1980, pp. 263–71

Diba, Darab, 'Iran: The University of Kerman', *Mimar* 42 (1992), pp. 62–4

Diba, Kamran, *Buildings and Projects*, Stuttgart, 1981;
—, 'Iranian Art', in Wijdan Ali (ed.), *Contemporary Art from the Islamic World*, London, 1989, pp. 150–8

Dix, Gerald (ed.), *Ecology and Ekistics*, London, 1977

Djait, Hisham, *Al-Kufa, Naissance de la ville islamique*, Paris, 1986

Doxiadis, Constantinos A., *Ekistics: An Introduction to the Science of Human Settlements*, London, 1968

Doxiadis Associates, 'Islamabad, the New Capital of Pakistan', *Ekistics* 18 (1964), pp. 331–6

Eade, John, 'Islam, Religious Buildings and Space in London' (unpublished paper), 1991

Effendi, M. Prasetiyo, *The Development of the Mosque in Indonesia*, Bandung, 1990

Ettinghausen, Richard, 'Arabic Epigraphy: Communication or Symbolic Affirmation', in Dickran Koumijiyan (ed.), *Festschrift for George Miles*, Beirut, 1973, pp. 297–317

Ettinghausen, Richard, and Oleg Grabar, *The Art and Architecture of Islam, 650–1250*, London and New York, 1987

Evenson, Norma, *Chandigarh*, Berkeley and Los Angeles, CA, 1966

Falamaki, M., and Kamran Adle, 'Al-Ghadir Mosque, Tehran', *Mimar* 29 (1988), pp. 24–9

Al-Farsy, Fouad, *Modernity and Tradition, The Saudi Equation*, London, 1990

Fathy, Hassan, *Architecture for the Poor: an Experiment in Rural Egypt*, Chicago, 1973;

—, *Gourna: A Tale of Two Villages*, Cairo, 1969

Fatma, Sabbah, *Women in the Muslim Unconscious* (translated by Mary Jo Lakeland), New York, 1984

Fethi, Ihsan, 'The Mosque Today', in Sherban Cantacuzino (ed.), *Architecture in Continuity*, pp. 53–63

Frishman, Martin, and Hasan-Uddin Khan (eds.), *The Mosque: History, Architectural Development & Regional Diversity*, London and New York, 1994 (reprinted 1997)

Geertz, Clifford, *Interpretation of Cultures: Selected Essays*, New York, 1973

El-Gohary, Osamah, 'Interview with Al-Wakil', *Al-Benaa*, 34/6, 1987;
—, *Mosque Design in Light of Psycho-Religious Experience*, London (in preparation)

Golombek, Lisa, and Donald Wilber, *The Timurid Architecture of Iran and Turan* (2 vols.), Princeton, NJ, 1988

Goodwin, Godfrey, *A History of Ottoman Architecture*, London and New York (paperback reprint), 1987 and 1997

Grabar, Oleg, *The Alhambra*, Cambridge, MA, 1978;
—, 'The Art of the Mamluks', *Muqarnas*, 2, 1984, pp. 1–11;
—, 'From the Past into the Future: On Two Designs for State Mosques', *Architectural Record*, June 1984, pp. 150–1;
—, *The Great Mosque of Isfahan*, New York, 1990;
—, 'The Mosque in Islamic Society Today', in M. Frishman and H.U. Khan (eds.), *The Mosque*, pp. 242–6

Guriz, Adnan, 'Mar'a', *Encyclopaedia of Islam* (2nd ed.), vol. VI, pp. 490–8

Haddad, Yvonne (ed.), *The Muslims of America*, Oxford and New York, 1991

Haddad, Yvonne, and Ellison Banks Findly, *Women, Religion, and Social Change*, Albany, NY, 1985

Haddad, Yvonne, and Adair Lumis, *Islamic Values in the United States*, New York, 1987.

Haider, Gulzar, 'Brother in Islam, Please Draw us a Mosque', in Hayat Salam (ed.), *Expressions of Islam in Buildings*, pp. 154–66

Haider, Gulzar, and Muhammad Mukhtar, 'Islamic Architecture in Non-Islamic Environments' (unpublished paper), 1980

Hanna, Sami A., *Arab Socialism. A Documentary Survey*, Salt Lake City, UT, 1969

Hannerz, Ulf, 'The World in Creolisation', *Africa* 57 (1987), pp. 546–59;

—, 'Cosmopolitans and locals in world culture', in M. Featherstone (ed.), *Global Culture: nationalism, globalization and modernity*, London, 1995, pp. 20–38

Hasan, Perween, 'The Indian Subcontinent', in M. Frishman and H.U. Khan (eds.), *The Mosque*, pp. 159–80

Head, Raymond, *The Indian Style*, London, 1986

'Hellmuth, Obata & Kassabaum: Airport', *Engineering News Record*, 27 October 1983

Hellmuth, Obata & Kassabaum, 'Saudi Arabia: King Saud University, Riyadh', *Mimar* 42 (1992), pp. 48–51

Herdeg, Klaus, *Formal Structure in the Islamic Architecture of Iran and Turkistan*, New York, 1990

Hill, Derek, *Islamic Architecture and its Decoration, A.D. 800–1500: A Photographic Survey*, with an introductory text by Oleg Grabar, London, 1967

Hillenbrand, Robert, *Islamic Architecture: Form, Function and Meaning*, New York, 1994;
—, 'The development of Saljuq mausolea in Iran', in O. Watson (ed.), *The Art of Iran and Anatolia from the 11th to the 13th century A.D.*, London, 1978, pp. 40–59

Holod, Renata, 'Patronage and the place of women in the monumental architecture of pre-modern and early modern Iran', in Guity Nashat (ed.), *Women in Iran* (in preparation)

Holod, Renata, and Ahmet Evin (eds.), *Modern Turkish Architecture*, Philadelphia, PA, 1984

Holod, Renata, with Darl Rastofer (eds.), *Architecture and Community: Building in the Islamic World Today*, Millerton, NY, 1984

Imamuddin, Abu H., 'Islamic Centre for Technical and Vocational Training and Research', *Mimar* 37 (1990), pp. 34–8

Imamuddin, Abu H., S.A. Hassan and D. Sarkar, 'Community Mosque: A Symbol of Society', in Robert Powell (ed.), *Regionalism in Architecture*, Singapore, 1985, pp. 60–9

Institut Musulman de Paris (brochure), Paris, n.d.

Islamabad (brochure), Capital Development Authority, Islamabad, 1985

Islamabad, the City of Peace (brochure), Capital Development Authority, Islamabad, n.d. (c. 1980)

Ismaili Centre, London, The (brochure), London, 1985

Ismaili Jamatkhana and Centre, Burnaby, B.C., Canada, The (brochure), London, 1985

Jamzadeh, Laal, and Margaret Mills, 'Iranian Sofreh: From Collective to Female Ritual', in Caroline Walker Bynum, Stevan Harrell and Paula Richman (eds.), *Gender and Religion: On the Complexity of Symbols*, Boston, MA, 1987, pp. 23–65

Jessup, Helen, 'Dutch Architectural Visions of the Indonesian Tradition', *Muqarnas* 3 (1985), pp. 138–61

Johansen, Baber, 'The mosques: places of religious integration or political agitation?', paper delivered at the University of Pennsylvania, March 1989 (unpublished)

Jones, Owen, *The Grammar of Ornament* (London, 1868), reprinted London, 1986

Kahn, Louis I., 'Address [to the Boston Society of Architects]', *Boston Society of Architects' Journal* 1 (1967), pp. 5–20

Kamal, Fawziah, 'A mosque for Penang', *Mimar* 1 (1981), pp. 38–9

Keddie, Nikki, and Beth Baron (eds.), *Women in Middle Eastern History: Shifting Boundaries in Sex and Gender*, New Haven, CT, 1991

Keddie, Nikki, and Lois Beck (eds.), *Women in the Muslim World*, Cambridge, MA, 1978

Khan, Hasan-Uddin, 'Mobile Shelter in Pakistan', in Paul Oliver (ed.), *Shelter, Sign and Symbol*, London, 1975, pp. 183–96; –, 'Meaning in Tradition Today: An Approach to Architectural Criticism', in Robert Powell (ed.), *Criticism in Architecture*, Singapore, 1989, pp. 53–64; –, 'Some Recent Large-Scale Projects in Asia', in Margaret Ševčenko (ed.), *Continuity and Change: Design Strategies for Large-Scale Urban Development*, Cambridge, MA, 1984, pp. 14–15

Khan, Sikandar A., 'The Shah Faisal Mosque', *Habitat Pakistan*, 2/2 (1987), pp. 22–3

Kiel, Machiel, *Studies on the Ottoman Architecture of the Balkans* (reprint ed.), Aldershot, Hampshire, 1990

King, Geoffrey R.D., *The Historical Mosques of Saudi Arabia*, New York and London, 1986

'KKIA: Riyadh's "Royal Airport"', *Airport Forum* 2 (1984), pp. 9–12

Kultermann, Udo, 'Architecture in South-East Asia 2: Indonesia', *Mimar* 21 (1986), pp. 45–52

Kuran, Aptullah, *Sinan: The Grand Old Master of Ottoman Architecture*, Washington, DC, and Istanbul, 1987

Lane, Edward William, *An Account of the Manners and Customs of the Modern Egyptians* (3rd ed.), London, 1842

Lewcock, Ronald, 'London Central Mosque', *Architects' Journal*, vol. 166, no. 32 (1977), pp. 265–9

Lewis, Bernard, *The Political Language of Islam*, Chicago, IL, 1988

'Loi no. 88-34 du mai 1988, relative aux mosquées', *Journal Officiel de la République Tunisienne*, 6 May 1988

McQuade, Walter, *Architecture in the Real World: the Work of HOK*, New York, 1984

Madrid Islamic Cultural Centre Competition, Union of International Architects, Paris, 1980

Makdisi, George, *The Rise of Colleges: Institutions of Learning in Islam and the West*, Edinburgh, 1981

Makiya, Kanan, *The Monument: Art, Vulgarity, and Responsibility in Iraq*, Berkeley, CA, 1991; –, *Post-Islamic Classicism: A Visual Essay on the Architecture of Mohamed Makiya*, London, 1990

Malti-Douglas, Fedwa, *A Woman and Her Sufis*, Washington, DC, 1995

Mardin, Serif, *Religion and Social Change in Modern Turkey: The Case of Bediuzzamen Said Nursi*, Albany, NY, 1989

Marefat, Roya, 'Beyond the Architecture of Death: the Shrine of the Shah-i-Zinda in Samarkand' (Ph.D. dissertation, Harvard University), 1991

Masjid al-Dawlah al-Kabir, Mutatallabat (The Great State Mosque: Requirements), Ministry of Public Works, State of Kuwait, n.d.

Masjid Negara (brochure), Malaysian Government Mosque Committee, Kuala Lumpur, 1965

al-Masri, Wael, 'Architecture and the Question of Identity: Issues of Self-Representation in Islamic Community Centers in America' (M.Sc. thesis, Massachusetts Institute of Technology), 1993

Mayet, Muhammad, 'The City Room', *Architecture SA*, July-August 1994

Meinecke, Michael, *Die Mamlukische Architektur in Ägypten und Syrien* (Abhandlungen des Deutschen Archäologischen Instituts Kairo, Islamische Reihe, Band 5), Gluckstadt, 1992

Mernissi, Fatima, 'Women, Saints and Sanctuaries', *Signs* 3 (1977), pp. 100–11; –, *Beyond the Veil: Male-Female Dynamics in Modern Muslim Society*, London, 1985; – (ed.), *Doing Daily Battle: Interviews with Moroccan Women* (translated by Mary Jo Lakeland), London, 1988; –, *The Veil and the Male Elite: A Feminist Interpretation of Women's Rights in Islam*, Reading, MA, 1991

Mernissi, Fatima, et al., *Femme et Pouvoir: Collection*, Casablanca, 1990

Mezquita del Sheykh Ibrahim bin Abdulaziz al-Ibrahim en Caracas, La (brochure), Caracas, 1993

Moghaddam, Valentine (ed.), *Gender and National Identity, Women and Politics in Muslim Societies*, London and Karachi, 1994

'Mohammad Makiya', *Middle East Times*, 4–11 February 1984

Mortimer, Rex, 'The Place of Communism', in J.J. Fox, R.G. Garnault, P.T. McCawley and J.A.C. Mackie (eds.), *Indonesia: Australian Perspectives*, Canberra, 1980, pp. 75–90

'Moslems making their mark on Ohio', *The New York Times*, 25 November 1984

Mottahedeh, R., *The Mantle of the Prophet: Religion and Politics in Iran*, New York, 1985

Mumtaz, Kamil Khan, 'Mistree Haji Ghulam Hussain', *Mimar* 10 (1983), pp. 8–13; –, *Architecture in Pakistan*, Singapore, 1985

Musallam, Basim, *Sex and Society in Islam*, New York, 1983

Neçipoğlu, Gülru, *Architecture, Ceremonial, and Power: the Topkapi Palace in the Fifteenth and Sixteenth Centuries*, New York and Cambridge, MA, 1991

'Negeri Sembilan State Mosque Architectural Competition', *PETA* (The Federation of Malaya Society of Architects), 4/3–4 (1963), pp. 42–50

New-Generation Mosques in Singapore and their activities, Majlis Ugama Islam, Singapore, 1986

'New Mosque Architecture' (special issue), *Al-Benaa*, April-May 1987

Norberg-Schulz, C., *Architetture di Paolo Portoghesi e Vittorio Gigliotti*, Rome, 1982

Noweir, Sawsan, 'The El-Miniawy Architects', *Mimar* 8 (1983), pp. 7–17

O'Kane, Bernard, *Timurid Architecture in Khurasan*, Costa Mesa, CA, 1987

O'Neill, Hugh, 'Southeast Asia', in M. Frishman and H.U. Khan (eds.), *The Mosque*, London and New York, 1994, pp. 225–40

Owen, Roger, 'The Cairo Building Industry and the Building Boom of 1897 to 1907', *Colloque International sur l'Histoire du Caire*, Cairo, 1969, pp. 337–50

Paccard, André, *Le Maroc et l'artisanat traditionnel Islamique dans l'architecture*, Paris, 1980

Palumbo, Marcello, 'La Moschea de Monte Antenne', *Storia dell'Arte*, Rome, 1990

Pope, Arthur Upham, and Phylllis Ackerman (eds.), *A Survey of Persian Art from Prehistoric Times to the Present* (Oxford, 1939), reprint Tokyo and New York, 1971

Portoghesi, Paolo, 'Elogio della Contamazione', *XX Secolo*, 1992

Powell, Robert (ed.), *Regionalism in Architecture*, Singapore, 1985

Prijotomo, Josef, *Ideas and Forms of Javanese Architecture*, Yogyakarta, 1984

Prussin, Labelle, *Hatumere: Islamic Design in West Africa*, Berkeley, CA, 1986

Puri, Aron, *Yeh Bhumi!* (booklet), *India Today*, n.d. (c. 1990)

Reid, Donald M., *Cairo University and the Making of Modern Egypt*, Cairo, 1990–91
'Regenerative Approaches to Mosque Design, Competition for the State Mosque, Baghdad', *Mimar* 11 (1984), pp. 44–63
'Riyadh: King Khaled Airport Mosque Interior', *Mimar* 12 (1984), pp. 8–10

Roaf, Susan, 'Badgir', *Encyclopaedia Iranica*, vol. III, pp. 368–70

Ronner, Heinz, Sharad Javeri and Alessandro Vasella (eds.), *Louis I. Kahn: Complete Works, 1935–1974*, Stuttgart, 1977

Rumler, E., "Institut Musulman et Mosquée de Paris', *La Construction moderne*, Paris, 2 November 1924

Sabbah, Fatma, *Women in the Muslim Unconscious* (translated by Mary Jo Lakeland), New York, 1984

Sadek, Noha, 'Rasulid Women: Power and Patronage', *Proceedings of the 22nd Seminar for Arabian Studies,* 19 (1989), pp. 121–36

el-Said, Issam, and Ayse Parman, *Geometric Concepts in Islamic Art,* London, 1976

Salam, Hayat (ed.), *Expressions of Islam in Buildings*, Geneva, 1990

Saliya, Yuswadi, Hariadi and Gunawan Tjahjono, 'The Indonesian Experience', in Hayat Salam (ed.), *Expressions of Islam in Buildings*, pp. 187–97

Samb, A., 'Masdjid', *Encyclopaedia of Islam* (2nd ed.), vol. VI, pp. 644–707

Schacht, Joseph, 'Wudu', *Encyclopaedia of Islam* (1st ed.), vol. VIII, pp. 1140–1

Schleifer, Abdullah, 'Hassan Fathy's Abiquiu', *Ekistics* 304 (1984), pp. 26–32

Schmertz, Mildred, 'Affording the Best', *Architectural Record*, March 1984, pp. 112–25;
–, 'Mosque as Monument', *Architectural Record,* June 1984, pp. 142–9

Serageldin, Ismail (ed.), *Space for Freedom: The Search for Architectural Excellence in Muslim Societies*, London and Boston, MA, 1989

Serageldin, Ismail, with James Steele (eds.), *Architecture of the Contemporary Mosque*, London, 1996

Ševčenko, Margaret B. (ed.), *Theories and Principles of Design in the Architecture of Islamic Societies*, Aga Khan Program for Islamic Architecture at MIT, Cambridge, MA, 1988

Sharabi, Hisham, *Neopatriarchy: a Theory of Distorted Changes in Arab Society*, New York, 1988

Siroux, Maxime, *Anciennes voies et monuments routiers de la région d'Ispahan, suivis de plusieurs autres édifices de cette province*, Cairo, 1971;
–, 'Les Caravansérails routiers safavides', in Renata Holod (ed.), *Studies on Isfahan, Journal of the Society for Iranian Studies,* 1974, pp. 348–79

Slessor, Catherine, 'Sacred Room', *Architectural Review*, March 1995, pp. 68–9

Slymovitz, Susan 'The Muslim World Day Parade and "Storefront" Mosques of New York City', in Barbara Daly Metcalf (ed.), *Making Muslim Space in North America and Europe*, Berkeley, CA, 1996;
–, 'New York City's Muslim World Day Parade', in Peter Van Der Veer (ed.), *Nation and Migration*: *The Politics of Space in the South Asian Diaspora*, Philadelphia, PA, 1995, pp. 157–77

Snelder, Raoul, 'The Great Mosque at Djenné: Its Impact Today as a Model,' *Mimar* 12 (1984), pp. 66–74

Sorkin, Michael, 'Counterpoint', in Robert Powell (ed.), *Criticism in Architecture*, Singapore, 1989, pp. 65–9
'Special Report on the Saudi Arabian Capital, A', *The International Herald Tribune*, 11 November 1983

Spigolature, Demetra (ed.), *The Mosque in Rome*, Palermo, 1993

Steele, James, *Hassan Fathy*, London and New York, 1988;
–, *An Architecture for People. The Complete Works of Hassan Fathy*, London and New York, 1997;
– (ed.), *Architecture for Islamic Societies Today*, London, 1994

Stowasser, Barbara Freyer, *Women in the Qur'an, Traditions, and Interpretation*, New York, 1994

Sukada, Budi A., 'The University of Indonesia Depok,' *Mimar* 42 (1992), pp. 65–9

Tabbaa, Yasser, 'The Muqarnas Dome; Its Origin and Meaning', *Muqarnas* 3 (1985) pp. 61–74;
–, *Circles of Power: Palace, Citadel, and City in Ayyubid Aleppo*, College Park, PA (in preparation)

Talib, Kaizer, *Shelter in Saudi Arabia*, London and New York, 1984

Tapper, Nancy, 'Gender and Religion in a Turkish Town: A Comparison of Two Types of Formal Women's Gatherings', in Pat Holden (ed.), *Women's Religious Experience*, London and Canberra, 1983

Taylor, Brian Brace, 'Directions in Diversity', *Mimar* 10 (1983), pp. 17–20;
–, 'Rethinking Colonial Archiecture', *Mimar* 13 (1984), pp. 16–25;
–, 'Hospital, Marrakesh', *Mimar* 14 (1984), pp. 45–49;
–, *Contemporary Houses, Traditional Values* (exhibition catalogue), London, 1988

Thys-Senocak, Lucienne, *The Yeni Valide Mosque Complex in Eminonu, Istanbul (1597–1665)*, (Ph.D. dissertation, University of Pennsylvania), 1994

Traub, James, 'The Road to Mecca', *New York Times,* 24 June 1991, pp. 36–48

Trexler, Richard C., *Public Life in Renaissance Florence*, New York, 1980;
– (compiler), *Gender Rhetorics: Postures of Dominance and Submission in History*, Binghamton, NY, 1994

Tyng, Alexandra, *Beginnings: Louis Kahn's Philosophy of Architecture*, New York, 1984

Vale, Lawrence, *Architecture, Power, and National Identity*, New Haven, CT, 1992
'View from a Jersey City Mosque', *The New Yorker*, 27 September 1992, pp. 30–6

Volait, Mercedes, *L'Architecture moderne en Egypte et la revue al-'Imara (1939-59)*, Cairo, 1988

El-Wakil, Abdel Wahed, 'An Island Mosque in Jeddah', *Mimar* 19 (1986), pp. 12–17

Weschler, Lawrence, 'Architects Amid the Ruins', *The New Yorker*, 6 January 1992
'Winners! Results of MIMAR Competition III' (on the Corniche mosques, Jeddah), *Mimar* 17 (1985), pp. 9–29

Wright, Gwendolyn, *The Politics of Design in French Colonial Urbanism*, Chicago, IL, 1991

Wurman, Richard Saul, *What Will Be Has Always Been: The Words of Louis I. Kahn*, New York, 1986

Yeang, Ken, *The Architecture of Malaysia*, Amsterdam and Kuala Lumpur, 1992

Glossary

In addition to the terms defined, specialized words and phrases occurring only rarely are defined in the relevant textual context.

adhan – the call to prayer delivered by the muezzin

badgir – wind-tower

bait – house or suite of rooms

chahar taq – a domed structure with openings on four sides

chhajja – eaves of a roof

chhatri – parasol, a small rooftop pavilion

claustra – a screen of open work in stone or brick

dewan – part of a palace; government department or royal reception chamber

dikka – raised platform from which the words and actions of the *imam* are relayed to members of a congregation

Eid – Muslim festival marking the end of Ramadan (the month of fasting)

hadith – a saying or action traditionally attributed to the Prophet Muhammad

hajj – pilgrimage to Mecca (see also *umra*)

hammam – public baths

hashti – a domed foyer or transition node, polygonal, often eight-sided

imam – leader; any adult male who leads prayers during congregational worship in a mosque

iwan – a chamber that is roofed or vaulted and open on one side (e.g. facing on to the courtyard of a mosque)

jamatkhana – a congregational building for the Ismaili community

khan – caravansary

khutba – oration delivered to the congregation at midday prayers each Friday

külliye (Turkish) – complex of buildings, especially associated with Ottoman mosques, including those used for medical, teaching and charitable purposes

madrasa – literally, 'place of study'; a school of theology and law associated with a mosque

maidan – a large open space for ceremonial use

masjid – a district or neighbourhood mosque

masjid-i jami – a congregational mosque or principal mosque

masjid-i juma – a Friday Mosque

mihrab – the recess or niche in a mosque indicating the direction of Mecca (*qibla*)

minbar – pulpit in a mosque, placed to the right of the *mihrab*, used by the *imam* for the delivery of the *khutba*

muezzin – the official (Arabic, *mu'adhdhin*) at a mosque who delivers the call to prayer (*adhan*) five times daily

muqarnas – ornamental vaulting composed of small concave elements, often employed to decorate an *iwan* or to fill the zone of transition between supporting walls and a dome

namaz – prayer

pishtaq – a large portal forming the open side of an *iwan*

qasr – palace or fort

qibla – the direction of prayer towards Mecca, indicated by the presence of the *mihrab* set in the wall of a mosque

riwaq – portico, a covered area usually along one side of a mosque courtyard (*sahn*)

sahn – courtyard of a mosque

sharia – the law of Islam

suq – market

sura – a chapter in the Qur'an

tadelakt (Morocco, Berber) – impermeable mortar

tawriq – a type of tile mosaic design based on vegetal motifs

umma – the Muslim community as a whole

umra – the 'lesser' pilgrimage to Mecca undertaken by the faithful outside the prescribed time of the *hajj*

waqf (pl. *awqaf*) – a charitable endowment

wilaya – province

yayasan (Indonesia) – a foundation

zakat – alms

zellij (Morocco) – cut-tile mosaic technique used in architectural ornament

ziggurat (ancient Mesopotamia)– a roughly pyramidal platform for a temple, consisting of stages; each successive stage being stepped back from the one below

Sources of illustrations

Illustrations are identified by page numbers, supplemented by the following abbreviations as necessary: a = above; b = below; c = centre; l = left; r = right.

Photographic illustrations were supplied by courtesy of the following:

The Aga Khan Award for Architecture / The Aga Khan Trust for Culture, Geneva 10; (photos by J. Bétant) 12a, 13a; 19b, 28a + b, 30–31, 42, 43, 44–45, 46, 52r; (photo by Christian Lignon) 55b; (photos by A. de Roux) 57, 58–59; (photo by Abu H. Imamuddin) 62; 64b, 68ar, 78, (photo by Vedat Dalokay) 79b; (photos by R. Günay) 95, 96–97, 98; 100l; (photos by R. Günay) 101b, 102–103, 104, 105; 110, 114b, 119; (photo by C. Abel) 134a; (photos by Kamran Adle) 144, 146, 147, 151; (photo by E.M. Balcioğlu) 155; (photo by Abu H. Imamuddin) 167; (photos by R. Gutbrod) 172, 173; (photos by Christian Lignon) 180a, 181; (photos by Kamran Adle) 185b, 187, 188b, 190, 191a; (photos by J. Bétant) 196a, 197a, 198, 199; 233b; 239, 240
Altug, Behruz & Can Çiniçi 101a
Arcop Associates 91, 92
Nader Ardalan 163, 164
Atelier Enam 145
Loghman Azar 217
Rasem Badran 86, 131, 132, 133
David A. Berkowitz 70br
Charles Boccara 178b
Ricardo Bofill 88, 115

Oscar Bracho 35
Caudill, Rowlett, Scott 160, 161
Abderrahim Charai and Abdelaziz Lazrak 180b
CSL Associates 117c + b
Vedat Dalokay 2, 63, 99
Dar al-Islam Foundation, Abiquiu, NM 19a (photo by Nuridin Durkee), 215 (photos by Cradoc Bagshaw), 216 (photo by Nuridin Durkee)
Kamran Diba 140, 141, 156, 157, 158, 159
Mohammad Abdallah Eissa 32
Douglas Ellis 93
Gamal El-Dowla Abdel Gadir 124b, 125
Sir Frederick Gibberd & Partners 231, 232
Vittorio Gigliotti 241a (photo by Aldo Ippoliti), 243b, 244–5, 246, 247
Mirže Golože and Dzeme Čelića 201ar + cr
Gulzar Haider 182, 218, 219, 220, 221, 222, 223, 224, 225
Hajeedar & Associates 94, 148, 149
Mokhless Al-Hariri 186b, 234, 235, 236
Hellmuth, Obata & Kassabaum 150, 174, 175 (photos by Robert Azzi), 176, 177 (photos by Robert Azzi)
Reproduced by permission of the Estate of Wolfgang Hoyt 248a, 249, 250, 251, 253
Abdulhalim Ibrahim 126, 127
Jurubena Bertiga International 73a, 74b, 75a
Amin Khan 208
Hasan-Uddin Khan 13b, 14c, 22, 52l, 54, 56r, 60, 64a, 65b, 68l + b, 70a + bl, 108b, 109, 153c + b, 154, 170a, 214, 226, 242, 243a
M.N. Khan 71, 72, 118a
Pervez A. Khan 76, 79a

King Abdul Aziz Foundation, Casablanca 53
Mohamed Makiya (Makiya Associates) 15b, 80, 81, 82, 83, 89, 142, 143
Mimar 139; (photos by Christian Lignon) 178a, 179; (photos by Kamran Adle) 192, 209a, 210, 211, 212
Kimberly Mims 233a
Hany Abdel Rahman El-Miniawy (photos by Véronique Dollfuss) 111a, 112–13
Akram Mohamed 136
Sami Moussawi 75b
K.L. Ng 20, 116, 117a
Achmad Noe'man 153a
S. Noorani 21, 204, 206, 207
Gary Otte 14a, 48, 49, 50, 51r, 66a, 67a, 170b, 171ar + br, 193b, 195b
Suha Özkan 14b
Doruk Pamir 13c, 165, 166, 167b
Piraz 168, 169
A. Sadali 11
A. Shuaibi / BEEAH 106, 128, 129, 130
Singapore Housing and Development Board 120
I.C. Stewart 121b, 122, 123
Nabbil Tabbara 24, 25
Kenzo Tange 162
Brian Brace Taylor 193a, 194, 195a
A.N. Tombazis & Associates 27
University of Pennsylvania Slide Library 200, 201b, 202–3
Juan Mora Urbano 33, 34
Robert Venturi 90
Abdel Wahed El-Wakil 12b, 15a, 23, 37, 38, 39, (drawing by Edwin Venn) 40b, 107, 134b, 135, 137
Woking Borough Council, Surrey (photo © Rob Reichenfeld) 227

Other items

Except as noted below, line drawings (copies of plans, sections etc.) were generously provided by the architects responsible for the individual projects illustrated. In a few such cases the drawings have been simplified or adapted to suit the requirements of this book (see Acknowledgments, p. 8), as have several items that were originally published as illustrations in official brochures.

The Aga Khan Award for Architecture 29, 32; 100; 108; 145; 172, 173; (plans and diagrams drawn by Raoul Snelder) 186a, 188a, 191r; 197; 238a + c
After drawings reproduced in 'The City Room' by Muhammad Mayet, *Architecture SA* (July-August 1994) 41
Capital Development Authority, Islamabad 77, 121a
After illustrations reproduced in *La Construction moderne* (Paris, November 1924) 228, 229
Islamic Cultural Foundation, Washington, DC 237
After plans reproduced in *The Ismaili Centre, London* and *The Ismaili Centre and Jamatkhana, Burnaby, B.C., Canada* (both Islamic Publications Ltd, 1985) 47, 51l
Courtesy, *Mimar* 95, 139, 209c + b
After plans reproduced in *La Mosquée Hassan II* 55a, 56l
Singapore Housing and Development Board 118
Union Internationale des Architectes, Paris 16

Index